ROUTLEDGE LIBRARY EDITIONS: ENERGY RESOURCES

Volume 12

THE NUCLEAR POWER DECISIONS

THE NUCLEAR POWER DECISIONS

British Policies, 1953–78

ROGER WILLIAMS

Routledge
Taylor & Francis Group

LONDON AND NEW YORK

First published in 1980 by Croom Helm

This edition first published in 2019
by Routledge
2 Park Square, Milton Park, Abingdon, Oxon OX14 4RN

and by Routledge
52 Vanderbilt Avenue, New York, NY 10017

Routledge is an imprint of the Taylor & Francis Group, an informa business

© 1980 Roger Williams

British Library Cataloguing in Publication Data
A catalogue record for this book is available from the British Library

ISBN: 978-0-367-23168-2 (Set)
ISBN: 978-0-429-27857-0 (Set) (ebk)
ISBN: 978-0-367-23166-8 (Volume 12) (hbk)
ISBN: 978-0-429-27856-3 (Volume 12) (ebk)

Publisher's Note
The publisher has gone to great lengths to ensure the quality of this reprint but points out that some imperfections in the original copies may be apparent.

Disclaimer
The publisher has made every effort to trace copyright holders and would welcome correspondence from those they have been unable to trace.

The Nuclear Power Decisions

British Policies, 1953-78

Roger Williams

CROOM HELM LONDON

© 1980 Roger Williams
Croom Helm Ltd. 2-10 St John's Road, London SW11

British Library Cataloguing in Publication Data

Williams, Roger b.1920
    The nuclear power decisions.
    1. Atomic energy — Great Britain — History
    2. Energy policy — Great Britain — History
    I. Title
    621.48'0941   TK9057
    ISBN 0-7099-0265-4

Typeset by Jayell Typesetting, London
Printed and bound in Great Britain by
Biddles Ltd, Guildford and King's Lynn

CONTENTS

ABBREVIATIONS

ACORD	Advisory Council on R & D for Fuel and Power
ACRS	Advisory Committee on Reactor Safeguards (US)
AEA	Atomic Energy Authority
AEC	Atomic Energy Commission (US)
AEG	Atomic Energy Group
AGR	Advanced gas-cooled reactor
APC	Atomic Power Constructions
APG	Atomic Power Group
ASLB	Atomic Safety and Licensing Board (US)
BEA	British Electricity Authority
BEEN	Babcock-English Electric Nuclear
BNA	British Nuclear Associates
BNDC	British Nuclear Design and Construction
BNEX	British Nuclear Export Executive
BNF	British Nuclear Forum
BNFL	British Nuclear Fuels Ltd
BRDC	British Research and Development Corporation
BWR	Boiling water reactor
C&AG	Comptroller and Auditor General
CANDU	CANadian Deuterium Uranium
CEA	Central Electricity Authority
CEGB	Central Electricity Generating Board
CFR (1)	Commercial Fast Reactor (1)
CPRE	Council for the Protection of Rural England
d	old penny (0.417p)
DFR	Dounreay fast reactor
DHSS	Department of Health and Social Security
DOE	Department of the Environment
DTI	Department of Trade and Industry
ECCS	Emergency core-cooling system
ETU	Electrical Trades Union
EURATOM	European Atomic Energy Community
FBR	Fast breeder reactor, or simply fast reactor or breeder reactor
FoE	Friends of the Earth
GE (US)	General Electric Co. (United States)

GEC	General Electric Company (UK)
GMWU	General and Municipal Workers Union
GW	gigawatt = 1,000MW
HTR	High-temperature reactor
IAEA	International Atomic Energy Agency
IBRD	International Bank for Reconstruction and Development
ICL	International Combustion Ltd
ICRP	International Commission on Radiological Protection
IPCS	Institution of Professional Civil Servants
IRC	Industrial Reorganisation Corporation
KW(h)	kilowatt (hour)
KWU	Kraftwerk Union
LWR	Light water reactor
mills	$0.001; in 1963-4 £1 = $2.78, i.e. 1d/KWh = 11.6 mills
Mintech	Ministry of Technology
MRC	Medical Research Council
mtce	million tons of coal equivalent
MW	megawatt (million watts)
MWD/tonne	megawatt days/tonne
MW (th)	megawatt (thermal)
NCB	National Coal Board
NCCL	National Council for Civil Liberties
NDC	Nuclear Design and Construction
NEC	Nuclear Energy Co.
NII	Nuclear Installations Inspectorate
NNC	National Nuclear Corporation
NPAB	Nuclear Power Advisory Board
NPC	Nuclear Power Company
NPPC	Nuclear Power Plant Co. Ltd
NPT	Non-proliferation Treaty
NRPB	National Radiological Protection Board
NSHEB	North of Scotland Hydro-Electric Board
PAC	Public Accounts Committee
PEP	Political and Economic Planning
PFR	Prototype fast reactor
psi	pounds per square inch
PWR	Pressurised water reactor
r & d	research and development
RCEP	Royal Commission on Environmental Pollution

SGHWR	Steam-generating heavy water reactor
SSEB	South of Scotland Electricity Board
TCPAct	Town and Country Planning Act (1971)
THORP	Thermal Oxide Reprocessing Plant
TNPG	The Nuclear Power Group
UPC	United Power Company
WAGR	Windscale AGR

Abbreviations to Notes

BNECJ	*Journal of the British Nuclear Energy Conference*
BNESJ	*Journal of the British Nuclear Energy Society*
HCD	House of Commons Debates
HLD	House of Lords Debates
NE(I)	*Nuclear Engineering (International)*
NP	*Nuclear Power*
WA	Written Answer

FOR RAE

PREFACE

I first became interested in civil nuclear power in 1965. I was amazed when I began that so little that was non-technical had been published on the subject, despite the time that had passed and the public money that had been spent. I refer in this book to the studies which have emerged since then. In my view they are still far from enough, and this book itself is no more than a contribution. Unhappily, what is true of civil nuclear power in particular is all too true of so many British policy questions in general. It must also be many years before the whole period of this book is finally covered in the excellent official histories.

I have concentrated on the major public decisions which have shaped British nuclear power development, and can only hope that I have not done too great a violence to what really happened. Certainly I am far from having persuaded myself that I have got it all right, and I have tried to remember that 'The truth about the events and arguments leading to decision-taking has, in many cases, only a modest resemblance to published statements' (J.V. Dunworth). As would be the case with almost any British policy study, I have necessarily had to depend heavily on published sources, supplementing these with interviews where this was possible. I have generally omitted those developments which I believe to have occurred but which I could not rigorously substantiate. I can certainly be criticised for having underplayed the scientific and engineering achievements of British civil nuclear power. My excuse is that I am concerned here with political decisions and that these are more than enough for one volume.

The events described in this book could be, and to some extent now have been, used to buttress many different conclusions. In this book I draw only one major one, but it is a conclusion I am now reasonably sure I would want to draw for most other such cases that I might have studied: Britain has settled for handling too many twentieth-century problems with nineteenth-century political and administrative attitudes and machinery, and this is one of the major reasons for her continuing decline. Vision and adventure in technology should now be part of the riches of a great nation, but for their fulfilment they need more than ever to be tempered with humility, with common sense and with wisdom.

There are at least two apologies I must make to the reader. First, this is a subject riddled with abbreviations: I can only hope that reference to my listing of these will not prove too tedious. There are also two short forms to which I would like to draw attention: I have throughout referred to the Commons Select Committee on Science and Technology as the Science Committee, and to the Royal Commission on Environmental Pollution as the Royal Commission. Second, this is also at root a very technical subject. Without attempting to write a technical guide, I have tried to help with two appendices outlining the functioning of a nuclear reactor and delineating the chief characteristics of the main reactor types. Nuclear scientists and engineers please forgive.

I owe many debts of gratitude: in particular to the many professionally and politically involved who have taken the trouble to answer my questions and to discuss nuclear power with me; to those of my students who have at one time or another offered comments; to the Nuffield Foundation for a small grant to permit further interviewing at one point in the work; to P. Gummett, M.J. Harris and P. Stubbs for reading drafts of the book; to the secretaries who assisted at different times, including in particular Marilyn Dunn, Stella Williams and Judith Lewis; and last, but not least, to my wife, who both encouraged and suffered. Responsibility for any errors of fact, as well as for all judgements in the book, naturally remains mine alone.

PART I: 1955-64

1 DRAMATIS PERSONAE

By the mid-seventies it was apparent to every reasonably informed member of the British public that nuclear power had become highly controversial and that there were important differences of view in respect of this technology and its contribution to the country's energy economy. It was also apparent that Britain's dilemmas were shared by other states, albeit with differences of emphasis. Having tacitly assumed that the basic facts were rooted in arcane science, the average layman was in an awkward position. Civil nuclear energy, it seemed, would indeed have a major impact on his future and on that of his descendants, but perhaps not inevitably for good, as he felt he had hitherto been led to believe.

Why had this subject become a matter for general political debate only in the seventies — why not in the fifties when civil nuclear power first got underway, or in the sixties when opposition to nuclear weapons prompted major demonstrations? There were, as it happens, some heated political arguments about British nuclear power during those decades, but these arguments were essentially 'private' ones between the principal institutional bodies directly involved. They centred on such questions as the amount of nuclear power to which Britain should commit herself in a given period, the type of nuclear reactor technology on which this commitment should be based, the industrial structure through which it should be constructed, the distribution of the financial burden as between the taxpayer and the electricity consumer, and the consequences for other energy industries, especially coal. The underlying premiss in all these earlier arguments was that the development of nuclear energy was desirable, even, in the long run, essential. To this belief there was in the fifties and sixties no significant dissent. Even the electricity authorities and the coal industry, both of which at different times questioned the scale and economics of Britain's nuclear programme, never seriously challenged the ultimate justification for the development of the technology.

The various 'private' nuclear issues were not all equally resolved when the situation was altered in the seventies by the activities of the international environmental movement. This movement, having established itself as a political force to be reckoned with, settled on nuclear energy as one of its targets, indeed in many senses its chief one. Even

17

then, for several reasons to be considered later, opposition to nuclear power in Britain was considerably slower to become mobilised than was the case in the United States and in Western Europe. Nevertheless, by 1975 the 'private' politics of British nuclear power had been overtaken by a distinctly 'public' politics. The new 'public' issues were quite different in character and consequence. They amounted to questioning the fundamental attractions of, and need for, nuclear power, particularly bearing in mind the doubts objectors had about the safety of the various types of nuclear facilities, their fear for the impact of nuclear power on civil liberties, and their wider concern that civil nuclear power development could not but promote nuclear weapon proliferation.

There was also a second transformation in the mid-seventies, the 'energy crisis' brought into sharp focus by the Middle East war of 1973. Those who had always regarded nuclear energy as the only long-term solution to the world's, and Britain's, energy needs, now felt the case for its rapid development to be even more urgent than they had all along maintained.

The environmental and energy crises necessarily made nuclear energy a target for worldwide political debate. Britain's circumstances were further complicated in that her short-term energy demand was depressed and her medium-term energy supply situation unusually healthy, the former largely due to the world recession, the latter thanks to North Sea oil and major coal reserves.

That nuclear energy had become so publicly political bewildered many in the British nuclear industry. After two decades of grappling with technical and managerial difficulties, and with the 'private' political problems, their frame of mind was already 'not unlike that of Cinders after the ball'.[1] On top of this they now found themselves plunged into an intense and public controversy, and furthermore, having become used to high public esteem, had now instead to get used to having their judgement, and even their motives, questioned. This book is concerned with both the private and the public politics of British nuclear power. To that end the rest of this chapter sets out some of the more basic facts, briefly noting in turn the British nuclear programmes, the reactors of which they were composed, the institutional actors and some of the key individuals in the story. These facts are expanded and discussed in subsequent chapters.

Britain embarked formally on a programme of civil nuclear power stations in February 1955. The provisional programme was for 1.5-2GW over ten years, twelve stations being envisaged, the first eight to be based on the same type of reactor, the last four perhaps drawing on a different one. (To get the scale of this programme into perspective, the public electricity system had an installed capacity of some 20.7GW at this time.) The rationale of the 1955 programme rested on three things: the technical feasibility of nuclear power stations; the apparently urgent need for them given the energy shortfall anticipated at that time; and the assumption that their economics would not compare too unfavourably with those of conventional power stations.

In March 1957 the 1955 programme was in effect about trebled. There would now, it was planned, be 5-6GW of nuclear power by 1965. In fact, by 1957 the economics of nuclear power had already begun to worsen relative to conventional power, and this deterioration continued thereafter. In the autumn of 1957 the target date for completion of the new programme was indeed put back to 1966, but it was not until June 1960 that the Government announced an official reduction in the construction schedule for nuclear power. There was now to be a maximum of 5GW of nuclear power in the first programme, and the programme was also to be stretched so that it would complete in 1968 rather than in 1965/6. In the event, reactor power output having increased more rapidly than had been foreseen, there were only nine stations in this first programme, and they were all based on the same type of reactor.

With the first programme coming to an end, it became necessary in the early sixties to consider the appropriate policy to be followed subsequently. There ensued a political crisis with technical, economic and institutional dimensions. This effectively began in 1961 and was not resolved until 1965. It centred on the reactor type to be adopted for use in the stations of a postulated second programme. The choice really lay between two varieties of American reactor and a new British reactor which had been developed from the one used for the first programme. On the basis of a comparative appraisal of alternative designs for an actual station, Dungeness B, a decision was made in 1965 in favour of the new British reactor. It was held that this decision had been arrived at strictly on economic grounds and that the new reactor would produce electricity not only more cheaply than the American alternatives, but even more cheaply than new coal-fired stations. Herein lay a new source of political disagreement, the opposition of the coal industry. In due course it also became clear that the reactor crisis of the early sixties had deflected attention from another pressing issue, the structure and health of the private nuclear industry.

When complete the second programme will consist of five stations totalling 6GW, but the first of these began to come on stream only in

1976. This was because the new construction programme encountered difficulties which were often extremely severe. Some of these were technical, others organisational. Cumulatively, the problems were such that by the early seventies it had come to seem very unwise to order further stations based on the same reactor until the type was proved in commercial service, which could not be for some years. As a result the early seventies, like the early sixties, were a time of crisis for British nuclear power, and again a technical question was central. The American reactor types which had been promoted a decade earlier were still in the offing, and even a return to the obsolete reactor of the first programme was half considered. In 1973 a Nuclear Power Advisory Board was established to assist the responsible minister.

In the end, as in 1965 so also in 1974, the eventual choice was a British-developed reactor, though not on this occasion from the technological mainstream of British reactor development. In this instance approval was given only for a deliberately modest programme, 4GW of starts over four years, for operation, given the lead times by now typical, some time in the early or middle eighties.

Almost at once the reactor crisis returned. The new reactor appeared after all not to be suitable. Yet again one of the American reactors had to be considered. But by 1977 the British reactor of the second programme had re-entered the picture, that programme's first two stations having at last begun to operate in 1976, and in 1978 it was for two stations based on this that government approval was forthcoming. In respect of subsequent orders however, the door appeared this time to have been left significantly more ajar than ever previously for an American reactor at a later stage.

The reactors of the first programme became known as Magnox after the magnesium alloy used as canning material for their fuel. Those of the second programme are advanced gas-cooled reactors (AGRs), and those of the third as laid down in 1974 were to have been steam generating heavy water reactors (SGHWRs). The two American reactors considered in 1965 were both light water-cooled reactors (LWRs), the boiling water reactor (BWR) and the pressurised water reactor (PWR). In 1965 the BWR was the front runner of these but in 1974 and 1977 only the PWR was seriously considered. The SGHWR had some features in common with the Canadian CANDU reactor, and this reactor was itself tentatively considered for Britain in the early sixties and again mentioned as a possibility in the seventies. In addition to Magnox, the AGR and the SGHWR, Britain also developed two other reactor types. These were the high temperature gas-cooled reactor (HTR), undertaken in conjunction with a European group, and the fast breeder reactor (FBR). There seemed in the late sixties/early seventies a possibility that the HTR would soon enter into Britain's commercial plans, but its development status and general prospects were ultimately judged in 1974 to be too problematic. Commercial ordering of the FBR having long been anticipated, at the time of writing (spring 1979) still remained an uncertain future prospect. By the mid-seventies the future of this reactor had become the most controversial of all nuclear power questions.

From the immediate post-war years Britain's work on nuclear energy was divided into three parts. These were research, weapons research, and production, and in 1954 the three became separate groups of a new Atomic Energy Authority (AEA). The production section of the AEA became known as the Industrial Group and upon it fell the main task of reactor development. The AEA Act of 1954 stipulated that three of the Authority's members should have had wide professional experience in nuclear energy, and the original members in this category were also given executive responsibility for the Authority's three groups. Christopher Hinton, later Sir Christopher and later still Lord Hinton, was thus both Member for Engineering and Production and Managing Director of the Industrial Group until, in September 1957, he was appointed chairman of the newly created Central Electricity Generating Board (CEGB). Sir Christopher was one of the original 'nuclear knights', Sir John Cockcroft in charge of the Research Group at Harwell and Sir William, later Lord, Penney in charge of the Atomic Weapons Research Establishment at Aldermaston (AWRE) being the others.

In the first decade the AEA had two chairmen, Sir Edwin, later Lord, Plowden from 1954 to 1960 and Sir Roger Makins, later Lord Sherfield, from 1960 to 1964. A deputy chairman was first appointed in 1961. This was Sir William Penney, who was afterwards chairman from 1964 until 1967, when he was succeeded by John, later Sir John, Hill. Both Plowden and Sherfield had previously been senior civil servants in the Treasury, and Penney, Member for Weapons Research and Development when the Authority were set up, was therefore the first chairman with professional experience of atomic energy, while Hill was the first chairman whose career had been on the civil side of the Authority.

Sir Christopher Hinton had continuous responsibility for the production side of Britain's work on atomic energy, civil and military, from its post-war beginnings. On his move to the CEGB his executive functions at the AEA were assumed by his deputy, Sir Leonard Owen and in January 1958, W.R.J., later Sir William, Cook, deputy director of AWRE Aldermaston, was appointed to the AEA Board with policy responsibility for production and engineering. By this time the Industrial Group, whose headquarters were at Risley, was undergoing organisational difficulties. One remedy proposed was for the Group to be broken up to form smaller and more manageable units, but a report by the Fleck Committee, set up after the major nuclear accident at Windscale in 1957, argued rather that 'great advantages' accrued from keeping the development of reactors, fuel manufacturing and fuel reprocessing plants together in the same organisation. This Committee therefore rejected any division of the Industrial Group, in spite of noting their particularly 'heavy burden' and the fact that they were 'considerably undermanned', especially at the more senior levels.[2]

By 1959 the Industrial Group had grown to twice their 1954 size of 9,700 and were expected to grow further. The case for a division thus seemed irresistible, and the group's functions were accordingly split between a Production Group and a Development and Engineering Group, the latter, with Cook also now in executive charge, taking over primary responsibility for reactor development. In 1961 the Authority decided to reorganise the resulting four groups into five, as far as possible concentrating in one all work on reactor design and development. This became the Reactor Group, Cook correspondingly becoming Member for Reactors. Cook's term of office was extended for a further five years from 1963 but in the event he left the Authority in August 1964 to become Deputy Chief Scientific Adviser to the Minister of Defence. His successor was J.C.C. Stewart, previously Managing Director of the Production Group and Member for Production. Stewart resigned in December 1968 on becoming deputy chairman and chief executive of Babcock-English Electric Nuclear, one of the new design and construction companies set up at that time. Hans Kronberger then became Member for Reactor Development, with R.V. Moore becoming a Member in 1971 on Kronberger's death, Moore having in 1971 already for some ten years been Managing Director of the Reactor Group. The Reactor Group had meanwhile in 1969 absorbed most of the Engineering Group's staff and functions.

What kind of body were the AEA meant to be? In the words of ministers, they were to be 'a very novel and exceptional authority', 'a curious halfway house between a government department and an ordinary industry', 'more or less an incubator which will hatch the ideas of research people'.[3] The Authority's nature closely reflected their origins. The security provisions of the United States Atomic Energy Act of 1946, the McMahon Act, had led to a wholly independent British development effort in nuclear energy. Most of Britain's leading scientists in the field had been transferred to the United States and Canada in 1943 following the decision to concentrate work on the atomic bomb there. Consequently, almost no specifically British progress had been made when the Atomic Energy Act of November 1946 placed with the Ministry of Supply the responsibilities for atomic energy development until then formally held by a directorate of the Department of Scientific and Industrial Research. This was at the time a logical arrangement in that the Ministry of Supply had had considerable wartime experience of 'quasi-industrial' problems and also because, the war being over, it had spare capacity. The infant atomic project, exclusively military, was at first characterised by a heavy research effort and the building of several large and exotic industrial factories.

By 1950 there was already some disillusionment with the Ministry of Supply's control of atomic energy, and in 1951 this was given clear expression, Lord Cherwell calling on the Government to transfer work on nuclear energy 'to a special organisation more flexible than the normal civil service system'.[4] Cherwell, long a close associate of Sir Winston Churchill, became Paymaster General in the administration formed by Churchill later that year, and as such assumed responsibility for advising the Prime Minister on atomic energy matters. Within a fortnight of taking office the Prime Minister announced that the Ministry of Supply's responsibilities for atomic energy were being reconsidered. Partly in view of the atomic weapons tests scheduled for 1952 concrete action was postponed, but the PM told Parliament in April 1953 that a decision in principle had been taken to create a new and non-departmental organisation for atomic energy. Thanks largely to Cherwell, the Government had by now concluded, not without internal resistance, that the new organisation had to be different from any existing one, both because they wanted overall policy control to stay unequivocally ministerial, and because of the complete dependence of the organisation on public funds. It was left to a committee under the chairmanship of Lord Waverley to plan the transfer of functions, and also to suggest an appropriate organisational structure for the new body.[5]

The Waverley Committee advocated giving general responsibility for the new body, a responsibility said to be 'special and rather personal', to a non-departmental minister of 'high Cabinet rank', whose other concerns were not to 'encroach upon' atomic energy.[6] This the Government accepted and the Lord President, who already had general charge of the Government's scientific projects, thereupon became the designated minister. In giving responsibility for the new organisation to a non-departmental minister the Government evidently hoped among other things to resolve the conflict of priorities which it was suspected might have come to exist by 1953 between the civil and military applications of nuclear energy. The other main recommendations of the Waverley Committee were embodied in the Atomic Energy Act of June 1954, and on 19 July 1954 the Atomic Energy Authority replaced the Department of Atomic Energy, which had been brought into being as a temporary arrangement that January.

Several members of the Labour Opposition, and notably G.R. Strauss, had made plain their disapproval of the Government's decision to set up the new corporation.[7] The Bill was described by some of them as 'Lord Cherwell's Folly', and under it, it was said, a potentially dangerous 'new form of technocracy' could emerge. The Opposition's case was that the Ministry of Supply's control of atomic energy had worked well, and that, the Government having failed to make a convincing case for change, the original arrangement should therefore have been allowed to continue. The Government, however, had majorities of 158 to 122 in December 1953, and of 266 to 244 in March 1954.

Strikingly, in view of later developments, one Opposition member, Arthur Palmer, afterwards chairman of the Commons Select Committee on Science and Technology, said he believed that if the civil nuclear energy function were given to the British Electricity Authority (BEA), then 'much of the taxpayer's money would probably be saved because of the avoidance of unremunerative and wasteful expense'.[8] Palmer also tried, during the Bill's committee stage, to insert a provision that one member of the Authority should at least have had wide experience in the electricity supply industry, and might even be asked to double as a BEA member. The Government, however, argued that since electric power was only one of the products of atomic energy, it would be wrong to single out the electricity industry for special treatment. Palmer raised the point again in 1956 and on that occasion the minister partly accepted the idea. It seemed that the Government had in the interim themselves come to believe that a degree of common membership was the best way to ensure a close and cordial working relationship between the nuclear and electricity authorities, and the minister now said that it was his intention to bring it about as regards perhaps two AEA members serving part-time on the CEGB. The reverse arrangement, being statutorily a little more difficult, could then be considered later.[9]

Palmer's proposal was eventually implemented, but not until October 1965 after Britain's first reactor crisis and the Dungeness B decision. E.S. Booth, CEGB Member for Engineering then became a part-time member of the AEA, and J.C.C. Stewart, AEA Member for Reactors, a part-time member of the CEGB.

The then chairman of the Central Electricity Authority (CEA), Lord Citrine, states in his memoirs that he too at the outset advised cross-membership between the AEA and the CEA.[10] He adds that in his time 'signs of friction did occasionally show themselves, although they never amounted to much'. During Sir Christopher Hinton's term as CEGB chairman it seems unlikely that any other CEGB board member could effectively have served on the Authority. Hinton was indeed translated to the CEGB to effect the commercial establishment of a technology whose chief architect he had been while with the AEA. What the Government did not adequately foresee in appointing him was that he would find increasingly unsatisfactory as CEGB chairman the influence he had over the AEA's subsequent policies. He became, in *The Economist*'s words, a most eminent 'poacher turned gamekeeper'.[11]

The 1954 Atomic Energy Act, then, provided for a body different from the more typical public corporations in two main respects. In the first place the Government felt that the political importance, the financial nature and the security aspects of the atomic energy project together made inadequate the standard formula whereby the responsible minister is supposed simply to give a public corporation general directions in instances where he thinks the national interest may be involved. In the case of atomic energy the minister was therefore given less restricted powers, though he was still not intended to exercise them except in a vital matter of the national interest. Second, since any prospect of the Authority paying their way seemed in 1954 a very long-term one, it appeared logical to finance them by Parliamentary Vote, after the manner of a government department and, the corollary of this, to make their accounts available to the Comptroller and Auditor General. The departmental responsibility for nuclear energy before the creation of the AEA, these two provisions and the consequences which flowed from them, were to make the AEA, as seen from within government, almost still a government department. And this circumstance in turn, reinforced by the prestige accruing to the AEA from the success of the military project and further protected by the esoteric nature of the Authority's concerns, was to confer on them a rather special autonomy.

The Waverley Committee had appreciated the need for the minister to whom the Authority reported to have his own small group of officials, and this was the group which came to constitute the Atomic Energy Office. The secretary of this office was made accounting officer for the Authority, but his position was formally recognised, in a Treasury letter to the first incumbent, to be anomalous, in that he neither had direct control over Authority personnel nor was he expected to have as thorough a knowledge of AEA affairs as would have been required of him as accounting officer for a normal government department. The Treasury also reached an early understanding with the Authority whereby they would be consulted by the Authority about any project costing more than £100,000, and about any having 'features of a novel or contentious character'. These moves were made in the spirit of the Waverley recommendation that the new Authority should in their financial transactions conform broadly to the procedures governing departments, while at the same time striving to operate in a more businesslike fashion than departments were able to do.[12]

In the development of civil nuclear energy the Authority were given a five-fold role.[13] They had to conduct an extensive r & d programme on nuclear reactors, including basic physics experiments and fuel element development; they had the initial task of training personnel from industry and the electricity authorities in the techniques of nuclear power; they had to act as advisers to the electricity authorities on the nuclear side of the new power stations; they had to procure adequate supplies of the special materials, primarily graphite and uranium, needed in the civil power programme, and they had to fabricate fuel elements and separate from irradiated fuel the potentially valuable plutonium residue. (In 1971 a new public body, British Nuclear Fuels Limited (BNFL), was set up to take over responsibility for the fuel side of the AEA, a measure of private shareholding being promised for the future. The new organisation's chairmanship was combined with that of the Authority but the Government stressed[14] at that time that there would be limits on BNFL's accountability to Parliament.)

On the one hand, then, there was from 1954 a new and rather unusual public corporation. On the other there were to be more traditional bodies, the electricity generating boards. The electricity supply industry had been nationalised in 1947, the Act providing for a British Electricity Authority (BEA) to be responsible for the generation and bulk transmission of electricity, and for area boards, to manage its distribution. Two of these boards were amalgamated in 1954 to form the South of Scotland Electricity Board (SSEB), and this board at the same time took over the duties of the BEA within their geographical area, the

BEA becoming the Central Electricity Authority (CEA) to mark the change. The CEA changed again when the industry in England and Wales was reorganised in 1957. The 1957 Act was based on the recommendations of the Herbert Committee, and under it the functions of the CEA were shared between the Central Electricity Generating Board and the Electricity Council.

The two generating boards central to the story of Britain's nuclear development are thus the CEGB and the all-purpose SSEB. The plant capacity of the CEGB has always been of the order of ten times that of the SSEB and, reflecting this, only one of the nine Magnox stations was built for the SSEB, at Hunterston on the Clyde, and only one AGR station in the second programme, also at Hunterston. The SSEB system was indeed not much bigger during the first nuclear programme than the minimum size capable of absorbing large nuclear stations, and since until the seventies the SSEB stayed close to the CEGB line in their specifications and approach, it is accurate enough for the earlier period to regard the CEGB as the effective voice of the electricity supply industry. (It should however be said that the SSEB were thought by some in 1957 to have opted for a more ambitious Magnox design than had the CEGB.[15])

The CEA chairman at the time of the 1955 White Paper was Lord Citrine. As noted above, Sir Christopher Hinton became chairman of the CEGB in 1957. Hinton's successors were Stanley, later Sir Stanley, Brown (1965-72), Arthur, later Sir Arthur, Hawkins (1972-7) and Glynn England (1977-). The SSEB's chairman when it distanced itself from the CEGB in the mid-seventies was Francis, later Sir Francis, Tombs.

It was arranged that the SSEB should report to the Secretary of State for Scotland, the CEGB, the Electricity Council and the area boards to the Minister of Power, and here again it is really only the latter ministry and its successors which are important for the purposes of this book. The ministry was in fact known as the Ministry of Fuel and Power until 1958, and as the Ministry of Power afterwards until its absorption in the Ministry of Technology in 1969.

The third element of Britain's nuclear industry, after the AEA and the CEGB, were the consortia, groups of companies undertaking to construct for the generating boards nuclear stations based on concepts developed by the Authority.[16] Even before 1955 the AEA had begun to prepare private industry for a commercial programme. A reactor school was opened at Harwell in 1954 and during the following two years the Authority trained design teams from industry, as well as groups seconded by the generating boards, in the technology of Magnox reactors. At the time the AEA felt strongly that the most effective industrial arrangement for developing nuclear power would be to have several groups, each wholly capable of executing the complete or turnkey contract for a nuclear power station. Interested companies were therefore firmly encouraged to form themselves into appropriate groups around selected parent firms. Four such consortia or quasi-consortia had been established by early 1955, each led by a heavy electrical plant manufacturer, a fifth consortium was formed in 1956 despite the opposition of the original four, and there was even talk of a sixth. Indeed, according to Sir Christopher Hinton, whereas some companies had joined a little reluctantly in 1954-5, by 1956 the AEA were having difficulty in restricting their numbers.

As adviser to the electricity authorities as well as the consortia, the AEA now had the difficult job of trying to be impartial while also preserving commercial security. 'Equivocal in the extreme' was how *Nuclear Engineering* for instance saw the Authority's position, though without suggesting any breach of faith.[17] There was also the problem that, with turnkey contracting, companies outside the consortia tended effectively to be excluded. On the other hand, membership of one consortium did not necessarily preclude a firm from supplying equipment to one of the others.

By 1958 the Government were acknowledging that the system was 'by no means perfect' and by 1960 shortage of work had led to amalgamations and withdrawals among the consortia, with the result that through most of the sixties there were in fact only three. The process by which these became first two, with a public shareholding, and then ultimately one was protracted and a major contributory factor to the poor health of British nuclear power in the late sixties and early seventies. Eventually, in 1973, the National Nuclear Corporation (NNC) was formed as a holding company, the Nuclear Power Company later being set up to act as its operational arm. The NNC was established as a mixed public-private body, the General Electric Company initially having a 50 per cent shareholding, the AEA 15 per cent, and the rest of private industry, grouped as British Nuclear Associates, 35 per cent.

The main co-ordinating body between the AEA, CEGB and consortia was originally the Nuclear Power Collaboration Committee, which first met in early 1955. This had subordinate working parties and study groups, separate arrangements initially being made for the fifth consortium. There was also other co-ordinating machinery between the AEA and the CEGB, and between the AEA and the consortia. Thus the

Authority Member for Reactors met regularly with the chief engineers of the consortia, with similar contacts at lower levels, and two technical members from each of the AEA and the CEGB met in a members' committee, again with expert subcommittees on appropriate subjects. The essentials of the internal AEA decision-making process were outlined by the Authority's chairman in 1963.[18] There was, he said, 'complete conviction' in the organisation that returns would eventually handsomely repay investment, though this could not then be proved, but the scale of nuclear projects made frequent policy changes inadvisable, and this implied 'exceptional care' in the initial selection of reactor systems for development. An elaborate committee structure within the AEA culminated in the Reactor Programmes Committee. Sir William Penney also mentioned on this occasion the then new Reactor Policy Committee, apparently designed to act as a vehicle for a fuller exchange of views between the AEA, generating boards and consortia, though by this time the key development decisions on the AGR, HTR and SGHWR had all been taken.

These then were the issues, programmes, institutional actors and reactors: what of ministerial responsibility for nuclear power development from 1955 to 1978? The nuclear programme of 1955 was announced while the AEA were still in their first year of independent existence. The Authority were then under the broad ministerial direction of the Marquess of Salisbury as Lord President of the Council. This arrangement continued until, on Salisbury's sudden resignation from the Government in March 1957, the Prime Minister, Harold Macmillan, himself took overall charge, letting it be known that he would be assisted by the Paymaster General, Reginald Maudling.[19]

In forming his 1959 Government Macmillan created the new office of Minister for Science and transferred to the minister, Lord Hailsham, the AEA responsibility. Hailsham retained this responsibility until the General Election of 1964, first as Lord Privy Seal and Minister for Science then, following the government changes of July 1960, as Lord President, and finally from April 1964 as Secretary of State for Education and Science. Following the setting up of the Ministry of Technology by the incoming Labour Government of 1964, statutory responsibility for the AEA passed from the Education Secretary (Michael Stewart) to the new minister, originally Frank Cousins, then after Cousins's resignation in 1966 to Anthony Wedgwood Benn. Benn continued to be responsible for the Authority until the defeat of the Labour Government in 1970, the Ministry of Technology meanwhile absorbing the Ministry of Power in the autumn of 1969. Geoffrey

Rippon then briefly became Minister of Technology, but both ministry and minister were soon changed, John Davies becoming Secretary of State in a new Department of Trade and Industry (DTI). Under the Secretary of State, and with particular responsibility for nuclear questions, Sir John Eden was Minister for Industry from 1970 to spring 1972, and Tom Boardman from then until the end of 1973. In 1973 Davies was succeeded by Peter Walker but in 1974 a new Department of Energy was created under Lord Carrington. On the return of Labour in 1974 Eric Varley was at first Energy Secretary but in 1975 he exchanged posts with Tony Benn, who thus returned to a policy field for which he had first had partial responsibility almost a decade before.

From their establishment in 1954 until the Conservatives left office a decade later, the AEA thus came under three ministers. Over the same period there were two Ministers of Fuel and Power (Geoffrey Lloyd 1954-5 and Aubrey Jones 1955-6) and three Ministers of Power (Lord Mills 1957-9, Richard Wood 1959-63 and F.J. Erroll 1963-4). Of these only Mills and Erroll were in the Cabinet. Under Labour from 1964-70 the AEA came under two ministers, but Power, throughout a Cabinet position, under five (Fred Lee 1964-6, Richard Marsh 1966-8, R.J. Gunter 1968, Roy Mason 1968-9 and Anthony Wedgwood Benn 1969-70 – as Minister of Technology). After 1969 responsibility for all sides of the nuclear industry, except the environmental aspects, was concentrated in one ministry, first Mintech, then the DTI, and from 1974, Energy.

The ministers responsible for the AEA were served by the Atomic Energy Office, first set up in 1955. This usually had a staff consisting of one under-secretary, one or two assistant secretaries, and one or two principals. The Office was absorbed into the Ministry of Technology upon the latter's formation and became a Division, a separate Reorganisation of the Nuclear Industry Branch also being formed. It is interesting in this connection to note the continuity established by two people, M.I. Michaels, under-secretary in the Atomic Energy Office when it was part of the Lord President's Office in 1955 and in the same field until 1971, by then responsible for the Atomic Energy Division in the DTI; and D.E.H. Peirson, AEA secretary over the same period.

Safety was from an early stage, and especially after the Windscale accident of 1957, a special concern in the civil nuclear context. Reflecting this, the Nuclear Installations Inspectorate were established as a licensing agency under an Act of 1959 and the Nuclear Safety Advisory Committee were created in 1960 to assist the responsible minister. This committee consisted, after 1972, of people whose interests were outside the nuclear industry. They were replaced in 1977 by an Advisory Committee on Nuclear Installations.[20] The Windscale accident of 1957 also led to the setting up of an AEA Health and Safety Branch. The research responsibilities of this branch, a Radiological Protection Service run by the Medical Research Council, and the functions of a Radioactive Substances Advisory Committee were all taken over in 1970 by a new National Radiological Protection Board, the AEA however retaining a Safety and Reliability Directorate.

Safety was naturally a focus also of the report on nuclear power and the environment published by the Royal Commission on Environmental Pollution in 1976. By this time the public debate on nuclear energy was in full swing and could be seen to have identified four main targets. These were the light water reactors, especially when contemplated for British use in 1974 and 1977; a proposal by British Nuclear Fuels Limited to install a new type of fuel reprocessing capacity at Windscale and to accept foreign contracts in respect of it; the exact location of nuclear waste disposal sites; and the future of the FBR and in particular of the projected first commercial fast reactor. Many groups were involved in contesting these issues, a leading role being taken by the Friends of the Earth organisation.

Civil nuclear power policy was by 1975 being more fully ventilated than ever before. Until 1967 there had been remarkably little public discussion of the subject, not least because public and Parliament had tolerated a situation in which relevant information was hard to come by. Some information had emerged in the late fifties as a result of the Fleck inquiries into the Windscale accident of 1957 and an investigation by the Commons Estimates Committee into part of the AEA. And in the early sixties a little more was forthcoming through an inquiry into electricity supply undertaken by the Commons Nationalised Industries Committee. Otherwise there was only the limited information provided by White Papers, annual reports, Parliamentary Questions and the occasional foray by the Commons Committee of Public Accounts. After 1967 the situation began to improve, in the first place because of the work of the Commons Select Committee on Science and Technology, who selected nuclear power for their first investigation and returned centrally to the area another four times in the following decade. The appointment in 1975 of an Energy Secretary who chose to make publication of relevant information into something of an issue of political principle, the report in 1976 by the Royal Commission, and the Windscale Inquiry of 1977 each then carried still further the process of opening up the public nuclear debate.

The structure of this book follows fairly naturally from the circumstances which have now been outlined. Chapters 2-10 deal with what were called above the 'private' nuclear issues, Chapter 11 with the 'public' ones, and the concluding chapter attempts to draw together the main political features of both.

The three foci of the private nuclear issues are taken to be the reactor crises culminating in the programme decisions of 1965, 1974 and 1978. Chapters 2, 3 and 4 discuss the three main inputs into the reactor crisis which was resolved by the 1965 decision. Broadly these inputs can be described as technological, economic and miscellaneous political — 'miscellaneous' because the economic and technological inputs produced their own politics. Chapter 5 then examines the policy of 1964 which led to the decision of 1965 and Chapter 6 examines the 1965 decision itself. Chapters 7, 8 and 9 trace the main political questions which arose in British nuclear power's second decade. Chapter 7 is concerned with the role of nuclear power in fuel policy, Chapter 8 with the structure of the nuclear industry and Chapter 9 with Britain's second reactor crisis. Chapter 10 deals with Britain's third reactor crisis and completes the first part of the book. A rather long Chapter 11 aims to do two things: first, to identify the main arguments about nuclear power as put by the nuclear 'establishment', the nuclear 'opposition', the 'quasi-official participants', and other interested parties; and second, to outline the circumstances of the government decisions which eventually led to approval for BNFL's Windscale reprocessing projects.

Coming to grips with the substance of the private and public nuclear issues is really task enough for two books. Despite that, it seems essential to try to put the British civil nuclear case into some sort of general context by asking of it some fundamental questions. The case, it is suggested, must be seen in terms of at least three fundamental political dilemmas. First, how is technical information and advice to be best integrated into general policy-making? Second, what kind of public accountability is it reasonable to look for in respect of issues like civil nuclear power? And third, what is the proper role of government in the development of a new technology? This book does not pretend finally to answer these questions but it is hoped that readers will with its help be able to formulate some tentative answers of their own.

Notes

1. R.L.R. Nicholson, 'The Nuclear Power Paradox in the UK', *Energy Policy* (June 1973), p. 38.
2. Cmd. 338; also HC 316-I (1958-9), p. 505.
3. HCD 529 c. 1532; HCD 526 c. 1795-886 (1881).

4. HLD 169 c. 461; HLD 172 c. 670-708 (670); also HLD 185 c. 24-63 (57).

5. See Lorna Arnold, 'The Birth of the UKAEA', *Atom* (July 1975), pp. 94-9; also HCD 493 c. 1160; HCD 498 c. 22; HCD 514 c. 1958-64.

6. Cmd. 8986; also A.W. Griffiths, 'Legislation on atomic energy in the UK', *Atom* (October 1958), pp. 9-12.

7. HCD 521 c. 2286-323; HCD 524 c. 844-966; HCD 525 c. 390-478.

8. HCD 524 c. 885.

9. HCD 562 c. 942-3, 1046-7.

10. Lord Citrine, *Two Careers* (Hutchinson, London, 1967), p. 347.

11. *The Economist*, 11 June 1960.

12. HC 348 (1955-6), pp. 491-2; Comptroller and Auditor General (1954-5), para. 184.

13. AEA 1st Annual Report, pp. 83-4; 3rd Annual Report, pp. 63-7; Sir John Cockcroft, 'The UKAEA and its Functions', *BNECJ*, 1, pp. 13-23 (January 1956); R.D'Arcy Best, 'The UKAEA', *Public Administration*, 34, (Spring 1956); K.H.B. Frere, 'Membership of the UKAEA', *Public Administration*, 36 (Autumn 1958).

14. HCD 867 c. 337-40 (WA); HCD 808 c. 1590-1658 (1647); HCD 809 c. 383-423.

15. See *NE* (January 1957), pp. 1, 5-9.

16. See for example, Sir Christopher Hinton, 'Industry's Role in Nuclear Development', *Atom* (October 1957), p. 5.

17. 'Structure of the British nuclear industry', *NE* (March 1963), pp. 96-9; *NE* (October 1956), p. 265; *NE* (August 1957), p. 307.

18. Sir William Penney, 'Research and Development in the AEA', *Atom* (February 1964), pp. 38-48: see also Sir Roger Makins, 'Nuclear Energy: A Year of Promise', *BNESJ*, 1 (1962), pp. 161-7 (164).

19. HCD 568 c. 105 (WA); HCD 577 c. 775-6.

20. HCD 654 c. 798; HCD 625 c. 117-18 (WA); *Atom* (1964), p. 213; *Atom* (1972), p. 109; *Atom* (1977), p. 283.

2 TECHNOLOGICAL MOMENTUM

The advanced gas-cooled reactor (AGR) came to be seen as really the only British-developed reactor which could be considered for the Dungeness B site in 1965. To explain how this came about, this chapter briefly traces the technical evolution of the AGR from its origins in the basic British philosophy of nuclear power. It then becomes possible to understand both the growth of the AEA's confidence in the AGR, and also the more important reasons why this confidence was, until 1965, essentially theirs alone. The outline which follows is far from being a technical history.[1] Much less ambitiously, one is concerned here only with the process through which the AEA came to concentrate their efforts on the AGR, with the way they went about overcoming technical development problems with this reactor, and with the consequent build-up of momentum within the Authority in its support.

Britain's original attachment to gas-cooled, graphite-moderated, natural uranium reactors was largely dictated by immediate post-war circumstances. First, the only fissile material then available to Britain was natural uranium. Second, the use of natural uranium meant that for technical reasons the use of ordinary, or 'light', water as a moderator was ruled out. Further, it seemed doubtful that adequate supplies of heavy water could be obtained, at least at reasonable prices, whereas the only other short-term alternative moderator material, graphite, was both readily available and familiar. Third, there was the question of coolant. It was inevitable that the first choice again here should be ordinary or 'light' water, since this was the coolant the Americans had settled upon for their graphite-moderated plutonium production reactors at Hanford. It was known that water-cooled reactors could under certain circumstances, and more or less instantaneously, become extremely dangerous, possibly leading to a serious release of radioactivity. Although this risk was not thought sufficient to outweigh the engineering simplicity of the water-cooled reactor, and the demonstrated fact from the Hanford experience that it could be made to work, it was still felt to be necessary to locate any such reactor at least fifty miles from the nearest town. It was also laid down that the site had to be coastal, have a plentiful supply of rather pure water, and be reasonably easily accessible, and in fact only one spot in Britain apparently managed to meet all these requirements, and even it had drawbacks. This was an unacceptable situation, and since a committee drawn from the atomic energy organisation and with independent experts declined to relax the safety requirements, the organisation was unable to conform to the directive it had been given to build a Hanford-type reactor. Its engineers were therefore encouraged to persevere with gas cooling. The Americans had earlier been discouraged from this approach by problems associated with gas circulation, in particular a lack of large gas-circulation blowers. Ways of overcoming these problems were now put forward in Britain, including the provision of fins on the fuel cans to promote the removal of waste heat. The plutonium-producing natural uranium reactor cooled by air at atmospheric pressure thus became possible, and two such reactors were thereupon built at Windscale to supply the military programme. The urgency of this programme meant that there was not enough time to equip these reactors with the means of converting their waste heat into useful power, but the Ministry of Supply's engineers and scientists, and also ministers and officials, had this prospect fully in mind from the beginning. The production group under Sir Christopher Hinton in fact suggested that the defence demand for plutonium might usefully be met in two stages, the second of which would have involved a dual purpose power/plutonium reactor. Had this proposal not been turned down — without apparently a very full consideration — the subsequent development of British nuclear power might well have been substantially different. Studies of the dual purpose concept were in hand by 1947 and industrial participation was soon invited. There was, in due course, a confluence between the results of these studies, the work done earlier at Chalk River in Canada, practical experience in building the Windscale reactors, and the Ministry of Work's experience with large pressure vessels. By September 1950 it had been shown that a gas-graphite power reactor could be designed with a thermal efficiency of around 20 per cent — the efficiency of conventional stations was then around 30 per cent. However, pressure of military work forced the Risley production organisation to drop out of power reactor studies, leaving this field temporarily to Harwell. After the Risley design team responsible for the Windscale reactors had completed their work there was a possibility that they might have been switched to designing power reactors based on the same concept, but because it had not become clear at what level financial support for this would be forthcoming, the decision was instead made to reassign the team to the fast breeder reactor (FBR).

The official historian, writing of the thousand different reactors which Harwell considered between 1948 and 1951, says that the 'only point on which there was general agreement throughout all these years was on the long-term future – on the ultimate and overriding importance of breeder reactors'.[2] Notwithstanding this, the FBR concept was already understood to be extremely complicated and necessarily very long term. Consequently, although FBRs were 'from the outset, the main goal of a nuclear power programme', it came to be believed that their development time scale left room for a 'transitional stage' using thermal reactors.

Of this early period one may conclude that the British decision, afterwards to be twice consciously reconfirmed in the fifties, to back gas cooling, was a choice which ensured that when commercial competition began between the United Kingdom and the United States, as it was eventually bound to do, then that competition would involve not only economics but also dissimilar technical philosophies. Because, from this time on, faith in the merits of gas cooling came to be, in Hinton's words, 'the cardinal belief of the British reactor creed',[3] both in that it promised higher temperatures, and therefore higher efficiencies, than water cooling, and in that it minimised the enrichment necessary for the fuel, a consideration especially important in the British context where power costs were high and enrichment therefore expensive. That gas reactors could for a long time be considered somehow safer than water ones was a welcome bonus, as also was the fact that they seemingly posed none of the metallurgical problems of corrosion met with in light water reactors.

Since Harwell was sceptical in the late forties about economic nuclear power despite its Power Conferences which began in 1948, studies of thermal reactors there initially focussed on enriched uranium models, with a particular view to submarine propulsion. The first thorough design study began in November 1949 and continued for two years. But this scheme failed to become an Admiralty priority, enriched uranium could not be made available in quantity for some years, and light water was still seen as technically unattractive both as coolant and moderator. Thus it was that a 'combination of circumstance and decision' reconfirmed Britain in gas-cooled natural uranium reactors.[4]

In the autumn of 1950 then, Harwell began turning back to these reactors, an unexciting but realistic proposition as it was then thought, if early nuclear power were the objective. The Harwell Power Conference of that year, at which the British Electricity Authority (BEA) were represented, discussed reactors of this sort and R.V. Moore, an engineer, made the first serious study of power costs.[5] Moore 'guessed' the capital cost of a nuclear station at about £100/kw for a 90MW reactor, with a power cost of 0.6d, this at an optimistic interest rate of four per cent but a pessimistic load factor of 60 per cent. He made no allowance for a plutonium credit, but suggested rather the 'carrying forward' free of cost of the potentially valuable but unseparated plutonium produced by power generation. Even so, he concluded that a natural uranium power station might 'begin to compete favourably' with coal stations at the comparatively low fuel irradiation figure of 2000MWD/ tonne, if the initial fuel cost were no more than £10,000/tonne. A generating cost figure of 0.6d was, in Sir John Cockcroft's words,[6] 'considerably lower than previous estimates and provoked a good deal of discussion especially by the supporters of the fast reactor'. In Lord Hinton's words,[7] written on R.V. Moore's retirement from the AEA in 1976, Moore's report was 'balanced and far-sighted' and his estimates 'were more realistic than those which were used as a basis for the 1954 [sic] White Paper'.

But even after this Harwell, as a whole, was far from enthusiastic about natural uranium reactors, and until 1952 there was substantially more interest in them outside the atomic energy organisation than inside. Despite its known disadvantages it still appeared that the moderator for a British natural uranium reactor must be graphite, and the coolant a gas. As moderator, heavy water continued to be ruled out on supply grounds and liquids and liquid metals were seen as infeasible coolants since they made necessary either cooling tubes, and hence again enriched fuel, or a pressure shell of a size and thickness then thought to be beyond construction.

Since the intention was now to extract heat usefully from the coolant gas, a pressure circuit was called for and the question arose as to which gas should be used. Of the more than a dozen gases which Harwell investigated, helium and, to a lesser extent, carbon dioxide seemed to be most attractive. Helium was then rejected because of its cost and an inevitable dependence on American supplies, and this left carbon dioxide. This was cheap, had good nuclear and heat transfer properties, and was soon shown to be stable at the temperature and radiation fluxes to be expected in a power reactor. There remained the problem that it was known to react with graphite, and extensive experiments had to be performed before it was established that the effect could be tolerated under the conditions which would obtain in the type of reactor then being considered. This problem was later to arise again, and much more critically, in the context of the AGR.

In moving from the Windscale plutonium-production reactors to power-producing ones it was also necessary to find a new fuel-canning material, as the aluminium cans used in the former were known to be unsuitable for operation at higher temperatures. Beryllium and zirconium both had particularly attractive characteristics, but these were again offset by a poor supply situation and also by the fact that not much was known about them. Gradually the choice devolved upon an alloy of magnesium with beryllium and other metals. This alloy became known as magnox and afterwards lent its name to the reactor family of the first commercial nuclear power programme.[8]

As well as settling the coolant and canning material the Harwell power reactor scheme of the early fifties, which became known as PIPPA, naturally implied many other detailed design changes, including for instance a vertical fuel channel arrangement as opposed to the horizontal arrangement used previously. Several industrial companies co-operated in carrying out the necessary design study under B.L. Goodlet in 1952, and BEA engineers also became involved. The atomic energy organisation, though now becoming increasingly persuaded that nuclear power was urgently needed, still had doubts about the natural uranium reactor, not least because of its apparently limited development potential, and even Hinton had come to share these doubts, despite his earlier proposal that the second Windscale pile be dual purpose. However, the 'determination and enthusiasm' of PIPPA's design team greatly helped to keep the project alive, and this small group thus 'powerfully influenced' subsequent British reactor development.[9]

By the end of 1952 the result of the combined effort on PIPPA was a blueprint for a 35MW plant which, when optimised for power production, promised an efficiency of 25 per cent, while simultaneously producing plutonium as a by-product. It is probable that a plant based on these specifications would shortly afterwards have been built for the BEA at East Yelland, but an increased military demand for plutonium in the autumn of 1952 encouraged the atomic energy organisation, after a tentative flirtation with a pressurised water reactor (PWR), to recommend to the Government that this demand be met by a reactor along the lines of the Harwell feasibility study, but optimised now for plutonium production and with electricity as a by-product. With Lord Cherwell's strong support the Government approved this proposal in March 1953 and there followed the building of Calder Hall.[10] Calder Hall was therefore a logical bridging step between the plutonium-production reactors at Windscale and commercial power stations. Government acceptance of this further step was itself only a couple of years away.

Before pursuing that further step there is a digression which is well worth making. As noted in the Introduction, Hinton was, until 1957, managing director of the AEA's Industrial Group and afterwards, until 1964, chairman of the CEGB. In 1952, as head of the atomic energy project's production side, he successfully bid to have his Risley organisation reassume responsibility for the Calder Hall project from Harwell and the AEA's Industrial Group thereafter became the womb of British reactors. An examination of Hinton's evolving opinions of the various types of nuclear reactor is therefore very valuable in trying to understand the CEGB's position in the early sixties.

During the fifties and early sixties Hinton lectured frequently[11] on nuclear energy and points from his later addresses are taken up below. His views at a critically formative time in the development of British nuclear power were set out in a lecture he gave to the Institution of Mechanical Engineers in 1954.[12] In the course of this he reviewed the most promising candidates among the many power reactor systems then being considered. The Calder Hall reactors were still being built and Hinton pointed out both their advantages, in particular their safety, partially deriving from their large thermal capacity, and their disadvantages, notably the large uranium investment and high-purity graphite they needed, and the difficulties involved in constructing their pressure shells. He took note of the design easement promised by enriched fuel, and of the cost reductions which could be expected to result from experience, and concluded overall that the gas-graphite reactor appeared to compare favourably with alternative thermal systems.

In the same vein, at the first Geneva conference on nuclear power, held a few months after publication of the first British White Paper in 1955, Hinton recalled[13] that it was the unavailability of suitable sites which had forced Britain to depart from the Hanford-type reactor, adding that 'in every engineering development there is an element of chance which may sway the balance between the choice of one design or another'. He suggested on this occasion that the basic gas-graphite reactor, with its tremendous advantages in terms of safety, avoidance of enriched uranium and of exotic materials, might perhaps be seen as the 'slow-speed reciprocating engine of the reactor world, reliable and almost conventional in design'.

Of the heavy water reactor Hinton's opinion in 1954 was that it had especially attractive features for the physicist, its good neutron economy holding out the promise of smaller cores and higher heat ratings. The chief drawback with it in 1954 was still, he felt, the poor availability of heavy water, a handicap which could be overcome only by substantial investment in a plant to manufacture this substance. What was to seem to many a damaging flirtation with the heavy water reactor by Hinton as CEGB chairman in the early sixties thus really had its origins in his much earlier assessment that, in spite of its drawbacks, this reactor might one day come to the fore.

The construction of a prototype heavy water reactor in Britain was in fact considered and rejected in 1953, partly on the grounds that it could not give the immediate results expected with the Calder reactors, partly on the grounds that if the Canadians, who had decided to back this system, made a breakthrough, then the relationship with them was such that licences would be easily forthcoming.[14] Until the increased plutonium demand of 1952 changed the whole picture, Hinton's preference had indeed been for close integration with the Canadians, Britain taking the lead on the FBR but leaving thermal reactor development to the Canadian Chalk River programme.

It was in his treatment of the light water reactors that Hinton managed in 1954 to be most percipient: 'To an engineer there is something particularly attractive about the light water reactor, both in its extreme simplicity and in its avoidance of any extravagant materials of construction. It is perhaps slightly inferior to the heavy water reactor in its economics owing to the use of enriched uranium; however, it has much the lowest capital cost of any type of nuclear reactor which we can at present envisage and this may be a very important consideration during the next few years.' In the light of this judgement it may be thought a little surprising that the AEA in the end chose not to construct a demonstration light water reactor. Hinton did however believe, as he said in 1956, that the merits of the Calder Hall type of reactor were such that it would not only give Britain a lead until the mid-sixties, but would also be built in some form fifteen years after that, gradually being superseded by liquid-cooled reactors with higher heat ratings. And he continued thereafter to affirm his confidence in gas-graphite as the right choice for Britain, stressing in 1958, for instance, that higher temperatures could be achieved with a gas than with a liquid, since at any given temperature gases are less chemically reactive than liquids.[15]

The first British nuclear power programme was announced in a uniquely entrepreneurial White Paper of February 1955. Yet, according to Sir Leonard Owen,[16] as late as January 1955 the (test bed) Calder Hall project itself 'was in jeopardy' because of problems with the fuel's magnox can. The fallback material was aluminium, but the use of this would have entailed a serious drop in reactor performance. Only 'at the last moment' apparently was the magnox can perfected.

And even then, when the 1955 decision was taken, there was, in Owen's words, 'very little information available on the irradiation behaviour of the individual materials and virtually none on their performance as complete fuel elements'. Owen adds that there was still 'no irradiation experience of any statistical value' when the first commercial tenders were accepted in late 1956.

The White Paper of 1955 tentatively outlined the reactor types likely to appear in the first commercial power programme. The choice of reactor at this time was still in principle wide open — it was said at the first Geneva conference on atomic energy in 1955 that about a hundred different systems were then not obviously infeasible, hence what Weinberg[17] called the 'enormous difficulty of choosing a proper path'. The 1955 plan was that the first four commercial stations would have reactors of the Calder Hall type, 'The only reactor for commercial power production that is within our present technical reach.' Somewhat less confidently, the White Paper[18] suggested that the next four stations might also have reactors of the same general type, but larger and more advanced versions. The last four it was thought might then be liquid-cooled reactors. Liquid cooling was sought because it offered higher heat ratings and lower capital costs. But it also meant enriched fuel, and the hope was expressed in the White Paper that the necessary enrichment might 'conveniently be provided by the plutonium produced in the early reactors'. It was considered probable that a prototype of a liquid-cooled reactor could be tested by 1963, paving the way for commercial stations by 1965. The White Paper added that the light water reactor, using light water under pressure as both coolant and moderator, was one type of liquid-cooled reactor which could probably be made commercial on this time scale. Carbon (graphite) and light water were spoken of as having 'obvious advantages' as moderators from the supply point of view, with graphite the 'most practical' in the immediate future, while carbon dioxide and light water were 'the most probable choices' as coolants in Britain over the following few years. Other possibilities mentioned were sodium-cooled, graphite-moderated reactors and heavy water reactors, but the White Paper made it plain that prototypes of neither the homogeneous reactor, a reactor having its fuel, coolant and moderator mixed in the form of a suspension, nor of the fast reactor could be ready before the mid-sixties.

At the outset, then,[19] the Atomic Energy Authority conceived the first commercial nuclear power programme as likely to consist of at least two kinds of reactor, the Calder Hall type steadily being improved, and a liquid-cooled variety, most probably a light water reactor (LWR) of some kind. The Authority's second annual report of 1956 reiterated this, describing Britain's exploitation of nuclear energy as likely to have three stages. As Sir John Cockcroft, the Director of the Authority's Research Group, explained in November 1956, these were still the gas-graphite reactors, where the immediate objective was to push up operating temperatures by at least a hundred degrees centigrade; the pressurised water reactor and the sodium-cooled, graphite-moderated reactor, both of which the Authority now said they had investigated in detail, as stage two candidates; and the fast breeder as the third-stage reactor on which a good deal of work had already been done. Beyond this Cockcroft reported that the Authority were working on two thermal breeder reactors on the U233-thorium cycle, and also that they were contemplating an ultra-high-temperature, gas-cooled experimental reactor for 1959. The latter soon began to have a high priority in their development programme. In part this was because they had come to suspect that the gas-graphite route might have greater potential than they had initially appreciated. In particular, straightforward engineering improvements were now expected to lead quite quickly to a fall of some 20 per cent in capital cost, and an increase of fuel element temperature by 200°C was also foreseen. The possibility of gas-graphite reactors of 400MW or more was now opened up.

With the trebling of the nuclear programme in 1957 there came also a change in its reactor strategy. All the stations of the programme were now expected to be of the Calder Hall type. The Authority's revised plan was that the second group of stations in the first programme would continue the straightforward engineering progress begun with the first group of three, the third group then perhaps having 'more radical changes in design', including perhaps a beryllium or beryllium-alloy fuel can, ceramic fuels, plate instead of rod-shaped fuel, and slight fuel enrichment.

In 1956 the AEA came to feel that 'too many reactor types were being investigated' and that 'the situation was getting out of control'.[20] A Committee on the Reactor Programme was therefore formed under W. Strath, Member for Overseas and Industry, and by 1958 the Authority had succeeded in establishing for themselves a more or less lasting set of development priorities. By then their studies had convinced them that the homogeneous aqueous and liquid metal-fuelled reactors, both of which had theoretical advantages over solid-fuelled reactors like Calder Hall, in fact threw up problems of corrosion and maintenance which could be overcome only by diverting resources from more worthwhile objectives. By 1958 also they had decided to curtail work on the sodium-graphite reactor. They had seriously considered building a prototype of this, but a design study completed in 1957 showed that while it might well have lower capital costs than the reactors it would displace, it would also need highly enriched fuel, leaving it with no definite balance of advantage over improved Magnox designs. Although the Authority did afterwards continue to pay marginal attention to more esoteric reactor concepts, for example the organic liquid-moderated system for use in small reactors, from 1958 onwards they essentially consolidated their reactor development effort on four systems. These were the fast breeder (FBR), the high-temperature, gas-cooled reactor (HTR), the steam-generating heavy water reactor (SGHWR) and the advanced gas-cooled reactor (AGR). What had in effect happened was that, in the view of the Authority, the improvements achieved and anticipated with gas-graphite reactors had substantially lifted the standards against which any potential substitute had to be judged.

As was explained above, the significance of the FBR had been appreciated from the beginning. The FBR owed its importance to two related features. First, an FBR would be fuelled with a mixture of fertile and fissile material. The fissile material, uranium 235 or plutonium, would produce the power output and in addition provide sufficient neutrons to convert (breed) the fertile material, uranium 238, into more fissile material, making possible a net gain of fissile material. At the outset this was the decisive consideration, but following the 1955 decision to start the Magnox programme it also came to be hoped that as a second fast reactor advantage the fissile material to be used in fast reactors would be the plutonium produced as a by-product of electricity production in Magnox reactors, since these would produce some half tonne of the material per GW/year of operation. The first of these two fast reactor features would increase very substantially the energy which could be extracted from a given supply of uranium, while the second would effectively reduce the cost of power generated by the thermal (Magnox) reactors. The use of plutonium produced in the first programme to help fuel a fast reactor programme was naturally an exciting and technically satisfying idea. Indeed, it was often suggested that Britain would not have a wholly satisfactory nuclear programme until this symbiosis had been brought about. But desirable as these ends might be, and despite the fact that the Authority began to construct a 60MW(th) experimental FBR at Dounreay in 1955, given the difficulties, the FBR was even then not really thought likely to be suitable for commercial power stations until sometime in the seventies, by which time of course the stations of the first programme would be producing the large amounts of plutonium necessary to start a full FBR programme.

The fast reactor will not figure significantly in this account again until the eleventh chapter and it is therefore convenient to summarise here its development up to the mid-seventies.[21] The Dounreay fast reactor (DFR) eventually started up in 1959 and in February 1966 the Government approved a 250MW prototype (PFR) at the same site, as an 'essential intermediate step' towards a 1000MW commercial station by 1978. This was after some 'locational politics' involving Winfrith Heath as an alternative site — the latter had the advantage of being in southern England rather than in northern Scotland and the HTR and SGHWR were by then already sited there. Capital costs for commercial FBRs were estimated by the late sixties as likely to be similar to those of thermal reactors contemporary with them, but fuel costs were expected to be only a half to two-thirds as great. The AEA were now planning for some 15GW of FBRs by 1986, or if plutonium availability were the only limitation, upwards of 20GW. Even in 1968, with the 250MW PFR far from complete, senior AEA staff were looking for 'another bold decision' in respect of the FBR: its exploitation would be 'the major event of the rest of the century'.[22] 'The UK has the firm intention of introducing fast reactors as rapidly as possible after the operation of our 250MW prototype,' was in fact how one AEA spokesman put it in 1969.[23] Many felt in the late sixties that Britain had a lead of up to five years in FBR development and the Minister of Technology was commended by the Prime Minister when he wrote to Dounreay staff urging them not to join Westinghouse of the US. A 2 x 1300MW first commercial fast reactor (CFR) was costed in 1970, and in 1971 the AEA were looking to a 'lead' CFR of 1300MW starting construction in 1974, but the prototype did not achieve regular power operation until that year and commitment to a CFR was still being lobbied five years later.

The Authority's main reason for giving a high priority to the HTR in 1957 was that it promised low fuel costs. Several alternative versions of it seemed technically practicable and the Authority felt that an experimental reactor would have to precede prototype construction, with commercial exploitation not until the seventies. The project was much favoured by Sir John Cockcroft, who believed his Research Group should test promising ideas by building small experimental reactors, but it was squeezed out of the UK's own development programme by the AGR commitment.[24] Cockcroft therefore spoke informally to certain atomic energy leaders in Europe to enlist their support for a collaborative scheme at Winfrith, his view that this Dorset site should be opened up having shortly before prevailed despite substantial controversy. Cockcroft also promised that the AEA would support a collaborative reactor scheme at Halden in Norway and this the Authority did in 1958. In 1959 the HTR concept became the Dragon project following an agreement providing for construction and development jointly by the AEA, Euratom and other European Nuclear Energy Agency members. By 1960, when construction started, the Authority were referring to the HTR as an 'increasingly promising' prospect, though still not a commercial proposition before the seventies. Like the FBR it was seen as a third-stage reactor, a near as opposed to a true breeder, but still with a small net fissile fuel consumption and low fuel costs, which would follow the natural uranium and slightly enriched uranium reactors of the first two stages. It also came to seem the best alternative to the FBR as a plutonium burner.[25]

The SGHWR on the other hand was always looked on as a possibility for the more medium term. This reactor became the physical expression of the Authority's general interest in water reactors. As mentioned above, work on light water reactors had begun at Harwell in the early fifties, and a reactor concept in which ordinary water could double as coolant and moderator was bound to be kept under close scrutiny despite the earlier doubts. By 1955 the Authority were describing light water reactors as 'particularly interesting'. They had begun the previous year on a design study of one, which became known as LEO and provided for a reactor producing saturated steam, which could then be superheated by a separate coal or oil plant. English Electric and Babcock and Wilcox collaborated on this, and the CEA appointed a consultant observer. But between 1955 and 1958 the Authority's attention shifted so far as water reactors were concerned, partly because of a growing familiarity with gas technology, towards a gas-cooled, heavy-water-moderated model with an indirect steam cycle and by the latter date they had come to think that this might after all represent the 'best possible alternative' to the AGR in the late sixties. The Authority certainly believed at this time that they needed a back-up to the AGR. It would, they said, 'be imprudent to base a future programme entirely upon the assumption that all the improvements which it is hoped to achieve with [the AGR] will in fact be realized at an economic cost'. Further study caused them to think that steam would make a better coolant than gas, since it would allow a direct cycle and hence cut capital costs, and consequently in 1959 they began a design study of an experimental steam-cooled, heavy-water-moderated reactor. This too

was eventually rejected, but the further step to core boiling was comparatively small — hence the SGHWR. The intention was that the plant
containing this reactor should be so equipped that it would be possible
later to add a second reactor if this came to seem desirable, and a boiling water reactor (BWR) was identified as one such possibility.

The US Argonne National Laboratory's experimental BWR had been
described at the first Geneva conference in 1955 and American proponents had suggested that large BWRs would in all probability be competitive,[26] but there was scepticism in Britain on grounds both of reactor
control and of safety. In 1956 an AEA scientist observed that most of
the information available on BWRs derived from the Argonne Laboratory.[27] And at the second Geneva conference it was reported both that
this reactor was 'clearly further advanced and more interesting' than
the PWR, and also that the 'quality and completeness' of its technology
now made it a close second to the PWR, itself easily the most extensi-
vely used reactor type in the US.[28] In 1957 Sir John Cockcroft noted
that 'far too little' was known about BWR stability,[29] but in 1958 the
Deputy Managing Director of the AEA's Industrial Group, P. G.
Fletcher, suggested that for installation in the late sixties Britain must
choose between gas reactors moderated with graphite or heavy water,
and the BWR: the AGR's advantage over the BWR might well one day,
he thought, be rather narrow.[30]

Nevertheless, the Authority were not persuaded by their studies that
the inherent simplicity of the BWR was an adequate inducement for
them to pursue its development themselves. The prevailing opinion was
that 'For use in the UK . . . the chief disadvantage of the BWR is that,
even with zirconium fuel cans, enrichment to about 1½% is necessary,
and a large programme of BWRs would, therefore, require supplies of
fissile material in substantially greater quantities and at a lower cost
than are at present available in the U.K.'[31] Similarly, the Authority's
conclusion as regards the PWR, on which they did a design study and of
which they built a zero energy version in 1957 for submarine propulsion experiments, was that while practical cost experience with it in the
United States gave confidence about its projected economics, here again
its enriched fuel made it unattractive for civil use in the United Kingdom.[32] They even thought at one point that the PWR's fuel might cost
as much as five times that of Magnox, more than offsetting its low capital cost. In short, while the Authority did not feel they were closing
their eyes to LWRs, they did regard their AGR as the soundest economic bet for British circumstances, at least until the plutonium to be
produced by the Magnox reactors became available as a substitute for

enriched uranium.[33]

It is of interest that in 1958 the AEA seemed to bracket their Magnox reactors with PWRs and their AGR with the BWR. Thus their economic adviser referred to the first two as the only ones which had reached the stage at which 'reasonably accurate' cost figures could be given, the second two as having been developed to the point where their costs could be estimated 'with some degree of reliability'.[34] It is also of interest that during what might be called the formative period of their reactor strategy, up to 1958, while the Authority saw their relationship with the US Atomic Energy Commission as 'close, cordial and continuous' they did not in the end seem to be much influenced by what they learned of American work on LWRs.

Thus it was that feeling they should not entertain the LWR, the AEA looked instead to the heavy water reactor for their insurance against AGR development failure. They became involved in a boiling heavy water reactor experiment through their membership of a European group, which, as noted, agreed in 1958 to operate such a reactor at Halden in Norway, and the steam-cooled, heavy water design referred to above was, as explained, gradually evolved into a steam-generating, heavy water concept, in which the coolant was evaporated in the reactor core instead of being used to raise steam in external heat exchangers. There followed a co-operative programme with Atomic Energy of Canada Ltd on some of the development problems encountered, and it was not until 1962 that the Authority decided that they wanted and were ready to build a prototype. Construction of this began in 1963 and was still in progress when the AEA announced in 1965 that they were sponsoring a design study by the consortia of a commercial SGHWR. At this time therefore the SGHWR was still some way from the point where it could be considered for immediate inclusion in a commercial power programme. In 1964-5 only the AGR could be represented as having reached that position. Whether it could have been otherwise had the AEA, say, lost confidence in the AGR in the very early sixties, is another matter. The important point is that if the option of a commercial SGHWR by the mid-sixties did initially exist, it had disappeared long before the 1964-5 crisis.

The AGR was a logical descendant of the Magnox reactor. Development of Magnox continued after its adoption for the first programme and the Authority's work on the system remained substantial until the early sixties. This, together with the growing experience of the consortia and Generating Boards, meant that the basic Magnox design improved significantly over the first programme. Among the gradual improvements were, for instance, higher operating pressures and temperatures, better fuel performance and more compact designs, and there were also more discontinuous improvements, notably the change, on safety grounds, from steel to concrete pressure vessels for the last two of the nine stations.[35] In spite of these improvements, the Magnox series had fundamental limitations which it was felt could be overcome only by going back to basic principles.

It needs emphasising just how cautious and conservative the British designers of nuclear plants thought it necessary to be in these early stages. The great public concern at Britain's one serious nuclear accident at Windscale in 1957 was an ever-present reminder to those designers of the risks they had at all costs to prevent. And apart from protecting the public from actual physical danger, they had also, they knew, to protect the overall image of nuclear power, so that one or two perhaps trivial accidents did not precipitate the public's latent fear of the new technology into open hostility. Sir Christopher Hinton more than once pointed out at this time that nuclear energy had to manage without the 'advantage of progressing on the basis of knowledge gained by failures',[36] a process which historically had been of great value in other branches of engineering.

In what direction were advances beyond the inherent limitations of Magnox to be made?[37] The pressing need was to reduce capital costs, and conventional power station development taught that this was primarily the result of pushing towards higher plant operating temperatures. The early Magnox stations with operating temperatures of the order of $380^{\circ}C$ were imitating conventional stations of twenty-five years before, and in their development of the gas reactor the AEA therefore thought it right to aim as quickly as possible at fuel element temperatures around 600°, together with higher fuel ratings and a longer fuel life. It was the pursuit of these temperatures which compelled a move from metal to ceramic fuel and started the search for a new canning material to replace magnox. It also made necessary a re-examination of the reaction between graphite and carbon dioxide, which had earlier been found to be tolerable at Magnox temperatures. The physics problems to which a new reactor configuration would give rise had also to be carefully studied. The consequent design changes were felt to be basic enough to warrant the building of a prototype reactor, and in July 1957 a formal proposal to this effect was submitted to the Authority's Executive Committee by Hinton as managing director of the Industrial Group. This was accepted, and in August the Group were instructed to propose a plan for the construction of the reactor. The Authority approved the plan in October 1957 and financial sanction was obtained from the Government by the turn of the year. Windscale again provided a site for the new reactor. The main design features were settled by March of 1958 and construction of a 28MW prototype began that November. Commissioning was commenced early in 1962, the reactor went critical in August and had become fully synchronised with the national grid by February of the following year. A 2 x 500MW design study for an AGR power station was started in 1960. Various other facilities were set up simultaneously to support the project, two of the most important being nuclear physics model assemblies, one of which, HERO, was to AGR physics what the Windscale AGR itself was to AGR fuel.

The AEA described the AGR as the 'largest step we think we can take with full confidence in time to exploit its advantages in the second half of the 1960s'.[38] The Windscale AGR (WAGR) had dual objectives. It was to be 'an experimental facility for testing fuel and graphites for a number of improved designs in a generation of AGR power stations', and also 'a prototype power station . . . enabling industry to build a large commercial station . . . in one step'.[39] The associated facilities, too, as well as yielding design information for the WAGR itself, were intended to assist in the speedy derivation of a generation of large AGRs. The deputy managing director of the Authority's Reactor Group summed the whole project up as 'a powerful investment . . . for future generations of AGRs'. However, one important respect in which the WAGR was to differ from commercial AGRs lay in its steel pressure vessel. Adoption of pre-stressed concrete for the later Magnox stations naturally led to the inclusion of this feature in the commercial AGRs, where it brought extra advantages.

The AEA hoped when they began that the results of the AGR project would begin to benefit commercial designs within a few years, and by 1959 further studies confirmed them in their view that the AGR system did indeed offer 'the best prospect' of commercial nuclear power in Britain. Their work on the AGR thereafter amounted to a major proportion of their total capability. This concentration was emphasised, for example, by the fact that construction of an SGHWR was made conditional on the availability of manpower and finance after providing for the AGR, and it was not until 1964 that the Authority were deploying equivalent effort on this reactor. They also thought it right in the early sixties to plan, as they had done with Magnox, for capital investment in AGR fuel facilities, this time standardising the fuel design. Effectively then, they were assuming by the beginning of the sixties that there would be a programme of commercial AGR stations, an assumption in which the Government tacitly acquiesced.[40]

In spite of this, almost eight years were to elapse between the decision to construct a prototype AGR and that to build a commercial station. The reason for this lay mainly in the highly complex nature of the technical problems which it turned out had to be solved to establish even the basic soundness of AGR technology. Two areas of particular difficulty need briefly to be mentioned here, because of their intrinsic importance, but even more as illustrations of the natural and gradual way in which the AEA became ever more sure of the quality of their AGR. The greater the difficulties which are overcome in the course of a project, the greater the momentum in support of that project which builds up amongst those who overcome those difficulties – a circumstance by no means true only of the AGR.

The first of the major problems with the AGR concerned its fuel cans. The magnox alloy which had given its name to the Magnox series of reactors melted at around 640°C. This was comfortably above the coolant gas outlet temperatures of these reactors, which ranged from 335°C at Calder Hall to 415°C at Wylfa, but the corresponding AGR temperatures were to be around 650°C. A new canning material was therefore necessary for AGR fuel, and the obvious first choice seemed to be beryllium.[41] A much higher melting point, good thermal conductivity, apparent compatibility with carbon dioxide and uranium dioxide, together with good nuclear properties all seemed to add up to 'powerful scientific' reasons for making beryllium the first choice. That beryllium would certainly be very expensive could be set against the high fuel burn-up it seemed likely to make possible.

But with beryllium the favoured material, the actual ways of using it pointed to slight enrichment of the fuel, a step requiring 'considered justification' in a country which had thus far confined itself to natural uranium. And enrichment in turn led to a really quite different basic type of gas-cooled reactor: 'In making one change,' it was said, 'we are forced to make several other changes.' Particularly reluctant to accept enrichment of the fuel with expensive U235 when plutonium was going to be so readily available, the Authority devoted considerable development effort to the problem of using the latter instead of U235 in the AGR. By the end of 1961, however, it was apparent that major technical problems would have had to be overcome to make this possible and the effort involved by then no longer seemed economically justified, though to demonstrate feasibility and 'increase the general confidence' one WAGR channel was loaded with plutonium fuel in 1964.

The Authority's experience with beryllium dated from 1949. Beginning in 1956 they set about building up stocks of the raw material beryl and the following year they decided to encourage industrial production of beryllium while it was still in the process of being proved by irradiation tests as suitable for the AGR. At least four firms began to interest themselves in the metal and there was some concern lest one of them, ICI, was being allowed a monopoly on a vital part of the work. Perfecting manufacturing techniques and running irradiation experiments in parallel was a risky course which the AEA decided upon only because each process was expected to take two or three years, so that performing them consecutively would have added more than two years to the AGR's development time schedule, a schedule which was itself closely tied in with the growing performance pressures on the commercial power programme.

The advantages of beryllium which had so attracted the Authority were well known, but so also, in the main, were its disadvantages. The most serious of these were its toxicity, necessitating extreme precautions to eliminate health hazards, the belief that it had rather poor mechanical properties under irradiation, its complicating effect on reactor control and, as mentioned above, its cost. The Authority in due course concluded from their experiments that these difficulties were in fact 'more limiting than expected'. The most important turned out to be the swelling of the metal under irradiation due to the formation of helium gas within it. Others were the corrosion of beryllium by all except very dry carbon dioxide, though the Authority said in 1961 that the rate at which this occurred could be made acceptable for AGR conditions, and the low ductility of the metal under irradiation, which could have caused cans made of it to fail, thereby contaminating the reactor. To correct for these various inadequacies would have meant producing a form of beryllium so different from that on which the original irradiation experiments had been done that these latter tests would have had to be repeated. Although a manufacturing process for beryllium had by now been proved, the cost, the need for new tests, the consequent delay plus remaining uncertainties, and above all the critical fact that they had by this time a better alternative, together impelled the Authority to stop their work on beryllium at the end of 1961.

The AEA were not necessarily wrong to have investigated beryllium: it was too intriguing a metal to have escaped attention for the kind of purpose they had in mind. That their work on it was 'most ably'[42] performed is equally probable. Nevertheless, some £10m was spent on beryllium, of which only some £3m was for r & d, most of the rest going to industry for the simultaneous development of the associated manufacturing processes. Given the well-known difficulties in halting ongoing research programmes, it is also likely that work on beryllium was continued beyond the point at which its use in the AGR had become distinctly improbable. *The Economist* reported in February 1960 that at least one of the consortia had decided to halt work on beryllium, and an AEA metallurgist suggested the same month that unless suitable alloys could be found its use in gas reactors was 'possibly limited'.[43] Yet at the same time it was being officially stated that the nuclear power programme would require the use of beryllium and its compounds 'in ever increasing quantities',[44] and almost two years were still to pass before the Authority decided finally to abandon hopes of the metal so far as the AGR was concerned. The whole case well illustrated, the AEA thought, the 'vicissitudes that sometimes attend work in the development field'.[45]

At least the AEA were not wholly committed to beryllium. Stainless steel had originally been passed over as first choice because its poorer nuclear properties meant either higher fuel enrichment than with beryllium, or else cans too thin to be feasible. But there was enough uncertainty within the Authority from the outset to ensure that experiments with alternatives to beryllium would be performed in the Windscale AGR. The steel industry co-operated in the development of a better steel and by early 1960 the Authority had begun to sound a little more hopeful about it than about beryllium. Gradually results obtained in Britain and in the United States began to show that stainless steel had far more promise than had originally been thought, and this happened at about the same time as experiments were demonstrating just how formidable were beryllium's problems. By this time it also seemed that the slightly higher enrichment called for by stainless steel would be almost balanced by the high fabrication cost of beryllium. When the time came in 1962 to charge the Windscale AGR with its first fuel, though it had been designed primarily for beryllium cans, only stainless steel ones were loaded. From this point onwards the question mark which had hung over AGR fuel began to disappear as fuel element behaviour in the AGR proved more and more satisfactory. Tests were performed with thinner cans, larger cans, cans deliberately holed, cans at higher temperatures, longer fuel elements, and on fuel enriched with plutonium. The Authority were able in 1963 to describe the results as 'excellent', in 1964 to record that the fuel had continued to perform 'faultlessly', and in 1965, when the Windscale AGR completed its second year, to report that it had had an availability, excluding planned shutdowns, of 85 per cent, without a single failure in 30,000 fuel elements.

It is instructive that although the AEA had elected not to pursue the BWR in large measure because of its enriched uranium requirement, they themselves with the AGR accepted the enrichment principle, albeit at a somewhat lower percentage. And when later it became clear that AGR fuel would have to be clad with stainless steel rather than with beryllium they also had then to accept the prospect of a 50 per - cent higher enrichment, so that the eventual enrichment was little different from that of the LWRs. A 'sop . . . to the original principles' was indeed how *Nuclear Engineering* in April 1961 described the attempt to use beryllium, adding that the AGR was 'so far removed' from the Magnox reactors that having accepted the principle of enrichment Britain could have started on a completely fresh reactor system with very little additional penalty.

The second of the two AGR problems to be mentioned here proved ultimately the more serious, especially in the sense that there remained some doubt as late as 1964 about whether or not it had been solved. This 'problem' was really a set of difficulties associated with the use of graphite as moderator. The Authority were aware from the outset that the behaviour of graphite under AGR operating conditions might constitute ' a limiting factor' on the AGR system. To simplify, one may say that there were problems both of chemistry and of physics.

The 'chemistry' problem stemmed from the fact that ordinary carbon dioxide is transformed, at a rate depending on the gas pressure and radiation flux, into a form which fairly readily oxidises graphite. This phenomenon was not new. On the contrary, it was one of the four major technical questions which the Windscale AGR was intended to investigate, and it was one of the first on which a supporting programme of irradiation experiments began. It was also the one AGR problem which the AEA came to regard as basic. Broadly, the reaction gave rise to two main fears: first, that the loss of graphite from the moderator might decrease the latter's mechanical strength and second, that it might lead to deposition of the carbon so removed in the cooling circuit. The Authority studied the possibility of protecting the graphite by coating it with some impervious material and, more fully, the alternative of producing less-porous graphite, since the reaction was known to take place primarily in the pores. They also established quite quickly that a small percentage of carbon monoxide mixed in with the carbon dioxide coolant slowed down the reaction, and priority experiments along these lines continued in order to discover exactly how this inhibiting effect worked, so that it could be enhanced. The optimum concentration of carbon monoxide had been determined by early 1962 and the Authority were by then confident enough to announce that there was no longer any fear that oxidation of the moderator would limit the life of an AGR. They went on to show that traces of other substances strengthened inhibition, and a variety of coolant mixtures were tried in the Windscale AGR before one containing a small percentage of methane as inhibiting agent instead of carbon monoxide was finally selected. This cut the rate of corrosion by between 10 and 40 per cent. The use of a coolant additive naturally called for some extra ancillary plant, but at least by 1965 the Authority felt able to extend their confidence on the graphite-carbon dioxide score to cover now the whole 'recognised development potential of the AGR'.[46]

This left the 'physics' problem, or rather problems, of graphite. An early graphite problem in this general category had been the energy build-up in graphite crystals caused by radiation. This became known as Wigner energy, and since the phenomenon was most marked at relatively low temperatures, the remedy adopted in the case of low-temperature reactors, such as those at Windscale, was carefully to raise the temperature of the graphite, when the stored energy was released as heat. It was while this technique was being carried out that the Windscale incident of 1957 had occurred. A necessarily pessimistic initial interpretation of this both delayed and added to the cost of the first two commercial stations, Berkeley and Bradwell, but when it became known that at Magnox temperatures no significant build-up of Wigner energy took place, it followed that the problem could be dismissed at the still higher AGR temperatures.

Of the remaining graphite physics problems by far the most important were the dimensional changes in the graphite known to take place under irradiation at AGR temperatures, and the differential growth or shrinkage in the graphite blocks caused by radiation and temperature gradients across them. It was, in fact, doubts on this score which more than anything else made the CEGB reluctant to move from a 20-year book life even for their Magnox stations. Simplifying considerably, the bulk dimensional changes arose from the fact that under irradiation graphite crystals tended to expand in one direction and contract in a perpendicular one, so that over a whole block of the material, with a preferred crystal orientation, there occurred an increase in length one way and a decrease the other. The AEA believed by 1963 that they could explain this phenomenon theoretically, and this they felt 'strengthened confidence' that it could be made tolerable in AGR stations, particularly since the same theory indicated that a 30-year life was possible with a specially designed core. But the dimensional changes, apart from their importance in their own right, also contributed, along with other irradiation-induced changes in the physical and mechanical properties of graphite, to differential stresses in the graphite blocks, and these it was feared would cause cracking. The Authority were evincing concern about this in 1964, at which time they were hoping to prove that another property of irradiated graphite, called 'creep', would help to cancel out the differential stresses. It was not really thought likely that graphite cracking would have serious implications, but there was a pessimistic interpretation which hinted at unsatisfactory safety and performance characteristics, and the Authority acknowledged in 1964 that if the problem had to be cured by a full redesign of the graphite structure, then this would add to the AGR's cost. By the spring of 1965 however, having taken AGR graphite specimens to half an ordinary lifetime using the high flux of the Dounreay fast reactor, the AEA were much more confident.

One possible way of neutralising any residual effects from the AGR's graphite physics and chemistry problems was to manufacture a form of the material less susceptible to them in the first place. With this in mind, the AEA mounted, concurrently with their experiments on the graphite problems, a programme aimed at producing an improved type of graphite, and in due course two British manufacturers undertook to supply trial batches. Both they and the Authority after their tests on it were sure that the large-scale production of 'improved' graphite was a straightforward proposition, and in 1964 the CEGB in their Dungeness B enquiry specified graphite of this type.[47]

Now with regard to that CEGB assessment, though it might demonstrate that the AGR had an economic edge over its rivals, lack of confidence in its graphite moderator could even then have prevented the reactor's adoption by the CEGB. The Board would quite properly have continued to be very unwilling to invest huge sums in the reactor so long as they felt that real doubts remained about its technical soundness. To guarantee the CEGB impartial advice, and to lay worries about graphite so far as possible to rest, the Authority conceived what in Authority-Board relationships may have been a unique arrangement. This was the so-called Emeléus Committee,[48] named for the Committee's chairman, Professor H.J. Emeléus, which the Authority convened in October 1964. The Committee had a membership of four professors, three of them Fellows of the Royal Society, and their meetings were attended by regular observers or representatives from the AEA, the CEGB and the Ministry of Power. The Committee's brief was to report on the likely life of the graphite in the AGR, and to this end they met six times to consider the data on graphite chemistry and physics then still emerging from AEA experiments. The Committee's conclusions were eventually forwarded to the AEA chairman, but they were naturally of equal moment to the CEGB. The Committee decided that under the conditions likely to arise in AGR reactors ordered in the following year or so, an AGR core could be designed to operate with a useful life of 30 years at a load factor of 85 per cent, and they were equally unequivocal about the reactor's development potential.

This chapter has gone in some depth into the AEA's reactor strategy and the AGR's main development problems up to 1964, more depth it might be thought than is necessary for an analysis primarily concerned with political choices, though obviously much less than would be necessary for a technical history. The justification for this chapter remains simple. Only by reflecting on the logic which brought the AEA to the AGR, and only by appreciating the hard problems they had to overcome in developing this reactor, can one properly understand where they stood in 1964. The decision to develop the AGR was *their* decision, its problems were *their* problems, the solutions to those problems constituted *their* success, what confidence existed in it in 1964 was essentially *their* confidence.[49] No other body was involved on anything like the scale that they were, and in particular not the CEGB. It is true that Sir Christopher Hinton initiated AGR development while with the AEA and was CEGB chairman when the reactor fell to be considered for the second nuclear power programme, but it is shown in the next chapter that by the early sixties, if not already in the late fifties, he was decisively, and properly, a CEGB man. The AGR was not exactly the AEA's total *raison d'être* − the HTR and SGHWR were in the wings and the FBR was on the far horizon − but if it were not to be adopted by the CEGB for a second commercial nuclear programme, then what had the AEA been doing in the eight years of its development? The Public Accounts Committee chairman, Douglas Houghton, put the unhappy possibility very bluntly to the AEA chairman, Sir Roger Makins, in 1963, referring to what he called an 'extraordinary' situation: 'You can, therefore, sit there developing your nuclear power with literally very little prospect of selling it at home and with little prospect in the export trade and you then become a dead loss to the community.'[50]

Notes

1. In addition to the sources cited separately, the account given here draws on Margaret Gowing, *Britain and Atomic Energy 1939-45* (Macmillan, London, 1964) and *Independence and Deterrence: Britain and Atomic Energy 1945-52* (2 vols. Macmillan, London, 1974) (these three volumes constitute the official history); see also K.E.B. Jay, *Britain's Atomic Factories* (HMSO, London, 1954) and *Calder Hall* (Methuen, London, 1956); also Sir John Cockcroft, *The Development and Future of Nuclear Energy* (Clarendon Press, Oxford, 1950); Sir Christopher Hinton, 'Nuclear Power Development: some experiences of the First Ten Years', *J. Inst. Fuel*, 31 (March 1958), pp. 90-5.

2. Gowing, *Independence and Deterrence*, vol. 2, pp. 266, 270.

3. Sir Christopher Hinton, 'Nuclear Power', *Three Banks Review* (December 1961), pp. 3-18 (3).

4. Gowing, *Independence and Deterrence*, vol. 2, p. 280.

5. Ibid., pp. 302-12.

6. Sir John Cockcroft, 'Harwell's 21st Anniversary', *Atom* (March 1967), pp. 51-8.

7. Lord Hinton, *Atom* (December 1976), p. 298.

8. For example, R.A.U. Huddle and L.M. Wyatt, 'Early Metallurgical Problems', *BNECJ* (April 1957), pp. 110-20 (113).

9. Gowing, *Independence and Deterrence*, vol. 2, pp. 289, 295.

10. HCD 510 c. 673; HCD 520 c. 1375-6.

11. Hinton's speeches as CEGB chairman include 'The Future for Nuclear Power' (Axel Axson Johnson lecture, Stockholm, 1957); 'The Development of Nuclear Energy for Electricity Supply in Great Britain' (BEPC, London, 1958); 'A Review of the Future of Nuclear Reactor Systems in the Light of the Available Research and Operating Experience' (World Power Conference, Montreal, 1958); 'Development of Atomic Energy and its Industrial Implications' (CEGB, London, 1960); 'The Economics of Nuclear Power in Great Britain' (World Power Conference, Madrid, 1960); 'The Evolution of Nuclear Power Plant Design' (Royal Society, London, 1960); 'Lessons of the Past Seven Years in Atomic Energy' (World Power Conference, Madrid, 1960); 'Nuclear Power', *Three Banks Review* (December 1961), pp. 3-18; 'The Problems and Prospects of Nuclear Power' (Atomic Industry Forum, Tokyo, 1962) *Atom* (March 1963), pp. 62-71; 'Nuclear Power Plants in England and Wales', *Atom* (May 1963), pp. 165-76; 'Power at the Source', *Electricity*, vol. 14 (January/February 1961), pp. 11-16.

12. Sir Christopher Hinton, 'Nuclear Reactors and Power Production', *Engineer* (March 5 and 12, 1954), pp. 357-60, 374-6.

13. Sir Christopher Hinton, 'The Graphite-moderated Gas-cooled Pile and its Place in Power Production', I Geneva, 3, pp. 322-9.

14. HC 236 (1962-3), Q 1118.

15. Sir Christopher Hinton, 'Nuclear Energy for Britain's Electricity Supply', *Engineer* (June 27, 1958).

16. Sir Leonard Owen, 'Some Experiences in the Industrial Group of the UKAEA 1947-58', II Geneva, 8, pp. 3-9 (7); also H.K. Hardy *et al.*, 'The Development of Uranium-Magnox Fuel Elements for an Average Irradiation Life of 3000MWD/te', *BNESJ*, 2 (1963), pp. 33-40 (33).

17. Alvin M. Weinberg, 'Survey of Fuel Cycles and Reactor Types', I Geneva, 3, pp. 19-25; J.V. Dunworth, 'Fuel Cycles and Types of Reactor', I Geneva, 3, pp. 14-18.

18. Cmd. 9389.

19. The discussion which follows is based on AEA Annual Reports, interviews and various lectures by Sir John Cockcroft, in particular: 'The Development of

Nuclear Power', Proc. Instn. Civ. Engrs., 1955, pt. I, 4, pp. 791-808; 'Development after 1960', *Atom* (November 1956), pp. 17-20; 'The Reactor Research Programme', *Atom* (January 1957), pp. 6-9; 'The Future Development of Nuclear Power', *Atom* (March 1957), pp. 15-18; 'Technical Developments in the Nuclear Energy Field', *Atom* (March 1958), pp. 19-22; 'Technical Aspects of the New Programme', *Atom* (March 1957), pp. 3-4; 'The UK Research Programme', *Atom* (July 1957), pp. 8-13; 'Nuclear Power', *Atom* (July 1958), pp. 8-13; *Atom* (May 1959), p. 15; 'Scientific problems in the development of nuclear power', *Brit. J. Applied Phys.*, Supplement 5 (1956), pp. 1-8; also J.V. Dunworth, 'Advanced Reactors', *BNECJ*, 4 (January 1959), pp. 61-77.

20. Lord Penney, 'Sir John Cockcroft and Atomic Energy', *BNESJ*, 7 (1968), pp. 295-301.

21. *Atom* (March 1966), pp. 46-8; Hans Kronberger, 'Fast Reactor Development in the UK', *Atom* (April 1968), pp. 92-100; R.V. Moore, 'Fast Breeder Reactor Power Stations', *Atom* (March 1969), pp. 59-74; H. Cartwright *et al.*, 'Review of the Progress of Sodium Cooled FRS in the UK', IV Geneva, 5, pp. 53-61.

22. T.N. Marsham, *BNESJ*, 8 (1969), p. 3 and P.W. Mummery, *BNESJ*, 8 (1969), p. 157.

23. Michael Davis, 'The Peaceful Use of Nuclear Energy', *Atom* (July 1969), pp. 198-211 (203).

24. Lord Penney, 'Sir John Cockcroft and Atomic Energy', *BNESJ*, I (1968), pp. 295-301. Also Sir Mark Oliphant and Lord Penney, 'John Douglas Cockcroft', *Bibliographical Memoirs of Fellows of the Royal Society*, XIV (The Royal Society, London, 1968); *Atom* (May 1959), p. 3 (Lord Plowden); L.R. Shepherd, 'The Ten Years of DRAGON', *Atom* (August 1969), pp. 218-36.

25. A.B. McIntosh and L. Grainger, 'Plutonium Fuel and Nuclear Power', *BNESJ*, I (1962), pp. 3-13, 141-4; M.B. Waldron, 'The Use of Plutonium in Reactors', *NP* (July 1961), pp. 58-62.

26. J.M. Harrer, *et al.*, 'The Engineering Design of a Prototype BWR Power Plant', I Geneva, 3, pp. 250-62; see also J.R. Dietrich, *et al.*, 'Design and Operating Experience of a Prototype Boiling Water Power Reactor', I Geneva, 3, pp. 56-68.

27. B.L. Goodlet, 'Nuclear Reactors for Power Production', The Institution of Mechanical Engineers, *Procs. of the Symp. on Nuclear Energy*, 28 March 1956, pp. 3-28 (16).

28. Clark Goodman, *et al.*, 'Experience with USA Nuclear Power Reactors', II Geneva, 8, pp. 23-39; W.H. Zinn, *et al.*, 'A 125 MW Indirect Cycle Boiling Water Power Reactor', II Geneva, 9, pp. 64-73.

29. Sir John Cockcroft, 'Technical Development in the Nuclear Energy Field', *Atom* (March 1958), p. 22.

30. *NP* (January 1959), p. 126; *NE* (December 1958), p. 513.

31. AEA, 5th Annual Report, para. 84. See also J.M. Kay and F.J. Hutchinson, 'The PWR as a Source of Heat for Steam Power Plants', *BNECJ*, I (July 1956), pp. 53-75.

32. Sir John Cockcroft, 'The Further Development of the UK Nuclear Power Programme', *BNECJ* (July 1958), pp. 157-65 and 'The Future Development of Nuclear Power', *Atom* (March 1957), p. 16; H. Kronberger *et al.*, 'Developments in Reactor Technology', *BNECJ*, 4 (April 1959), pp. 107-14.

33. Sir John Cockcroft, 'Nuclear Power and Radiobiology', *Atom* (May 1959), pp. 13-19.

34. J.A. Jukes, 'The Economic Problems of Nuclear Power', *Atom* (October 1958), pp. 17-28.

35. See, for example, H.M. Curruthers, 'The Evolution of Magnox Station Design', *BNESJ* (July 1965), pp. 171-80.

36. This is from the Axel Axson lecture.

37. E.g., R.V. Moore *et al.*, 'Advances in the Design of Gas-cooled Graphite Moderated Power Reactors', II Geneva, 9, pp. 104-14; the remainder of this chapter draws generally on the Symposium on the AGR, *BNESJ*, 2 (1963), pp. 95-294, 335-54. Also *NE* (April 1961), pp. 151-8. R.V. Moore, 'The AGR: Design Concept', *Elec. Rev.* (17 November 1961), pp. 774-92. Sir William Cook, 'The AGR: Britain's New Power Reactor', *New Scientist* (23 April 1964), pp. 205-6.

38. Sir William Cook, 'Nuclear Power in Western Europe', *Atom* (January 1959), pp. 4-6.

39. Symposium on the AGR, Kronberger, p. 225, para. 6.

40. AEA Annual Reports (4th, p. 83; 6th, pp. 56, 74, 102; 7th, p. 86; 10th, p. 57); HCD 622 c.68 (WA); N.L. Franklin, 'Nuclear Fuel Cycle Services in the UK', *Atom* (May 1968), pp. 126-30; HC 622 c.68 (WA).

41. Sources on beryllium, apart from those separately cited, include AEA Annual Reports; J.G. Ball, 'Metallurgical Research in Nuclear Power Production', *BNECJ*, 3 (January 1958), pp. 1-14; HC 275 (1962-3), paras. 149-51; H.M. Finniston, 'Some Metallurgical Features of Nuclear Reactors', *BNECJ*, 5 (1960), pp. 37-48; L. Rotherham, 'The Role of Metallurgy in a Nuclear Energy Project', *BNECJ*, 2 (January 1957 supplement), pp. 91-5; *NP* (March 1958), pp. 112-14 (January, 1960), p. 71 (July 1960), pp. 94-6; *NE* (January 1958), pp. 9-18 (March 1958), p. 125 (January 1960), pp. 31-2 (April 1960), p. 145-6 (April 1961), pp. 149-50 (December 1961), pp. 531-3; *Journal of Metals* (1960), p. 793 (1958), p. 738; HCD 664 c.75-6 (WA); HCD 677 c.189 (WA).

42. Sir Christopher Hinton, 'The Evolution of Nuclear Power Plant Design' (Royal Society, London, 1960), p. 12.

43. *The Economist*, 27 February 1960; A.J. Martin, 'Beryllium as a Structural Material', *Atom* (March 1960), pp. 12-22 (22).

44. *Atom* (April 1960), p. 5.

45. Sir Roger Makins, 'Nuclear Energy in 1962', *Atom* (1962), p. 69.

46. But see R. Lind and H.G. Lewis, 'Graphite Corrosion in AGRs', *Graphite Structures for Nuclear Reactors* (Institution of Mechanical Engineers, London, 1972) (Symp. 7-9 March 1972), pp. 59-68; Christopher J. Wood, 'Solving Moderator Corrosion Problems in AGRs', *NEI* (January 1977), pp. 29-32.

47. See P.T. Nettley *et al.*, 'Irradiation Experience with Isotropic Graphite', *Atom* (December 1968), pp. 329-39; J.M. Hutcheon and K. Prince, 'Graphite for the Commercial AGR', *NE* (October 1965), pp. 368-70.

48. AEA 11th Annual Report, para. 97.

49. For example, A.D. Evans and L. Barton, 'Operating Experience with the WAGR', *BNESJ* (April 1965), pp. 109-18; J.C.C. Stewart, *NE* (September 1964), pp. 311-12.

50. HC 275 (1962-3), Qs 3558, 3560.

3 ECONOMIC CONFUSION

It was estimated in the 1955 White Paper[1] which established the first nuclear programme that the cost of electricity from that programme's early stations would be approximately 0.6d per unit, 'about the same', it was said, as the generating cost of contemporary coal stations. This chapter is concerned with the political outcome of that estimate.

Nuclear power economics were obviously not of importance in regard to Calder Hall: since the central object there was plutonium production, it was enough that costs be lower than those of the original Windscale piles, which they clearly would be. But it was fully understood at the time, at least among those closest to events, that this was a special case and that nuclear power could not be represented as economic unless a substantial allowance were made for its plutonium by-product, or unless it were compared with high-cost marginal or imported coal. At a Harwell conference of 1953 for instance, B.L. Goodlet suggested a capital cost of £227/KW and a generating cost of 1d, without a plutonium allowance, this for a 35MW reactor at an 80 per cent load factor, an 'optimistic' 20-year life, a 4 per cent interest rate and an initial fuel cost of £15,000/tonne.[2] On the other hand, the official historian has pointed out that while in the early fifties the Ministry of Fuel and Power's economist would have preferred to see the limited resources available concentrated on the fast breeder reactor, the department's chief scientist wanted instead to press ahead immediately with a real power station, even if it were obsolescent when complete, on the grounds that its economics could be proved only by building it, and that such an enterprise should not be left to the Americans.[3] Considerations of national prestige grew in importance over the next few years and, in conjunction with a general sense of urgency with regard to energy availability, came to entail a more relaxed, if not cavalier, attitude to economic justification.

That said, the first point to be clear about is that there was specifically no official intention to justify the 1955 nuclear programme on the grounds either that there had been a spectacular advance in technology or that nuclear stations would achieve an exact parity of generating cost with conventional plant. The 'compelling' justification for the programme, to use Sir Edwin Plowden's word, was rather the fear of a gap developing between Britain's rapidly growing energy requirements and the capacity of her coal industry.[4] The case of electricity was thought especially serious, with demand expected to grow from 20GW in 1954 to as much as 55-60GW in 1975. The corollary of this increase would ordinarily have been a parallel growth in demand for coal, power station consumption alone rising from 40 to some 100m tons a year over the same period. The ability of the coal industry to meet this target was judged pessimistically, for although the industry's output had expanded by more than 20 per cent since the war, demand had increased faster still, and neither open-cast mining nor coal imports had entirely overcome the resulting problem. Further, the coal industry's manpower shortage was thought likely to remain a chronic difficulty, and even the heavy capital investment programme which the National Coal Board (NCB) had put in hand was regarded as largely a holding operation.

In these circumstances the prospects for oil as a power station fuel assumed a new importance, the Government announcing in July 1954 that it had been decided to equip a first power station with dual coal and oil firing apparatus. But the relief which oil would bring was nevertheless viewed only as a breathing space until nuclear power was in a position to make a 'massive contribution' to the energy economy: 'timely if not providential' was how the Ministry saw the advent of nuclear power.[5] This concern with an energy shortfall was in a very few years to prove completely misplaced, or at any rate highly premature, and it is therefore only fair to remember that in the mid-fifties other European countries shared Britain's sense of alarm — their fears were for instance to be an important stimulus in the creation of Euratom in 1957.

The threat of an energy gap would presumably of itself have produced a determined British effort to develop nuclear energy, but for the adoption of the ten-year commercial nuclear programme of 1.5-2GW announced in the 1955 White Paper it was also necessary that the projected economics of nuclear stations should appear in their own right not too unfavourable. The Government were now persuaded that this really was the case, though it was acknowledged that the initial estimate of nuclear generating cost was 'subject to a wide margin of uncertainty'.

Inevitably, much of the uncertainty was a consequence of the technical novelty of nuclear plant. Capital costs were derived, allowing for anticipated improvements, from Calder Hall figures, although in 1955, with operation of the latter still more than a year away, these themselves were not finally known. It was assumed that a nuclear station would have a useful life of some fifteen years, and that its low operating costs would mean that it was used throughout to meet base load, giving a utilisation or load factor of up to 80 per cent. Works and operating costs were estimated from the relevant figures for coal plant and the Windscale military reactors. Fuel costs were arrived at by taking into account the price of uranium ore, processing costs extrapolated from experience with the military processing factories at Springfields and Windscale, the expected behaviour of the fuel, and finally, by allowing a credit value for the by-product plutonium which was to be extracted from spent fuel. Overall the AEA felt they were 'on fairly firm ground' in their estimates of capital cost but that there were 'much greater uncertainties' in regard to fuel costs.[6]

Sir Christopher Hinton said in 1956[7] that the 1955 White Paper had been based, 'with some developments and modifications', on an AEA report by J.M. Kay, G.R.H. Geoghegan and D.R. Poulter which had put the power cost for a series of Calder Hall-type reactors at about 1d a unit. Hinton noted that this report had also pointed out that while the plutonium produced in these reactors could be used as a fuel for other reactors, such an arrangement would almost certainly not be satisfactory using gas-cooled reactors, but rather would require development of liquid-cooled reactors of higher rating.

A somewhat different account of the estimates in the 1955 White Paper was given by J.A. Jukes[8] in a paper to the first Geneva conference on atomic energy later in 1955. (Jukes was Economic Adviser to the AEA from 1954-64 and became a CEGB Member in 1977.) Describing his figures as cautious, Jukes put the generating cost of the early nuclear stations at 0.76d, made up of 0.36 for capital charges and 0.40 for fuel. These were gross figures which made no allowance for the sale or use of the plutonium produced. The latter consideration was therefore potentially crucial in determining whether the early stations would be competitive with coal plant. The White Paper spoke only in terms of a value of 'many thousands of pounds a kilogram' for plutonium, admitting that without a plutonium credit the nuclear power cost would be 'substantially more' than 0.6d.

The actual analysis of plutonium value was conducted in terms of the uses to which plutonium might eventually be put. Its most wasteful use was thought likely to be as a substitute for natural uranium, the plutonium then simply being fabricated into fuel elements and recycled through the original reactors. Making a 'reasonable guess' as to how this could best be done, Jukes suggested that the nuclear generating cost would fall from 0.76 to 0.65d. There were also, though again only in theory, more efficient ways of using the plutonium, the upper limit here being fixed by the cost of separated uranium 235. Taking into account these other ways of using the material, Jukes felt that the value in practice of plutonium would remain near the theoretical upper limit for at least fifteen years, falling thereafter towards the lower limit as the element became more plentiful. The resulting reduction in nuclear generating cost then came out at between 0.17 and 0.33d, with the larger figure, Jukes thought, the 'more reasonable'. On what he again described as cautious grounds, the net cost of nuclear electricity from the early stations could thus be expected to lie in the range 0.59 to 0.43d.

The Central Electricity Authority (CEA)'s projections in 1955[9] were in line with those of the White Paper. The generating costs of 200MW coal and nuclear plants they put at 0.519 and 0.698d/unit respectively, the latter falling with the plutonium credit to 0.432. The electricity 'gap' the CEA saw as growing from 3.9GW in 1965 to 23GW by 1981, and while they did not feel that nuclear energy could by itself meet the 1965 gap, they did not see this objective as too unrealistic for later years. It was therefore 'important that all concerned should set out their stalls to cater for this and the export business which might well be achieved'.

The economic rationale of the first nuclear programme therefore derived from the threat of an energy gap, coupled with the belief that nuclear electricity could be roughly competitive from the outset. In addition, the Government said that they wished to create as soon as possible a sound industrial foundation in the new industry, which would then act as a springboard for 'a rapid expansion both at home and overseas', at which time 'a valuable export trade' could be established. The final two paragraphs of the 1955 White Paper acknowledged that the programme which had been adopted might prove too optimistic and that for a number of reasons nuclear power might turn out to be more expensive than had been assumed. 'The stakes,' it said, 'are high but the final reward will be immeasurable.'

It was repeatedly stressed in the 1955 White Paper that the initial programme was provisional, and when in March 1957 the Government revealed their decision to expand the programme to 5-6GW by 1965 they refused to see the need for a new White Paper. Eventually they relented somewhat and the main details of what was effectively a new programme were published as a brief appendix to a White Paper on capital investment in the fuel industries.[10]

In the same month as the nuclear programme was trebled Sir

Christopher Hinton gave a lecture[11] in Sweden which was immediately recognised as of major importance, given the British expansion. Hinton's most critical economic conclusion in this paper was that nuclear stations coming on stream in 1962/3 would probably have marginally lower generating costs than conventional ones completed at the same time. By 1970 nuclear power would be 'appreciably cheaper' and its advantage would continue to increase thereafter. These developments would, however, come about only by pushing ahead with courage.

Several factors contributed to the 1957 decision that the programme should be trebled (or, taking the lower figure of 1955 with the higher figure of 1957, quadrupled). The Government were still thinking in terms of a 40m ton gap in coal availability by 1965, and of a growing balance of payments cost for energy imports, then already running at £250m a year. In addition, oil supplies had seemed to be at particular risk following the Suez crisis of the previous year. October 1956 also saw the opening of Calder Hall. Represented as a 'world first' for Britain in the provision of civil nuclear power, this understandably cast a favourable light upon the prospects generally for nuclear energy, as did the discovery the same year of new uranium reserves in Canada. Finally, whereas station size in 1955 was limited both by the conventional parts of projected stations and by the reactor output expected to be available, it had become clear with the submission of the first Magnox tenders, another event of October 1956, that a station size about double that proposed in the 1955 White Paper was now feasible and would be more efficient. To keep the programme at the same size the number of stations would thus have had to be halved, which in turn would have meant a much more uneven work load for private industry.

Under the 1955 programme there had been tentative plans for twelve stations. The 1957 revision increased this to a projected nineteen, plus one for Northern Ireland. The 1955 programme had provided for an expenditure of £300m for stations completing before 1965 and the electricity authorities were to have met some £230-240m of this, the remainder being AEA expenditure. The 1957 programme now increased to some £919m the charge on the electricity authorities, with a further £160m to be found by 1966 for stations completing later. The real significance of the new programme was that it was expected to require a total capital investment by the electricity authorities in the period to 1965 some £750m greater than would have been necessary with no nuclear stations. The 1957 White Paper cautioned that it was impossible in forecasting to 'claim any precision' given the ten-year period involved, and that its figures were therefore best regarded only as order of magnitude ones.

In announcing the 1957 programme the Minister of Power admitted that the generating cost at the first three nuclear stations would be 'very slightly more' than that of new conventional plant, but added that he remained confident that the efficiency of nuclear stations was improving more rapidly than that of their conventional rivals.[12] AEA and CEGB representatives said much the same thing at the second Geneva atomic energy conference the following year. J.A. Jukes[13] then suggested that the 1955 nuclear cost estimates had 'stood up well'. The whole of the slight increase which had occurred could be accounted for by the inclusion of site and engineering charges amounting to 5-10 per cent of capital cost, charges which in error had been overlooked in 1955, and by a rise in interest rates from 4 to 5-6 per cent. The notional load factor for nuclear stations had in the interim been reduced from 80 to 75 per cent, their notional life increased from 15 to 20 years, but a fall in the value attributed to plutonium was said by Jukes to have been offset by newly expected increases in thermal efficiency from 20 to 27-35 per cent. That the plutonium credit was now only some 10 per cent of the generating cost should be seen, Jukes suggested, as 'an improvement in the reliability of the estimates'. CEGB projections in 1958,[14] at interest rates of 6 per cent, were 0.63-0.70d (best nuclear) and 0.54-0.65 (coal), these figures applying to plants completing in 1962/3, the coal plant being assumed to have a 25-year life and the coal cost range being entirely dependent on the site cost of coal.

In fact, even before the first commercial nuclear stations were ordered the comparative economics of nuclear power had begun to deteriorate. Two of the reasons for this were those mentioned by Jukes in 1958, though not fully elaborated on that occasion, the fall in plutonium credit and the rise in interest rates. The plutonium credit fell for several reasons. First was an easing of uranium supplies, starting in 1956. This eventually halved the price of uranium, but could not be immediately reflected in the generating costs of the first stations since under the terms of an AEA-CEGB agreement these were to be fuelled with uranium contracted for at the earlier higher price. Second, in late 1956 the US Atomic Energy Commission (AEC) cut by more than a third their quoted price for enriched uranium. And third, by 1956 it had been virtually established that plutonium was really unsuitable as a fuel for the existing thermal reactors and could be fully utilised only in fast reactors, already understood to be much longer-term prospects. The first of these factors depressed the bottom of the theoretical plutonium value bracket, the second and third had a similar effect on its top. The net result was that the credit value which the AEA felt able to offer for plutonium was reduced to 0.1d by the autumn of 1956, and to 0.07d by the spring of 1957. In Jukes's words at that time, 'Because of the uncertainties over its method of use it is usual to be cautious in estimating its value and to allow only a low value.'[15] This was obviously a decisive change from the expectations of 1955.

It is important to be clear that the plutonium allowance was quite unconnected with any military aspect. It was announced in 1958 that the Government had asked the CEGB to modify the design of three of their Magnox stations to allow military-grade plutonium to be obtained from them if this should become necessary, but a year later it was decided to confine the arrangement to the Hinkley Point station and in any case the provision apparently had no economic bearing.[16]

The general rise in interest rates, which increased from 4 per cent when the 1955 programme was drawn up to 5 per cent by 1957, 6 per cent by 1961 and 7 per cent by 1963, amounted to a further relative handicap to nuclear power in that capital charges constituted about two-thirds of nuclear generating costs, but only about one-fifth of conventional generating costs.

A third serious economic problem which nuclear energy began to meet in the late fifties was renewed competition from conventional fuels. Coal and oil supplies both began to improve, so that by 1959 the NCB had coal stocks of 40m tons, there was considerable spare oil-tanker capacity and plenty of cheap oil. In addition, the size of conventional generating sets had begun to increase, and their capital costs correspondingly to decrease, so that by 1961 the capital cost of conventional plant, at about £40/KW, was roughly a third lower than it had been in 1955. On top of this, the efficiency of conventional generation was steadily being enhanced by r & d, and the careful siting of power stations near to coal supplies was also helping to keep costs down. The overall effect of these changes was that the conventional generating cost target at which nuclear energy had to aim was nearer to 0.5d than the 0.6d assumed in 1955.

The AEA were very surprised both by what they saw as 'violent changes' in fossil fuel availability and by the fall in the capital costs of conventional power stations. But allowing for price inflation of 10 per cent and an increase in interest rates from 4 to 5½ per cent, their economic adviser continued to regard nuclear estimates in mid-1959 as being very similar to those of 1955.[17] These two factors, he judged, put up the cost of nuclear power by 'a little over 0.1d' per unit. He looked now, however, to a substantial fall in uranium prices in the mid-sixties to cut the nuclear generating cost by perhaps 10 per cent.

As the first nuclear programme was carried through it began to suffer still other economic embarrassments. In particular, the capital cost of the first two stations proved to be about 25 per cent higher than the £140-145/KW which had been predicted. Faulty estimates, price inflation and design improvements during construction all contributed to this increase. Also, as mentioned above, the capital cost of site development and of engineering overheads had been overlooked when the original estimates were made. The corresponding increase in unit generating cost worked out at between 0.1d and 0.15d, depending on the interest rate applied. A much small increase, less than 0.03d, stemmed from three other sources, the higher price being charged by the AEA for graphite so that a new factory, needed for the expanded programme, could be written off more quickly, the installation of additional safety devices in the reactors following the Fleck Report on the Windscale incident of 1957, and modifications in the CEGB's accountancy procedures.

Thus, within a few years of the original commitment to a nuclear power programme, the immediate economic prospects of nuclear power had for several reasons become much poorer. While there had been pluses, such as the achievement of a thermal efficiency for the first station a third higher than planned, in total these were insufficient to counter-balance the series of blows to nuclear economics. It was therefore hardly surprising that the programme had by 1959 begun to 'slip a bit'. The expanded programme of March 1957 had actually been marginally changed almost immediately, in October of the same year, but formally at least this had been done as part of the Government's general strategy for checking capital expenditure, and not in response to nuclear economics. The effect of this move had been to extend the nuclear programme by a year, so that it would complete in 1966 instead of 1965.[18]

In June 1960 there appeared the second White Paper[19] wholly devoted to the nuclear programme. It was recognised in this short document both that there was no longer a case on fuel supply grounds for a rapid build-up in nuclear capacity, and that conventional generating costs were by this time about 25 per cent lower than those of nuclear plant. The White Paper argued that although the generating costs at the first nuclear stations would be 'rather higher' than had been forecast, the downward trend was closely in line with the 1957 projection: what had not been foreseen was the extent of the fall in conventional generating costs. Seven nuclear stations totalling 3GW were building or had been approved by 1960. Instead of ordering 2-3GW more in 1960-1 to commission by 1966 and so fulfill the 1957 programme, the new White Paper indicated that roughly one station a year would be ordered in each of the following four years. This was thus the third revision of the 1955 programme. In the event, only two more stations were to be ordered before 1965.

Since station capacity was tending to increase from order to order, the 1960 revision was expected to produce a steady annual growth to some 5GW by 1968. This was the lower of the two target figures of 1957, and the programme was, of course, also now being stretched over an extra two years. No detailed costings were given for the new programme but it was suggested in the White Paper that the CEGB would save some £90m over the following seven years, though at some loss to the AEA. The official justification for the revised programme was still that Britain would eventually require a third fuel, but later now rather than sooner, since nuclear generating costs below those of conventional plant were not in the new circumstances expected, even for base load, until about 1970. But the technological progress necessary to accomplish even this could be ensured, the White Paper stated, only by building sufficient nuclear stations in the interim.

The early sixties brought little relief for nuclear power. By 1963, after further cuts in the USAEC's enriched uranium prices, the AEA were unable to fix any precise value at all on plutonium and the CEGB therefore reduced their allowance to zero.[20] The capital cost of conventional plant continued to fall so that nuclear's target was now some 30 per cent below 1955 assumptions, while delays in commissioning nuclear plant began to inflict yet another economic penalty on the plant, and specifically on the generating boards. This arose because the loss of electricity scheduled for generation by nuclear plant had to be made good by retaining existing or bringing in reserve plant with much higher fuel costs. The first two nuclear stations ended by being between a year and fifteen months late, while the next two were about two years late, the resulting cost to the CEGB being about £2½m for the first two and more than double this for the second two.

The Board also came to feel that the 6 per cent interest rate which they were now applying to nuclear power was artificially low, in that it had become their practice to look for a return of 10 per cent on expenditure over and above that necessary to meet demand. In the light of this they could, they said, see a case for charging 10 per cent on the difference between the capital costs of nuclear and of conventional stations.

Detailed capital costs for nuclear and conventional stations were given to Parliament in March 1963.[21] For fifteen conventional plants completed in the previous three years the capital cost was shown as ranging from 58.2 to 50.8 £/KW, and for thirteen under construction from 61.8 to 31.8 £/KW. At this time only Berkeley and Bradwell of the Magnox stations had commissioned and for them the comparable figures were given as 176.7 and 171.7 £/KW. More realistic for comparison were the figures for the next five Magnox stations, expected to commission between 1963 and 1966, the latest estimates for which then ranged from 142.5 £/KW for Hinkley Point to 106.0 for Sizewell. In line with these figures the CEGB's nuclear generating cost estimates at the end of 1963 ranged from a high of 1.23d/KWh at Berkeley to a low of 0.66 at Wylfa, the other six stations dividing between a group of three at 0.97-1.12 and another group of three at 0.73-0.74: the Ferrybridge C coal station then under construction was by contrast quoted at 0.48. Actual running costs were of course estimated to be firmly in favour of nuclear, a range of 0.22-0.38d/KWh compared with one of 0.39 to 0.52.

The AEA were unhappy in the early sixties with the ground rules for costing nuclear power, thinking them 'unduly conservative'. Thus in 1962 Sir Leonard Owen[22] suggested that instead of a load factor of 75 per cent one of 90 per cent 'would not be unduly optimistic', at least for the early stations. Owen said he also knew of no reason why the book life of nuclear plant should be less than that of conventional plant. And, acknowledging that not all his colleagues would agree, he suggested that a Magnox fuel burn-up a third higher than then assumed would be achievable. These changes, together with a reduction in interest rates, he saw as significantly altering the nuclear-conventional comparison. On the other hand, at the CEGB Sir Christopher Hinton's view of the ground rules in 1963 was that a 75 per cent load factor was 'very high' for a life of 20 years and 'even more remarkable' if a longer life were assumed. Hinton also pointed out that it was the summer night load, then running at only 12-15 per cent of the winter peak, rather than reactor availability which would ultimately constitute a limitation on the achievable load factor.[23]

This chapter has so far dealt only with the unhappy economic side of the first nuclear programme, but there are some economic points to be made in part mitigation. There was, for example, the fall of some 40 per cent in capital costs per KW capacity between the first two nuclear stations and the last two. It must also be remembered that whereas the CEGB assumed a 25/30 year book life for coal plant, they felt compelled at the outset to be cautious with nuclear plant simply because there was no definite evidence about its safe working life. Initially nuclear stations were therefore regarded as having only 15-year lives, and though this quickly became 20 years, there it stuck throughout most of the sixties, in spite of the later Magnox stations having design lives of 30 years. In the course of the sixties such developments as the 1965 entry into an AEA reactor by suitably clad staff to recover a camera demonstrated that certain quite extensive repairs to reactors could probably be carried out if they became necessary, thereby strengthening the argument of those who had long believed a 20-year book life to be excessively harsh. It was still not until 1969 that the CEGB relaxed their position, maintaining the 20-year period for the earlier Magnox stations but going over then to a 25-year book life for AGR stations, and a 30-year one for those later Magnox stations having concrete pressure vessels. Time may well show that the earlier assumptions were too pessimistic, and the generating board may in due course be left with plant which is fully written off and technically obsolete, but which is still safe and reliable. If this should happen, then unlike old conventional stations, since the fuel costs of the Magnox stations will continue to be comparatively very low, their contemporary generating costs will ultimately appear extremely attractive. Indeed, as explained in Chapter 7, even by the mid-seventies this point was already important to the CEGB, despite the fact that the first Magnox stations were then only half way through their book lives. The Magnox stations are likely, in short, to be operated for as long as they are safe. Finally, it may also eventually have to be counted in the first nuclear power programme's economic favour that its nine stations have a substantial annual output of plutonium because, despite the long confusion about the credit allowance to be made for this, Britain's plutonium stockpile will become an economic boon if eventually a fast reactor programme is undertaken.

Observations like these do not add up to a retrospective justification of the Magnox programme on economic grounds, but it is important that such considerations should not be forgotten in a chapter which otherwise dwells on the disappointing economics of that programme as it unfolded. In any case, a fundamental economic question in connection with the Magnox stations must be how far their cost disadvantage in comparison with conventional plant should really have been foreseen, either when the programme was established in 1955, or at worse when it was trebled in 1957. Nor can this question easily be passed over on the grounds that both the 1955 programme and its 1957 revision

were undertaken against the fear of a fuel shortage.
Take first the plutonium credit. An easing of the supply situation
with regard to uranium and enriched uranium was arguably foreseeable
in 1955/6. But in any case there is another and even firmer reason for
thinking that the plutonium credit was originally set much too high.
The paper of 1955 by J.A. Jukes, referred to above, envisaged five
possible uses for plutonium, the three at the top of the material's value
bracket all being as fuel for new types of reactor. Development of
those reactor systems then lay almost entirely in the future, and the
difficult technical problems associated with the use of plutonium as a
fuel also remained to be overcome. Yet while conceding that 'it is anybody's guess as to exactly what price such systems will be able to pay
for their plutonium and remain economic', Jukes settled for the top of
a £6-12/gram range. He recognised that 'The use of a large arbitrary
figure leaves one with an uneasy feeling that it may have been selected
to achieve the right answer,' and therefore described as 'a reassuring
result' the value obtained by considering recycled plutonium, the floor
of the value bracket at £3/gram. Unfortunately, as his paper also stated,
this too was based on 'a reasonable guess' about the unsolved problems
connected with plutonium recycling. Jukes concluded fairly that his
estimates of plutonium values were 'the result of crystal gazing rather
than scientific analysis', but less convincingly that these estimates
justified the claim that the generating costs of the earliest nuclear
stations would be about the same as or less than those of conventional
plant.

It should not be thought that in the mid-fifties optimism about the
value of plutonium was confined to the AEA. In the United States for
example, it emerged early in 1955 that some interests had apparently
been counting on plutonium prices double those fixed by the US
Atomic Energy Commission soon afterwards, and even in late 1957 at
an American Nuclear Society symposium there was still talk of a significant plutonium value.[24] But the matter was less immediately vital in
the United States, and in conditions of such uncertainty Britain's 1955
White Paper was at best naive in its treatment of the plutonium credit,
particularly so when the allowance constituted 25 per cent or more of
the 0.6d target cost at which nuclear power had to aim.

As to the failure to allow for the fall in conventional generating
costs, the Advisory Council on Scientific Policy, in commending civil
nuclear power experiments, had emphasised as early as 1951[25] that
there was a risk of overlooking scientific developments for the more
efficient use of coal in power production. This was a prescient warning.

In early 1955 the British Electricity Authority ordered their first 200MW turbogenerator. This was twice as large as any then in commission, yet by 1956 they were looking forward to a 550MW set as part of their 1962 programme. This increase in size was coupled with higher operating temperatures, and the whole was seen as promising considerable economic advantage. This was brought out by F.H.S. Brown, then a Central Electricity Authority engineer and later CEGB chairman, at a Calder Hall symposium in 1956.[26] Virtually alone in his cautious reservation on that occasion, he pointed out that while he shared the general confidence in the future of nuclear costs, a very great change in conventional generating economics could be foreseen, with the result that nuclear engineers had to aim at a moving target.

Thus, when the nuclear programme was trebled in 1957, it should really have been better appreciated that the nuclear stations were probably going to meet a more severe challenge from conventional plant than had been allowed for in 1955. Lord Hinton has in fact suggested that it was known at the time of the 1957 expansion that there would be a 25 per cent difference between conventional and nuclear generating costs. For Hinton, the additional cost was 'part of the price to be paid for the Suez incident, for without Suez it is inconceivable that the 6,000MW programme for 1957 would have been given approval'.[27] Hinton himself had returned to Britain in October 1956 from a six-month recuperation abroad and had been far from happy with the programme expansion then being contemplated.

With respect to interest rate increases during the first programme, although this was in one sense a given external factor, it was not widely enough realised in the early years, though there were warnings, just how dependent the economics of Calder Hall and the Magnox stations were on the low-cost financing they initially enjoyed. Influenced by the high cost of enriched uranium and the prevailing low interest rates, British development was significantly more concerned at the time with low fuel costs than with low capital costs, whereas in the US the opposite held true. Contemporary American practice was based on fixed charges of 14 per cent for conventional plant and 15 per cent for nuclear plant, to cover that is debt service, amortisation and depreciation. The comparable figure for Calder Hall was only a little over 8 per cent, and a comparative study in 1957, for instance, of Calder Hall and the American pressurised water reactor under both American and British conditions and rules concluded that while Calder Hall retained the better power costs in each case, both reactors were a long way from being economic under American rules.[28] In addition, there were good grounds from 1956 for anticipating an increase in the interest rate appropriate to the nuclear programme. The Report of the Herbert Committee[29] on the electricity supply industry, published in January of that year, criticised the principle of making capital available to the industry on terms more favourable than those obtaining in the market, and the Government quickly made it clear that they were in broad sympathy with this opinion. During the debate on expansion of the nuclear programme in 1957, Reginald Maudling for the Government actually spoke of the interest rate applying to the programme, then 5 per cent, as 'a little artificial' and 'a little optimistic'. But the minister also said he thought this optimism quite reasonable — 'if we cannot be optimistic about our nuclear advances what can we be optimistic about?' — an approach which overlooked the extra distortion involved in applying artificially low interest rates to capital intensive plant. The real trouble was that there were many technical and economic un-knowns at this time, and virtually no real operating experience. Really those American commentators were right who maintained that the estimated cost of nuclear power still depended mainly on whether one wanted to be optimistic or pessimistic.

A rare and powerful critique of British nuclear economics was put forward in December 1958 by K.L. Stretch, Works Manager at Calder Hall from 1954-7 and in 1958 an Engineering Director with the NCB.[30] Stretch was concerned that Sir Christopher Hinton's reputation had dis-couraged the ruthless examination which a paper as important as his Swedish lecture of March 1957 properly demanded, with the result that Hinton's suggestion that nuclear power should be cheaper than coal by 1965 was, as Stretch saw it, being quoted as an established fact, even though Hinton himself, Stretch thought, now appeared to be hedging his forecasts following his translation to the CEGB. Stretch's analysis of Hinton's figures suggested to him that they were 'seriously biased in favour of nuclear power'. Hinton's estimate of coal costs was already too high while his estimate of nuclear fuel costs had no real evidence to support it. It was questionable whether the postulated plutonium allowance could be justified on civil grounds alone; it was wrong to compare base-load nuclear energy with peak-load coal plant; nuclear plant availability was not analysed; the capital charges applied were artificially soft; and, 'possibly most important of all', nuclear stations did not carry their full r & d charges, or perhaps any at all. Stretch himself did not expect nuclear power to be competitive with coal until 1980-90. It was therefore 'extremely rash for this country to rush into building a large number of obsolescent nuclear stations', and over-optimistic forecasts of nuclear costs were 'likely to rebound very awkwardly'.

As well as the question of comparative generating costs, another controversial economic issue which the Magnox programme began to give rise to as it unfolded was the distribution of its cost as between the generating boards and the AEA.[31] A Ministry of Technology estimate in 1967 put the total cost to the boards, including the initial fuel, at some £740m. This was the cost borne ultimately by the electricity consumer. The AEA's expenditure on Magnox development for civil purposes, the expenditure shouldered by the taxpayer, was put at a further £21m — since the Magnox reactors were derived from the reactors originally developed for the nuclear weapons programme, this latter figure could not properly be compared with development expenditure on the later, wholly civil, systems.

There was no difficulty over consultancy work performed by the Authority for the boards: this was paid for annually as an ordinary service. Similarly with regard to fuel elements, the Authority's objective was to cover their costs in the price they charged the boards, but not to make a profit. The Authority also had the task of ensuring the availability of such special materials as were required for the nuclear programme, and this did become an embarrassment when the programme slowed in the late fifties. To meet the 1957 programme, and also the military demand, the Authority had entered into substantial new uranium supply contracts, but even before the end of 1957 they were trying to reduce their commitment under these. In this they had some success but nevertheless reckoned two years later that the contracted supply, intended for the next six years, would be sufficient for more like eleven. Another special material needed for the programme was reactor-quality graphite. To guarantee supplies of this the Authority offered incentives to two companies, including an undertaking covering the capital costs of the requisite plant. The contracts in this case had to be on a non-competitive basis and there were no break clauses. Here again by 1960 it was clear that there was excess capacity, and the Authority found themselves in discussions with the CEGB about the financial responsibility for this situation, and also with the graphite manufacturers with a view to cutting back procurement.

Although the Government did not indicate whether or how the AEA were to recover development costs on reactors later adopted by the generating boards, the Authority chose to interpret their remit as requiring them, so far as conditions permitted, to seek royalties from the boards. Consequently, when the boards grew restive about Magnox economics, the royalty issue became a source of considerable friction between them and the Authority. Since any royalty imposed by the Authority on the consortia was bound to be passed on to the boards, it was logical that negotiations on this subject should be conducted directly between the public bodies themselves. Initially the generating boards were unwilling to pay royalties until their nuclear stations were truly competitive, but following tripartite discussions between them, the Authority and the Treasury, in 1956 a compromise was arranged. Under this, royalties were to be waived on the first four stations, then charged at a rate of 0.015d per unit of electricity for twenty years on the two stations expected to complete between 1963 and 1965, after which there was to be a review in 1965 of the position in regard to later stations. There were provisions in the 1956 agreement both for a higher royalty, if the nuclear stations turned out after all to be more economic than conventional ones, and on the other hand for the Board to seek an extension of the waiver if the nuclear stations failed to measure up to what was expected of them. According to the Comptroller and Auditor General the actual term used was 'proved their worth', which, as he understood it, 'was a phrase on the interpretation of which the Authority and the Board never reached complete agreement'. In due course the Board apparently claimed that the earlier stations had *not* proved their worth, in that their economics compared unfavourably with those of conventional stations, the Authority that the fair test was whether they had come up to expectation in their own right. In any case, the outcome was that the Board 'resisted' payment of royalties on the two 1963/5 stations, and in addition the discussions between them and the Authority on the royalties for the remaining Magnox stations broke down. The issue then became one for the two sponsoring departments and the Treasury and not until January 1967 was it announced that a settlement had been reached. This then covered both the Magnox programme and the AGR programme up to 1975 and under it the royalties on all nine Magnox stations were waived. The AEA accepted that there were grounds for treating the Magnox programme as a whole, but pointed out that its last three stations were expected, even on the CEGB's ground rules, to be just competitive with coal stations constructed away from the coal fields — Wylfa, Sir William Penney said, would generate at 0.55d, whereas the 1955 estimate of 0.6d was now equivalent to 0.8d.[32]

(The AGR royalty as set in 1967 was to be 0.014d for stations commissioning before 1975. Since, in the event, none commissioned in this period, no royalty fell to be paid.[33])

This chapter has now sketched the economic unfolding of the Magnox programme and it is appropriate against this background to look briefly at some of the projections of AGR economics made before 1964.[34] In starting development of the AGR the AEA's principal economic aim had been to achieve for it a capital cost lower than that which could be attained with Magnox, as low as possible in fact, consistent with minimum enrichment.[35] There was also a need to offset the decreasing load factor AGR stations had to be prepared to encounter as a result of the Magnox stations having taken over much of base load. The AEA's expectation in 1958 was that the fourth station of the first programme, due to come into operation in 1962, would, at a load factor of 80 per cent, break even with coal or oil stations. The AGR, they then thought, should bring down capital costs by a further 20 per cent by the late sixties, even at a load factor of 70 per cent. A joint study carried out with the CEGB in 1959-60 confirmed, so far as the AEA were concerned, that the AGR really did offer considerable advantages over Magnox, and with respect both to capital and generating costs. On the other hand, Sir Christopher Hinton as CEGB chairman believed at this time that initially the AGR might have 'little if any' cost advantage over a 500MW Magnox station, so that orders for the two types might actually overlap for a time until the AGR did finally establish itself as definitely the more economic.[36]

The AEA's design studies continued, along with development of the AGR, and in 1962 they gave further details of the AGR's economic prospects as they then saw them. Assuming the same load factor and plant life as for Magnox, taking a 6 per cent interest rate and spreading overheads over a 6,000MW programme, then the capital cost of a 2 x 500MW AGR station they now put at about £80/KW, and the generating cost at 'rather less than' 0.5d, perhaps 0.45d without allowing for royalties. The generating cost was shown as falling by 0.04d if an 85 per cent load factor were secured, and by 0.03d if the plant life were taken as 30 years. Realising development potential was expected 'quite early on' to improve still further on these figures, and calculations made in 1963 were said to demonstrate that a reduction was possible to below 0.4d. Even allowing for an interest rate of 7½ per cent the Authority in 1964 still held firmly, at least for later reactors, to a generating cost figure of 0.4d, or 0.35d 'or even less' on favourable life and load factor assumptions, 'far below what a conventional coal-fired station is ever likely to achieve'.[37] When the CEGB were comparing the AGR with alternatives in 1962/3, however, more conservatively they settled for an estimated AGR generating cost in the

range of 0.47-5d, though with a capital cost of only £65/KW at 700MW.
One problem with the various cost estimates, as *Nuclear Engineering*
said, was that the 'continued coyness' over enriched fuel prices gave
them all a 'haze of unreality'.[38]
Bearing in mind the extra capital investment entailed and the comparative generating costs of nuclear and conventional plant, the decisive
political consequence of the first nuclear programme's economics was
that it was the CEGB which carried nearly all of the burden. It was
they, as it were, who paid the piper, though, as shown in Chapter 4,
they could scarcely be said to have called the original tune. Twice
bitten, in 1955 and again in 1957, they understandably came to institutionalise economic resistance to nuclear power. This was evidenced
both by their general attitude and by their specific views on the question of Magnox royalties. They, after all, had to pass the costs of
nuclear power on to their consumers, and electricity prices were necessarily much more visible publicly than were the consequences of the
much smaller financial burden borne by the AEA, consequences in any
case routinely encompassed by a parliamentary vote. The 1960 cutback
of the nuclear programme marginally eased the CEGB's problems but
also strengthened their determination not to be landed, if they could
possibly prevent it, with any second nuclear programme whose economic premises were as doubtful as those of the first had proved to be.
This consideration, the economic dimension of the first nuclear programme, together with its implications for AEA projections of AGR
economics, would necessarily have caused a crisis before any second
nuclear programme could have been undertaken. The technological
aspects outlined in the last chapter and the political circumstances to
be mentioned in the next then complicated this crisis still further.

Notes

1. Cmd. 9389.
2. Sir John Cockcroft, 'Harwell's 21st Anniversary', *Atom* (March 1967),
pp. 51-8.
3. Margaret Gowing, *Independence and Deterrence: Britain and Atomic
Energy 1945-52* (2 vols., Macmillan, London, 1974), vol. 2, p. 289.
4. Sir Edwin Plowden, 'Nuclear Power in the UK and Abroad', *Atom* (November 1956), p. 14; also Cmd. 8647.
5. G.H. Daniel, 'The Energy Requirements of the UK', I Geneva, 1, pp. 239-44.
HCD 529 c.2509.
6. Sir Edwin Plowden, 'Nuclear Power in the UK and Abroad', *Atom*
(November 1956), pp. 14-17; J.A. Jukes, 'The Cost of Nuclear Power', *Atom*
(December 1956), pp. 27-31.

7. Sir Christopher Hinton, 'The Place of the Calder Hall Type of Reactor in Nuclear Power Generation', *BNECJ* (April 1957), pp. 43-6; also see R.V. Moore, 'Development of Gas-cooled Reactors for Power Production', *BNECJ* (April 1957), p. 220. Also HC 316-I (1958-9) Q 2340.

8. J.A. Jukes, 'The Cost of Nuclear Power and the Value of Plutonium from Early Nuclear Power Stations', I Geneva, 1, pp. 322-6; also HC 316-I (1958-9) Q 2340; and J.M. Kay, 'The Economics of Nuclear Power' and 'The Economics of Enriched-fuel Reactors', *NE* (1956), pp. 54-5, 141-2.

9. For example, V.A. Pask, 'The Place of Nuclear Energy in UK Power Development', *BNECJ*, 1 (January 1956), pp. 13-23.

10. Cmnd. 132.

11. Sir Christopher Hinton, 'The Future of Nuclear Power', *BNECJ* (July 1957), pp. 292-305.

12. HLD 202 c.192-3.

13. J.A. Jukes, 'Economics of Nuclear Power', II Geneva, 13, pp. 499-504.

14. J.C. Duckworth and E.H. Jones, 'Economic Aspects of the UK Nuclear Power Programme', II Geneva, 13, pp. 575-81.

15. J.A. Jukes, 'Cost Factors in Nuclear Energy', *Atom* (May 1957), pp. 11-21.

16. HCD 590 c.246, c.857; HCD 607 c.849; HCD 608 c.24.

17. J.A. Jukes, 'Economic Factors – Past and Present', *Atom* (August 1959), pp. 13-15.

18. HCD 575 c.53, c.66 (WA); HCD 579 c.123 (WA). See Sir Richard Clarke, *Public Expenditure Management and Control* (Macmillan, London, 1978), p. 12.

19. Cmnd. 1083; see also *NE* (March 1960), p. 95 and *NP* (July 1960), pp. 73-5. Also HCD 625 c.15-16.

20. See for example, HCD 694 c.125 (WA); 695 c.198 (WA); H. Kronberger, 'The Role of Plutonium in the British Nuclear Power Programme', *Atom* (August 1963), pp. 240-50. Also C.E. Illife and J.K. Wright, 'A Method for the Economic Assessment of Nuclear Power Reactors', *BNESJ*, 2 (1963), pp. 41-8.

21. HCD 674 c.16-18, 123-4; HCD 680 c.13-14 (WA).

22. Sir Leonard Owen, 'Nuclear Power Costs: A Re-examination', *Atom* (April 1962), pp. 48-50; See Sir Roger Makins, 'Nuclear Power Policy in the UK', *Atom* (February 1961), pp. 10-15.

23. *BNESJ* (1963), 2, p. 338. See P.W. Cash and F. Faux, 'Planning for Nuclear Power in the CEGB's System', III Geneva, 1, pp. 254-60.

24. For example, *Nucleonics* (March 1955), p. 42 (January 1958), p. 53.

25. 4th Annual Report (1950-1), Cmd. 8299, pp. 13-14.

26. *BNECJ* (July 1957), p. 238.

27. Sir Christopher Hinton, 'Nuclear Power', *Three Banks Review* (December 1961), p. 11.

28. *Nucleonics* (December 1956), p. 530 (June 1957), p. 75; *NE* (July 1957), p. 269 (December 1958), pp. 538-40.

29. Cmd. 9672, para. 349 and HCD 554 c.529; HCD 568 c.606-8.

30. K.L. Stretch, 'Is Britain on the Right Track?', *NP* (December 1968), pp. 580-4; see also his *A Power Policy for Britain* (Ernest Benn, London, 1961). See also the remarks of J.R. Cuthbertson and J. Broderick (FBI Eastbourne Conference on Nuclear Energy), reported *NP* (May 1958), p. 244.

31. The discussion which follows is based on the reports of the Comptroller and Auditor General, Public Accounts Committee and AEA: See also HC 381-XVII (1966-7), Appendix 20; HLD 756 c.58, 79, 82 (WA).

32. Sir William Penney, 'Nuclear Power', *Atom* (June 1967), pp. 136-44 (138); *The Times*, 19 February 1966.

33. HC 534-ii (1976-7), p. 243.

34. AEA Reports. Also Symposium on the AGR, *BNESJ*, 2 (1963), pp. 98-294,

335-54 (especially R.V. Moore and J.D. Thorn, 'AGRs — An Assessment', paras. 52-7, 75-88). Sir John Cockcroft, 'Nuclear Power', *Atom* (July 1958), pp. 8-13.

35. Sir William Cook, 'The First Generation of Nuclear Power Stations', *Atom* (July 1959), pp. 32-8.

36. For the CEGB's position see, for example, Sir Christopher Hinton, 'The Evolution of Nuclear Power Plant Design' (Royal Society, 20 July 1960); 'The Problems and Prospects of Nuclear Power', *Atom* (March 1963), pp. 62-71; HC 236 (1962-3) Q 3594.

37. H. Kronberger quoted in *Atom* (August 1963), p. 233.

38. *NE* (April 1963), p. 109.

4 POLITICAL ARGUMENTS

The economic and technological aspects of nuclear power outlined in the previous two chapters, with the CEGB vitally concerned about shortcomings in the former and the AEA increasingly convinced about the soundness of the latter, would by themselves have produced a crisis before the AGR could have been adopted for a second nuclear programme. The circumstances to be identified in this chapter and the next deepened that crisis, while also creating something of a 'nuclear cacophony'.[1]

The decisions which established the civil nuclear programme in 1955 and expanded it in 1957 were both formally government ones, but obviously neither could have been taken without strong positive advice from the AEA. The Ministry of Supply's atomic energy organisation communicated to the Government as early as 1953 its confidence that the Calder Hall type of reactor had a vital part to play in the energy economy, and also its belief that stations bigger than Calder Hall needed to be built to allow a more accurate idea of nuclear economics than could be obtained with Calder Hall itself. As noted in the last chapter, an AEA report by Kay, Geoghegan and Poulter acted as a trigger. This report was studied by an interdepartmental committee chaired by B.F. St J., later Lord, Trend, under-secretary at the Treasury, and the 1955 White Paper followed on directly.[2] Naturally, only the AEA had the knowledge to compose the technical parts of the White Paper but that document's remarkable, though undetailed, confidence in regard to costs contrasted with the earlier caution of the nuclear engineers, especially on the matter of the plutonium credit. According to D.E.H. Peirson, AEA secretary, the White Paper was in fact largely the work of the AEA chairman, Sir Edwin Plowden – 'the supreme planner, knowing exactly how to achieve the desired ends and what strings to pull'.[3]

The Government did not consider they were routinely approving an AEA scheme. There were evidently very great risks involved which it fell to them to recognise and accept, and this was exactly what they felt they were doing in instituting the 1955 programme. As the Minister of Fuel and Power explained: 'Owing to the secrecy of much of the knowledge on which this programme is based, it was necessary for the Government themselves to take the initiative in the matter, but they gave the BEA an opportunity of undertaking this programme as part of its normal activities.'[4] But having thus involved themselves, as far as the Government were concerned, the limitations on the programme would now be technical, and not financial.

In the early sixties the Select Committee on the Nationalised Industries heard a slightly fuller account of the BEA's role from the Electricity Council. The Council then said, in reference to the 1955 White Paper, that: 'The CEA had no part in the detailed preparation of this. . . and were given only a month or so in which to comment on it in draft. Nevertheless, on the information available they accepted the proposals as a reasonable approach to nuclear energy development in the United Kingdom.'[5] The BEA had begun in the early fifties to prepare for the new technology, and in their 1954 report had looked forward to the time when working with nuclear power stations would be part of their ordinary activities. Indeed, Lord Citrine,[6] the BEA chairman, reveals in his memoirs that he went to a meeting in 1953 armed with the authority from his board to meet some £3m of the cost of the station which later became Calder Hall, keeping discreetly quiet when it emerged that this station was going ahead anyway for military purposes. The CEA still thought the 1955 programme 'a bold step'[7] in the absence of operating experience on an industrial scale with Magnox reactors: Calder Hall was of course still more than a year from completion.

The CEA were associated rather more closely, though hardly more effectively, with the 1957 decision to expand the programme. They participated, together with the AEA, the South of Scotland Electricity Board and several government departments in a review carried out by the Ministry of Fuel and Power at the end of 1956. The CEA had received the first orders for their nuclear stations in October 1956 and oil rationing had been announced in November. The review committee, under the chairmanship of M.T., later Sir Martin, Flett, deputy secretary at the Ministry, apparently had 'the usual fierce argument about the costs involved' and experienced 'considerable difficulty in picking their way between the conflicting arguments'.[8] The committee's estimates of the difference between coal and nuclear generating costs was within the limits of accuracy of the estimates, but the CEA understandably felt happier with their coal figures. In the light of Suez, power at almost any cost seemed acceptable and even on the assumption of oil supplies of 8.5 million tons of coal equivalent (mtce) in 1965, it was thought that there would still be a fuel gap of at least 9mtce. The 'main case' for the new programme as the Government saw it was thus the persisting coal shortage. The cost to the balance of payments of importing energy also continued to be important. In addition, it was thought right to demonstrate the 'tremendous confidence' the country had in its nuclear scientists. The lesson to be drawn from the past was that in energy policy 'our outlook must be bold and one in which we are prepared to take risks'. The Paymaster-General, Reginald Maudling, indicated that the stations were all now likely to be of the Calder type. He saw no reason to depart from the 1955 estimate of generating cost but acknowledged that the calculations were liable to a 'considerable margin of error in either direction'.[9] The 1955 programme had been well received but 1957 saw some public criticism: *The Economist*, for example, wondered whether 'the Cabinet was any more competent to make this decision than official spokesmen proved themselves able to explain it'. *The Times* had already warned that atomic energy possessed 'the power to evoke fantasies'.[10]

Of the three alternative programme expansions discussed by the review committee, 3.4, 4.5 and 6GW, the largest was chosen, in spite of the CEA's preference for the middle one.[11] This evidence of a fairly cautious CEA attitude to nuclear energy is particularly striking when it is remembered that the review was conducted in the immediate aftermath of the Suez crisis, and at a time when the CEA's oil consumption had for four months to be cut by some 90 per cent.

The CEA apparently feared they had been saddled with an uneconomically large programme and continued to be uneasy, especially when within a month the NCB indicated that an extra 10m tons of coal might be available in 1965. This in turn led to the setting up of another committee, bringing together the Ministry, the NCB and the CEA under the chairmanship of R.J., later Sir Reginald, Ayres, deputy secretary at the Ministry of Fuel and Power, but apart from concluding that some 3m more tons might be available in 1965 than had been assumed when the decision was made to treble the nuclear programme, this committee's deliberations had no other effect.[12]

The 1957 expansion, while much influenced by the AEA's enhanced confidence of 1956, was again none the less a government decision. While the review was in progress the Government declared their keenness to expand the programme 'as far and as fast' as was practicable, because, it was said, 'the whole national situation absolutely demands it': to reap full benefit the country must 'undergo the sacrifice' the huge nuclear investment entailed.[13] Similarly, in the appointment of a new Minister of Power in January 1957 reference was specifically made to extending the use of atomic energy, and in the debate on the bill reorganising the electricity supply industry, Geoffrey Lloyd, who as

Minister of Fuel and Power had announced the 1955 programme, specifically suggested that the key question to be asked about the bill was whether or not it would create an efficient organisation for the rapid exploitation of nuclear energy. He was summing up the general preoccupation: the 1957 decision was the Government's, but it is probable that any other Government would, *faced with the same situation*, have acted in the same way.[14]

James Callaghan for the Opposition had expressed the hope in late 1956 that the nuclear programme would be speeded up, standardising on Magnox, but he had also acknowledged that the electricity authorities were being asked to take 'a tremendous gamble' and had therefore suggested they should receive financial assistance. In welcoming the 1957 expansion, another leading Opposition spokesman, Alfred Robens, pressing for a new White Paper, argued that a trebling of planned nuclear capacity amounted to a new programme rather than flexibility in the old one. In the light of events a decade later it is also interesting that Robens, though still supporting the new programme, repeatedly stressed that under it 18mtce were being obtained for an investment of £919m.[15]

By mid-1959 it was widely appreciated that the comparative economics of nuclear power had significantly deteriorated, projected conventional generating costs now lying in the range 0.5-0.65d per unit, those for nuclear plant in the range 0.65-0.7d. The difficulty experienced by those who had become uneasy about the size of the nuclear power programme in the new circumstances was brought out by Arthur Palmer in a Commons debate.[16] Palmer said he yielded to none in his admiration for 'the nuclear knights', had no wish to blame anyone for what had happened to nuclear economics, and accepted that the existing programme must continue. Yet his fear remained that Britain might have to accept unnecessarily expensive electricity, having invested 'too much, too hastily, in high-cost nuclear stations'.

It was the post-1965 programme which Palmer wanted rethought, but the Government were not quite ready to act. Without a 'real push' Britain could not expect to reap the full benefits of her enormous nuclear expansion, Maudling told Palmer. The Government felt they enjoyed 'the advantage of very comprehensive advice from a remarkably efficient range of people' and did not think, in the words of the Parliamentary Secretary to the Minister of Power, Sir Ian Horobin, that they should 'run any risk of completely unbalancing the structure of the industry by interfering with the programme'. The programme was a long-term one, not to be interrupted by 'fits and starts and lurches in response to short-term considerations'. Nuclear energy would certainly break even with coal sometime in the late sixties. Meanwhile, it was necessary to take a 'big view': Britain was not just a major civil nuclear power, she was *the* major civil nuclear power.

The 1960 cutback, when it came, really amounted only to formal government approval of a situation which had already come about as a result of a more or less calculated slippage in the rate of ordering. It was still not an easy course for the Government to accept, especially given the leading role they had played in creating the nuclear industry. The new Minister of Power, Richard Wood, in announcing the stretched programme, chose to represent it as 'a deferment of the acceleration which was planned in 1957'.[17] This was not well received and the Parliamentary Secretary, J.C. George, was more explicit. Admitting that a programme of one station a year was not much to ensure progress in the nuclear industry, he added that 'the Government believe that it is enough but that it is no more than enough. We could not have stretched the programme out any more and have been satisfied that we were giving the industry a fair deal.'[18]

The halcyon days of late 1956 and early 1957 had fostered a rapid increase in the work capacity of the consortia. There were even hopes initially that despite the increase in station size as compared with the 1955 projections, the programme would still be held to nineteen stations. One consortium reckoned it could take on a new nuclear station each year from 1958 and extend this by half from 1959, and all the groups judged it prudent to train larger staffs than were immediately needed. Three of the consortia had received contracts by the end of 1956 and the English Electric Group were awarded Hinkley Point A in autumn 1957. The fifth consortium, Atomic Power Constructions, had however to wait until 1959, when they received the Trawsfynydd order. Two of the consortia also secured export orders in the late fifties, the Parsons-Reyrolle Group at Latina in Italy and the GEC-Simon Carves Group at Tokai Mura in Japan. Some of the companies in the consortia also started showing interest in foreign reactor types, AEI in the BWR for instance.

With larger, and hence fewer, stations being ordered, and with the programme already having begun tacitly to slow down by 1959, the embarrassment of permanent excess capacity had by then to be faced. The depressing picture was made very plain in the evidence the consortia gave to the Commons Estimates Committee in April 1959.[19] Excluded of course from fuel development, all five of them had, they said, varying amounts of spare resources, all were anxious to undertake more r & d under contract from the AEA, and all felt they could play a bigger part in long-term reactor development than was being asked of them. They were particularly dismayed at the £¼m cost of tendering to the CEGB: this was wasted money for the consortia not awarded the contract, even though they would expect to pass the loss on to the CEGB via future contracts. There was a feeling among the consortia that the Authority did too much detailed design work, and that this could be done equally well and more cheaply by private industry. There was also a belief that, the AEA's own resources being limited, a more efficient deployment of the total national resources available, including, that is, those of the consortia, would permit development on a broader front. This was seen as being in itself desirable. One of the consortia had at this time still to receive a first order and did not reckon it would be fully occupied even when this arrived. Another acknowledged that there was inadequate work in prospect even for four consortia and that, failing a substantial improvement in the situation, the only alternative was a reduction in the number of consortia.

When, as 1959 went on, the situation worsened, this latter course became inevitable and the first merger between the consortia was completed in early 1960, the Nuclear Energy Company, builders of the first Magnox station, and the Nuclear Power Plant Company, builders of the second, linking to form The Nuclear Power Group. By the end of 1960 a second merger had, a little less smoothly, been arranged between Atomic Power Constructions Limited and the Atomic Energy Group, the new company becoming known as the United Power Company. The original five consortia had thus become three. Moreover, after the official slowing-down of the programme in June 1960 the workload even for these three looked uncertain,[20] and indeed only three further contracts were placed to 1965. The 1960 cutback also left the AEA with some excess capacity, heavy capitalisation having occurred before it was required.[21]

The Government's decision of 1960 was taken mainly on representations from the CEGB. As explained in the last chapter, the overall fuel position had changed radically since 1957. In October 1959 the NCB published a 'Revised Plan for Coal', which estimated total demand at 200-215m tons by 1965.[22] As with nuclear energy, there had had to be a reduction in the industry's target, for the 1956 plan had put the 1965 demand at 240m tons. The difference between the 200 and 215m tons target figures was of critical significance to the coal industry in that it was the equivalent of thirty-five extra colliery closures, and the industry was also by now fully aware that it had a vigorous competitor in oil.

The CEGB were inevitably at the centre of this coal-oil competition and as a result of some tough negotiations with the Ministry of Power they agreed at this time to delay the conversion to oil-firing of five of their stations. All things considered, October 1959 was not really the best of times for the Minister of Power to cease to be a member of the Cabinet.

Sir Stanley Brown, Sir Christopher Hinton's successor as CEGB chairman, later explained the latter's role in the 1960 nuclear cutback.[23] Hinton had come to the CEGB when 'increasing doubts were being felt both as to the necessity and the economics of the large nuclear programme . . . within six months he had weighed up the situation and informed the Ministry of his view . . . that the rate of expansion aimed at at this early stage of development of nuclear power was too great'. According to Brown, it was at Hinton's request that there were then further discussions between the Board and the Ministry, full culmination not coming until the White Paper of 1960. Of Hinton's role in getting it officially accepted that the 1957 assumptions were out of date Brown's conclusion was that 'it is at least open to doubt whether anyone but Sir Christopher Hinton could have obtained the frank recognition of this fact, and the quite drastic change of Government decision . . . He was an acknowledged expert who could by no conceivable stretch of the imagination ever be accused of prejudice against nuclear power, but he took the initiative in recognising the changed facts and recommended dispassionately and unemotionally . . . this quite considerable change in the short-term fortunes of the lusty child of commercial nuclear power, of which he more than any other single person was perhaps the father. This was not the least of the many decisions which he took in the country's interest.'

Much later, discussing Britain's failure in the nuclear export market, Hinton himself argued that 'technological progress in this country was retarded by the large, obligatory, nuclear power programme of 1957'.[24] Hinton said on this occasion that while he did not wish to criticise the people who had been responsible — 'indeed, I had some part of it myself' — the 1957 programme had drawn attention from advanced forms of reactor and 'even worse, it gave a guaranteed programme to the nuclear power industry, and that industry knew that, irrespective of economics, the Electricity Boards were bound to go on ordering nuclear power stations'. In fact, Hinton did make clear as early as June 1958 that once nuclear stations had taken over base load, a development then expected to occur with plant beginning construction in 1966-7, nuclear orders subsequently might have to be confined to increases in base load.

In view of the previous rapid growth of the nuclear industry the

CEGB were satisfied with the scale of the 1960 reduction. They conceded that an even more drastic reduction would have been unfair to the industry, but Hinton did later indicate that if it had been possible to start again from scratch, then he would have wanted to build a reactor only every two or three years, possibly interposing a smaller model of a new type when this was justified technologically. The Board's understanding in 1960 was that the size of the programme would in future be determined by more objective criteria than had previously obtained. As they saw it, the immediate programme was to be the minimum one required to make up any shortfall in conventional fuel, to maintain the health of the industry, and to secure technological advance: when nuclear costs had broken even with conventional ones then the programme was to be the economically justifiable one. On the other hand, the construction the AEA put upon the 1960 cutback was that it amounted to 'a change of pace rather than a change of policy'.[25]

The formal deceleration of the nuclear programme in 1960 having been mainly at the instigation of the CEGB, in 1961 it was the turn of the AGR to be threatened by the Board's increasingly active involvement in nuclear affairs. Or at least, that was the interpretation which many both within and outside the AEA placed upon the publication in December 1961 of an article by the CEGB chairman in the *Three Banks Review*.[26] As the Board's competence in the field of nuclear energy grew it is certain that under any chairman they would gradually have moved from their initial somewhat passive role to a far more active involvement in the making and execution of nuclear energy policy. On the other hand, there is not much doubt that when eventually they did take up a distinctly independent view, the expression of that view was more forceful and carried more weight precisely because of Hinton's personal authority as Britain's leading nuclear engineer.

In his evidence to the Estimates Committee in April 1959[27] Hinton revealed that the CEGB were even then weighing up the risks of ordering an AGR before the AEA had any operating experience with their prototype. He had in mind a 300-400MW plant, but only if the AEA chose stainless steel for the Windscale AGR's cans. To the extent that this was a serious suggestion, Hinton was presumably considering whether the technical faith he had had in the AGR while with the AEA could perhaps be translated into a commercial proposition. It will be remembered that in the event six more years were to pass before the CEGB ordered an AGR. Definitely convinced in 1959 that the AGR should be exploited 'as soon as possible' was the General Electric Company, the main contractor for its consortium. To build an AGR station this company said it would have wanted a relaxation of the guarantee it normally gave the CEGB, but only by some 10 per cent, and only in regard to output, as the company were already happy about the reactor's inherent safety. Another consortium, the Nuclear Power Plant Company, commented that for the CEGB to request AGR tenders in 1960 and start building in 1961 would be to run no greater risk than had been implicit in the first nuclear programme, even though, as the consortium admitted, there remained real uncertainties. A third consortium, the English Electric Group, by contrast felt at this time that the limited information made available to them by the Authority was inadequate to allow them to evaluate the AGR, though they had learned the Authority would shortly be rectifying this situation. One trouble in 1960 was that no one could be sure that the early AGRs, even if they worked properly, would not be more expensive to operate than the Magnox reactors contemporary with them.

Hinton said in 1960 that the AGR was 'unquestionably the logical step forward in British reactor technology', and at the press conference held in conjunction with the 1960 White Paper he kept open the possibility of a relatively early CEGB order for it, suggesting now that this might be placed in about two years. He was still talking in the spring of 1961 of a generating board programme in which the AGR would follow on from Magnox.[28] Then, in December 1961, came his controversial article in the *Three Banks Review*.

This article marked a definite change of attitude towards the AGR and also, almost as a generalisation of this, offered a broad philosophy of national technological development. Hinton's perspective on Britain's nuclear power troubles was not wholly unsympathetic, but his essay contained several arguments of startling significance for the future of the nuclear power programme, and especially for the AGR. Hinton noted first that different countries had adopted different reactor philosophies, that it was still not possible to say how many of these would prove successful, and that at any given time a reactor developed abroad might have the edge over one developed in Britain. His second and more general observation was that to ensure a satisfactory position in any technical field, it was not necessary for a country to make every invention in that field, but enough simply that it have the all-round scientific and technological capacity to stay with the leaders, in which case a reasonable proportion of inventions would in fact be made nationally, while the rest could easily and rapidly be taken up under licence. This proposition was well enough served by the specific examples Hinton cited in its support, but it was obviously much more provocative, though not necessarily unsound, to suggest as he did that it should apply also in the case of nuclear energy.

Hinton's third major point, actually the last sentence of his paper, must be read in the light of the AEA-CEGB dialogue, or the lack of it, in the early sixties with respect to the selection and development of reactor systems: 'Ultimately everyone connected with the development, design and construction of nuclear power plants must decide his research and development programme on the basis of what his customers find most economical and what he can develop and sell to give him a profit and them power at the lowest possible cost.' Hinton elaborated on this last point in the evidence he gave to the Select Committee on the Nationalised Industries in 1963[29] in connection with the AEA's decision to embark on a prototype SGHWR. This is taken up below.

The *Three Banks Review* article was undoubtedly painful for the AEA. Most cruel was the possibility it held out that the CEGB might wish in due course to build a foreign reactor, a threat scarcely latent before this. The article appeared to signal a profound shift in CEGB policy, or at any rate in declared policy, something rather different given that such organisations do not always say what they mean or mean what they say, and that this organisation could not expect ultimately to be allowed to act independently of government. That the AEA should be ruffled was understandable, though some thought the Authority showed an excessive sensitivity to criticism.

Against the background of the *Three Banks* article it is easy to see how potentially damaging were the AGR's development problems, especially those connected with graphite. In the ordinary way these problems, though taxing enough, would have remained essentially an internal AEA concern, but the interest shown in them by the CEGB chairman, with his personal technical grasp of their severity, ensured that they remained sharply in focus at the highest decision-making levels. Hinton had naturally been aware from the outset of the AGR's development that there was a 'major uncertainty'[30] about the behaviour of its graphite moderator and in his *Three Banks* article he spoke of graphite's use as presenting 'grave difficulties'. As a last resort he suggested there that 'it might be necessary to abandon the use of graphite as moderator and use heavy water instead'. The CEGB also had their own programme of research on graphite and right up to 1964 struck a wholly uncompromising tone in their annual report: 'Further confirmatory graphite and fuel element performance data will be required before an [AGR] order could be placed.'[31]

The SGHWR arrived too late to be a prospect for the second nuclear programme, but by 1962 the CEGB had begun to give the impression that they thought the Canadian heavy water reactor (CANDU) a definite possibility for that programme. Hinton himself visited Canada in October 1962 to arrange for the CEGB to be furnished with the information needed to evaluate the system properly. If this reactor were to be built in Britain then Hinton was clear that, given the extensive Canadian experience,[32] it should be of commercial size, and he was equally confident as regards the competence of the consortia to build it under licence. It seemed to the CEGB that they would incur no extra costs as a result of licensing, since the Canadians were asking identical royalties to those the AEA were then seeking for Magnox, and adding the inducement of rebates on all materials bought in Canada.

As for the light water reactors, while the Board continued to watch progress made with them, in 1962 they remained pessimistic about both the PWR and the BWR: 'Both of these use fairly highly enriched fuels, and neither of them seems to us to give the future development potential which we think it is essential to look for.' Anxious as they were to move on to a reactor with lower power costs than Magnox, the Board still thought it 'far more important to be right than to be quick', and it was in the spirit of this maxim that Hinton excused the CEGB's continuing failure to order an AGR, despite his speculative hint three years before that they might soon place one. There had been no decision against the AGR: the CEGB had simply thought it more prudent to wait. The information on AGR performance which had been obtained in the three years was not, Hinton now said, of a kind to persuade him to take the risk he had then contemplated. He realised how much of a disappointment it would be to the AEA if the AGR were to be passed over, but he none the less wanted the eventual choice of reactor made on technical grounds, and he could only hope that the AEA would not object in principle to the introduction of a foreign reactor. He appreciated that the Authority might take their grievances to the Government, but in effect was claiming for the CEGB a superior entitlement to strong views, on the grounds that it was they who would eventually be called upon to pay.

At least the AGR remained in the running, and the CEGB accepted that they would have to finalise their review of all the reactor types in conjunction with the AEA. A joint evaluation was in fact under way in 1962, but the CEGB remained dubious about its usefulness as a method for getting agreement on the next step forward. Specifically, in calculating power costs for CANDU, the BWR and AGR, they were not yet persuaded that predicted differences exceeded the margins of error. Nor did they expect unanimity between themselves and the AEA as to the weight to be attached to the impact of each reactor on their financial policies. The Government agreed that the time was not yet ripe for a decision.

It was with good reason that *Nuclear Power* spoke of 1962 as 'Hinton's Year'. Having begun it with the chill *Three Banks* statement, Hinton ended it with two important lectures in Japan.[33] In these, granting that projected AGR economics looked more promising than those of Magnox, he emphasised the importance of development potential and again said that the key to this remained the ability of graphite to tolerate the more demanding conditions it would meet in advance versions of the reactor. The chances of its doing so successfully were, he now thought, 'reasonably promising', but if further experience did not confirm this, then it would be necessary to turn to reactor types which allowed replacement or reconditioning of the moderator. The HTR was one possibility here but its development problems were still formidable, and that left the light and heavy water reactors. Of the former Hinton now had this to say: '. . . there is no doubt that these reactors (and particularly perhaps the BWR) can today produce power at costs which (particularly in countries where interest rates are high) compare reasonably with nuclear power costs from other reactor types'. But still there remained doubt about their development potential and he was not best pleased that, like the AGR, these reactors used enriched uranium. Given that, apart from the AEA's very small civil capacity, enriched uranium could then be obtained only from the US Atomic Energy Commission, he feared that the commercial freedom of the reactor buyer was being circumscribed. He had shortly before told the Parliamentary and Scientific Committee — in a seminar with senior AEA and industry figures — that he would be unhappy for Britain to be entirely in the hands of the US for her supplies of nuclear fuel:[34] this was a political aspect which ought to be an important consideration in deciding Britain's line of nuclear development. It was a further clue to his thinking therefore that he ended his Tokyo lecture with some remarks on the CANDU. He explained that CEGB studies had shown that this reactor should have power costs comparable with those of the AGR and BWR, with the important advantage that it used natural uranium. Again he identified the vital question as being development potential, but although he indicated several alternative paths in terms of materials, configuration and fuel, he was careful to note that there were still difficult problems awaiting solution. Not surprisingly, in view of the pluses and minuses he had awarded to the AGR, the BWR and CANDU,

Hinton concluded by hoping that the experience to be accumulated with all three during the next year would make possible a more rigorous choice between them at the end of 1963.

But no decisive technical gap appeared and so, all things being equal, the CEGB would, as Hinton put it, have felt 'impelled' to adopt the home-produced system. After all, as he said at an AGR symposium in March 1963: 'What is certain is that the AGR is a simple and logical step forward from the Calder Hall Magnox reactor and that that reactor is the most highly developed and best tried system in the world. This must strongly recommend it for careful consideration by practical engineers.'[35] What dramatically changed the position later in the year, after the CEGB had in fact issued a preliminary AGR specification to the consortia in October, was direct intervention by the interested American firms, who now 'came along suggesting prices based on the prices which General Electric quoted for Oyster Creek and which Westinghouse is quoting elsewhere'. These prices were lower than those the CEGB had used for LWRs in their earlier comparisons, but informal offers, even when confirmed on paper, naturally could not have been accepted at face value. Substantial detailed supporting information was also essential, and in Hinton's words, 'The only way to do this is to get firm tenders.'[36] He stressed that he had made clear to the Americans that he would not in any case want to place orders directly in the US. The American intervention is discussed further in the next chapter.

Even when commenting favourably on a foreign reactor, Hinton never argued for a broader British approach, one, that is, which would have included other reactor types: the Americans could afford to cover more options but Britain's restricted means had left her no possibility of pushing on with all the half dozen or so attractive designs which had earlier circulated within the AEA. As he told the Estimates Committee[37] in 1959: 'We in this country have always had limited resources, and the success that we met in the first ten or eleven years of atomic energy was by a rigid and relentless concentration of those resources on a limited number of projects.' The lesson he drew from this was that it would be unwise to widen the programme because if effort became diffused over many different types of reactor, this might jeopardise the chances of success in each of them. He was prepared at that time to recognise the case for working on a reactor using a moderator other than graphite and capable of AGR temperatures, that is a gas-cooled or steam-cooled heavy water reactor, but that was as far as he wanted to go. Not even in his *Three Banks* article did Hinton suggest that Britain's reactor development programme had taken a wrong turning, or that it had been too narrow. It was rather part of an historical panorama in which each country had made its choice, or had had that choice dictated to it, by its own particular set of circumstances. It was for posterity to assess which country had been most successful. It was even possible that technical choices and constraints might in the end cause the British and American streams of development 'starting so far apart' to flow 'logically together'.[38] If Britain had failed thus far to make her reactors competitive, it was 'because of adverse economic and commercial changes and not because scientists and technologists have fallen short of their hopes'.[39]

The differences in the early sixties between the CEGB and the AEA received almost their only public airing as a result of an inquiry by the Select Committee on the Nationalised Industries[40] into the electricity supply industry, though only one of the nineteen chapters of this Committee's report dealt with nuclear energy. That the Generating Board 'must have found the Committee's support in this matter extremely welcome'[41] is certain. The Committee recognised that their inquiry did not properly extend to the AEA, the Authority being outside their terms of reference, and their previous inquiries and the nature of their general remit made it easier for them to understand the CEGB's problems than those of the AEA. Their observations on the state of the AEA-CEGB relationship were nevertheless, from the point of view of the public interest, timely, serious and sensible.

The evidence they had received suggested to the Committee that 'defects in the existing structure and organisation' might be responsible for the very large sums of public money involved 'not being spent to the best advantage'. They were in no doubt that the Generating Board 'harboured some resentment at the way in which they had been treated by the Authority', and they were disturbed by the manifestations of the differences between the two bodies. In welcoming the appointment of an official committee under the chairmanship of Sir Richard Powell, permanent secretary at the Board of Trade, which they heard had been set up to investigate reactor choice, the Select Committee said they thought there was 'room for co-ordination in other matters besides the choice of the next reactor'. More specifically, because they were not satisfied with the equity of the existing allocation of charges for the nuclear programme as between the Board and the Authority, the Committee were anxious that the Powell Committee should examine 'as a matter of urgency, the extent to which the Board and the Authority should bear responsibility for research and development of civilian types of reactor'. They also wanted the Powell Committee to consider 'how the additional cost of making power by nuclear means under the present programme should be apportioned between the taxpayer and the electricity consumer'. The Committee saw that their proposals might involve amending the Authority's statute, and this too they wanted the Powell Committee to look at. They hoped that that Committee would solve the problem of the next reactor to the satisfaction of both the CEGB and the AEA, but if the reactor eventually chosen were one which the Board judged not to be 'in their best commercial interests', then the Select Committee felt that the Board should be compensated 'to the extent of their disadvantage'.

These were sweeping recommendations, but the evidence the Committee had taken scarcely warranted less. They might well have steered a fairer path between the position of the Board and that of the Authority, but even had they done so this could have changed only the balance and not the tone of their conclusions. There was too much wrong, and even more important, too much more which seemed likely to go wrong, with the AEA-CEGB relationship for there to have been at this time any room for complacency.[42]

The most succinct summary of the AEA-CEGB dispute was a one-paragraph CEGB comment[43] to the Select Committee on the earlier evidence of the AEA: 'Some of the statements made do not exactly accord with the picture as we see it but we do not think that this is unnatural. The Atomic Energy Authority is primarily a research and development organisation and is staffed by people who have been trained for these activities; the picture that they paint is naturally of the view as seen by an enthusiastic research staff. The picture painted in the CEGB memoranda and evidence shows that same view as it appears to an organisation carrying heavy financial and commercial responsibilities.' Essentially the same point was made by Hinton in his oral evidence. Asked whether it was fair to conclude that the AEA's r & d programme was guided by the CEGB's requirements, his reply was that 'I think that their activities are guided by what they think our requirements ought to be'. This observation related less to the choice of reactor for the second commercial programme than to the Authority's longer term development programme. Hinton thought it would be wiser, and more normal, for the Authority to take their r & d only to the point where a commercial organisation, in this case the CEGB, were prepared to pay for a pilot model. He saw no reason why the electricity consumer should pay for such r & d 'blindly'.

Hinton defended his view with particular reference to the Authority's decision to construct a prototype SGHWR, as mentioned above. In effect he told the Nationalised Industries Committee that the CEGB would have preferred that a heavy water reactor of the Canadian type be built, but that the Authority would have none of this. The Authority, by his account, had even declined to furnish the Board with the technical reports on which their decision was based. The Board were having to be content, he complained, with discussions between their own and the Authority's technical staff as to the reasons for the Authority's decision. The CEGB were not therefore 'fully with the plan' that was being followed. It was 'a mistake in policy for a research organisation to launch out into expensive prototype work without taking their main potential user with them'. Generalising further, he said that he believed it wrong for a research organisation in any field to be the 'ultimate arbiter of commercial policy'; that was the task of the commercial risk-taking body which, if it were a competent one, would pay due regard to the evidence of research. (It was also not immaterial in this connection that in 1961 the CEGB had opened their own nuclear laboratory at Berkeley.)

The Nationalised Industries Committee did not highlight as well as they might have the cause of the Board-Authority disagreement on heavy water reactors. The Board were essentially saying that they might be interested in proceeding immediately to a commercial reactor of the Canadian type, using Canadian experience and know-how. The Authority agreed that, if it were decided to build such a reactor, then there was no need for a British prototype, at least unless further development work were shown to be necessary. But of course, for the next commercial station, which a British CANDU would thus effectively have been, the Authority were running their own AGR. Therefore, recognising the desirability of getting into the heavy water field now that they had the resources available, the Authority wanted to move to a more advanced reactor, in particular, and unlike CANDU, to one using enriched fuel, since they thought that this promised better economics. They naturally did not accept that their r & d programme was determined by what they thought the CEGB's requirements ought to be. The CEGB 'knew very well' what the Authority's reactor programme consisted of, and there was regular consultation with them on it. Nevertheless, a new Reactor Policy Committee was established in February 1963, to strengthen co-ordination between the AEA, the CEGB and the consortia.[44]

It emerged that the permanent secretary to the Ministry of Power, Sir Dennis Proctor, had been sufficiently worried by the Board's disagreement with the Authority over the SGHWR that he had himself tried to mediate through the Treasury, and also by means of a direct approach to Sir Roger Makins, the Authority's chairman.[45] The Authority, Proctor said, had taken the line that they had statutory responsibility for r & d on nuclear reactors, and their position apparently was that while they took note of the Board's suggestions, 'They [the Authority] are having to pay for it, and in the last resort they had to back their own judgement and do it in the way they thought best.' He had thought it highly relevant that, before sanctioning the Authority's projected expenditure on the SGHWR, the Treasury should ensure that it knew of the Board's views, especially with respect to the Board's eventual willingness to include an SGHWR in a commercial programme. Proctor told the Nationalised Industries Committee that he had been in a very embarrassing position on this issue since, strictly, the SGHWR belonged in the Authority's r & d programme, and that lay wholly outside his own area of responsibility. Not wanting to give the Authority the impression that he was 'ganging up with the Generating Board against them' he said that he had 'intervened entirely on my own responsibility and have not said anything to Sir Christopher about it — but I do not know that it is proper for me to say this'.

Apart from the disagreement between the two public bodies centring on the SGHWR, the investigation by the Nationalised Industries Committee naturally turned up the other matters on which in 1962-3 the Board and the Authority did not see eye to eye. These included the matter of royalties, ground rules, uranium procurement and plutonium credit, but the choice of the next commercial reactor was inevitably the most important of them. So far as the impression the Board gave was concerned, this question, as pointed out above, was closely involved with the choice of an appropriate heavy water reactor for development in Britain. The CEGB pulled few punches in their evidence. They were, they said, in close contact with the AEA as regards the AGR but felt 'that it would be wrong to overlook reactor developments which have taken place overseas and in particular . . . in Canada': CANDU might prove to have advantages as compared with the AGR which should not be dismissed without examination. It was also said by the Ministry of Power's witness that the Generating Board were 'quite emphatic' that they would not order a station based on a new type of reactor until a prototype had been running for a year. Hinton in his evidence to the Committee in May 1962 expressed the hope that this would be by the autumn of 1963, but when the permanent secretary to the Ministry of Power gave evidence the following February it was clear that while CANDU might meet the criterion of a year's operation by mid-1963, the AGR could not hope to do so before early 1964. There could therefore be no government decision until 'sometime in 1964', but the CEGB had meanwhile indicated that they would act to minimise the delay by getting on with the preparation of a specification on the assumption that the AGR would eventually be chosen, postponing the actual commitment until they had the results of a year's operating experience with the Windscale prototype. The AEA stressed that they had no wish that the CEGB should order an AGR until this prototype had been in operation 'for some time', though they themselves still had 'great confidence' in the AGR.

Hinton's opinion that progress on the fast reactor had been 'disappointingly slow' was possibly directed more at the frustrating technical problems which had arisen than at the AEA for their conduct of the project, though some thought he was angling to have the CEGB made responsible for the next, or prototype, phase. But he also implied that the slow progress was one of the factors which had stimulated his interest in CANDU, a reactor which he thought, because of its high fuel burn-up, did not, unlike Magnox and the AGR, depend for its economics on the development of a fast reactor to burn its by-product plutonium. The Authority's response to this was that progress with the fast reactor would not affect the economics of a programme based on Magnox or the AGR much more than it would one based on CANDU: the penalty for not recovering the plutonium was 'broadly the same' for all three, and in any case the value attributed to recovered plutonium amounted to only about one-twentieth of the total generating costs.

Whatever the shortcomings of the Nationalised Industries Committee's inquiry, the evidence taken was at least published. There was never a likelihood that this would be true of the Powell Committee's work.[46] The Powell Committee were set up 'under the auspices of the Cabinet Office' in the early summer of 1962. The Committee were something of an administrative innovation in that, remarkably, this was the first forum in which representatives of the CEGB, the AEA, the Treasury and the Board of Trade had all come together. The permanent secretary to the Ministry of Power told the Nationalised Industries Committee in 1963 that, although the Committee were awaiting a joint techno-economic report on reactors from the AEA and the CEGB, early meetings had seemed to be very successful. He expected that the two public bodies would agree up to a point on a joint factual appraisal, but that beyond that there would be a difference of judgement. The CEGB also indicated that they had hopes the Powell Committee would turn out to be the appropriate machinery for removing disagreements between themselves and the Authority. Very little was made public about the role or function of the Committee because of the position taken by the Prime Minister, Harold Macmillan, in a reply to a Parliamentary Question of 11 July 1963, when he indicated that he wished to continue the practice of not disclosing details of the work of Cabinet Committees. In line with this, Lord Carrington had said the previous day in the course of a Lords debate that the Committee had 'never been officially acknowledged', adding that while the body's terms of reference had 'never been publicly stated' they were none the less 'very comprehensive'. Later in the same debate Lord Hailsham, the Minister for Science, managed to be a little more forthcoming, revealing that it had been he and the Minister of Power who had initiated the Committee. In Hailsham's words: 'although I should not like to recite its terms of reference, broadly speaking it is designed to reconcile the differences of view which are quite legitimately held about the economics of nuclear and of conventional power, and about, to some extent, the economics of particular types of reactor'.

Criticism began to mount in late 1963 about the length of time the Powell Committee had been at work and in February 1964 Austin Albu and Richard Crossman, both afterwards ministers in the 1964 Labour Government, pressed the Prime Minister, by now Sir Alec Douglas-Home, about 'the increasing concern at the mystery surrounding this Committee'. Albu was disturbed that firms in the manufacturing industries concerned had, he understood, been asked to give evidence to the chairman of the Committee, though they knew neither the Committee's terms of reference nor the other members. Albu also later wrote a scholarly article in general support of a more useful role for MPs, and in this he declared that information about the proceedings of the Powell Committee had been available only informally to MPs fortunate enough to know one of its members.[47] What Crossman was upset about was what he called the 'vast amount of irresponsible information coming out' as a result of 'leaks and counter-leaks from the AEA and from the CEGB'. Douglas-Home took the same line as his predecessor had done, adding that since the report of the Committee was based on information given in confidence, naturally it could not be published. He did promise to consider what relevant facts could be made available to the House, but in the event this undertaking was redeemed only through the medium of the subsequent White Paper on the second nuclear power programme.

The Powell Committee were established primarily to dispel a gathering crisis, but it was really somewhat optimistic of the Government to think that such a body might resolve difficulties which more usual channels had failed to prevent. On the other hand, without the almost last-minute developments in the United States, the outcome might have been different. There was a second issue with respect to which the creation of the Powell Committee might have been much more relevant. When the AGR and SGHWR were selected for development by the AEA there existed no central machinery for reviewing the AEA's decisions. It was too late when the Powell Committee were established for any such review to affect a second nuclear programme, but it would not have been too late in regard to a third. Sir Dennis Proctor had indeed agreed with the Nationalised Industries Committee in this connection that it was 'anomalous' that the Powell Committee were looking at the next reactor, yet not at the next development project. The fact was, however, that the Committee were too involved in trying to provide for a second programme to be much worried about a much more remote third.

The investigation by the Nationalised Industries Committee having confirmed rumours about the unhappy condition to which the relationship between the AEA and the CEGB had deteriorated by the early sixties, an unusually stormy Lords debate of 10 July 1963[48] was no less significant in demonstrating how thoroughly dissatisfied one of the consortia felt with its treatment at the hands of the Generating Board. The focus of this debate concerned the placing of the contract for the last station of the first nuclear programme, which was to be at Wylfa in Anglesey. The contract for the penultimate station of the first programme, Oldbury, had gone to The Nuclear Power Group (TNPG) for a pre-stressed concrete pressure vessel design, the first major departure from AEA guidelines. But TNPG's had apparently ended up as the highest bid and so, despite the CEGB's known wish to get away from an effective 'buggins turn' principle — they had in 1960 requested the consortia henceforth to tender fully for all stations — the two unsuccessful consortia had somehow to be placated. The Lords debate was initiated by Lord Coleraine and, foreshadowing his attack, he announced that he had resigned from three relevant directorships so that he might speak without the handicap of personal interest.

By Coleraine's account the 'Wylfa imbroglio' had begun in 1961, just after the formation of the United Power Company (UPC). Partly to cement a union they had themselves encouraged, the CEGB had at that time agreed to negotiate with UPC a contract for one reactor at the Wylfa site, telling UPC that they would be negotiating with another company, the English Electric Group, for a second. Beginning in

February 1962 there were some 150 design meetings between CEGB and UPC personnel, and by December 1962 UPC were in a position to submit a full priced-design to the CEGB. UPC then received a questionnaire of the kind usually reserved for successful tenderers, replied to its more than 2,000 questions, and were given to understand that the CEGB were satisfied with their replies.

According to Coleraine, UPC had criticised this procedure in two respects. First, they had pointed out that two main contractors working on a remote site would inevitably increase overheads. The Board, they thought, had yielded to this view and in March 1963 they therefore put in a revised tender for a two-reactor 1,000MW station, informing the English Electric Group of the consequent threat to their position.

Coleraine said that UPC's second criticism had been that the CEGB's specification for a 500MW reactor was unnecessarily and uneconomically restrictive. A 600MW reactor would, UPC had thought, have been much better, and they had tried to persuade the CEGB of this from the first. The Board had, however, resisted the suggestion for nine months, giving in too late for UPC's offer to be uprated beyond 535MW. Worse had then followed for UPC. A series of meetings between their chairman and the CEGB chairman in the first half of 1963 had led to a rejection of the UPC tender by Sir Christopher Hinton on 24 May, and on 9 July the CEGB had announced that both the Wylfa reactors would be built by the English Electric consortium. A fortnight before the Lords debate the Minister of Power had said in a Commons reply that he did not think it unreasonable 'that the CEGB should have refused a tender which was not only high but which was for a design that it did not like'. But Coleraine, describing the business as a 'dishonourable transaction', felt that the Minister, who was listening to the Lords debate from the steps of the throne, had been misled, and that a Committee of Inquiry would establish this. Coleraine said he himself was deeply afraid for the future of UPC's technical and scientific staff as a result of a decision which seemed to him arbitrary, irresponsible and unjust.

UPC's chairman, Lord Aldington, previously as Sir Toby Low the first chairman of the Select Committee on the Nationalised Industries, also spoke in this debate, not, as he confessed, without having had serious doubts about the propriety of his doing so. He was far more circumspect than his ex-colleague, and far more ready to accept that there might be a reasonable explanation for the CEGB's behaviour. His firm knew only their own side of the dispute, but judgement could be based only on knowing both sides. He was anxious, from his own earlier experience with the Nationalised Industries Committee, that the nationalised industries should be free of outside interference when reaching their decisions, and he regretted that what had happened was being raked over in the Lords at all. Nevertheless, he clearly felt that some onus of clarification lay with the CEGB — 'even yet not all the circumstances have been made public' — and he overcame his doubts to the extent of firmly refuting what he described as the 'damaging' government statement that his company's tender had been high compared with that of English Electric.

The Government replies to this debate fell short of clearing up the matter. Lord Carrington indicated that the details of the CEGB-UPC negotiations were effectively known only to the two parties themselves, and not to the Government, but he did explain that in using the term 'high' of UPC's price the Minister of Power had meant high in the context of a design the Generating Board did not much like rather than in terms of excessive profits. (Four years later the CEGB in fact still maintained that UPC had failed to produce 'an acceptable design at an acceptable price'.) Lord Hailsham, in following Carrington, observed that it would be difficult and undesirable for the Government to elicit or reveal in public the substance of commercial negotiations. Hailsham also told the House that the opinion of the AEA, though it had not entered into the CEGB's decision, was that 'having regard to the peculiar circumstances of the case' it was in the public interest that the two reactors should be built by the same company, and that the Board had made the right choice of company. Pressed by Coleraine to explain what he meant by 'the public interest' Hailsham said he was not clear whether the Government would be justified in overriding the CEGB's decision. What had been announced was 'the decision of the Board, not the decision of the Government', but the Minister of Power might in the end feel that he must support the CEGB on principle.

Hailsham had a particular interest in UPC's problems in that Richardsons Westgarth of Hartlepool were a constituent company of UPC, unemployment in the North East was well above the national average, and Hailsham had been given responsibility for tackling this. The CEGB, however, had already said that they would ensure Richardsons Westgarth received a substantial subcontract for Wylfa even though their consortium would not now be building the station itself.

The wider issues which Lord Coleraine raised in the 'Wylfa debate' were the 'economic dictatorship on a pretty wide scale' which he considered that Sir Christopher Hinton exerted in the nuclear field, and what he saw as the failure in this context of the Ministry of Power, which had not 'effectively controlled nuclear policy at all'.

Coleraine's attack on Hinton was severe. Four points stood out. Coleraine claimed first that when UPC's tender had been rejected on 24 May both the CEGB's Engineering Member, who had had chief responsibility for the negotiations with UPC, and the deputy chairman, who had previously been Engineering Member, were in Japan. Second, Coleraine resented the practice he insisted existed whereby to receive an order a consortium had first to comply with the Board's suggestions. Third, he disliked Hinton's public criticism of the AGR and Magnox which had, he thought, greatly hampered export efforts with Magnox as well as harming relationships between the AEA and the CEGB. Finally, he regarded as a diversionary affront to the House a CEGB statement which had appeared in the press that morning. This dealt only briefly with the Wylfa affair, and concentrated rather on the AGR, for which the CEGB now indicated they would place an inquiry, subject to satisfactory experience with the prototype, at the latest by early 1964.

Hinton was not without his defenders in the House. In particular Lord Geddes, who until six months before had been a part-time member of the CEGB and was then acting in a similar capacity at the AEA, described him as 'a great man and a great public servant', even if 'a little ruthless in pursuit of efficiency'. And to be fair, even in criticising Hinton, Coleraine had himself referred to Sir Christopher as perhaps 'the most brilliant engineer that we have in this country'.

As regards the second wider issue he had identified, Coleraine asserted that the Minister of Power's failure to formulate a clear-cut nuclear policy had resulted in policy drifting in midstream between the AEA and CEGB, with catastrophic effects in terms of losses and insecurity for the consortia. In their reporting of this debate, which they referred to as 'a big industrial dispute' which had been 'seething below the surface for some time', *The Times* and the *Financial Times* both focussed on the urgent need to secure a better understanding between the AEA and the CEGB. This, the question of how much extra money it was worth spending on nuclear power, the allocation of this between the taxpayer and the consumer, and the overall organisational structure were together likely to be, the *Financial Times* thought, too much for the Powell Committee. Coleraine made essentially the same point when he returned to the parliamentary attack later in July. Lord Carrington, however, stood by the position that the Committee was a 'high-powered one — part of the confidential machinery of government'.

In view both of the accusations made against him in 1963-4 and of his overall role in the development of British civil nuclear power, Lord Hinton's later reflections[49] on the subject of British nuclear development are of very considerable interest. In December 1975 he told the Lords that he had always believed that it had been an 'over-ambitious nuclear programme' which had undermined the pre-eminence Britain had earned by 1956. And the following January he suggested to the same audience that the public image of nuclear power had deteriorated in the previous decade partly because of an 'over-ambitious extrapolation of designs' and partly because the authorities had 'played their cards very much too close to their chests'. Probably his most pointed observations however came in a *New Scientist* article of October 1976. Writing then of 'Two Decades of Nuclear Confusion', he attributed this to the division of responsibility which had existed between the AEA, the CEGB, the consortia, the Government and the NII. Design by consensus needed to be replaced by an organisation which put final responsibility with a single competent engineer: 'Unless we can have such an autocratic organisation . . . I suggest that we should consider whether we might not save money by getting out of the business of reactor development.'

Notes

1. R.M. Bankes-Jones, 'Nuclear Organisation?', *NE* (October 1963), pp. 354-5.

2. Sir Leonard Owen, 'Nuclear Engineering in the UK – The First 10 years', *BNESJ*, 2 (1963), pp. 23-32.

3. D.E.H. Peirson, 'Twenty-one Years On', *Atom* (July 1975), pp. 100-4.

4. HCD 537 c.187-8; 542 c.342-3.

5. HC 236 (1962-3), appendix 39.

6. Lord Citrine, *Two Careers* (Hutchinson, London, 1967), p. 302.

7. CEA Annual Report 1956-7, para. 56.

8. Sir Stanley Brown, 'The Background to the Nuclear Power Programmes', *BNESJ*, 9 (1970), pp. 4-10.

9. HLD 202 c.1010; HCD 569 c.33-159; HCD 566 c.184-90.

10. *The Times*, 6 February 1957; *The Economist*, 9 March 1957.

11. HC 236 (1962-3), appendix 39; HLD 262 c.14-85 (64).

12. Brown, 'The Background to the Nuclear Power Programmes'.

13. HCD 562 c.901-3, 938-1057 (940).

14. HCD 558 c.109 (WA); HCD 560 c.553, 1560; HCD 562 c.901-2, 962; HCD 569 c.59, 61.

15. HCD 562 c.962, 967, 992; HCD 566 c.186-7; HCD 569 c.59, 61.

16. HCD 605 c.149-50; HCD 608 c.569-82; HCD 607 c.21, 24, 847, 849; see HLD 218 c.65.

17. HCD 625 c.14, 954.

18. HCD 633 c.1389; HCD 662 c.6 (WA); HCD 663 c.20-3; HCD 699 c.347 (WA).

19. HC 316-I (1958-9). See also HCD 623 c.126 (WA); 725 c.499 (WA); Sir Edwin Plowden, 'The Impact of Nuclear Energy upon Industry', *Atom* (June 1958), p. 8-14; *NE* (March 1960), pp. 112-13.

20. *NP* (November 1960), pp. 90-1.

21. Sir Leonard Owen, 'Nuclear Plant Experience in the UK', *Atom* (October 1962), pp. 245-8; HCD 663 c.138, 163 (WA).

22. NCB 14th Annual Report 1959.

23. Brown, 'The Background to the Nuclear Power Programmes'.

24. HLD 291 c.1477-549 (1501); see also Sir Christopher Hinton, 'Outlook for Generation', *NE* (July 1958), pp. 287-8.

25. Sir Roger Makins, 'Nuclear Power Policy in the UK', *Atom* (February 1961), pp. 10-14.

26. Sir Christopher Hinton, 'Nuclear Power', *Three Banks Review* (December 1961), pp. 3-18.

27. HC 316 (1958-9); *NP* (November 1959), p. 86; *NE* (November 1959), p..382; *NP* (November 1960), p. 67.

28. *NE* (July 1960), pp. 317-19; *NE* (July 1961), p. 270; *NP* (July 1960), p. 61; Sir Christopher Hinton, 'The Evolution of Power Plant Design' (Royal Society, 20 July 1960); Sir Christopher Hinton, 'Power at the Source', *Electricity*, 14 (January-February 1961), pp. 11-16.

29. HC 236 (1962-3).

30. Sir Christopher Hinton, 'The Problems and Prospects of Nuclear Power', *Atom* (March 1963), p. 68.

31. Para. 247.

32. For example, D.S. St John and J.W. Wade, 'Economics of Heavy Water Reactors', *Nucleonics* (December 1962), pp. 52-5; J.L. Gray *et al.*, 'Heavy Water Moderated Natural Uranium Power Reactors', 6th World Power Conference (Melbourne, October 1962), paper 66; L. Gray, 'Why Canada is Developing Heavy Water Reactors', *New Scientist* (1961), pp. 668-71; W.B. Lewis, 'Some Highlights of Experience and Engineering of High-power, Heavy Water Moderated Nuclear Power Reactors', *BNECJ*, 5 (1960), pp. 30-6.

33. Sir Christopher Hinton, 'The problems and Prospects of Nuclear Power', *Atom* (March 1963), pp. 62-71, and 'Nuclear Power Plants in England and Wales', *Atom* (May 1963), pp. 165-76.

34. *NE* (September 1962), p. 39; *NP* (September 1962), pp. 339-40.

35. *Atom* (May 1963), p. 164; *NE* (November 1963), p. 385.

36. *Electrical World*, 24 August 1964, pp. 42-4.

37. HC 316-I (1958-9), Q 2360.

38. Hinton, 'Nuclear Power Plant Design'.

39. Hinton, 'Nuclear Power'.

40. HC 236 (1962-3).

41. David Coombes, *The Member of Parliament and the Administration: The Case of the Select Committee on the Nationalised Industries* (Allen and Unwin, London, 1966), p. 111.

42. See for example, Mary Goldring, 'Replanning Britain's Nuclear Power Programme', *BNESJ* (January 1964), pp. 11-15; L. Grainger, 'Some Personal Views on the Status of Nuclear Energy in Britain', *NE* (November 1962), pp. 429-34.

43. Appendix 10; Qs 3576, 1025, 3574-86.

44. *Atom* (April 1963), p. 115; HCD 682 c.113 (WA); HC 375 (1971-2), p. 555.

45. HC 236 (1962-3), Qs 3927-30.

46. Powell Committee: – HLD 251 c.1449, 1452; HCD 680 c.1413, 197-8; HC 236 (1962-3), Qs 480, 3919, 3924, 3573, 3575, 3595; HCD 686 c.1035.

47. Austin Albu, 'The Member of Parliament, the Executive, and Scientific Policy', *Minerva*, II, 1 (Autumn 1963). HCD 684 c.808; HCD 689 c.1019-20; HCD 687 c.910-11; HCD 690 c.620-1; HCD 693 c.157-8.

48. HLD 251 c.1380-457.

49. HLD 367 c.1174-216; HLD 366 c.482-562; Lord Hinton, 'Two Decades of Nuclear Confusion', *New Scientist*, 28 October 1976.

PART II: 1964-5

5 1964: CRISIS

The last three chapters have established that Britain's nuclear power crisis of the early sixties had its origins in economic, technological, and institutional and political factors. On top of all this there now intruded in late 1963 a new and threatening consideration: American nuclear power companies were claiming a cost breakthrough and offering its advantages to Britain. 1964 must be the year of policy, but with this final complication, what policy?

AEA spokesmen said repeatedly in the late fifties that 'the strength of the British programme derives from its narrow front'.[1] The 1958 Geneva conference was told that Britain had had perforce to choose one development route, a pressing need for nuclear energy and limited resources ruling out any attempt to emulate the broad front approach adopted by the USA. Britain's problem it was said was to 'steer carefully between premature decisions for large-scale investment in relatively primitive systems, and the fascinations of a search for perfection that will never end'.[2] At the same time the Americans explained the 'very great breadth' of their programme in terms of their relatively favourable fuel position and the plurality of their objectives.[3] Their programme as they saw it had been shaped by its military inheritance, in particular the early concentration on a submarine propulsion unit, making necessary the use of enriched uranium; by the needs and aspirations of other countries; by the uneven distribution of energy supply and demand within the United States; and by the belief that the rate of increase in energy consumption would call for large scale nuclear power in the United States within a generation. By 1958 the 60MW Shippingport pressurised water reactor (PWR) was producing more electricity than any other reactor in the world, and an experimental boiling water reactor (BWR) had achieved more than three times its design output, suggesting to some that the BWR, the product of an experimental development programme, might even prove eventually to be better than the PWR, the end result of a much more severely practical naval reactor development programme. Plans for power stations based on both reactor types were well advanced.[4]

In March 1962 President Kennedy asked the Atomic Energy Commission (AEC) to 'take a new and hard look at the role of nuclear power in our economy'. The Commission's report[5] was forwarded to

107

the President the following November, and in view of the economic breakthrough which was to be claimed for nuclear power in the US just over a year later, it is relevant to dwell briefly on the economic status of the new technology as it appeared to the Commission in 1962. Until this time civil nuclear power in the US had very much ridden on the back of the submarine propulsion programme. The Commission's main conclusion in 1962 was that 'nuclear power is on the threshold of economic competitiveness and can soon be made competitive in areas consuming a significant fraction of the nation's electrical energy; relatively modest assistance by the AEC will assure the crossing of that threshold and bring about widespread acceptance by the utility industry'. In his covering letter to the President the AEC chairman also pointed out that 'largely as a result of early optimism' the United States had 'a competitive nuclear equipment industry which is over-capitalised and underused'. The report gave details of nuclear energy's approach to the 'economic threshold'. It was naturally the two classes of light water reactor (LWR) which the Commission held had 'definitely "arrived"'. Manufacturer's estimates, it was said, put generating costs for plants of this type ordered in 1962 at '6 mills/KWh or less' (approximately 0.5d/KWh), and the Commission foresaw a fall of 0.5-0.6 mills/KWh over the lifetime of such plants. With the generating cost range in the US then extending from about 4.1 mills/KWh to 6.2 mills/KWh, the AEC judged that nuclear plant ordered in 1962 might be able to compete with contemporary conventional plant in areas accounting for about a third of US electricity consumption. Each 0.1 mill/KWh reduction in the cost of nuclear energy would thereafter make it competitive for very roughly 5 per cent more of new plants, neglecting the fact that nuclear plants had to be ordered in large sizes to be economic, and that this was not always possible. But the AEC's supplementary tables suggested that the 5 mills barrier might not be broken by plant entering service much before 1970, or the 4 mills barrier by plant entering before 1975, and even then the tables implied that these barriers would not be crossed until five years or more from the start-up of such plants, when lower fuel costs and enhanced output might allow the magical targets to be achieved. Yet it was the 4 mills barrier which, as explained below, Oyster Creek ordered at the end of 1963, was to be represented as having crossed. The dramatic significance of the latter order, seen in this context, needs no further emphasis.

In view of what was to happen at Oyster Creek, it is interesting to note that on the basis of their assessment, and having regard to the importance of the 'psychology' factor in encouraging the use of nuclear energy by the electricity utilities, the Commission in this report to the President made specific proposals for financially assisting the exploitation in the immediate future of the most nearly competitive reactors. They believed that once the economic prospects of LWRs were demonstrated to the utilities' satisfaction, only a little further financial assistance by them would thereafter be necessary as industry increasingly assumed the cost of improving these reactors. They hoped, they said, that the various methods they had in hand of providing financial assistance would 'bring about a marked increase in the number of full-scale installations', but if they failed to do so then 'more attractive forms of incentives or other means' would have to be found to assure the construction of commercial-scale plant. To repeat, the Oyster Creek 'breakthrough' was but a year away, and the beginning of a nuclear power boom in the US little more than two.

Even before the 1963 'breakthrough' orders for large LWRs were starting to come forward. As well as Shippingport (eventually 140MW), three other large LWRs were now operating, the 200MW Dresden BWR from 1960, the 140 (later 175) MW Yankee PWR from 1961, and the 255MW Indian Point PWR from 1962. Westinghouse's contracts now included San Onofre at 430MW and Haddam Neck at 575MW, both however with government design aid and waiver in respect of fuel use charges. Westinghouse already dominated the PWR field, with the Shippingport and Yankee stations, but Babcock and Wilcox, having supplied most of the nuclear parts of Indian Point, were also involved in PWRs. Similarly, while the General Electric Company (US) were coming to dominate the BWR scene, with Dresden operating, the 65MW Humboldt Bay reactor nearing completion and a 70MW reactor at Big Rock Point well advanced, Allis-Chalmers were also an interested party in BWRs, their 22MW Elk River reactor being almost finished and a 50MW reactor at La Crosse being started. It should additionally be said that quite apart from these various large and intermediate size LWRs, a number of smaller experimental projects, LWR and other, were also going ahead and firms of architect-engineers like Bechtel were beginning to play a major role.

Three events of 1963-4 in the US stand out: the result in December 1963 of the Oyster Creek competition; an important speech by President Johnson in June 1964; and the publication by General Electric in the autumn of 1964 of a price list for reactors.

Proposals for the Oyster Creek station had to be submitted to the utility, Jersey Central Power and Light Company, by July 1963. Jersey Central then analysed the offers and compared the economics of the

nuclear plant with those for a conventional plant, the latter on the
assumptions both of same-site and of mine-mouth operation. In December 1963 they announced their choice of General Electric's BWR reactor. Widespread interest in the assessment prompted the utility to publish a 46-page explanatory report,[6] and it was the economic implications of this which appeared to some to amount to ' an historic turning
point in the quest for broadly competitive nuclear power'. In essence
this was because first, nuclear plant had emerged economically superior
to a coal plant on the same site, and even a mine-mouth plant, over
most of a wide range of assumptions: second, its generating cost was expected to break the 4 mills/KWh 'barrier' over most of the plant's lifetime, again on all but the harshest assumptions; and third, it seemed
possible that Jersey Central's analysis might even on several points be at
least a little conservative. The analysis was actually performed for a
range of nuclear plant outputs from a 515MW guaranteed minimum to
a 620MW stretched maximum, these being compared with a conventional plant of some 600MW. The present-worth annual advantage of
the nuclear plant over the same-site and mine-mouth coal plants ranged
correspondingly from $2.5m and $1.1m respectively at 620MW, to
$0.4m and a disadvantage of $0.8m respectively at the 515MW output
figure.

Jersey Central's analysis was not really as conservative as a first
reading of their report suggested. This seemed to emerge even at the
time from a comparison of their figures with those released by Niagara
Mohawk in connection with the 500MW Nine Mile Point nuclear station
which they were simultaneously ordering from General Electric. Like
Oyster Creek, this was also to be an unsubsidised station, and the utility
were again in this case satisfied that it was more competitive than a conventional plant would have been. Yet whereas Jersey Central's expected
power costs were under 4 mills/KWh, those of Niagara Mohawk were
almost 6.7 mills/KWh, the capital costs of the two stations being put
at some $69m and $90m respectively. It was possible to explain much
of the difference as being due simply to different utility practices, site
conditions, construction procedures, and so on. But there was also a
difference of approach, and the widely read *Nucleonics Week* concluded that, since there was as yet no 'truly definitive cost experience',
distortions were caused 'by the wide variations in optimism that different utility managements choose to factor into their planning in
today's fluid situation'.

Over and above this, Oyster Creek was also undoubtedly a calculated loss-leader for General Electric. Even if they proved in the event

to be very optimistic, the Oyster Creek figures were bound when announced to be received as little short of sensational. Nuclear power,
they shouted, was suddenly in a position to compete for the great proportion of new power plant orders in the United States.

President Johnson's speech of 10 June 1964 was the second major
American nuclear event of 1963-4. In his speech, basing his remarks on
the developments of the previous six months, the President claimed
that the US had at last achieved an economic breakthrough with
nuclear energy, and that as a result it was years ahead of its own plans.
The President's remarks were naturally widely reported and were
obviously very helpful to the American reactor manufacturers, even
then gearing themselves up for the marketing opportunities presented
by the third Geneva atomic energy conference.

The third, and psychologically telling, development of 1963-4 was
General Electric's spring announcement that they intended to publish a
'definitive price schedule for nuclear power plant equipment'. Such a
price list, for that is how it was intended to be seen, if it could be taken
seriously would, more than anything else could do, confirm that
nuclear power had at last come of age. Indeed, when in September
1964 General Electric duly released their 'price list' they stressed that
in itself this demonstrated that 'conventionality' and 'standardisation'
would henceforth be the normal characteristic of nuclear power plant.
The catalogue figures were actually some 12 per cent above those for
Oyster Creek, but General Electric excused this on the grounds that it
merely reflected normal cost escalation and the fact that the list prices
were meant to be ceiling figures.

It was not necessary to believe that General Electric's price list was
the nuclear equivalent of a motor car price list to appreciate that they
had found an excellent sales technique. The Oyster Creek price and the
1964 price list were evidently both meant to persuade the many prospective purchasers to convert their interest into orders and, after a
necessary interval for general reflection and local interpretation of the
new figures, this is broadly what happened. General Electric's chief
rivals, Westinghouse, were rather less imaginative with their PWR, or
perhaps perforce more straightforward. There was, they thought, not a
lot of point in issuing a price list when the prices it contained were
necessarily highly conditional upon the customer's requirements and
circumstances. Their greater orthodoxy did not, however, prevent
them from sharing in the nuclear order boom when in due course it
began in 1965.[7]

The British Government's eagerly-awaited policy statement on the future of nuclear power was published as a three-page White Paper in April 1964.[8] Both the delay in its appearance, and the fact that it put forward an essentially temporising solution, reflected clearly enough the Cabinet's embarrassment at the impasse which had been reached. The Powell Committee having failed to resolve the reactor issue, the Cabinet could have decided in favour of the AGR, and therefore of the AEA, only at the expense of the CEGB, in effect accepting one piece of specialist advice but setting aside another. This might have been a possible outcome, though even then not really a likely one, had either of the two ministers most closely involved been prepared to abandon their charges, the AEA and CEGB, in Cabinet. But this they were not ready to do. F.J. Erroll was now Minister of Power, having replaced Richard Wood in the autumn of 1963, the office again becoming a Cabinet one at this time. Lord Hailsham (Quintin Hogg) continued to be responsible for the AEA and in the circumstances was necessarily rather more on the defensive. Significantly, when in 1965 the decision eventually went the AGR's way, Sir Edward Boyle suggested that credit was due not least to Hogg, for his 'repeatedly expressed faith' in the AEA and the AGR.[9]

The way found out of the political stalemate of 1964 involved transposing the problem so that instead of a highly controversial Cabinet decision that year, an apparently straightforward commercial one by the CEGB in 1965 was to be the instrument which determined the medium-term future of British nuclear power. The White Paper specified the procedure to be followed: 'The CEGB will issue an enquiry for tenders for an AGR station. They will also be ready to consider tenders from British industry for water-moderated reactor systems of proved design, provided that full supporting evidence is submitted with the tenders and that requirements of safety and performance comparable with those of the AGR are met. They will ensure that these tenders are judged on a comparable basis. The Government will review with the supply industry and the AEA the results of this enquiry in order to decide the type or types of reactor to be built.' The White Paper no doubt represented the highest common factor in the AEA and CEGB viewpoints and Sir Christopher Hinton's position had ensured that Britain would at any rate not routinely adopt the AGR. As late as February 1964 the Government had said that they and the AEA already had all the information they needed to assess the American developments.[10]

Relations between the AEA and the CEGB were now said to be 'most amicable',[11] but the frustrations met by the Powell Committee had left their mark. At the press conference arranged for the White Paper's release, Hinton denied that the document was a compromise and insisted that the policy embodied in it was 'an entirely sensible and logical solution to an extremely difficult problem'. He added that the Powell Committee's decision had been a unanimous one, but also said 'I don't agree with things I think are wrong. That is why so many people dislike me.'[12] On the same occasion, Sir William Penney for the AEA said that while they agreed with the new policy, the 5GW programme proposed was 'rather on the small side'. The Authority accepted that 'two or three' reactors now seemed competitive with conventional stations and that 'the only reliable way' forward was to get firm quotations, though it would not be easy to judge them on a fully comparable basis, because unlike the LWR tenders those for the AGR would be the first of their kind. And at another press conference later in the year Penney, while again reaffirming the AEA's agreement with the White Paper, left no doubt that the Authority would do all they could to prevent a repetition of Powell, so that if possible no Government would again be called upon to make a technical choice between reactors.

While the White Paper was indecisive on the most critical question, it nevertheless contained, more implicitly than explicitly, several very material conclusions.[13] First of all it was made clear that there would be a second *programme*, a planned 5GW to be commissioned between 1970 and 1976. The White Paper referred to 'detailed studies' which it said pointed to a place on economic grounds for nuclear power in Britain by 1970. This had thus come to be the prevailing CEGB opinion, the AEA having for some time thought the costing rules for nuclear power too harsh. The new programme was in principle to be flexible, but the assumption which was bound to be drawn from the White Paper was that the second programme would almost certainly be based on only one reactor system, as in practice the first had been. The provision laid down in the 1964 White Paper for comparing the alternative systems and deciding the 'type or types' to be built might in theory have been justified even for a single station, but remembering the serious hold-up the problem had already caused, it was quite apparent that any further competition would be very unattractive to all the parties. Only unanticipated disaster with the reactor initially selected could have been expected to persuade the CEGB to undertake a second new system while they were still familiarising themselves with the first. The stakes of the 1964-5 competition were therefore seen to be not simply a one-station contract, but at least the full 5GW programme.

This presumption was afterwards borne out, the CEGB hinting from time to time in the late sixties that other reactors might be tried,[14] but also continuing to emphasise that the significance of the 1965 assessment was not, in their view, confined to one station. They actually said in 1966, in fact, that while they continued to keep all systems under review, they were not likely to conduct a second major assessment unless there were 'firm evidence' of 'significant changes' in the relative economics of those systems. And in particular, for the remainder of the sixties they showed no real interest in adding an LWR to their system.

A second feature of the White Paper was that it represented official confirmation of a national shift to enriched uranium reactors, a shift which the AEA had effectively predetermined more than seven years before when they decided to develop the AGR. The Government's effective approval of a move to enriched uranium had two immediate consequences. First, with four Magnox stations still building and export orders for this unit still being sought, the attempt had to be made to put its obsolescence into a commercially acceptable perspective. The AEA's difficulties on this point were much in evidence, for instance, at an Anglo-Spanish Nuclear Power symposium in November 1964. Even if, as was claimed, Magnox were the best-proved reactor in the world, and even if, as was maintained at this symposium, it still had development potential, the implication of the 1964 White Paper was that only a country which valued self-sufficiency in nuclear fuel above cheap power would choose Magnox in preference to an enriched uranium reactor. As the AEA chairman himself put it quite bluntly on this occasion, why was Britain thinking of adopting an enriched uranium system while at the same time saying what great merit Magnox had? Other AEA speakers at this symposium argued that there was no real inconsistency in the British position, and the managing director of the AEA's Reactor Group, asked why Spain should standardise on a reactor when Britain had not, replied pointedly that there were 'many of us in England who think a policy of replication would be a good thing'.[15] One of the consortia, TNPG, were in fact claiming at this time that they could build a 'super' or 'flat-bar' Magnox station which would compete with coal. But low US enrichment prices, the higher return now looked for on capital, and the very long endurance expected of oxide fuel were between them widely felt by 1964 to have swung the balance finally away from natural uranium fuel.[16]

The second consequence of the British switch to enriched uranium concerned its implications for Britain's own self-sufficiency. At the press conference on the White Paper the AEA chairman, referring to promising discussions with the Americans on the subject of fuel supply, disclosed that the AEA had also examined the possibility of producing their own enriched fuel. They were, he said, of the opinion that they could get within 10-20 per cent of the American price if, whichever reactor were selected, Britain elected to produce some of the fuel for it herself.

A third, and remarkable, feature of the 1964 White Paper was that it seemed, taken at face value, to show a willingness to pass over British technology, if in the end the facts should warrant this. This willingness was predicated on an estimate that even so not more than 15 per cent of any station's hardware would need to be manufactured outside Britain.[17] There was also a requirement that it must be British industry which undertook the construction work. But still, as one informed commentator put it: 'For a country investing hundreds of millions of pounds annually in the gas-graphite line, the importance of accepting light-water tenders could not be overemphasised.'[18] At the same time, the Government rather contradicted themselves in the White Paper by recording their confidence in the 'important part' the British development line had still to play in the future of nuclear power. Had the choice not fallen on the AGR in 1965, this must certainly have proved, for several years at least, a misplaced confidence.

A fourth outcome of the 1964 policy was that, the choice of reactor having been postponed until 1965, the status of the AGR remained uncertain in the interim. The White Paper, noting only that it was 'accepted as one of the most promising' of the available reactors, maintained that the delay would not adversely affect the health of the nuclear industry, but in fact one result of it was severely to hamper British efforts to sell reactors abroad during what proved to be a vital formative year in the commercial establishment of nuclear power. As one American nuclear industry journal commented: 'The conclusions of the White Paper are likely to have repercussions far beyond Britain and US . . . The mere fact that LWR's are being seriously considered by a nation which has invested heavily in developing its own commercial power plants enhances the prestige and competitive position of the US nuclear industry everywhere.'[19]

It was thus especially galling for Britain that, whereas the first two Geneva conferences on atomic energy in 1955 and 1958 had been mainly science and engineering affairs, the third in 1964 turned out to be, following the American lead, to a considerable extent a salesmen's forum, with cost comparison a 'major preoccupation'.[20]

Inevitably the British delegation had to fight a defensive action,[21] the White Paper proving an 'enormous millstone'.[22] The country's first nuclear programme, with its emphasis on engineering progress rather than 'mass production' meant that there was little to offer in terms of experience with quantity construction, or as regards the benefits of 'replication'. Nor was there now a new British reactor to display as a world beater. In complete contrast, the Americans, primed by the exciting Oyster Creek and Nine Mile Point domestic orders, were poised to capture and expand the foreign market. Distrust of American figures on the basis of their incompleteness and AEA faith in the AGR were weak salvoes in the propaganda battle which, in many ways, Geneva became. Yet there was little else in the Authority's armoury because, as their chairman was forced to admit, 'the choice for the next stage of the UK programme is still open'. It would also, he indicated, not be easy even when the choice was made to judge the tenders offered on a comparable basis, 'because it will be necessary to extrapolate from the tenders for possible first UK stations in order to get figures for a run of stations'.[23] This was scarcely fighting talk.

The 1964 White Paper was not well received by the Commons.[24] The Minister of Power, declining to publish details of the Powell Committee's work, took the position that he had provided MPs with all the information he had which was useful, and that the White Paper made it plain where such information was lacking, namely in regard to the comparative economic merits of the various reactors. There had been a good deal of discussion as to how exactly to make a comparative assessment, the Commons were told, but it was a fair inference that the AEA and CEGB now agreed on the proper ground rules. There was 'no question yet of having taken a wrong turning': the key decision lay in the future and the Government were determined that the comparison should be made 'fairly and thoroughly'. As the Prime Minister rather charmingly put it, 'a little more experimentation' was necessary. It did emerge from Parliamentary Questions that the CEGB had issued their preliminary inquiry for tenders on 20 April, that while being ready to accept alternatives they had specified their requirements only in terms of the AGR, and that tenders were to reach them by February 1965.

Uneasiness at the White Paper was not confined to the Opposition. In the week it was published the Minister of Power and the AEA chairman both met with members of the Conservative backbench committees on power and on science and technology, and the following week these members had a similar meeting with the chairman of the CEGB. The Lords were rather more sympathetic towards the White Paper, as was shown by the second debate which Lord Coleraine now initiated on nuclear power within twelve months.[25] The organisational short-comings of the nuclear power industry were a recurring theme in this debate. For Coleraine himself the gulf between the AEA and the CEGB had been both 'wide and deep', with the CEGB pressing for action inimical to British interests in part because of the irreconcilable conflict of functions which the Board faced, having both to provide the cheap-est possible electricity and in practice promote nuclear development. There had been no dramatic breakthrough in the US: the manufac-turer there simply had more freedom in his design and was allowed to repeat it, whereas in Britain the CEGB simultaneously circumscribed the tenderer and insisted on technical advance, with the result that each nuclear station became virtually a new design. Coleraine was here re-turning to a position he had taken in the *Daily Telegraph* in an article attacking the White Paper.[26] 'Policy decisions,' he had written, 'which in this field are inseparable from technical decisions, have been dele-gated by the Minister of Power to the Generating Board. The chairman of the CEGB is in fact the best Minister of Power we have. In this con-text, and as the record shows, the best is nothing like good enough.' The *Telegraph* had agreed. 'A firm political decision,' it had averred, 'seems to provide the only way forward out of this technocrats' dead-lock.'

Another speaker in the Lords debate, Viscount Caldecote, a director of English Electric, referred to the 'strong impression . . . that the CEGB and the AEA have not got on too well together; that their poli-cies have been unco-ordinated, even in opposition'. Where, as in Britain, there was a monopoly customer, there was the possibility of 'just one big mistake, and no counter-balancing opinion'. For the Government, Lord Derwent replied that such differences as there had been were inevitable, and also healthy, in that they facilitated better policy-making. To dramatise them into personality clashes as some news-papers had done was to misunderstand them.

One point made by Coleraine, that the water-moderated reactor was 'substantially the same animal as it was ten years ago', was also made elsewhere. *Engineering*[27], for instance, dismissing the White Paper as a 'damp squib', gave its own explanation for the rumoured low American prices: 'There have been recent changes in the hierarchy of the American G.E. board and this company now adopts a logical mar-keting policy towards nuclear power. Series manufacture is the aim. There is no miracle. . . '

That the White Paper contained so little in the way of hard com-parative information after all the work the Powell Committee were supposed to have done was a feature which came in for criticism both in Parliament and outside. *Nature's*[28] opinion was not untypical: 'the secrecy maintained over the proceedings of the Powell Committee is indefensible. Informed comment and discussion are both impossible if the Government withholds from publication all the technical considera- tions on which its decision — so far as that goes — is based . . . the White paper is not very convincing.' *New Scientist*[29] had already sugges- ted that controversy should be regarded as normal before difficult technological decisions, and that poorer decisions were to be expected from a secret technocracy than from a more open policy system. *Nuclear Engineering*[30] thought that in the last resort the decision would have to be political.

Between the White Paper of April 1964 and the tender assessment of spring 1965 there occurred two events which might have been expected to have some bearing on the final outcome of the crisis. First, import- ant changes occurred at both the AEA and the CEGB. At the CEGB it was announced in June 1964 that Sir Christopher Hinton would retire as chairman on completing his term of office at the end of December. His successor turned out to be F.H.S. Brown, previously deputy chair- man. Hinton later[31] said that although his years at the CEGB had been 'probably the pleasantest and happiest' of his working life, 'far less complex and anxious than the first ten years of atomic energy', he still felt by 1964 that the time had come for a move. At the AEA, Sir William Cook, Member for Reactors, whose appointment had been extended for a five-year period from February 1963, left in August 1964 to become deputy chief scientific adviser at the Ministry of Defence. This was part of that Ministry's scientific strengthening fol- lowing its creation as a unified department in the spring of 1964. Cook was succeeded by J.C.C. Stewart, AEA Member for Production since September 1963. These changes attracted relatively little attention, although it had inevitably been rumoured before the publication of the White Paper that the Government were contemplating a change at the CEGB at least as a way out of their difficulties.[32]

The second potentially significant event of 1964-5 was the election of a Labour Government in October 1964. However, within three months a new Minister of Power, Fred Lee, and the Government's spokesman in the Lords, Lord Hobson, were both stressing that they were continuing with 'precisely the same policy' as had been pursued by their Conservative predecessors.[33] Hobson's assurance was given in the context of yet another Lords debate touching on nuclear energy, a debate noteworthy for the contribution of Lord Sherfield (previously Sir Roger Makins).[34] Sherfield, chairman of the AEA until early 1964, while seeking 'to lay the ghost of the supposed bitter antagonism between the CEGB and the AEA', made abundantly plain his unhappiness on several counts. He expressed his dislike of the monopoly positions held by both organisations, carefully noting that the AEA's position was weaker, and, in applauding the devotion of the electricity authorities to cheap power, qualified this by observing that it did not follow that 'what is good for a public board is good for a country'. On the contrary, there were judgements which neither the AEA nor the CEGB, nor the two together, but only the Government of the day could properly make. One specific CEGB practice which Sherfield attacked was the tendency he believed might exist for the Board to insist on far more detailed, and therefore costly, tenders for domestic gas reactors than they might accept for foreign-designed ones, where their lesser experience might incline them, he felt, to take more on trust. 'I know of no way,' he continued, 'of moderating the power of a large public monopoly otherwise than by governmental influence. I suggest that the present situation is having a harmful effect on the chances of our industry competing with foreign suppliers or maybe even of staying in business and that there is a prima facie case for Government intervention.'

On the systematic comparison of alternative reactors, then approaching its climax, Sherfield made some telling remarks. Taking for granted that all the advanced reactors being considered would be cheaper, 'if built on a sufficient scale', than alternative sources of electricity, he suggested that the estimated economics of the British, American and Canadian types 'would be the same within the margin of error', and added that if this did indeed prove to be the case, then 'the presumption in favour of the British system must surely prevail'. In any case, the projected 5GW of the second programme was 'at the bottom end' of the desirable range. Further, since the reactor chosen would most probably use enriched fuel, it would be an 'act of folly' not to modernise the Capenhurst enrichment plant, as a complementary rather than as an alternative source, and whether or not its costs could be brought into line with American ones.

Thus was a political crisis weathered in 1964 and the stage set for a nominally techno-economic decision in 1965: 'Chaos umpire sits/And by decision more embroils the fray' – but chance was certainly not now to govern all.

Notes

1. For example, P.T. Fletcher, 'Commercial Prospects of Atomic Energy', *Atom* (February 1960), pp. 16-23.

2. W. Strath, 'The UK Programme for the Development of Nuclear Power', II Geneva, 1, pp. 73-9.

3. U.M. Staebler, 'Objectives and Summary of USAEC Civilian Power Reactor Program', I Geneva, 3, pp. 361-5.

4. Clark Goodman *et al.*, 'Experience with USA Nuclear Power Reactors', II Geneva, 8, pp. 23-39; J.W. Simpson and H.G. Rickover, 'Shippingport Atomic Power Station (PWR)', II Geneva, 8, pp. 40-5; P.G. Dehuff *et al.*, 'Experience in the Design, Construction and Operation of the PWR at Shippingport', II Geneva, 8, pp. 47-85; E. Beckjard *et al.*, 'Operation of a High Performance Light Water Boiling Reactor', II Geneva, 9, pp. 455-67; 'Comparison of Pressurized Water and Boiling Water Plants', *Power Reactor Technology*, 2 (1959) pp. 13-16; N. Hilberry, 'Full-scale Power Reactor Projects in the USA', II Geneva, 8, pp. 479-82 etc.

5. *Civilian Nuclear Power . . . A Report to the President* (USAEC 1962) (with appendices).

6. *Report on Economic Analysis for Oyster Creek Nuclear Electric Generating Station* (Jersey Central Power and Light Company, 1964).

7. For example, John F. Hogerton, 'The Arrival of Nuclear Power', *Scientific American* (February 1968), pp. 21-31.

8. Cmnd. 2335.

9. HCD 713 c.240.

10. See HCD 689 c.534.

11. HLD 262 c.37, 79.

12. *Daily Telegraph*, 16 April 1964.

13. See Ryukichi Imai, 'The Dungeness B Appraisal', *NE* (October 1965), pp. 379-80.

14. For example, E.S. Booth, 'Electricity from the Atom — Britain's Second Decade', *Atom* (1967), pp. 299-311.

15. See Proceedings (Madrid, November 1964) vol. 2, p. 50.

16. For example, N.L. Franklin, 'Striking a Balance in Uranium Fuels', *Atom* (January 1963), pp. 15-18.

17. *The Times*, 16 April 1964.

18. Imai, 'The Dungeness B Appraisal', pp. 379-80.

19. Atomic Industrial Forum, New York, Forum Memo, May 1964, p. 7.

20. For example, G.W.K. Ford, 'The Commercial Atom', *BNESJ* (October 1964), pp. 244-51, para. 26.

21. See D.R.R. Fair and R.L. Rutter, 'Early Operation of the CEGB Nuclear Power Stations', III Geneva, 5, pp. 19-25; R.J. Coe and W.L. Beattie, 'Operating Experience with Pressurized Water Systems', III Geneva, 5, pp. 199-206; V.L. Stone, 'Operating Experience with BWRs', III Geneva, 5, pp. 209-16. See, K. Saddington *et al.*, 'The Contribution of the WAGR to the Development of a Commercial Power System', III Geneva, 5, pp. 90-7; G. White, 'Developments in BWRs', III Geneva, 5, pp. 147-55; J.C. Rengel and W.E. Johnson, 'Developments in PWRs', III Geneva, 5, pp. 137-44.

22. *NE* (October 1964), p. 344.

23. Sir William Penney, 'Nuclear Power Costs in the UK', III Geneva, 1, p. 93.

24. HCD 693 c.158 (WA), c.1491, c.230, c.1488; HCD 695 c.594-5; HCD 697 c.56, 188 (WA).

25. HLD 258 c.895-959.

26. Lord Coleraine, 'Nuclear Energy: Why Britain Has Lost the Lead', *Daily Telegraph*, 16 April 1964.

27. *Engineering* (24 April 1964), p. 562.

28. *Nature*, 202 (27 June 1964), pp. 1247-8.

29. *New Scientist*, 19 March 1964.

30. *NE* (May 1964), p. 151.

31. Lord Hinton, 'Good Management: The Foundation of Good Technology', *Proc. Instn. Mech. Engrs.*, 181, pt. 1 (1966-7), p. 9.

32. David Fishlock, 'Critical Days for Nuclear Power', *New Scientist* (13 March 1964), p. 734; HCD 707 c.1106; *Observer*, 14 February 1965.

33. HCD 703 c.1306, 36 (WA) and 156 (WA); 704 c.57 (WA); HLD 262 c.14-85 (77).

34. HLD 262 c.44-52.

6 1965: TRIUMPH OF THE AGR

This chapter explains, so far as the information available allows, the shortcomings of the process by which the British AGR was chosen in preference to an American LWR in the Dungeness B appraisal of 1965: there is really no shortcut if the limitations of this particular example of technological decision-making are to be properly appreciated. But first there is a case for going back some seven years, because the confrontation between gas-graphite and light water reactors at Dungeness B was in many ways foreshadowed by the Italian Project ENSI in 1958, and one might perhaps have expected the latter to have had more influence on subsequent developments in Britain than in fact it did.

The International Bank for Reconstruction and Development (IBRD) in July 1957 agreed with the Italian Government to sponsor a study of the prospects for a large nuclear power station in southern Italy and SENN, a group formed later that year, became responsible for the resulting Project ENSI. SENN, foreseeing that the reactors offered to it would mostly be American or British, secured the services of two firms of consulting engineers, one American and one British, and arranged that the US Atomic Energy Commission (AEC) and the AEA respectively would conduct reviews of such enriched and natural uranium reactor tenders as were received. In addition, an international panel of experts was established to oversee the whole project.

It was a specific objective of Project ENSI 'to introduce, to the maximum extent feasible, the concept of competitive international bidding', thereby providing 'the first firm data on the relative costs of competing nuclear power systems'.[1] Nine tenders had been received by April 1958, four American, three British, one Anglo-American and one French. Four were for gas reactors, there were two PWRs, two BWRs and one organic liquid reactor. The tender evaluation by Project ENSI's working group and the examination of individual tenders by the AEA, the AEC and the international panel were to find a parallel seven years later in the Dungeness B assessment.

The IBRD's atomic energy adviser explained at the 1958 Geneva conference that Project ENSI had to consider other factors as well as generating costs, lest differences in these turned out to be less than the difference between designed and actual performance. He added that 'the only real test of the validity of the estimates' would come when the plant eventually began to operate.[2] Both of these observations may be said to have retained their validity at Dungeness B.

On 25 September 1958 it was announced that the successful tender was a BWR from the American General Electric Company. The basis of SENN's choice was said to be first, that this BWR had the lowest generating cost, second that there were no technical doubts about it, third that it had high operational flexibility, and fourth that there were good prospects of performance improvements with the existing design, though this last point had not been included in the selection process. Other factors which it was understood might have helped to tip the balance were the possibility that a BWR would allow more of the associated work to be done locally, the fact that the Magnox reactor was less competitive at 150MW than it could have been at 200MW, and of particular importance, the fuel warranties apparently available with the American reactors. A second Italian group already had at this time an agreement with Westinghouse for the construction of a PWR, and a third group one with a British consortium for a Magnox station. Selection of a BWR by SENN thus provided Italy with all three reactor types then judged to be commercially viable. With so much uncertainty surrounding nuclear economics, and with Italy contemplating at the time a rapid growth of nuclear generating capacity, it made a great deal of commercial sense to investigate nuclear economics in the only really satisfactory way, by building actual power plants.[3]

A fairly typical American reaction was that the outcome of 'the first head-on bidding' between British and American reactors had helped to give the US 'an undisputed lead in the world reactor market'. The Americans were particularly gratified that while British and American reactors might be closely comparable on a generating cost basis, the capital cost of the former appeared on SENN's figures to be at least 30 per cent higher. There were some in Britain who accepted that Project ENSI had indeed constituted an objective comparison which would influence other potential buyers to Britain's disadvantage, and that Britain should therefore put her house in order. An alternative view was that Project ENSI had not been a real test case in that there had been special influences peculiar to it, but such a view, however correct, was none the less an obvious encouragement to complacency.[4] The last word on the case may be left with the President of SENN. It was not, he said, uncommon for economic comparisons to lead to different and confusing results, especially when 'the breakdown of costs or prices is not completely specified'.[5] These observations had not lost their significance when a different group of tenders were compared at

Dungeness B in 1965.

There were many in the British nuclear industry in 1964 who considered the early introduction of an 'alien theme'[6] into the country's nuclear programme to be virtually inevitable, and it fell to the consortia to work up tenders using light water as well as AGR technology. The Nuclear Power Group (TNPG) had an arrangement with the American General Electric Co. and in due course submitted a BWR tender to the CEGB in 1965. The English Electric/Babcock and Wilcox/Taylor Woodrow consortium developed their links with Westinghouse, who already had an association with Rolls-Royce, and this led to a PWR tender in 1965. The United Power Company (UPC) settled for a priced design of the reactor part only of a PWR station, and Babcock and Wilcox also independently submitted a similar PWR priced-design.

UPC had experienced a thin time after their reverse at Wylfa. Their loss there meant that as a consortium they received no order in the first programme, their only work on that programme coming from the orders their constituent elements, Atomic Power Constructions (APC) and GEC-Simon Carves, had received before their merger in 1960, (Trawsfynydd and Hunterston A respectively). The Wylfa outcome had also not been helpful to GEC's position in Japan, where they had secured one of Britain's two Magnox export orders, for Tokai Mura, in 1959. Already unhappy at losing the Sizewell contract to the English Electric group in 1961, following on the Wylfa decision GEC eventually withdrew from UPC in early 1965. APC then effectively resumed as a consortium in their own right while GEC operated only as a subcontractor. There were suggestions at the time that this move was not unconnected with the type of AGR tender APC now submitted.

Tenders for the Dungeness B station had to reach the CEGB by 1 February 1965. Six weeks later there were rumours that the AGR had won.[7] *The Economist* was even able to point to UPC (APC) as the likely winner. It was, the newspaper thought, the 'surprise of the year'. Yet it was not until mid-May that the CEGB forwarded the results of their appraisal to the Ministry of Power, and not until 25 May that the minister made his official announcement to the Commons.[8] Extolling the virtues of the AGR, Fred Lee now claimed that it was a 'jackpot' which represented 'the greatest breakthrough of all time'. He stressed that he had simply accepted the joint recommendation of the AEA and CEGB, but even in the Commons he was himself congratulated on having shown preference for the British reactor. It seemed that what UPC had lost on the Wylfa swings its descendent APC had now gained on the Dungeness roundabout.

Lee was evidently determined on maximum publicity, and his speech was clearly intended to be the counterpart to President Johnson's after the American 'breakthrough'. But Lee gave no details, and it was left for the CEGB to open the overseas sales drive. On 29 July the Board gave a press conference[9] at which they released two techno-economic summaries[10] explaining their selection of the AGR. They saw their decision as having 'very considerable international interest', and to meet their indirect responsibility as a shop window of British technology had therefore had the summaries translated into six languages. More than 15,000 copies were eventually distributed. Since Dungeness B was seen as a 'special case to enable comparisons to be drawn between British and American reactor systems',[11] no similar documents were published for the later AGR contracts.

At the press conference the new CEGB chairman, F.H.S. Brown, twice asserted that the Board had taken a hard-headed commercial decision: 'There were no political pressures of any sort put on us in forming our decision. It was a completely dispassionate decision made on our own responsibility . . . it was we who recommended to the Government that the best buy . . . was the AGR.' Asked whether the decision had not nevertheless been influenced by consideration of what might happen to British nuclear research were the AGR passed over, the CEGB chairman replied that the question 'just didn't arise by a factor of about 10 per cent'. There was, he felt, a twofold significance in what had occurred. First, nuclear power was now economic in Britain, and second, 'receipt of these tenders has permitted us to compare the competing technologies of the different types of reactors now available and . . . it is quite clear that the British concept of AGR is in fact the most economic'. In the course of questions he later qualified this second conclusion more than somewhat, to 'in the British context', and 'in the present stage of development', but it remained a very positive assertion.

To represent the AGR as having won a competition, as the CEGB thus did, was to talk the language of international marketing. But viewed in this way, and not just as a domestic affair, the presentation of the AGR as 'winner' was deficient in at least two major respects. To start with, more than two months elapsed between the first whisper of APC's triumph and the formal confirmation of it, and another two before any quantitative underpinning was forthcoming. This did nothing to allay suspicions, particularly foreign ones, that the whole assessment had somehow been 'fixed'. The seeds of such suspicions were going to be there anyway, but five months of anticlimax allowed them exceptionally good conditions for germination.

The second shortcoming in the presentation of the AGR as winner was that the CEGB's technical summaries were so brief, their account of the methodology of comparison so sketchy, as to be tantamount to asking the technical world to take the result virtually on trust. It was at best naive of the Board to suppose that the specialist reader would be satisfied with the outline of the assessment process given in the summaries: yet for what other readership were these summaries produced?

The CEGB received, in all, seven tenders for Dungeness B. There were tenders from each of the three consortia for the AGR, also three for the PWR, and a tender from TNPG for the BWR. The appraisal itself had several stages, the first preceding the receipt of the tenders. The CEGB were already well acquainted with gas-graphite reactors from their Magnox experience, and from working with the AEA on the Windscale AGR, but they had no experience with water reactors. During the nine months before February 1965 they therefore established contact with the AEA personnel working on the SGHWR, and also with the consortia and American firms in respect of the LWRs.

The core of the appraisal involved the breaking down of each tender into 71 parts, the writing of at least two detailed critiques on each part by mixed AEA-CEGB teams, and the resynthesising of these into full reports on each tender. In the final stage a steering committee made up of the senior Board and Authority engineers who had guided the whole operation brought the reports together into one document. This recommended acceptance of APC's AGR tender. The assessment proper involved some 15 man-years of work, the preparation about 10: as a comparison, examination of the tenders for the first four Magnox stations had taken a hundred professional staff six weeks.

The Board took pains to emphasise the distinction between their own and the Authority's role in the assessment. They had, they said, 'made it plain early on' that they would take the BWR or the PWR were they to be satisfied that either was preferable to the AGR. Theirs had also been the dominant voice in the appraisal, and in the event 'The final choice of the AGR system was made independently by the Board and they take full responsibility for it.' On the other hand, the Board stressed the value of the AEA's assistance. As they said, 'There were exponents in the Authority of both water and gas-cooled reactor systems and it was vital that the bodies of expertise which they represented should be properly deployed in the critical evaluation that had to be made.' Reasonable though this sounded there were two obvious reservations. First, the AEA's SGHWR technology was different from that of the PWR or BWR, and second the AEA's SGHWR personnel could have felt intimidated by the knowledge that it was the AGR which the Authority wished in 1965 to establish. Whether or not these things mattered, they were both the sort of feature which critics could and did cite as casting doubt on the assessment. As to the overall result of their appraisal, the CEGB implied that the task of the steering committee had largely been formal in that their reports on the two best tenders, APC's AGR and TNPG's BWR, had these offers 'still in the same relative positions as they were when the tenders were first examined'. It was said of the remaining tenders that they were 'grouped together and failed by a fair margin to win the competition'.

The CEGB compared the Dungeness B tenders using the present-worth method of financial analysis. This was itself something of a benchmark at the time, in that another two years were to pass before the Treasury formally recommended the nationalised industries to use such techniques.[12] One further general aspect of the Dungeness B appraisal also calls for mention: the general validity, at least in 1965, of comparative reactor evaluation.[13]

The absolute significance of any comparison between advanced technological products is limited at root by the complexity of the products, the associated uncertainties and the detailed circumstances in which the comparison is made. So it was with nuclear power stations in 1965, especially when these were projected rather than real. In the first place, there was a long inventory of technical parameters, such as operating temperatures and pressures, and values for the fuel rating and plant thermal efficiency. These parameters had in common that, at least in theory, they could be assigned numerical values. Then there was another list of factors for which quantification was less feasible, if indeed it was possible at all. Under this heading could be included a reactor's safety characteristics, development potential, reliability and so on. Next, both sets of factors required to be converted into capital, fuel and operating costs. Here the particular circumstances of the utility came into play. Externally imposed determinants such as interest rate, load factor and book life, could in practice make any assessment critically dependent upon the time and place at which it was conducted. Furthermore, since some suitable criterion had to be found to compare the station with alternatives, this normally meant boiling everything down to expected unit generating cost. All in all, it is obvious that in reactor comparison there was in 1965 considerable scope for argument.

It may reasonably be pointed out that such difficulties were not in 1965 confined to nuclear plant, that they occurred even with familiar conventional plant. So they did: it is simply that there was in 1965 so

much more complexity and uncertainty attaching to nuclear plant. Nor
could a prospective purchaser avoid all difficulty and protect himself
by negotiating cost escalation provisions and performance warranties.
It was stated[14] at the Geneva conference of 1964 that such guarantees
were of no great value, because if they were strong enough to be effica-
cious then they were too complex to be enforceable. Minor infringe-
ments, it was said at that time, made poor subjects for litigation, and
the multiplicity of variables diminished the chances of a successful suit
even where a major complaint existed.

The weakness of comparative reactor evaluation may be summed up
from official documents contemporary with the Dungeness B appraisal.
For example: 'Probably the most important consideration when reviewing published information on nuclear power costs is that in most cases
the cost data given is specific to one situation only, generally in the
country of publication, and is conditioned by local accounting procedures'; and: 'the methods of calculating nuclear power costs differ
widely from country to country . . . it is not always possible to obtain a
valid comparison of construction costs in different countries simply by
applying the official rates of exchange for their currencies.'[15] Or in the
words of Ryukichi Imai of the Japan Atomic Power Co.: 'Sometimes
evaluation is just another name for justification . . . It is the manufacturer's or utility's liberty and privilege to carry out cost calculations
and announce the results. But unless such announcement is accom-
panied by a detailed explanation . . . it has little application to other
reactors on other sites.'[16]

What from one point of view was surprising in 1965 was that, there
being no standard international method for evaluating reactors, the
CEGB were seemingly entrusted with the full responsibility for reducing the tenders to unit generating cost figures. Imai's observation was
that 'To adopt current economic parameters of CEGB for long term
evaluation of national policy must have been a result of a difficult
policy decision.'[17] It seems much more likely however that the Government did not deeply concern themselves with the latitude for techno-
economic judgement which had been left to the Board by the 1964
White Paper.

Analysis of the Dungeness B appraisal necessarily depends in the first
place on the two explanatory summaries of the event prepared by the
CEGB and referred to above. The economic details given in these documents were those for the successful AGR and for the BWR which
proved its nearest rival. They have long since been overtaken by events
but the main comparative items where there was a difference between

the AGR and the BWR need briefly to be mentioned to pu⁺ in perspective the conclusion which the Board drew from them in 1965, as well as subsequent events.

The CEGB found the technologies on which the offers they had received were based to be 'fundamentally sound in every case'. Specifically, they felt APC had made 'bold but well substantiated advances' on the Windscale AGR. The calculated unit generating cost of APC's AGR at 0.457d/KWh was some 7 per cent less than that of the BWR at 0.489d/KWh, and it was primarily on this difference that the choice of the AGR rested. The total capital cost of construction was given as £78.40/KW for the AGR and £70.86/KW for the BWR. In arriving at these figures the adjustments made by the CEGB to the original tender prices were more severe on the BWR than on the AGR, by some £2m, although the Board acknowledged that in contract negotiations the tenderer might in fact agree to amend his design at no extra cost. A more important question was why the BWR price in the UK had turned out to be so much higher than contemporary quotations in the United States and in W. Germany had led commentators to expect – a maximum for the LWRs of about £60/KW and a minimum for the AGR of about £70/KW was the general expectation. The high LWR prices appeared to have several contributory causes. The CEGB declined to discuss the make-up of the tenders, on the grounds that the responsibility lay with the consortia, and each had 'put in presumably his best effort'. The Board did, however, note three considerations which could marginally have increased LWR prices in Britain – the consequences of the British 50-cycles system, as compared with the American 60; the special civil engineering difficulties of the Dungeness site: and duty amounting to £0.8m on LWR imports.

Critics of the appraisal offered somewhat more substantial reasons. Burn,[18] singled out three: far higher construction costs in Britain; the CEGB's insistence on more detailed and lavish tenders; and their restriction of the tenders to 'proven designs'. The first two of these factors would have borne roughly equally on the AGR and the LWRs, but Burn argued that the third 'acted exclusively against light water reactors . . . the estimate for the AGR was . . . for the most advanced design available, that for the BWR was for a design and design-capacity relation slightly obsolete'. Beyond these reasons too there were almost certainly others. Thus the tenders were prepared by British companies drawing at second hand on American designs. In addition it is likely that the tenderers set their asking prices partly with reference to their estimates of the likely winning bid. Since APC's turned out a much cheaper AGR offer than had been anticipated, and since the other two consortia knew their AGRs were dearer than their LWRs, they may well have sought too high a profit margin on their LWR tenders. Finally, the CEGB were certainly right to some extent in their scepticism about many of the published figures for LWRs. Four years later the Board chairman in fact said that the CEGB, having made 'every effort' to identify the sources of the US-UK LWR cost differential, had been most impressed by this one: 'We concluded that a large part of the discrepancy could only be ascribed to the differing commercial policies of vendors, and recent upward price movements in the USA water reactor market confirm that this must have been the case.'[19] Unscrambling the effects of all these factors, and perhaps of others, is neither rewarding nor necessary. The elementary point is that the BWR price *was* high, the reasons for this were unclear, and outsiders could find in this another reason to be suspicious of the Dungeness B comparison.

Two other cost differences between the AGR and BWR were minor. One, 'other works costs', again disadvantaged the BWR, by £2.17/KW, but the vagueness of the explanation for this really only exemplified in miniature the frustrating lack of detail in the appraisal documents as a whole. The other item, arising from the need to protect the grid, fractionally disadvantaged the AGR.

The really critical item in the appraisal was the availability adjustment or penalty, £8.97/KW for the BWR, but nil for the AGR. Since the total cost difference between the reactors was, at £8.81/KW, less than this, in this single item, as the Board Member for Engineering said, lay 'the telling advantage of the AGR'. In on-load refuelling had lain the basic difference between Calder Hall and the first commercial Magnox stations, and when it came to the AGR the CEGB warned the consortia that stations refuelling off-load would be treated as having an availability below the notional 75 per cent assumed for on-load reactors. In spite of this, APC's AGR was the only tender which incorporated the principle. The CEGB's preference for on-load refuelling[20] stemmed partly from their belief that off-load refuelling was inflexible. They were also concerned that whereas the AGR was expected to have regular manpower requirements, those for the LWRs would peak at refuelling and maintenance shutdowns. With off-load refuelling, as well as the generation loss during refuelling the CEGB were concerned about outages to remove failed fuel elements, and also about the need for increased enrichment and possible control problems resulting from this. They were satisfied that on-load refuelling of the AGR was much simpler than in 1965 it was proving to be for Magnox — with Berkeley and

Bradwell, two of the three British Magnox stations to have commissioned up to 1965, it had proved a 'major source of difficulty'. The LWRs on the other hand were all designed to refuel off-load and American opinion generally was that the advantages of on-loading refuelling were offset by the cost and complexity of the extra equipment needed.

The penalty for off-load refuelling of the LWRs was put by the CEGB at 19½ days per annum. This implied an outage considerably in excess of the American manufacturer's claims or West German contemporary practice. It had also been stated at Geneva in 1964 that an LWR shutdown of 15 days per annum was compatible with an availability above 90 per cent. And the CEGB's notional load factor of 75 per cent would anyway have allowed the station to be out of commission for three months in the year, if it worked at maximum capacity for the other nine, 'more than ample for the most pessimistic fuel-change operation', in the words of R.F.W. Guard.[21] Hence his conclusion that 'It is . . . in the area of availability that the CEGB assessment is most partisan . . . these are treacherous waters indeed.'

The AEA's view of on-load refuelling at the time was that it constituted one of the AGR's three 'outstanding advantages' (modern steam conditions and safety being the others).[22] According to D.J. Berry[23] of the AEA, the CEGB's availability adjustment 'was not made because it was considered that some systems were not capable of the 75% load factor assumed, but because extra outages such as those incurred by the necessity to refuel off-load would be detrimental to the load factors achieved in practice'.

Of the engineers who had designed the Windscale AGR it was said that their backgrounds had 'impressed on them very forcibly' the considerable problems of reactor refuelling – especially on-load. And three years after the Dungeness appraisal it was being concluded that 'we are almost certainly now in a position to free ourselves from the bogey associated with fuel handling on Magnox stations . . . There can be little doubt that during five years of "on power" fuel handling at Windscale the reliability of the basic system has been amply demonstrated.'[24] On the other hand, there were refuelling problems with the Windscale AGR due to vibration and it was recognised that these problems would be exacerbated on the commercial AGRs with their higher pressure drops. For this reason, and because the problems were not properly understood even by specialists in the aircraft industry, a full-scale test rig was built at Windscale. This was done between 1965 and 1967 and in the first test on this rig, for Dungeness B refuelling in 1967, three fuel elements were shaken to pieces.[25] Ten years of development using the rig were however said to have made on-load AGR refuelling fully feasible a decade later.

There was another interesting, though less controversial, aspect to the availability adjustment. The financial penalty corresponding to the BWR's lower availability was determined by calculating the cost of generating the lost units elsewhere on the electricity system, by bringing in, that is, reserve and therefore less efficient plant. This necessarily made the major cost difference between the AGR and the BWR directly dependent on the cost characteristics of the electricity system, so that where the cost of replacement units was lower – the CEGB cited America and Australia as examples – then the advantage of the AGR could be expected to be correspondingly less.

From the figures given in the appraisal documents for the initial fuel it was possible to deduce approximately the charge made for AGR fuel fabrication and this seemed to come out substantially below equivalent American prices. This was the more surprising since the American figures related to less complex fuel elements than those of the AGR. The resulting possibility that the fabrication costs might be benefitting from a hidden subsidy did not go unnoticed: 'The cost of the complete AGR core is astonishing . . . Clearly the UK AEA are not expecting to make a profit.'[26] The suspicion that AEA fuel prices were too low persisted thereafter, even cropping up in 1967 in the EEC Commission's opinion[27] on British membership, when it was suggested that the AEA's fuel cycle prices were 'such that one may legitimately ask whether they are not subsidized'.

The statement in the appraisal documents that most of the fuel fabrication costs would be reduced after five years by 25 per cent was therefore all the more remarkable. The documents also showed that the BWR had incurred small penalties because of the need to pay import duty on its American-manufactured fuel (£0.9/KW), and because more capital would have been tied up in its transport (£0.25/KW).

The fuel costs in the assessment itself were calculated in terms of current American prices for uranium enrichment, but those in the published summaries were based on estimated enrichment costs using the AEA's Capenhurst plant.[28] This was because by mid-1965 the CEGB had come to expect that this plant would be supplying the enriched fuel required, at a cost in 1970 'not much above' published American prices, and falling as capacity expanded. The Board had been consulted by the AEA and were in favour of this but separate government approval was necessary. This came in December 1965, the Minister of Technology, Frank Cousins, then expressing his pleasure that Treasury clearance had been won for a scheme which he recognised was commercially rather uncertain.[29] It had been decided that £13½m would be spent in modernising and reactivating the Capenhurst plant, £7½m of this in a first phase which was to begin immediately. Capenhurst had effectively been mothballed in 1962-3 when the demand for weapons-grade uranium had stopped, and since then had only been ticking over to supply the small civil demand. The minister was advised by the AEA that the gap between American and British enrichment prices was nearer 10 than 15 per cent and that this would narrow progressively in the seventies as Capenhurst prices fell and American ones quite possibly rose. The minister also gave supporting reasons for his decision. These were a reluctance to depend on foreign supply in view of the projected growth of nuclear power, a balance of payments saving amounting eventually to over £10m a year, an unwillingness to wind up the nation's capacity in an important technology, and the export possibilities — 'supplying tailor-made material to tailor-made stations'. Cousins had also been informed by the Authority that experiments on the centrifuge alternative to diffusion were not at this time giving results which implied any threat to the economics of diffusion before the late seventies.

(The hour of the centrifuge however was soon to come. The Capenhurst diffusion plant as modified was expected to be capable of meeting UK requirements for enriched uranium until the mid-seventies. With the delays to the AGR programme to be discussed later this date in the event receded, but meanwhile, in November 1968, British, West German and Dutch ministers met to discuss collaboration on a centrifuge project, and a formal agreement was announced in December 1969.[30] At the time there was a good deal of public concern about this project from several angles, not least its military implications,[31] but it went ahead and a first commercial plant came into operation in the late seventies.)

That British enrichment costs were likely to be within 10 per cent of American ones was widely seen in 1965 as surprising. The impression had emerged from the Geneva conference in 1964 that AEA prices would be perhaps 25 per cent above American ones, and even in 1966 AEA sources were reported as admitting to a 20 per cent initial differential, though with an overall programme surcharge to the CEGB of only 5 per cent. The issue promised to be of great commercial significance and was therefore highly controversial. The AEA were anxious that Capenhurst should have an opportunity to prove itself competitive, while American interests were keen to defeat at the outset any challenge to the existing American monopoly. Both sides knew that prospective reactor purchasers might be decisively influenced by enriched uranium supplies and prices.[32]

The fact still could not really be disguised that reactivating Capenhurst was at the time more a political act of faith than a commercial decision, the politically almost inescapable corollary of what the CEGB insisted was their wholly commercial decision to choose the AGR. The Government's approval in 1965 was also of course the direct outcome of the AEA's decision in 1956-7 to accept fuel enrichment as integral to their medium term reactor development strategy.

In addition to the quantitative differences between the AGR and the BWR there were also more qualitative differences which did not appear directly in the Dungeness cost comparison. Two of these were spotlighted in the CEGB's summaries, namely the issues of safety and development potential. The CEGB were satisfied that both the AGR and BWR could meet the safety conditions applying to the Dungeness site. They also believed that the Dungeness AGR design was suitable for urban locations and that with 'relatively small changes' it should be able to meet 'much more severe criteria than any currently suggested in the UK for urban sites'. What they were less sure of was the BWR's suitability for sites in more populated areas. The crux of the matter was that the safety characteristics of the two reactors were seen as resting on different bases. The AGR was regarded as inherently[33] safe, not least because of its concrete pressure vessel, while the BWR was described as relying more on engineered safeguards, in that special containment arrangements seemed called for to prevent release of radioactive material in the event of its steel pressure vessel or pipework failing. For sites near centres of population the CEGB feared it might be mandatory on them to upgrade the BWR's containment, and that this would cost money.

BWR sponsors by this time felt the early doubts about this reactor's stability, corrosion weakness and overall safety had been removed, but there were still some grounds for the CEGB's caution. An appropriate example, in view of Oyster Creek's significance, is the treatment of that station at the hands of the US Atomic Safety and Licensing Board (ASLB). In their initial decision of December 1964 this Board criticised several features of the Oyster Creek design, and the safety angle was prominent among their reservations: 'In a notable and historic effort to obtain competitive nuclear power, especially in terms of $/KW capacity, the Board cannot help but gain the impression that the numerator has been reduced by sharpening the considerations involving installed safety provisions and similarly increasing the denominator by pushing the design power and power density to the upper limits of present day prudence, if not beyond. The combination effect of these factors has a dramatic effect upon $/KW but the fact that the hazards are inversely affected has not escaped the attention of the Board. At some point in the continued reduction in the secondary safety equipment costs and increasing power densities the accumulation of the uncertainties prevents the attainment of the assurance for the findings on safety that the Board must make.'[34]

The US Advisory Committee on Reactor Safeguards had previously noted the incomplete status of the Oyster Creek proposal as presented, but thought that there was 'reasonable assurance that it can be operated without undue risk to the health and safety of the public'.[35] The ASLB, however, withheld an unqualified provisional construction permit at the original hearing, requesting more data in two key areas, one of which concerned the allocation of responsibility for safety between Jersey Central as operator and General Electric as manufacturer. And even in their subsequent order of January 1966, recording Jersey Central's compliance with the conditions attached to the provisional permit, the ASLB described the data supplied in fulfilment of these conditions as 'minimum but adequate'.[36]

The CEGB could certainly have claimed in 1965 that the willingness of the American authorities to allow a BWR to be constructed near a city had not at that date been tested. (For various reasons, plans for a 1,000MW PWR in the heart of New York city had come to nothing.) Two years after the Dungeness assessment the CEGB continued to defend their suspicions about BWR safety, citing, in a memorandum to the Commons Science Committee, Boston Edison's resiting of a proposed BWR 50 miles from Boston and 5 miles from the nearest small town, at a time when they themselves were contemplating two AGRs within 4 miles of highly populated areas. In their words: 'The American AEC have recently indicated that further improvements to standards and more operating experience will be required before there is a more general move towards metropolitan siting.'[37] (A more relaxed siting policy for AGRs was in due course approved by the Government, on the advice of the Nuclear Safety Advisory Committee, in February 1968.)

Of the other important qualitative difference between the AGR and the BWR, development potential, the CEGB reported that, for the following five years, the assessment panel had concluded that the cost advantage of the AGR was 'likely to increase rather than diminish'. The target was a 20 per cent reduction in generating costs, but while a general indication was given of how this might be achieved, the specific sources of the AGR's advantage were not detailed.[38] Here again the CEGB's vague presentation should not have been expected to make much impression on the international technical community.

The AGR-BWR competition which turned out to be the heart of the Dungeness appraisal has been discussed here at some length. The vital competition having been that between APC's AGR and TNPG's BWR it is difficult to explain why this should have been so. Why in particular was APC's the cheapest of the AGR bids? Both the other consortia proposed novel engineering variations in their AGR tenders, and one of them, like APC, also incorporated a higher gas pressure and turbine rating than had been specified. But the most controversial difference between APC's AGR and the others lay elsewhere,[39] a point fully brought out by the Commons Science Committee in 1967. In the words of the appraisal in 1965, 'APC . . . drawing encouragement from the successful operation of the Windscale prototype and the successful outcome of other research and development work . . . adopted a larger fuel element cluster developed by the UKAEA.'

More than one observer concluded that in their unique fuel cluster lay the key to APC's success.[40] APC admitted that it had indeed made a contribution, perhaps between £2 and £3/KW, but their chairman still insisted that this was not much in comparison with the total cost reduction they had accomplished with their design. In fact, the exact consequences for the overall economics of such a design modification were inevitably unclear and the fuel cluster issue therefore became an especially unsatisfactory feature of the Dungeness assessment.

The fuel element on which the AEA had concentrated for the AGR was a 21-rod, two-ring cluster, this being the type used in the Windscale prototype. TNPG later claimed that they had drawn attention to the potential benefits of larger clusters, including a 36-rod, three-ring one, as early as August 1961, but according to them, the AEA had been unconvinced that the promise justified the expenditure of an estimated £100,000, there having been at the time, in TNPG's words, 'no thought' of American competition. The AEA were said by TNPG to have reaffirmed their position in July 1963, and when the Dungeness inquiry was issued on 20 April 1964 among its key requirements were an 18-rod, two-ring cluster, maximum gas pressure of 330 pounds per square inch (psi), increased the same month to 400psi, and 525MW turbogenerator sets. TNPG also later claimed that they had regarded a certain clause of this inquiry as intentionally discouraging tenderers from submitting alternative fuel assemblies.

Working outwards from the reactor core of an AGR station there was a progressive increase in the scope for independent design, and it is this which distinguished the different AGR designs and led to their differing costs. APC, exercising their creativity in this way, had apparently taken their main design decisions by early 1964. The CEGB's inquiry called for design principles to be made available to the Board in advance of the tender date, and APC's documented proposal was presented to the Board at the beginning of May 1964. Its basic principles were accepted and in the ordinary way would have been consolidated into a tender by January 1965. APC therefore proceeded to work along these lines from May to October 1964.

TNPG later told the Science Committee that they had similarly frozen their key design parameters in early May. The AEA then began, by TNPG's account, to show 'serious interest' in a 36-rod fuel cluster, and in more advanced AGR parameters generally, Sir William Cook, the Authority Member for Reactors, informing the consortium in July that APC were to be given the costing exercise for a new AGR design since it was understood from their chairman, Colonel Raby, that they would not be tendering for Dungeness B. TNPG's 'great concern' at this was, they claimed, shared by the third consortium, and also by the CEGB at a meeting of the Reactor Policy Committee on 17 July. The AEA again confirmed, according to TNPG, that APC would not be tendering, but at the September meeting of the same Committee announced that in view of the 'strong views' which had been expressed, the arrangement with APC had now been terminated, the information which had come out to be available in February 1965 for discussion with interested parties.

TNPG said they had been greatly relieved by this, since they would have found it impossible to change their major design parameters at that stage and keep to the tender deadline. Yet this is precisely what APC apparently did decide to do, and at an even later date. APC's chief engineer wrote later that it had become clear to the consortium by October 1964 from information made available by the AEA, and from informal discussions with them, that a fuel element based on a 36-rod cluster had been brought to the point where it was suitable for Dungeness B: 'This seemed at first a late stage at which to make such a radical change, but further examination of the layout showed that there were remarkably few changes of engineering principle, and that the main task would be to redraw existing designs to suit the new dimensions.' APC thought there were sound reasons for the change, and they also wanted a fuel element which could be expected to become standard for AGRs. Having decided to amend their design APC also then took the opportunity of benefitting from the most recent Windscale results, increasing the gas pressure to 450psi.

AEA personnel referred to the 36-rod cluster during the Anglo-Spanish symposium of November 1964, also on that occasion alluding to the merits of higher pressures and better fuel element irradiation: 'it now appears possible to incorporate some of what was formerly considered to be development potential into a much earlier stage of any programme'.[41] Then, on 30 November 1964, eight weeks before the tender deadline, the CEGB amended their specification, and in effect cleared the way for the 36-rod cluster.

It was not easy to interpret these events. The CEGB, for example, saw a clear lesson in APC's action. They had avoided 'the danger of premature standardisation in the early development of a technology'. In sharp contrast was the impression formed by a member of the Science Committee, Sir Harry Legge-Bourke: 'It appears that immense pressure was brought to bear at some point with a result that the specification was changed and eventually the AGR was accepted when the other two consortia believed that the AGR was not on.' The Authority's deputy chairman emphasised how meticulous the AEA tried to be in ensuring all the consortia were treated equally. At the time of the Dungeness B tenders all the consortia had been free to consult the Authority. As he saw it, 'The information was available to all three equally, but APC paid most attention to it and made most use of it.'

APC's chairman stressed to the Science Committee in 1967 that while APC had taken up the 36-rod concept because they thought it attractive, the idea itself had originated with the AEA. It was after all, said APC, the AEA which in late summer 1964 had circulated to the consortia and the CEGB an AGR design with a 36-rod fuel element arrangement. APC's chairman emphasised the risk APC had then run: 'We made up our mind to put forward the 36-rod cluster as agreed with the AEA. I had to take the risk that the CEGB might turn it down because it did not meet the specification . . . in the end the CEGB themselves accepted the position . . . any of the other two groups could have done the same thing . . .'

The third consortium also offered an uncomplicated view of what had happened. As they chose to see it, the competition had been one between the consortia, APC had more or less had to win simply to stay in existence, and as a result had come up with the only AGR able to beat the LWRs.

This left TNPG's criticisms. TNPG reckoned that both the AGR and the BWR which they had tendered to the CEGB were obsolete designs. They had thought this was what the CEGB wanted, but the winning AGR design had then turned out to be 'tomorrow's design'. TNPG's managing director, while not doubting the soundness of APC's proposal, thought that, with 'very little to lose', APC had 'stuck their necks out'. But attributing this, as TNPG did, to the 'value of competition', seemed at odds with another of their statements: 'We were not allowed, during our pre-tender discussions, by the CEGB to deviate from the specification, so we stuck to it; but for reasons best known to APC they deviated from the specification very considerably . . . when the APC were allowed to revise the specification it was regarded as a great breakthrough and they did something that we desired to do but we were not allowed to do it.'

TNPG's managing director also offered the Science Committee his personal opinion in 1967 that his consortium had been awarded the next AGR station contract, Hinkley Point B, without competition, because 'something went wrong with Dungeness B . . . The CEGB may have thought that they had not been altogether completely fair to TNPG.'

The CEGB's explanation of the fuel rod amendment to their specification was that it had been made not to allow APC to submit their 36-rod cluster but rather because they had been unable to dissuade one of the other tenderers from pressing a new fuel handling concept unrelated to the cluster. This had perhaps been a 'little unwise', but in any case, they had not at this time expected a tender from APC: 'They said they were not going to quote.' This latter point was in itself one of the more puzzling features of the Dungeness B episode. For, as noted above, TNPG had apparently learned the same thing from the AEA in the summer of 1964, yet in his account APC's chief engineer afterwards represented APC's work on the AGR design as a smooth progress until October 1964, with at that time last minute thoughts rather than fundamental hesitation.

The CEGB said they had been even more surprised when APC's tender turned out to have a 36-pin fuel cluster. They had heard about it 'over the grapevine' only about three weeks before the tender date. If a 'special relationship' had evolved between the AEA and APC over the AGR they had, they said, definitely been unaware of it. On the same point, even TNPG affirmed that they did not for one moment doubt that in this case as in all others the Authority had treated the three consortia equally. APC agreed that this was invariably the Authority's practice: 'We were asked if we would be interested and prepared to do some homework to establish the AEA's view that [a 36-rod cluster] would be better . . . I am pretty certain, knowing the AEA that this would also have been put to the other two consortia. I have never known a case yet where the AEA have given any sort of information to one consortium without giving it to the others . . . after we had done a study and some work . . . we thought we might be on to a winner.'

APC had needed the AEA's support in establishing the 36-rod concept with the CEGB: 'This was not my company alone but my company and the AEA.' It is also interesting that whereas the other two consortia saw APC as having responded to the pressures of competition, APC themselves saw the 'spur of competition' as having rather impelled the AEA to bring forward a more advanced fuel design. There may have been truth in both perspectives. It may have been that only APC realised how vital to the AEA's interests the AGR was. They may have hoped, by hastening to carry through refinements originating with the AEA, either to identify themselves with the AGR's success, if this were the outcome, or else to have still had the best AGR tender if an LWR emerged ahead and the decision were then set aside, or both reactors built, as a result of government intervention. At the time TNPG knew their BWR was better than their AGR by a good margin, and they may also have had grounds for believing that their licensing facilities were better than those available to the other two consortia. They therefore were in a position to view their BWR as possibly the overall favourite, and this may have lessened their inclination to redraft their AGR tender at a late stage so as to include those improvements which they had themselves earlier canvassed unsuccessfully.

A little more light was thrown on the 36-rod cluster and its part in APC's successful tender as a result of the Science Committee's 1969 inquiry. Following APC's success they had been joined in September 1965 by Gordon Brown, previously the AEA's director of gas reactors. As APC's managing director he admitted to the Science Committee that the APC offer had not been 'a tender in depth to the degree that some of the other tenders were'. He said that he did not want to get into a controversy on the matter but dated reports existed which showed that all the information which the AEA had had in late 1964 was made available by him to all three consortia. In the course of the same inquiry by the Science Committee, ICL, a constituent company of APC, explained the AEA's actions of 1964 in terms of the Authority's fear that the AGR's development potential might not be fully realised.

The Authority, as ICL saw it, had therefore decided to undertake a full-scale priced design, giving ICL a contract for the boiler design in June 1964, and telling them that it might form the basis of an order. Later however this procedure by the AEA had turned out, ICL thought, to be 'politically unacceptable'.

Departing from the reactor design specification as APC did was not unprecedented and the CEGB had previously profited from this sort of flexibility, the classic instance before Dungeness B having occurred at Oldbury, where TNPG had ignored the stipulation for a steel pressure vessel. What was particularly unfortunate about the 36-rod cluster business was that, as has been shown, it was only one of several puzzles in the Dungeness B assessment. One final curious aspect of the whole affair was the sharp contrast between the CEGB's almost ecstatic attitude towards the AGR in 1965 and their clear reservations about the successful consortium, APC. They in fact made it a condition of the award of the Dungeness contract that APC strengthen themselves by the recruitment of some senior personnel: 'They had so much design work on their hands to implement a sketched out design into working detail.' The CEGB also had had, and were having, problems with APC's Magnox station at Trawsfynydd, and the Wylfa affair too had suggested that the APC were not their favourite group. The CEGB were also to become sure at an early stage that the Dungeness B design was 'not the one to replicate'.

The outcome of the competition between reactors, and between consortia, at Dungeness B has been considered here in some detail, above all to bring out its serious shortcomings. It remains to examine the result of the further comparison between nuclear and coal generation which was made in conjunction with the Dungeness appraisal. This was of much more than incidental interest given that the CEGB's insistence on the cheapest possible power had been one of the major causes of the 1964 crisis.

The CEGB's published summaries gave the result of the comparison between coal and nuclear generation as calculated by two different methods. The first, and simple one, was a straight juxtaposition of unit generating costs over the first years of operation of contemporary stations at a load factor of 75 per cent and at lifetimes of 20 years for nuclear and 30 years for coal. The relevant figures were then 0.457d for Dungeness B and 0.54d for Cottam, the coal station chosen for the comparison. The weakness of this method was that it made no allowance for the different lifetime load factors nuclear and coal plant would ordinarily be expected to have. The more complex method therefore sought to meet this objection by projecting the whole life record of both types of plant.

From the CEGB's figures the total capital cost of Dungeness B at £92/KW was more than double that of Cottam at £43/KW, but its fuel cost, at 1.1d/therm, was less than a third of Cottam's 3.8d/therm. The CEGB practice being naturally to operate generating plant so far as possible in 'merit order', so that the lower the plant's fuel cost per unit generated, the more intensive its use, regardless of its capital cost, for each forward year a picture could then be built up showing the contribution of each station when operated in merit order. Both nuclear and conventional plant would enter at the top of the order when new because their fuel costs would then be lower than those of virtually all existing plants, the conventional plant because it would be the most modern of its type, the nuclear plant simply through being nuclear. However, the conventional plant would drop down the merit order more quickly because of new nuclear, and even new conventional plant, coming into service. The CEGB's figures thus showed a 75 per cent load factor for Dungeness B over the whole of its book life, but an eventual lifetime average for Cottam of only 38 per cent. For each the total annual capital charge was then divided by the corresponding lifetime output and the lifetime to give an annual capital charge. The conventional plant still came out ahead, £10.7/KW per annum for Cottam, £12.5/KW per annum for Dungeness B. The final step was to work out the effect of the new plant on the rest of the system, because a new plant, apart from bringing its own block of cheaper energy, would also reduce marginally the costs of all the energy generated on the system, less efficient plants towards the bottom of the merit order then being run at lower load factors. It was here that nuclear power forged ahead of coal, the 38 per cent average lifetime load factor for Cottam representing a significantly smaller contribution to the general fall in system costs than that produced by the 75 per cent load factor of Dungeness B, £1.7/KW per annum compared with £4.7/KW per annum.

Now this procedure no doubt gave 'a more realistic assessment of the practical worth of alternative plants', but it had its own shortcomings, not least that this was a comparison at only the planning stage with a great deal in terms of national fuel policy hanging on it. The analysis clearly had to be done, but in the way they presented their conclusions the CEGB laid themselves open to yet another criticism. This was because only they possessed the relevant data about the existing merit order, predicted demand and fuel prices, projected new plant and so on. As a Political and Economic Planning group complained:

'criticism of the figures produced becomes impossible for an outsider . . . When a nationalized industry presents data which it alone is in a position to produce it seems necessary that it should produce more than a rather stark table and give a wide range of alternative assumptions, which should be explicitly stated, so that the implications of its esoteric calculations can be fully understood.'[42]

It is tempting to draw a parallel between the AGR case and that of the TSR2 aircraft, though as in most such comparisons, there are plenty of pitfalls. Indeed, the value of the exercise may lie entirely in pointing out that the two cases were roughly contemporary. The cancellation of the TSR2 aircraft programme, essentially in favour of the American F-111, was announced in the budget statement of 6 April 1965. This decision earned the new Labour Government, with its precariously slender majority, much unpopularity. To have announced at about the same time that the American BWR was to be preferred over the British AGR would have been, to say the least, doubly embarrassing, especially to a Government whose Prime Minister while in Opposition had talked of creating a new Britain in the white heat of a technological revolution. Nor would it generally have been regarded an adequate defence that the situations in both cases were not of the incoming Government's making.

It would be safest to leave the parallel at that, but it is intriguing to push it a little further. Thus in both cases there had been mistrust between the prospective purchaser (the CEGB/the Ministry of Defence) and the manufacturer (the AEA/private industry). In both cases there was need to decide between complex products, the fruits respectively of British and American technology. The potential ramifications also appeared to be similar, domestically in terms of technological independence and morale, internationally in terms of prospective exports. In both cases the decisions reached were officially justified on economic grounds, although in the case of the TSR2 there were those, mostly in Britain, who adhered to a conspiracy theory, and in the case of the AGR those, especially abroad, who also suspected that politics had proved stronger than economics. There were also differences between the two cases. In the AEA the AGR had a strong institutional backer, but while the TSR2 was also not without its supporters, especially in industry, this support was not gathered in one body; the TSR2 also had more powerful enemies than did the AGR. Then again, while both the AGR and the TSR2 had initially been undertaken without a full cost-benefit analysis, and while both became late, it finally proved possible to justify the AGR in this respect, though not to everyone's satisfaction, in a way that apparently could not be done for the TSR2. And, when the hour of decision arrived, the AGR could be represented as a more-or-less finished product, whereas for the TSR2 this apparently was not feasible. Finally, while it was possible to resolve the reactor crisis by an analysis which, despite all its shortcomings, could culminate in the easily grasped concept of unit generating cost, no such straightforward study could have commanded agreement in the case of TSR2. It is instructive to note the conclusions Geoffrey Williams[43] reached in his study of the TSR2 case: 'By quantifying the quantifiable, therefore, the 1965 TSR2 decision can be shown to be correct, though the gains from its cancellation were so small that a slight alteration of estimates could easily have produced a contrary argument. However, when the unquantifiable elements are added, the issue becomes an even more open one, so much so that it is difficult to arrive at a clear cut answer by rational analysis. In short, the TSR2 cancellation decision was a very difficult one to take because of the multitude of countervailing factors involved, and must have been a very close-run thing.' It is especially ironical that Williams should add that: 'from the availability point of view TSR2 was a better aircraft . . . had the normal accounting conventions been altered . . . and greater account taken of the increased reliability and availability of TSR2 . . . it would have been valid to argue that the TSR2 ought not to have been cancelled for the F-111 . . .' In the light of all this, and of later events, it is interesting to speculate on what might have happened had the Government in 1965 chosen the TSR2 instead of the F-111 and the BWR instead of the AGR.

The point has now been reached in this summary of the Dungeness B appraisal where it is necessary to stand back and draw some conclusions from the episode in the context of 1965. Three comments from independent, though not necessarily unbiased, sources give an indication of professional response at the time:[44] 'To sum up, it seems that the CEGB have made a predictable decision, and probably the only one they could make in the circumstances. Uncommitted observers elsewhere will hardly agree that the decision would be the same under different circumstances'; 'There is good enough evidence to indicate that the assessment was genuine . . . At the same time . . . the Dungeness B was a UK evaluation leading to a UK conclusion'; 'It is odd that the CEGB, while manifestly trying to be scrupulously fair, should appear nationalistic or even biased to the rest of the world when dealing with such an affair of global significance as Dungeness B. This accusation is not fair and not true.'

Echoing 1955 the British press gave the AGR's success an enthusiastic, and mostly uncritical, reception.[45]. The stock words were used: 'triumph', 'breakthrough', 'decisive advantage'. The appraisal, the *New Scientist* thought, 'must surely rank among the most searching scrutinies to be applied to any technical project'. More than one newspaper personalised the affair by focusing on APC's chairman, Colonel Raby, formerly deputy director of engineering in the AEA's Research Group. 'I waved the Union Jack' the *Observer* had him as saying, and the same metaphor cropped up in the *Financial Times*, though there it was said that 'The flag was never unfurled.' Only the *Daily Telegraph* entertained real reservations: 'It is well that the Minister should feel able to make this decision on technical and economic grounds . . . the Government is freed from the complications of a political decision . . . There is much that needs explaining in greater detail.' It was, according to the international edition of the *New York Times*, a 'set-back' for General Electric and Westinghouse: a 'bitter blow' agreed *Business Week*, especially after the 'major coup' implicit in the 1964 White Paper.

Between the announcement of the AGR's success in May and the publication of the CEGB's summaries in July the AGR's defenders sometimes lost the initiative and 'Every gullible journalist and MP . . . had it hinted to him . . . that political pressure had been brought to bear . . .'[46] There was no hard public evidence for this and against the CEGB's own defence of the decision as a 'genuine commercial' one. Few outside the technical community recognised, however, that it was on the basis of the CEGB's assumptions and not on basic technological and economic merit that the AGR had won.[47] The Board might have found more sympathy, and even helped the AGR more, had they simply published a statement and brief explanatory details to the effect that they saw nothing to choose between the best offers and so felt it right to follow the domestic line. As for the AEA, one judgement was that they had 'fought legitimately for [their] own candidate'.[48] It was left to the future to show whether or not the AGR had as a result been oversold.

Overall, it can be seen how the political method of solution, comprising delay in 1964 and appraisal in 1965, permitted each major source of the 1962-4 reactor crisis to be accommodated. The objection that AGR technology was unproved was seemingly dissolved by the further results in the interim from the Windscale AGR and other tests, by the deliberations of the Emeléus Committee, and by the CEGB's own investigation of the AGR's technology in the course of the 1965 appraisal. The objection on the grounds of unfavourable international comparison was removed by demonstrating that, for whatever reasons,

American costs did not translate, and the objection based on economics was dismissed by comparing Dungeness B with Cottam. Of the truly political difficulties, to the extent that they still existed in 1965, by then there had been changes at the most senior level in both the AEA and the CEGB, and although the change of Government made no direct difference, indirectly the change of responsible ministers can only have helped. In addition, what the 1964 White Paper did do was to provide that the 1965 decision would be made by the CEGB alone, at least in the first place. Had an LWR emerged from the 1965 appraisal ahead of the AGR, then the Government would again of course have had a problem, its severity this time depending upon the percentage advantage of the LWR. At a few per cent, and equal promise, the Government would almost certainly have directed the CEGB to take the AGR, possibly compensating the Board appropriately for taking a less economic reactor; above a few per cent it would have become increasingly difficult for the Government to justify intervention. As the Minister of Technology said, not perhaps without overtones of relief, in a congratulatory letter to the chairman of the AEA, it was 'particularly gratifying that on sheer technical and economic merit', the AGR had shown itself 'capable of more than holding its own', and that Penney's own 'constant faith in the AGR' had been vindicated.[49]

A problem which the appraisal did not solve was the weakness of the private nuclear industry. It is indeed now quite clear, if it was not at the time, that Dungeness B exacerbated the difficulties of the consortia by keeping the weakest one, APC, alive. The Dungeness outcome also foreshadowed a new problem: the arrival of a truly 3-fuel electricity economy. There was also now the increasingly important question of the AEA's own future, given the organisation's great proportion of the nation's r & d resources. Here the Science and Technology Act of 1965 made a start, empowering the Minister of Technology to require the Authority to undertake r & d outside the atomic energy field. At least what there did not seem to be in summer 1965 was a thermal reactor problem. On the contrary, with the Dungeness B decision nuclear energy in Britain had, in the words of the Minister of Technology, 'turned an important corner'. 'We have gone a very long way — further than anyone else — in producing an objective comparison,' said the Ministry's Parliamentary Secretary, Jeremy Bray, two years later.[50] Most were happy to agree: there had indeed been a 'popular win for the home side'.[51]

Notes

1. See Felice Ippolito and Corbin Allardice, 'Project ENSI', II Geneva, 8, pp. 380-91 (385). Also Carlo Matteini, 'The SENN Nuclear Power Plant Project', II Geneva, 8, pp. 392-7.

2. Ippolito and Allardice, 'Project ENSI', p. 391.

3. Sir John Cockcroft, 'The Future Prospects of Nuclear Power', *Atom* (June 1960), pp. 13-16.

4. *NE* (April 1958), pp. 137-9 (November 1958), p. 468; *Nucleonics* (November 1958), pp. 20-1; *NP* (November 1958), pp. 526-7.

5. Carlo Matteini, *NP* (January 1959), p. 75; Carlo Matteini, 'Why SENN Chose GE Reactor', *Nucleonics* (May 1959), p. 95-9; *NP* (October 1959), pp. 87-91.

6. *NE* (May 1964), p. 152.

7. *Financial Times*, 17 March 1965; *The Economist*, 20 March 1965; *Engineering* (5 March 1965), p. 305; *Nuclear Industry* (March 1965), p. 19.

8. HCD 712 c.1197; HCD 713 c.237-40; HLD 266 c.793-7.

9. Verbatim report of the press conference on tender assessment of nuclear reactors for Dungeness B, held at Sudbury House 29 July 1965. (Quotations are taken from this.) See also 'Will Britain Export the AGR?', *New Scientist* (21 October 1965).

10. *An Appraisal of the Technical and Economic Aspects of Dungeness B Nuclear Power Station* (CEGB, London, 1965); *Dungeness B AGR Nuclear Power Station* (CEGB, London, 1965); see also G.R. Bainbridge, 'Factors Affecting Costs of Export Nuclear Power Stations', *Atom* (December 1967), pp. 312-20; HC 381-XVII (1966-7), Appendix 12.

11. HCD 743 c.20 (WA).

12. See Cmnd. 1337 and Cmnd. 3437; see also C.E. Illife, 'Balancing the Cost of Electrical Power by the Technique of Discounted Cash Flow', *Atom* (March 1966), pp. 58-9.

13. For example, *Introduction to the Methods of Estimating Nuclear Power Generating Costs* (IAEA, Vienna, 1961), Technical Reports Series No. 5; *Problems Regarding the Competitiveness of Nuclear Power Reactors* (Council of Europe, Strasbourg, 1965); M. Willems *et al.*, *Euratom Economic Handbook* (Euratom, Brussels, 1966) EUR 3079e; see T.W. Berrie, 'The Economics of System Planning in Bulk Electricity Supply' in R. Turvey (ed.), *Public Enterprise* (Penguin Books, Harmondsworth, 1968), pp. 173-211.

14. G.F. Kennedy and R.F.W. Guard, 'The Initiation of a National Nuclear Programme', III Geneva, P/131, p. 148.

15. IAEA General Conference GC (IV) 123 (27 August 1960), para. 13; IAEA General Conference GC (V)/INF/38 (13 September 1961), paras. 3-6.

16. Ryukichi Imai, 'On Power Reactor Evaluation', *NE* (February 1965), pp. 46-8.

17. Ryukichi Imai, 'The Dungeness B Appraisal', *NE* (October 1965), p. 379.

18. Duncan Burn, *The Political Economy of Nuclear Energy* (IEA, London, 1967), p. 61. See also *Nuclear Industry* (August 1965).

19. *BNF Bulletin*, 5 (10 October 1969), p. 2.

20. For example, K.H. Dent, 'On Load Refuelling Problems', *NP* (August 1961), pp. 69-76. D.T. Evans *et al.*, 'The Performance of Nuclear Power Station Plant', *BNESJ*, 4 (July 1965), pp. 217-26 para. 77; D.R.R. Fair , 'Comments on Performance of British Power Reactors', *BNESJ*, 8 (1969), p. 133. HC 381 (1966-7) Q921; E.E. Jenkins 'Refuelling of Gas-cooled Reactors: Fuel Handling Equipment for Dungeness B', Symposium Nuclear Energy Group of Institution of Mechanical Engineers, Procs., 1968-9, 183, pp. 91-8; P.C. Warner, 'The Dungeness B Nuclear Power Station', *BNX Review*, no. 1, pp. 15-20 (German Forum, Frankfurt, April 1966).

21. R.F.W. Guard, 'The Year Since Geneva', *Euronuclear* (September 1965), pp. 440-1.

22. Sir William Penney, 'Nuclear Power Development in the UK', *Atom* (October 1965), pp. 198-205.

23. D.J. Berry, 'The Dungeness B Decision — Some Economics and Technical Factors Affecting Reactor Choice', *Atom* (1966), pp. 37-43.

24. E. Slater *et al.*, 'WAGR Fuel Handling Equipment', Institution of Mechanical Engineers Procs., 1961-9, 183, part 3G, Symposium, 12 December 1968, *Refuelling of Gas Cooled Reactors*, para 2, p. 19, p. 27; also E. Slater, 'Operating Experience with the WAGR Fuelling Machine', *NE* (August 1967), pp. 600-3.

25. M.E. Ginniff, 'The Windscale CAGR Handling Rig — 10 Years Testing', *Atom* (March 1978), pp. 69-73.

26. Guard, 'The Year Since Geneva'.

27. *Opinion*, para. 135; also J.D. Thorn, 'Development Trends in CO_2-cooled Nuclear Power Stations', *Atom* (August 1966), p. 175.

28. See generally, Ryukichi Imai, 'The Utility Fuel Dilemma', *NE* (July 1966), pp. 546-7.

29. HCD 722 c.623-8.

30. HCD 783 c.1600-12. The AEA's objectives were set out, for example, in C. Allday *et al.*, 'Planning for Future Enrichment Plants', *Atom* (February 1969), pp. 36-42; D.G. Avery and R.B. Kehoe, 'The Uranium Enrichment Industry', *Atom* (June 1970), pp. 120-30; G.R.H. Geoghegan and R.B. Kehoe, 'Uranium Enrichment in the UK', *Atom* (November 1970), pp. 224-30.

31. For example, C.F. Barnaby, 'The Gas Centrifuge Project', *Science Journal* (August 1969), pp. 54-9; Leonard Beaton, *The Times*, 23 January 1969.

32. For example, N.L. Franklin, 'Great Britain — An Alternative Economical Source of Enriched Uranium Fuel', *Atom* (January 1968), pp. 8-12; *Nucleonics* (November 1965), p. 21 (February 1966), p. 27.

33. See for example, G.R. Bainbridge *et al.*, 'The Safety of UK Gas-cooled Reactors — A Review', III Geneva, 13, pp. 341-50.

34. *USAEC, Initial Decision Upon Application for Provisional Construction Permit in the Matter of Jersey Central Power and Light Company*, Docket No. 50 — 219 (4 December 1964), p. 32; see also S.G. Kingsley, 'The Licensing of Nuclear Power Reactors in the US', *BNESJ*, 5 (1966), pp. 49-59.

35. Ibid., p. 38.

36. *USAEC, In the Matter of Jersey Central Power and Light Company, Order Determining Compliance with Conditions in Initial Decision in Reference to Provisional Construction Permit*, Docket No. 50 — 219 (10 January 1966), p. 4.

37. HC 381 (1966-7), Appendix 14; also L. Cave and R.E. Holmes, 'Suitability of the AGR for Urban Siting', IAEA Symposium on *The Containment and Siting of Nuclear Power Plants* (April 1967); *Nucleonics* (January 1966), p. 17.

38. See also Thorn, 'Development Trends', pp. 175-80.

39. The discussion here is based *inter alia* on P.C. Warner, 'Development of the Dungeness B Design', *NE* (October 1965), pp. 375-8; HC 381-XVII (1966-7) evidence and Appendices 26 and 31; HC 401 (1968-9) APC evidence and Appendix 13; *Nucleonics* (November 1965), p. 42; HCD 697 c.132 (WA).

40. For example, *New Scientist*, 27 May 1965. See *Euronuclear* (August 1965), p. 371.

41. Anglo-Spanish Nuclear Power Symposium (Madrid, November 1964), vol. 2, paper 12, para. 36. See G.B. Greenough, 'Progress Towards the Design of AGR Fuel Elements for Power Reactors', III Geneva, 10, pp. 114-20 (114).

42. Jack Hartshorn, *A Fuel Policy for Britain* (PEP, London, 1966), p. 222; see also K.P. Gibbs (CEGB) 'Ground Rules for Costs', *Financial Times*, 9 September 1966.

43. Geoffrey Williams *et al.*, *Crisis in Procurement: A Case Study of the TSR2* (RUSI, London, 1969), pp. 8, 45, 65-6.

44. Guard, 'The Year Since Geneva'; Imai, 'The Dungeness B Appraisal', pp. 379-80; *NE* (October 1965), p. 362; also *NE* (March 1966), pp. 175-6.

45. For example, *Observer*, 30 May 1965; *Financial Times*, 26 May 1965; *Daily Telegraph*, 26 May 1965; *New York Times*, 27 May 1965; *Business Week*, 29 May 1965; *Daily Express*, 22 May 1965; *The Times*, 28 May 1965; *Euronuclear* (July 1965), p. 328; *Sunday Times*, 30 May 1965.

46. *New Statesman*, 6 August 1965; HCD 714 c.222.

47. *Euronuclear* (August 1965), p. 371.

48. *NE* (June 1965), pp. 205-6.

49. *Atom* (June 1965), p. 100.

50. HCD 743 c.1339-53.

51. *NE* (January 1967), p. 25.

PART III: 1965-74

7 THE QUARREL WITH COAL

On taking office in 1964 the Labour Government began formulating a co-ordinated fuel policy and in October 1965 their first White Paper[1] on the subject was published. This took as reference figures for nuclear energy the generating cost estimates for the Dungeness B station. These, 'on cautious assumptions' 0.46 and 0.38d/KWh, depending on the severity of the ground rules, were compared with figures of 0.52 and 0.54 for contemporary coal stations, and with others of 0.52 and 0.41 for a contemporary oil station with and without fuel tax. The conclusion was inevitably drawn that the nuclear stations of the second programme would be 'fully competitive' with conventional ones, and in the light of what were described as 'the encouraging tenders' received for Dungeness B the Government announced that, in agreement with the supply industry and the AEA, they had decided to plan for an average of one nuclear station a year to commission between 1970 and 1975. This was expected to amount to some 8GW as compared with the planned figure of 5GW in the 1964 programme. The amended programme, it was said, would be based on the AGR but the possible introduction of another reactor type was not ruled out: in any case there would be flexibility and review. In providing for a programme, in settling upon a single reactor type, in nominally leaving scope for a different type, and in promising flexibility, the 1965 White Paper was more than a little reminiscent of that of 1955. There were also to be parallels in the way things turned out.

The fact and manner of the CEGB's selection of the AGR in 1965 were together instrumental in converting their longstanding doubts about the economics of nuclear power into a lasting enthusiasm. *Nuclear Engineering* may also have been right in suggesting that the new generation of CEGB managers were 'nearly all bright boys with a nuclear background and training, very close to the Authority in their thinking'.[2] In any case the CEGB's first annual report after the Dungeness appraisal stated unequivocally that 'the capability of large nuclear power stations to supply electricity continuously over long periods to the national grid system at low running cost has been firmly established'. In their next report the fact that Britain's nuclear stations had generated more electricity than the total generated by nuclear plant in the rest of the world was said to constitute 'ample proof of the Board's

153

lead in the industrial use of nuclear power'. It was recognised that the
AGR's generating cost was still higher than that of untaxed oil, but it
was also again pointed out that the reactor had a 10 per cent advantage
over coal at 1965 prices, and that the gap was expected to widen after
1970. The Board said they had now re-examined their requirements for
the Hinkley B station, with the result that their new specification incorporated a number of features which they hoped it would be possible
to repeat unchanged for several further nuclear stations.

The Board's 1966/7 report, written in the context of a new government review of fuel policy, noted that the total costs of the later
Magnox stations, 0.7d/unit or less, were 'already comparable' with
coal plant away from the coal fields; that the AGR would be cheaper
than all coal plant; and that nuclear generating costs were far less sensitive to fuel price rises than were those of fossil plant. These statements
were juxtaposed with the argument that it would be 'grossly inequitable
and probably self-defeating' for the electricity consumer to be required
indefinitely to bear the cost of supporting coal beyond the economically indicated level. Sir Stanley Brown's opinion was that with the first
AGR undercutting the best coal station, later ones would 'undoubtedly
do even better'. Sir Ronald Edwards, Electricity Council chairman,
agreed. With a move also taking place to a 'more realistic approach' to
the siting of nuclear stations, the implications for the coal industry
could hardly have been more pointed. The Ministry accepted in 1967
that the CEGB felt themselves limited for the time being in their plans
for building AGRs: these plans were understood to be a 'compromise
between what would be the most economic for them and what is likely
to be acceptable in the light of government policy'.[3]

It had universally been seen as a virtue in 1955 that the Magnox programme would reduce substantially the electricity industry's demand
for coal, and the stations in operation by 1970 indeed displaced almost
10m tons, the equivalent of nearly 18,000 jobs in mining according to
Lord Robens the NCB chairman. Robens afterwards wrote, in a chapter
headed 'Nuclear Scandals' in his book *Ten Year Stint*,[4] that 'The battle
of nuclear power versus coal began as far as I was concerned in October
1960, the month that I took up my post as Chairman Designate of the
Coal Board.' The real battle between these fuels was not, however,
despite earlier skirmishes,[5] properly joined until 1965. For this there
were three main reasons.

First, in the early years nuclear energy was viewed not as a challenge
to the coal industry but rather as a desperately needed substitute for
coal supplies which were, despite the best efforts of the industry, un-

available. Then, second, as it became clear that new coal stations were going to have better immediate economics than the Magnox stations, there was still little incentive for the NCB to lobby against the Magnox reactors; since the commitment to build them had been made, everyone recognised without the intervention of the NCB the unsound economic premises of the programme; and anyway, it was not until the mid-sixties that the Magnox stations actually began to affect the market for coal. The third reason for identifying 1965 as the year in which the coal-nuclear confrontation first became of major importance is even clearer. It was then, following the Dungeness B appraisal, that the CEGB ceased to institutionalise the call for restraint in the exploitation of nuclear energy and became instead the new technology's firm champion.

Since the official interpretation placed on the Dungeness appraisal undoubtedly led in the late sixties to some distortion of the premises of national fuel policy in general, and of the CEGB's policy in particular, it is important to establish the basis and strength of the Coal Board's opposition to nuclear energy in the late sixties. It needs also to be remembered that this was only one of the arguments during these years between the NCB on the one hand and the Ministry and CEGB on the other. The wider argument, taking in as it did oil and North Sea gas as well as nuclear energy, naturally lies outside the scope of this book.

The NCB's annual report for 1965/6 left no doubt that they had in that year become directly aware of the nuclear challenge. Power station use of coal, which had been expanding rapidly, was, at some 68m tons, slightly down on 1964/5, and the Board pointed to the cause of this, the commissioning in the year of four nuclear power stations and the consequent doubling of the nuclear power output, from 3.2 million tons of coal equivalent (mtce) in 1964 to 7.8mtce in 1966. Board members now began insisting that coal would long remain both necessary and competitive. The Board's report for 1966/7 offered a vigorous statement of such views. Of nuclear energy, which had provided some 8mtce in 1966, it argued that: 'Estimates that the cost of providing electricity from nuclear stations will be less than the cost of doing so from thermal stations need close and dispassionate examination. Nuclear stations cost huge sums in capital and account needs to be taken of the use to which the excess capital expenditure could be put if it were not sunk in these stations. To the extent that the basic technology remains unproved, the justification for spending these large sums of capital must be open to question . . . The mistake of an over-large experiment which was made in the first nuclear programme ought not to be repeated.'

These observations were somewhat out of place in a report on the coal industry, and were clearly provocative. It was not, the Board said, that they did not welcome new sources of fuel: simply that they feared 'precipitate short-term action' which might prevent their achieving their goal of an efficient and viable coal industry.

The following year, 1967/8, was critically eventful for the coal industry. There were two tactical engagements with nuclear energy, over a project to construct aluminium smelters and over a power station planned for Hartlepool, and the argument with nuclear energy was also part of a wider campaign waged by the Board in the context of the fuel policy review being conducted by the Ministry of Power. There were as well two appearances by the Board before Select Committees of the House of Commons. The first of these took place in April 1967, when Lord Robens told the Nationalised Industries Committee[6] that he saw nuclear power as the 'great competitor to coal' over the following 10 to 15 years. His most specific complaint at this time was that he had been unable to discover the exact target cost of nuclear power at which coal had to aim. The only figures with which the Ministry had been prepared to furnish his Board included no breakdown showing how nuclear costs were arrived at, particularly regarding the return looked for on the extra capital invested in nuclear stations. Robens criticised the wider policy-making structure for fuel and also the Ministry of Power. The latter, he said, had neglected its co-ordinating role, was organised in such a way as to encourage parochialism, and had an inadequate staff, whose normal career development moreover militated against their acquiring sufficient expertise in the problems of the power industries. Robens called instead for a Fuel Industry Investment Board provided with an expert staff and equipped to apply a 'total sum' approach to fuel policy, including the social costs of, and mutual interaction between, major decisions taken by the respective industries.

Just a month after his appearance before the Select Committee Robens met with the chairmen of the other nationalised fuel industries and the Minister of Power for a much publicised conference at the Selsdon Park Hotel, Croydon, called by the minister in the course of his revision of the Government's fuel policy of 1965. The argument which ensued about the comparative economics of coal and nuclear power stations was, according to Robens, 'fast and furious'.[7] The NCB had heard only shortly before of a Ministry Working Party, which had been in existence for a year, with representatives from the AEA, the CEGB and the Electricity Council. The report of this group, it emerged, had included assumptions about the cost of coal, and Robens was later to describe himself as 'outraged' that the Board had, as he saw it, been 'deliberately excluded' from the group's work. He had therefore, he said, 'kicked up merry hell' until the Board's scientific member, Leslie Grainger, formerly assistant director of Harwell, was allowed to join.

Following the Selsdon conference the Working Party, with the addition now of Grainger, reconvened. In due course another report was arrived at, the NCB supplying a still dissenting addendum, and both this second report and the addendum were later published by the Science Committee.[8] Grainger told this latter Committee that although the Board had at last been given an opportunity to look at the figures, the time and circumstances were such as to limit the effectiveness of the NCB's representation. The Board had raised four main objections to the Working Party's initial report. They had questioned whether there might not be a disguised subsidy in the fuel prices charged by the AEA, given that the Authority were not compelled to behave as a commercial body; they had expressed their doubts that the AGR's costs would be recovered in the royalty to be levied; they had explained that they felt an inadequate allowance had been made for technical problems arising in the execution of the AGR programme; and they had queried the methods of economic analysis which had been employed. The Board's opinion was that the cost difference between nuclear and coal generation was then 'certainly less than the errors in forecasting', and estimating the excess capital required for the existing 8GW AGR programme at £330m, they suggested that the return on this avoidable expenditure was 'probably the most important factor of all'. They wanted therefore an independent financial and technical assessment of the AGR programme.

Observations of this sort, however reasonable, were obviously not unexpected from this quarter. What was remarkable was that the Coal Board also took it upon themselves to question the technical standing of the AGR. Naturally they could not remotely rival the expertise of the AEA, but their addendum was a rare critical assessment of the AGR at this time. The NCB's various technical reservations with regard to the AGR need not be itemised, though in view of the technical problems which were to befall the reactor, they ought not to be overlooked as querulous irrelevancies. The Board's main point deserves quotation: 'Much the most serious doubts . . . are related to the technical performance of the commercial AGRs . . . the evidence provided by the Windscale AGR is of strictly limited value . . . It is scarcely credible that the reactors will function as assumed by the economic analyses.'

In his evidence to the Science Committee in June 1967 Robens[9] stressed that while the cost of coal was known, that of nuclear energy was not, and that this was because 'The total sum has never been done.' It had become possible to derive from the published accounts of the AEA and the CEGB the 'reasonable and true costs', but these were not added together. Robens was therefore convinced that the AGR programme was being subsidised. He repeated his criticisms of the civil servants in the Ministry of Power: they were 'birds of passage . . . never there long enough really to do more than get the top of everything'. His scientific board member added that since neither the Ministry of Power nor the Ministry of Technology had a nuclear expert, he thought the AEA's figures were challenged much less than were those put forward by the NCB.

One unusual admission in Robens's evidence to the Science Committee was that the Board had asked MPs to put questions in the House in order to obtain cost information which the Board regarded as essential but which they were otherwise unable to obtain. Here it is also of some interest that Michael Posner, in 1966/7 Director of Economics at the Ministry of Power and later the author of an important economic study of fuel policy, had written of the fuel policy White Paper of 1965 that, while planning necessarily involved 'Whitehall knowing best', the really important point was that 'the calculations are made publicly, and publicly criticised'.[10]

Shortly after the NCB chairman's appearance before the Science Committee a group of six Labour MPs from mining constituencies carried on his attack on the AGR programme in a letter to *The Times*.[11] In this they cited his illustration that the avoidable cost of the generating capacity supplied by the Magnox programme would have bought 5 new universities, 20 new hospitals, 150 new schools and 200 miles of motorway. In July 1967 Robens himself told the National Union of Mineworkers (NUM) that the Magnox programme had cost 28,000 jobs in mining, and £525m extra capital over and above the £225m a comparable coal station programme would have cost. The AGR programme should not, he thought, be one station larger than was necessary to get to the fast breeder reactor. The Board's statutory obligation, to manage the coal industry so as to further the public interest in all respects, compelled them to demand an examination of all the figures in detail, or else an independent inquiry.

By the autumn of 1967, with publication eagerly awaited of the new White Paper on fuel policy, the position of coal seemed still to be worsening. In June, for instance, the chairman of the Electricity Council went on record as being confident of the future superiority of nuclear power.[12] And in July the Minister of Power indicated that he was convinced of the AGR's competitiveness even under what he considered the pessimistic ground rules then being applied to it. In a Commons debate the minister emphasised the unanimity on this point of the AEA, the CEGB, and his own Chief Scientist's division: if they were wrong, then so were all the nuclear scientists of every other industrial nation.[13] (Sir William Penney had made it clear in 1966 that he thought a book life of 35 years and a load factor of 85 per cent more reasonable than the 20 years, 75 per cent still being being assumed by the CEGB.)[14] The minister's statement and a press briefing were interpreted as removing any remaining doubts about the Government's commitment to a policy of cheap fuel. And even when the Government asked the Coal Board in September 1967 to postpone for a few months sixteen projected pit closures, it was stressed that this move was a response to the overall employment situation and in no way implied a change in fuel strategy.

The month scheduled for the publication of the White Paper was October. For the NCB it began inauspiciously, the CEGB presenting their annual report as an 'historic moment', in that they claimed nuclear energy now enjoyed an advantage in generating cost over coal of some 0.1d/KWh − 0.48 compared with 0.58d/KWh. 'It is clear,' said *The Times Business News* 'that, unless the nation is being taken for a gigantic ride by its technocrats, the age of cheap power from nuclear energy has, after several false starts, now arrived.' 'He may have convinced himself,' Robens retorted of Sir Stanley Brown's claim, '[but] he's not proved it to our satisfaction.'[15]

Ironically, at this same time Robens's most basic criticism of nuclear power found support in a paper given by the head of the European Nuclear Energy Agency's Economics Office to a London conference organised by the AEA.[16] According to this expert, whose motives, unlike those of the NCB chairman, obviously did not include a brief for an alternative fuel, it was 'likely to be some considerable time before adequate economic operating experience is available from a representative range of nuclear power stations in the OECD area to demonstrate the actual relation between *a priori* and *a posteriori* calculation, which are the only true measure of competitivity'. This conclusion, had it been accepted by the Ministry, would clearly have served Robens's case to perfection.

Later in October 1967 came a highly controversial lecture by E.F.

Schumacher, the NCB's Economic Adviser. In this Schumacher argued that the decision between coal, oil and nuclear stations was being taken on economic grounds, with only a small element of regard being paid to social consequences. Schumacher also offered what was for its time a very unorthodox opinion, to the effect that nuclear stations represented an incredible, incomparable, and unique hazard to human life: worse still, this did not enter any calculations and was never mentioned. The reaction of the injured parties was bitter. The Ministry of Power at once issued a statement dismissing Schumacher's remarks as 'so inaccurate that they cannot be regarded as a serious contribution', and a spokesman for the CEGB saw them as 'maybe . . . just part of the anti-nuclear campaign [of] the past few months'.[17]

Schumacher's remarks were naturally widely reported, and a final move by Robens also helped to ensure that the 1967 White Paper would appear in a highly charged atmosphere. The occasion for this initiative was a private meeting between the NCB chairman, the President and Secretary of the NUM, and the chairmen of the seven Regional Economic Planning Councils in which the coal fields were situated. In his briefing of the chairmen, Robens apparently suggested speculatively that the continuation of existing trends would mean a coal output of only 80m tons in 1980, and a labour force reduced from the current 390,000 to a mere 65,000. The reaction was immediate; expressions such as 'kiss of death', 'frightening', 'annihilation of mining communities' were commonplace, and there were reports that some NUM lodges were voting to end the political levy paid to the Labour Party.[18] But after a meeting between Robens and the Minister of Power it was officially stated that the offending remarks had been taken out of context and were therefore misleading, and when the White Paper was published a few days later it was clear that this last storm had had no effect.

The economic comparison made in the White Paper[19] between coal and nuclear generation seemed to leave the advantage decisively with the latter. The generating cost at Dungeness B was now put at 0.52d/KWh, and at Hinkley Point B, the second AGR station, at 0.48, compared with 0.53 and 0.56 at the Cottam and Drax coal stations. The Dungeness B figure had risen since 1965, but it was maintained that there had been no increase apart from inflation in the cost of its nuclear sections. The White Paper put at £170m the additional capital cost of the 5.5GW of the second nuclear programme scheduled to follow Hinkley B, as compared that is with an equivalent programme of coal stations. On the worst possible assumptions as far as nuclear power was concerned, the minimum internal rate of return on this excess capital was calculated at 10 per cent, and the probability of a much higher figure, up to a maximum of 34 per cent, was firmly indicated. To complete the case against coal, the White Paper rejected the principle of a 'breakeven' price at which coal could still compete, on the grounds that any cheaper coal which became available should simply displace the most expensive coal then being used. A notional breakeven figure was nevertheless estimated. This came out as at best 3.2d per therm, 0.7d per therm below the lowest price then being paid by the CEGB and 1.8d per therm below the average they were paying. From all this the conclusion for coal was unmistakable. The 1965 White Paper having put the 1970 output target for coal at 170-180m tons, the actual domestic demand for coal in 1970 was now estimated at 146m tons, and production under existing plans at 152m tons. To bridge this gap the White Paper explained that the gas and electricity industries were being asked to burn the 6m excess tons, the additional cost, up to £45m to be borne by the taxpayer, rather than by the consumer as provided for in the 1965 White Paper. By 1975 domestic coal demand was expected to have fallen to 118m tons, and beyond this the prospects for coal were not set out in detail. It was stated only that the Government expected coal to contribute a 'substantial though declining' part of the country's fuel requirements.

Nuclear energy was itself spoken of in the White Paper as 'proven and increasingly competitive'. There were said to be 'good grounds' for believing that AGR stations after Hinkley B would show further cost reductions, 'further considerable reductions' were 'confidently expected' after 1975; and between then and 1980 the AGR would become 'fully competitive' with generation by untaxed oil, with the construction costs of AGR stations commissioning at that time 'little greater' than those of conventional stations. All in all, nuclear power was judged to be 'on its way to becoming the principal fuel for new generating capacity', so that conventional stations would in future be built only where sites were 'specially favourable' to them. It was admitted that the choice between nuclear and conventional generation rested mainly on estimates and a 'regular sequence' of new nuclear stations was said to be desirable if their full development potential were to be realised. It was also acknowledged that 'in a young technology the risk of disappointment must exist'. But these considerations were not allowed to diminish the firm underlying confidence in nuclear energy, and specifically in the 'ample scope' for development with the AGR.

The new approach was fairly generally seen as a courageous attempt to bring order into fuel policy, *The Times* going as far as to say it was 'the first real fuel policy we have had . . . the sort of achievement for which the present Government will be remembered when some of their other works have been completely forgotten'.[20] The almost immediate devaluation of the pound and the Science Committee's first report on the nuclear industry briefly had some MPs from mining constituencies demanding that the figures in the White Paper be recalculated, and new generating costs were in fact published in January 1968 which, including royalty and devaluation allowances, and at a uniform 8 per cent discount rate, put Dungeness B at 0.57, Hinkley Point B at 0.52, Cottam at 0.56 and Drax at 0.60d. But apart from giving these figures the minister was not to be drawn as regards any wider reassessment.

The 1967 White Paper did have at least one strong pro-nuclear critic, Lord Sherfield, as emerged in a Lords debate.[21] 'Unlike coal,' Sherfield argued, 'nuclear power has no lobby . . . There are indeed only a limited number of people who speak up for nuclear power, besides the AEA and the CEGB.' Even the Government, Sherfield thought, had a 'probably subconscious . . . built-in bias against nuclear power in relation to coal'. The White Paper left the impression that every conceivable disadvantage had been loaded onto nuclear power, yet it still came out ahead: a much stronger official endorsement was called for. The Government's spokesman in the Lords accepted Sherfield's criticism but in general, as a parallel Commons debate showed, the Government were well pleased with the techniques and principles which underlay their White Paper.

Lord Robens's defence of coal, and his attack on nuclear energy and by implication on its advocates as he saw them, the Ministry and the CEGB, continued into 1968.[22] That his frequent and vehement criticisms of fuel policy did not precipitate his forced resignation was due above all to the Government's paramount need of his prestige and abilities in maintaining an orderly contraction of the coal industry. At his New Year press conference Robens again asked for an independent inquiry into nuclear costs. He also alleged on this occasion that the NCB had not been consulted on the 118m tons coal target figure for 1975. It even appeared that the Coal Board had definite people in mind as suitable chairmen of an independent inquiry into costs, people such as Sir Solly Zuckerman, or Lords Plowden or Hinton. In March 1968 Robens was widely reported as having told mining MPs that the Prime Minister, Harold Wilson, and George Brown had broken promises given to the miners in 1964, and in May he condemned the 'structure of the Civil Service inside the economic ministries' as being inadequate to cope with the enormous investment decisions called for in the energy field.

Then, shortly after Ray Gunter's resignation as Minister of Power, Robens blamed the Government for their over-concentration on the 'whizz kids who think that technological advance is the be all and end all'. The 1975 coal target of 118m tons he now described as 'an utter misjudgement', and he was able on this occasion to quote in further-ance of his case two economic studies which reached conclusions different from those of the White Paper. These were an Economist Intelligence Unit report commissioned by the NCB and the study of the British economy by the Brookings Institution. The Economist Unit's report is considered below.

The Brookings report[23] described energy policy as being 'at a water-shed', and the associated problems as 'unusually complex'. Since fuel costs were probably only some 7-8 per cent of average costs of manu-factured goods the report argued that even a 20 per cent average reduc-tion in fuel costs would reduce total costs by 'only a sliver'. Yet, it added, 'the pursuit of these gains may well be leading to over-commit-ment of investment in this direction during the 1970s . . . the latest plans probably exceed the optimal rate of substitution of, in effect, nuclear power for coal; they involve an exceptionally and unnecessarily capital-intensive method which will yield only modest gains in fuel economy and a relatively small release of miners for other industries. Coal output should probably be cut back more slowly than is planned and the investment programme for electricity (especially nuclear generation) should be substantially reduced.' Innovation in the elec-tricity industry, the report suggested, had 'probably been too rapid, in the first nuclear power programme after 1956 and probably now in the second generation of reactors'. Its overall conclusion was that the existing plans amounted to 'small gains in fuel prices and transferable labour at the cost of a large intake of capital'.

Gunter's successor as Minister of Power was Roy Mason, MP for a mining constituency, but known even on his appointment to be no simple standard-bearer for coal. There was some optimism in the mining community following his announcement to the NUM and his fellow mining MPs that he was re-examining the implications for coal of the Government's fuel policy, but no easement of the industry's circumstances was forthcoming.

In August 1968 Robens received some new ammunition, in the form of a report by the Public Accounts Committee.[24] The PAC con-tinued to be concerned about the question of royalties. They were still 'unconvinced' of the justification for waiving royalties on the Magnox stations, but said they might more readily have swallowed this had the electricity authorities been required to accept a hard bargain in respect of the AGR. In settling royalties on this at 0.014d/unit of electricity the Treasury had 'come down in the middle' of the 0.03d advantage the Dungeness B appraisal had shown the AGR to have over the BWR. On the 8.4GW AGR programme then expected to commission up to 1975 this royalty was projected to produce a lifetime return, even on the AEA's calculations, of only some £26m present worth, whereas AGR development had historically cost £89m and was expected then to cost a further £20m. The Comptroller and Auditor General had thought the CEGB should bear a higher proportion of the AGR's costs and with this the PAC agreed. They did not think the balance between the taxpayer and the electricity consumer had been fairly struck in an arrangement which left the CEGB with four-fifths of the savings the AGR was expected to effect as compared with conventional generation. They thought it would have been inducement enough had the CEGB had to pay the full 0.03d by which the AGR was calculated to be cheaper than the BWR. A fair comparison between nuclear and conventional generation was invalidated if the true nuclear costs were obscured by indirect Exchequer subsidy.

The AEA and Mintech were agreed that there was a disguised subsidy in LWR prices in that American companies were not required to pay the US Atomic Energy Commission royalties. The Treasury spokesman to the PAC also expressed satisfaction that it had not been necessary to 'import political considerations' into the 'essentially commercial transaction' at Dungeness B. In settling the royalty the Treasury had seen no 'vital economic point' or 'great point of principle'. The AEA and CEGB were 'two worthy parties' and both had a good cause. The desirability of a nuclear programme and the royalty issue were not really related in any clear-cut way. The provision of an alternative system of generation was a good in itself and it would be 'entirely unreal' to require nuclear to carry its full development cost. The permanent secretary to Mintech assured the PAC that a 'complete apparatus of calculation and ground rules' for making investment decisions had existed for several years. Any wrongness in setting royalties did not flow into the quite different investment decisions, at least in principle, though there was 'not really a scientific way of doing it'.

It was mentioned above that as well as the general argument in 1967/8 about the comparative generating costs of coal and nuclear power stations, the issue also figured prominently in the case of the aluminium smelter project and in that of the power station which the CEGB decided to build near Hartlepool. Both of these cases extended over a considerable period of time, with the proponents of coal and nuclear power skirmishing throughout.

The Hartlepool episode effectively began in March 1967 with a CEGB application to the Minister of Power, then Richard Marsh, for permission to construct a nuclear power station at Seaton Carew near Hartlepool. The issue from the outset meant much more to the mining industry than a few million tons of coal a year. Hartlepool was on the edge of the Durham coalfield, and it seemed clear that if coal could not compete successfully with nuclear energy there, then its future was bleak indeed. The psychological stake for the mining community was thus enormous. Yet in no sense was this a decisive test between coal and nuclear energy in the eyes of the CEGB. That had occurred for them at Dungeness B. As a result, at Hartlepool they were predisposed to choose nuclear energy. This was made perfectly clear, for instance, in their evidence to the Science Committee. In the words of one of the members of that Committee: 'the CEGB hierarchy, particularly their engineers, have really made up their minds that they want to deal in nuclear and not in thermal stations . . . There is no doubt that everybody in the CEGB — and not just those in authority . . . — are keen that [Hartlepool] should be nuclear.'[25] In fact, it was understood that if the Hartlepool station were not to be nuclear, then the Board had no interest in building any station there.

Faced with such a major challenge Robens played a dramatic card, offering the CEGB coal for Hartlepool at 3.25d per therm, substantially less than the average figure then being paid by the Board of 4.7d. This offer considerably embarrassed the Government, already on the defensive because of the close connection between the mining community and the Labour Party. The NCB's offer was curtly received by the CEGB, and the gulf between the two organisations was clearly brought out in a sharp exchange of letters between the respective chairmen in the columns of *The Times*.[26] Robens's position was that his offer of coal at 3.25d a therm was a hard one, the underlying calculations being open to inspection by the CEGB and the Ministry, while the nuclear generating cost was not only higher but also based on unproven estimates. The essence of Sir Stanley Brown's reply was that the NCB's offer was not really firm; that, even if it were, a nuclear station at Hartlepool would still be £1m a year cheaper; and that if coal could be made available at 3.25d a therm, then this should be done not at Hartlepool but elsewhere, in order to reduce the average figure which the Board were paying. Brown's final point was that 'The CEGB have nothing to gain, and a good deal to lose, from deceiving themselves about future nuclear – or indeed coal – costs.' To retard the development of nuclear energy so as to maintain the Board's demand for high-cost coal made, he argued, no sense so far as the CEGB were concerned. Brown also insisted at this time that the criticism that the electricity industry was turning its back on coal was 'so ludicrous that it scarcely deserves a denial'. But he continued to underline the realities of the situation as he saw them: 'The plain fact is that the trend for the last five years has been for nuclear power to get steadily cheaper and for coal to get steadily dearer, and further, the technology of nuclear power is still in its infancy whereas that of generation from coal has been intensively developed over many years.'

The decision that Hartlepool would definitely be a nuclear station was eventually announced by Roy Mason in August 1968. A press notice[27] described the Government as confident that there was a substantial net advantage, to the nation as well as to the CEGB, in building a nuclear station as compared with a coal one. The CEGB's figures were said to show a present-worth financial advantage to nuclear power of £37m, with the nuclear station generating at 0.52d, including a royalty payment, and coal at 0.70d, both at 75 per cent load factor, though it was argued that the coal plant would in practice have had a lower load factor, and also coal usage, than this because of its high fuel costs. There was criticism that the Government had chosen to make the announcement when the House was in recess, but it was thought politically courageous, even if still more damaging to the coal industry, that the decision had been taken by a minister who was himself an ex-miner. This, for example, was the view of the *Financial Times*,[28] which as an advocate of cheap energy welcomed the decision. This newspaper nevertheless had doubts, and in this it was not alone, as to whether the growth of nuclear power at the expense of coal was 'as yet' in the national interest. Like others it was unhappy with the Government's consistent refusal of Robens's demands for an independent inquiry into fuel costs, and concerned that there might have been a commitment to a policy 'to the point where the facts are no longer always looked at impartially'. At the very least, the newspaper suggested, there was need for greater disclosure. For his part the minister, whilst acknowledging that the decision had been a 'particularly difficult one', continued to reject any outside investigation into comparative generating costs.

The decision to offer government support for the establishment of an aluminium smelting capacity in Britain was announced by the Prime Minister in a speech to the Labour Party Conference at Scarborough in October 1967. In his speech Wilson emphasised that it was advances in nuclear generation which had made feasible in Britain the creation of new industries heavily dependent on electric power. He indicated that power would be supplied at a price dependent on the generating cost of the power station concerned, and added that he was discussing with the NCB chairman the possibility of associating the Board with the venture. The original idea had been for a smelter or smelters to share the output of an AGR station with the AEA's enrichment plant at Capenhurst, so that both would enjoy cheap power. This scheme and the one eventually adopted each involved the supply of power at a preferential tariff.

In January 1968 the Alcan company announced that they would meet the power requirements for their proposed smelter by building their own coal generating station and operating it with coal obtained from the NCB on a 25-year contract. This decision was hailed by Robens as demonstrating that coal could still compete with nuclear energy, but the Electricity Council, launching what was described by one commentator[29] as 'an unprecedented public attack' on the NCB, questioned whether the Board's arrangement with Alcan did not contravene the provisions in the 1946 Coal Nationalisation Act forbidding preferential pricing. Critics of the CEGB pointed out that coal at a preferential price was also available to them at Hartlepool. The Government in due course announced support for all three smelter proposals made to them, those from British Aluminium and RTZ as well as Alcan's.

It was not really surprising that in their annual report for 1967/8 the NCB took the unusual step of effectively dissociating themselves from the Government's fuel policy. This was really the final step Robens could take, short of actually resigning. This report complained that there had not been adequate discussion before the preparation of the 1967 White Paper, specifically with respect to the future of coal after 1970-1. Any error in the AGR programme would involve the country in 'abortive capital investment' totalling hundreds of millions of pounds. That the 'larger than normal' return to be looked for from this 'avoidable investment' would not be obtained was in the NCB's opinion a 'real risk' given the 'identifiable areas of technical uncertainty in the AGR system'. Again they asked for an independent inquiry: the hypothetical cost advantages of nuclear power were 'at best, narrow'. It was not, the Board insisted, that they were opposed to the development of nuclear energy: they merely thought that the AGR stations already committed were sufficient to ensure technical progress until the inquiry they suggested was completed.

The NCB's annual report was published in September 1968 and in this month the Board delivered a second public challenge by issuing the study which had been prepared for them by the Economist Intelligence Unit. The NCB had commissioned the latter report some months before, apparently in despair of getting an independent inquiry. Given its sponsors, the report was bound to be regarded with some suspicion, especially since its preference was for a 'middle of the road policy', with a domestic coal demand of 144m tons in 1975. The expansion of nuclear energy should, the report suggested, depend 'on evidence of technical progress as it accumulates'. The Ministry's response was sharp. They had, they said, reservations some of which were 'fundamental to the approach' of the report, and it did not therefore seem to them to constitute 'a valid basis for policy decisions'.

In October 1968 the Minister of Power held another 'country retreat' meeting with the chairmen of the nationalised fuel industries, this time at Sunningdale. The official statement after the meeting stated only that no new decision had been taken and that a further review of fuel policy was being conducted by the Ministry. Robens was later to be again scathing about the outcome.

The Minister of Power, already the butt of criticism from mining MPs, in November 1968 also came under fire from the Science Committee. In their first report on nuclear power in 1967 the Committee had complained about the time it had taken to obtain from the Minister of Power information he had promised on his appearance before them. On the occasion of his appearance[30] Marsh had made the point that although he had been surprised on becoming minister at the extent to which his Ministry was a technical one, nevertheless it was not set up to run the CEGB, only to evaluate and question what the CEGB were doing and, in the nuclear case, to adjudicate on the technical activities of the Board and the AEA. The CEGB and the AEA did not have a common interest and the AEA's policies received a 'very powerful check' from the CEGB. The minister agreed that he would not be in a position in a technical argument to judge between the AEA and the CEGB, but the Chief Scientist's Division in the Ministry of Power 'would generally be regarded as a reasonably convincing team', and together with the AEA and CEGB nuclear people it constituted 'a reasonable amalgam of expertise'. There had been 'no real division' between these people on nuclear costs. 'If they are wrong, I am not qualified to judge . . . there is nothing more I can do . . . to commission anything further on this particular issue.' Marsh accepted Robens's criticism that there had been a high turnover of ministers and permanent secretaries at the Ministry of Power, but argued that at under-secretary and assistant secretary level there had been reasonable stability.

The Science Committee's opinion in 1967 was that there was 'a certain amount of wishful thinking' in the minister's confidence in his technical staff on the nuclear side. The Committee also said that, being unable themselves to reconcile the cost figures presented to them, the 'most authoritative and independent' ones available, in the words of the PM, they suspected that they were not the only ones to be confused. They therefore recommended 'an examination by an independent outside agency of the purely financial aspects of costing of all methods of energy supply'. The failure to have such an independent costing performed was, they thought, 'a serious weakness of present British energy policy'.

It was November 1968 when the Committee eventually received a reply.[31] Asking an outside body to make such a study meant, the new minister, Roy Mason, said, imposing on them a 'heavy task' which would not yield 'commensurate benefits'. This answer did not satisfy the Committee. However efficient and painstaking internal reviews might be, it seemed to the Committee natural that outsiders should retain doubts about the validity of the conclusions reached. In December the minister gave a different and more remarkable reason for refusing to have an independent inquiry. Addressing Yorkshire miners at Barnsley, Mason explained that he was fully satisfied both that nuclear power was competitive and that any independent inquiry would confirm this. Since this would 'shatter the morale of the miners' and lead ultimately to the killing of coal, he wanted to avoid such an inquiry. The paradox was not lost on Robens, who afterwards wrote that he had 'known ministers to utter nonsense' but that this had been 'the limit, and a crushingly inept way to enhance morale'.[32]

In February 1969 the Government said they had been assured by the CEGB that the engineering difficulties by this time being encountered with Dungeness B had no implications for other AGR stations, and that there was therefore no occasion for an independent inquiry into costs or for a delay in further AGR orders. In March 1969 generating cost figures of 0.56d and 0.52d were officially quoted for Dungeness B and Hinkley Point B, but these were not strictly comparable with earlier estimates because the CEGB had in the interim moved from a 20 to a 25-year book life for AGRs.[33] As noted above, the AEA had long been urging a change in this direction, as well as a higher load factor. The Minister of Power now rejected the suggestion made by Sir John Eden that it had been 'disingenuous, to say the least, to have allowed the ground rules to be changed and go through as a footnote in a written answer'.[34] The minister's position was that he could have announced the change in book life before the Hartlepool decision, but that if he had done so he would then have been accused of bias.

Right through 1969 the argument about fuel policy continued, making it, as *The Times* said, 'one of the longest running debates in politics'. In March Robens again criticised civil service inadequacy in the context of fuel policy decisions, and again stressed the need for independent advice to ministers. The minister repeated his unwillingness to have an independent inquiry lest it shatter mining morale, but the cost figure he continued to quote for generation at Dungeness B was by now completely out of date because of the construction troubles at that site.

In April it emerged that the Coal Board had applied for permission to put up the price of certain coals, an application obviously embarrassing to them at a time when they were making special low-cost supply offers at specific sites, and especially since it was the CEGB which would bear half of the £15m increase being sought. July 1969 also proved an important month for the coal-nuclear contest. The minister told the Nationalised Industries Committee of a 'ring of protection' around the coal industry, some of which would have to go by 1971; the CEGB revealed that they wished to obtain consent for another nuclear station, at Connah's Quay in North Wales; and both the minister and Lord Robens addressed the annual NUM conference in Blackpool.[35] The minister promised this conference sympathetic consideration for the proposal that a Drax B coal power station be proceeded with ahead of the CEGB's plans for nuclear stations, but the following day Robens attacked both the Ministry's delay in respect of Drax and the 'veil of secrecy' and 'thicket of ambiguity' over nuclear power costings. The Dungeness B station was now, Robens suggested, no 'Pilgrim Father' of the new world of nuclear power, only a 'Tired Tim'.

It was again an embarrassment that in presenting his Board's 1968/9 report Robens had to warn that the NCB were incurring a deficit likely to amount to some £10m in the financial year 1969/70. This did not prevent the Board regretting in their report that in their Hartlepool decision the Government had apparently rejected 'a positive policy of preserving a balance of opportunity between nuclear power and conventional forms of generation'. This would have meant building coal stations on the coal fields and nuclear ones elsewhere: the nuclear-conventional cost difference would for a very long time remain less than the errors in forecasting. The Board's own output target figure for

1975 was reaffirmed at 135m tons.

Drax B had now become, as *The Economist* said, a 'test case . . . of massive importance to the miners'.[36] The CEGB meanwhile were pressing for permission to proceed with a nuclear station at Heysham in Lancashire, formal consent for this having been granted in 1967. The Government's decisions on these two issues were eventually announced in October 1969 by Harold Lever, Paymaster General and, as the second Cabinet minister in the Ministry of Technology, responsible for fuel policy after the Government reorganisation of that month. Lever, in a departure from usual practice, announced a package of four new power stations, two of them, Heysham and Sizewell B, scheduled to be nuclear, one, the Isle of Grain, oil, and the fourth, Drax B, coal. Only the first of the four was to go to immediate tender, the other three waiting on growth in demand, but the decision was seen as offering something for everyone, and the inclusion of Drax, the minister stressed, symbolised the Government's confidence in the long-term future of coal. One fairly typical interpretation of the underlying rationale found the two AGR stations unsurprising, since they were 'tried, tested and cheap to run', but saw the logic of the Drax decision in the 'psychological rather than objective . . . crisis of morale' amongst miners.[37]

By 1970 the prospects of the coal industry had begun to stabilise. The productivity increase was below target and the relative price increases approved in August 1969 had soon to be followed by a further flat 10 per cent increase. But in spite of this, confidence had begun to return. The Coal Board now thought that they could discern a market swing back to coal, not least because of delays and difficulties the world over with nuclear stations. Coal stocks had declined sharply in 1969 and it seemed that annual output could perhaps be held at 160m tons. Indeed, in the light of what was proving to be a 'less dynamic takeover' by nuclear power, oil and natural gas than had been expected, there were even fears of coal shortages.[38] Thus it was that the Minister of Technology was able to say that although there was agreement between the Board and the Government on a maximum rate of rundown of 10 per cent, the actual contraction was well below this and was thought likely to stay below, at least for some time. This was in the context of a new Act extending for a further three years, but at a lower rate, the financial support provisions laid down for the coal industry in the 1967 Act, only some half of the earlier funds having actually been used.

With a refusal by the new Conservative Government to allow a 12-14 per cent price increase for coal, a sluggish rate of productivity, an outstanding wages claim by the NUM, and an accumulated deficit over the two years 1968-70 of some £35m, the Coal Board's finances were again in trouble. Nevertheless, the Board could now afford to be a little more relaxed as regards the challenge from nuclear energy. The demand for coal in 1969-70 had been high, at 158m tons, 10.5m tons higher than output, and the 1967 White Paper was now said by the NCB both to have clearly underestimated the demand for coal and to have overestimated the contribution of nuclear electricity. The Board were also able to point to the delays in commissioning new generating plants, both conventional and nuclear, which had meant the burning of more coal in older and less efficient plant; to the Magnox corrosion problem, which had reduced nuclear output by some ½mtce compared with the previous year; and to the increasing flexibility of the CEGB's system, which made it capable of burning such additional coal as became available.

Coal continued in short supply and in December 1970, with stocks dangerously low, permission had to be given for the CEGB to import: 'as a turnabout situation it takes some beating' was one very fair comment.[39] 1971 quickly showed that this was no false new dawn for coal. In addition to the coal shortage, the oil-producing countries were now becoming firmly embarked on a policy of price rises, and the construction delays with the AGR stations began to make clear the short-term limitations of nuclear energy. The combination of cheap energy and fuel flexibility which had been the goal of the 1967 White Paper could now be seen as largely illusory, and the time had evidently arrived to rethink fuel policy. By mid-1971 the CEGB had decided to halt further power station conversions from coal to oil, at least until oil prices stabilised, and when in July Derek Ezra took over from Lord Robens, although it was known that he would soon face a very large wage claim from the NUM, there was nevertheless general optimism about the future of the industry for the first time in many years. Indeed, in their annual report for 1970-1 the Board described the prospects for coal as brighter than they had been at any time since 1957, and by the year-end the new NCB chairman was pressing the CEGB and the Government to undertake the construction of two new coal stations, one of them the long-canvassed, half-promised Drax B. In fact, for the first time ever in 1970-1, coal provided less than half of Britain's primary energy, 154.4 out of a total of 328mtce. But whereas coal consumption in 1970-1 was slightly above the 152m tons target figure in the 1967 White Paper, the contribution of nuclear power was some 4mtce below. Coal had come through an anxious time: it had not had the last laugh at the expense of nuclear power, but it could in 1971 allow itself something of a sober chuckle.

But coal's change of fortune was in no sense the result of a change of heart on the part of the CEGB. This can be seen by tracing through to 1977 the Board's evolving attitudes towards coal and nuclear power.

By the late sixties nuclear reactors were proving much more maintainable than had been expected, and contemporary designs were further extending the scope for repair.[40] AEA personnel had first entered the Windscale AGR in 1966 and 1967/8 saw the first occasion on which CEGB staff showed it was possible to enter a reactor (Oldbury 2) to rectify an installation fault. The Board's report for that year complained that 'the penalties of rising fuel costs' were 'plainly apparent' to them since they were major users of high-priced coal and of heavily taxed fuel oil. The Board also drew attention on this occasion to the support given to their confidence in nuclear power by the 1967 White Paper on fuel policy, stressing that this had been 'published only after a further examination of the costs of nuclear generation by a Working Party, on which the National Coal Board were represented'. And they pointed out that while £45m was available to the electricity and gas industries to compensate them for maintaining a higher coal burn than was economically justified, they, the CEGB, also incurred substantial non-reimbursable costs because of their support for coal.

Welcoming a year later the consent to build the nuclear station at Hartlepool, both because it upheld their choice of nuclear power and because it confirmed the less restrictive siting policy previously agreed for the AGR, the CEGB again emphasised that their support for coal remained well in excess of the reimbursement provided for under the Coal Industry Act of 1967. They were 'strongly of the opinion that practices so damaging to the supply industry should not be continued beyond the period allowed for in the statute'. 1970 once more found them 'deeply concerned' about the continuing upward trend in coal prices, and extremely anxious to be free to exploit whatever economies were offered by oil, nuclear power, and now, natural gas. With the predicted cost of nuclear power 'similar' to that from oil-fired plant, the Board said they thought it wise to mix the introduction of nuclear and conventional plant. Even the oxidation troubles which had now emerged with the Magnox reactors they described as only marginal in their effect on total output, this because of the high availability and reliability of these stations.

That the Magnox corrosion problem was serious and yet did not shake the CEGB's confidence in nuclear energy was itself instructive.

This problem emerged at a time when the Board were already experiencing severe difficulties with new conventional plant. In connection with Magnox there had naturally been substantial investigation of steel corrosion in hot gas, but this had mostly been confined to the steels used for critical components. That there might be trouble with the steel used only for minor components was first suggested by research done in the context of Wylfa in 1965 and confirmed at Bradwell in 1968. It turned out that there had been substantial corrosion of one particular quality of steel, and although this had been used only for components under no stress, it now became clear that over the life of the Magnox stations the effect had to be taken into account. The corrosion rate proved strongly temperature-dependent, and so in September 1969 the top operating temperature of affected reactors was dropped to a point where damage became negligible. This ensured the reactors would at least achieve their projected economic life, but the restriction initially meant an effective loss of some 700MW. It was however pointed out that even so the Magnox stations could still accomplish their load factor targets, and that it was really a hoped for 'bonus' which had been lost. The CEGB's attack on the problem included an investigation of the thermodynamic cycles of the reactors and, by suggesting a reduction in the bottom operating temperature of the reactors as well as that already made as an emergency measure in the top, quickly allowed the recovery of an effective 200MW. The financial loss to the CEGB caused by the problem was put at £7m for 1969-70 and a projected £10m per annum subsequently.[41] It was somewhat surprising, the Science Committee observed[42] in 1970, that the 'now obvious vulnerability of the bolts and associated parts' had escaped the attention of all the engineering teams concerned, a failing the Committee attributed in part to the fact that corrosion chemistry was not included in the training of engineers.

An accident in 1969 eventually led in 1970-1 to the shutdown of the Hinkley Point A turbines for repairs which cost almost £30m, and there were continuing delays in commissioning Wylfa, but the CEGB continued to see the 'economic generation of electricity . . . fairly evenly balanced between oil and nuclear energy'. Since it was now seen as necessary to limit the total amount of long-term oil-fired capacity, the Board said they expected that most of the increase in primary energy after the seventies would have to be met from nuclear sources. (The AEA had for some time thought that at least 70 per cent of new generating capacity should be nuclear.[43])

The CEGB found 1970-1 a particularly testing year. Following a 10 per cent rise in the price of all coals in January 1970 there was a 16 per cent rise in the price of industrial coals in the following November, and this meant that, including the rise in the price of East Midlands coal in October 1969, there had been a 40 per cent rise in the price of the cheapest coals in just eighteen months. Furthermore, as was noted above, coal stocks had deteriorated to the point where ministerial consent for coal imports became necessary. Finally, 1970-1 was a year of oil tanker and refinery shortage, and of pressure by the oil-producing countries for higher prices. In all, the coal price increases added £23m to the Board's costs and the oil price increases £20m. For only the second year since their formation they made a loss. The conclusion they drew was that: 'Experience of the last winter has reinforced the Board's conviction that they must have the opportunity to develop a more flexible system of fuel use which will save them from being the captive purchasers of a single or largely preponderant basic fuel — coal.'

In February 1972 electricity supplies had to be drastically restricted as a result of a strike by mineworkers and their picketing of power stations. This, the picketing especially, left an exceptionally bitter taste with the Board. They had been placed in an 'intolerable situation' and this was 'ironical indeed' given that the electricity industry was coal's biggest user. Oil and nuclear stations, though amounting to only about a quarter of the Board's total capacity, on certain occasions during this strike contributed half of the electricity supplied. 'Quite irrespective of the miners' strike and its repercussions,' the Board insisted, 'fundamental reappraisal of coal's place in the energy picture was already overdue at the beginning of 1972.' Their pattern of generation had to be flexible as well as economical, and these criteria pointed in the same direction — 'that of less reliance on coal obtained from a single producer'. The Board spelled out the roles of nuclear power, and of oil and coal, as they now saw them: 'Nuclear power will predominate in the longer term although oil will have a major place whilst nuclear power remains at the crossroads . . . Ultimately . . . the hedge against excessive oil prices must be nuclear power and not coal.'

It is important to understand why the Board saw nuclear power as being in 1972 again, in a sense, back at 'the crossroads', however temporarily. To begin with, it did not help that the Magnox stations were still having because of their corrosion problems to be operated at reduced power, with no obvious end to the restriction in view. This continuing irritation was offset to some extent by good prospects of increasing the Magnox fuel rating by up to 10 per cent, this in addition to an earlier increase of 20 per cent, though the price of Magnox fuel had also now risen by 35 per cent. Much more important than the Magnox problem however was the fact that delays and uncertainties in the AGR programme were by 1972 a 'matter of major concern' to the Board. This is taken up in Chapter 9.

Following a new Coal Industry Act in 1973 the CEGB stressed that, if the price were right, they could substantially increase their coal burn without new coal plant. They would remain coal's largest customer 'indefinitely'. Then came the winter of 1973/4 with its four-month coal dispute, the effects of the October war, and an overtime ban by the Electrical Power Engineers Association. With the price of oil trebling and that of coal increasing 50 per cent the CEGB felt their case strengthened for greater flexibility in respect of fossil fuels, and also for an early decision on nuclear ordering. They were still experiencing trouble at Wylfa but it was now that they talked of a 'possibly critical situation' with fossil fuels in the eighties, and of its being 'essential' to launch the 'maximum prudent' nuclear programme. They had in mind some 41GW of nuclear power by 1989, a target figure bound up with a move they simultaneously wanted to make to light water reactors. They also now saw a clear case for promoting a faster growth of nuclear electricity than was required simply to meet demand forecasts. By the next year, 1975, the Board were still protesting strongly at NCB price increases, this time totalling 130 per cent in less than a twelve-month, but 1976 found them addressing a quite new problem, a large surplus of generating plant. Coal prices had risen again, but despite this coal was now cheaper than oil. A further coal price increase in 1976/7 was, the Board felt, yet another 'heavy blow' after all they had done to help this industry.

This chapter began by arguing the importance of the Dungeness B appraisal in converting the CEGB from nuclear sceptics to nuclear advocates. The serious consequences for the NCB of the CEGB's conversion were then traced. But as will emerge in Chapter 9, the appraisal was a paper exercise which came to seem increasingly irrelevant from the late sixties onwards. However, even as this happened another development was occurring which in shaping the CEGB's attitude to nuclear power, eventually more than offset the disappointment of Dungeness B. This, a real development as compared with the theory of the appraisal, was the coming on stream of the Magnox programme. While the Magnox stations were building it was their high capital costs which naturally most concerned the CEGB, but as each joined the grid it was their low fuel costs and high reliability which more and more came to dominate.[44] Thus by 1973 the Board were emphasising that these stations enjoyed 'by far the lowest generation cost' of any of their plant. Nuclear investment, they said in 1974, was 'tremendously rewarding' as regards fuel costs — these would be perhaps half those of fossil fuels in the eighties. In 1975 they chose to illustrate nuclear's advantage by pointing out that although these stations cost £49m more per annum in depreciation, they saved £133m in fuel. 'Britain's nuclear workhorses' was how the CEGB chairman referred to them:[45] for a peak three-month period in 1974-5 the Board's seven fully commissioned stations had achieved a 98 per cent load factor, and over twelve years their fuel failure rate had been only 0.1 per cent. Still more dramatic were the CEGB's figures for comparative generating costs as given to Parliament between April 1974 and November 1977:

Average Generating Costs (p/KWh) of CEGB Stations Commissioned in Previous 12 Years

	Nuclear	Coal	Oil
1971-2	0.43	0.43	0.39
1972-3	0.48	0.49	0.40
1973-4	0.52	0.53	0.55
1974-5	0.48	0.74	0.88
1975-6	0.67	0.97	1.09
1976-7	0.69	1.07	1.27

The Government stressed that these figures were not of course a guide to investment decisions, but the appeal of the nuclear figures to the CEGB after 1973-4 remained obvious.

In 1977, the year when they first began to set aside funds for decommissioning their nuclear plant, the CEGB found yet another way of bringing out the virtues of the Magnox stations: Berkeley and Bradwell, they reported, both commissioned in 1962, had already generated more electricity than fossil plant contemporary with them would do over thirty years. After a prolonged outage and some five months work by a large team inside the reactor pressure vessel, even Wylfa was now back in full service. The CEGB's new chairman, Glyn England,[46] summed up in August 1977. The Magnox stations had proved tough, reliable and prolific power producers, and since the explosion in coal and oil prices in 1973 were more economical than ever. They were all now expected to last beyond their book lives and would automatically be kept in service as long as possible. The CEGB's corporate plan the following year even accepted that it could prove economic to install new nuclear plant before it was actually required to meet increased demand.

Notes

1. Cmnd. 2798.
2. *NE* (June 1966), p. 20.
3. HC 371 III (1967-8), p. 92.
4. Lord Robens, *Ten Year Stint* (Cassell, London, 1972), p. 179. Many of Lord Robens's speeches, and those of his opponents, were widely reported in the press between 1966 and 1970, and there was also much editorial coverage. This chapter draws heavily on the author's cuttings from this period but only the most important instances are separately cited.
5. For example, Sir John Hacking, *NP* (August 1958), p. 376.
6. HC 371-II (1967-8), memo p. 135, paras. 17-19; Qs 508, 529.
7. Robens, *Ten Year Stint*, p. 215.
8. HC 381 (1966-7), Appendix 44; Qs 1307, 1334.
9. HC 381 (1966-7), pp. 271-98.
10. *New Statesman*, 19 November 1965, and Michael Posner, *Fuel Policy* (Macmillan, London, 1973).
11. Lord Robens, 'Consider the Record', NUM (Eastbourne), 6 July 1967; *The Times*, 24 June 1967.
12. *The Times*, 2 June 1967.
13. HCD 750 c.1865.
14. Sir William Penney, 'The Future of Nuclear Power as Seen from the UK', *Atom* (January 1967), pp. 5-11.
15. *The Times*, 4 and 6 October 1967.
16. Klaub B. Stadie, 'The Implications of Generalized Nuclear Power Cost Comparisons', Symposium 9, 13 October, paper 13 (ENEA, Paris, 1967).
17. *The Times*, 20 October 1967.
18. *The Times*, 15 November 1967; *Financial Times*, 10 November 1967; *Observer*, 12 November 1967; *Guardian*, 13 November 1967.
19. Cmnd. 3438; see also P. Lesley Cook and A.J. Surrey, *Energy Policy* (Martin Robertson, London, 1977), Ch. 2 for another retrospective view.
20. *The Times*, 15 and 19 November 1967; *Financial Times*, 15 November 1967.
21. HLD 289 c.143.
22. For example, *Financial Times*, 6 March, 18 May 1968.
23. Richard E. Caves and associates, *Britain's Economic Prospects* (The Brookings Institution, Washington, 1968), pp. 390, 393, 397, 493.
24. HC 314 (1967-8).
25. Tam Dalyell, *New Scientist*, 22 August 1968; also 5 September 1968.
26. 8, 9, 12 and 14 August 1968.
27. *Atom* (October 1968), pp. 258-9.
28. *Financial Times*, 23 August 1968.
29. *Financial Times*, 25 January 1968. Robens, *Ten Year Stint*, p. 79.
30. HC 381-XVII (1966-7) pp. 314-34.
31. HC 40 (1968-9); also HCD 758 c.235; HCD 798 c.256-7 (WA).
32. *The Times*, 24 December 1968; Robens, *Ten Year Stint*, p. 173.
33. HCD 756 c.185 (WA); HCD 759 c.187 (WA); HCD 760 c.51 (WA); HCD 775 c.70 c.515 (WA); HCD 777 c.201 c.1102; HCD 788 c.178 (WA) c.271 (WA).
34. HCD 779 c.355 (WA); HCD 780 c.52, c.260 (WA); HCD 781 c.80 (WA) HCD 782 c.97 (WA) c.1135.
35. Lord Robens, 'Working Under Pressure', NUM (Blackpool), 10 July 1969; also 'The Only Real Asset We Have', NUM (Swansea), 4 July 1968.
36. *The Economist*, 5 July 1969.
37. *The Times*, 31 October 1969; *New Scientist*, 6 November 1969.

38. *The Times*, 27 February 1970.

39. *Financial Times*, 21 December 1970.

40. See R.V. Moore, 'A Review of Experience with Gas-cooled Reactors', *Atom* (January 1969), pp. 6-22.

41. HCD 788 c.38 (WA); HCD 792 c.188-9 (WA); HC 108 (1968-9).

42. HC 223 (1969-70).

43. For example, G.R. Bainbridge and G. Beveridge, 'The Future Operating Role of Nuclear Power Stations', *Atom* (September 1969), pp. 248-62 (250).

44. F. Dixon and H.K. Simons, 'The CEGB's Nuclear Power Stations: A Review of the First 10 Years of Magnox Reactor Plant Performance and Reliability', *BNESJ* (1974), 13, pp. 9-38.

45. Sir Arthur Hawkins, 'Britain's Nuclear Workhorses', *BNESJ*, 14 (October 1975), pp. 293-4.

46. Glyn England, 'Nuclear Power – A Report on Progress', *Atom* (October 1977), pp. 254-6.

8 INDUSTRIAL CHAOS[1]

The Nuclear Power Group (TNPG) were very surprised to be beaten at Dungeness B. Other things apart, they had built Dungeness A and were thought to have an advantage on the site. They had not, their chairman later said, appreciated the effectiveness of the AGR design. In the mid-sixties, TNPG saw the consortia as 'the only sources of diversity and informed criticism in an otherwise monolithic industry', and were therefore opposed to a single British design authority for nuclear plant, which they feared would lead, among other things, to a loss of British design engineers to the United States. To the extent that such an arrangement implied a lack of confidence on the part of the Government in the efforts the consortia were then making, it could also damage Britain's export prospects. It was essential that there be domestic technical and commercial competition in the development of new reactors. There had, it was true, been merger discussions between the consortia at the time of Dungeness B, but it had been found that 'oil and water did not mix', and TNPG's position was that there should be a minimum of two competing groups working on a particular reactor type.

Nuclear Design and Construction (NDC) thought that the maintenance of three consortia was desirable if the work were forthcoming to support them, but in any case for them also in the mid-sixties two consortia were a minimum. They admitted that the consortia arrangement had not always worked perfectly, but felt that adjustments could be made to it without the need for radical changes at a time when the industry should be consolidating to meet the American challenge. They believed that the existing system provided the 'inestimable benefits' of competition at 'relatively low cost', and that going over to a single design organisation would save very little. It might be very unpalatable to the AEA when the consortia stood up to them, but it was to the country's good.

Atomic Power Constructions (APC's) view was very different. It did not seem to them that the consortia had the resources to compete among themselves domestically at the same time as they were trying to co-operate against foreign manufacturers. Immediate action was necessary to produce a single definitive design for both the domestic and the export market. It was 'absurd' to separate the design of the reactor core from that of the fuel, and this implied a single small design group composed of senior people who would lay down the three or four most basic parameters. The onus in this matter would lie with the AEA, though the consortia and the CEGB would be associated with the decisions. Responsibility would then be taken up by private industry, and here it was necessary to retain three groups, but they would behave not as the consortia had done but instead as architect-engineer organisations along American lines. It would be their task to integrate a given basic design into a total 'reactor island', or overall station layout for a particular site.

The CEGB could see no logic in APC's proposal since it seemed to them to mean that no consortium would be able in future to take the initiative as APC themselves had done at Dungeness B. On the other hand, given that three consortia meant a triplication of much of the design work, on top of the work already done by the AEA, and given also that on the programme contemplated for the late sixties each consortium could expect a contract only about once every three years, the Board recognised that the shape of the industry was capable of improvement. They had necessarily to take into account other considerations than those confronting the consortia. They felt, for example, that the nuclear boiler would gradually displace the conventional boiler, yet the four existing British manufacturers of the latter were already in their view too many. Then again, it had for some time been their intention to move away from turnkey contracts – they might in fact have done this from the first with the AGR had it not been for the opposition of the consortia and the impossibility of comparing a 'separated-out' AGR tender with a turnkey BWR or PWR. But they had informed the consortia that a change in this regard was likely and they were, they said in 1967, simply waiting for the right moment to make it so as neither to harm export prospects nor to lose the special competence the consortia had built up. So far as the actual number of consortia was concerned the Board looked for evolution via a process of 'argument, erosion and optimisation'. Their guiding principle was clear: 'We must have competition . . . unless [the cost of] maintaining competition is too high'. That it was expensive to maintain competition they fully accepted, and in one effort to reduce costs they had asked the AEA to investigate ways of reducing the complexity they (the Board) wrote into their design requirements.

By mid-1967 the AEA had evolved what they described as 'very tentative conclusions' in regard to the future of the nuclear industry. In fact, their conclusions as presented to the Science Committee at that time gave every appearance of being considerably firmer than this, and furthermore, they differed significantly from the proposals of the CEGB. The essence of the Authority's case was that, while making due allowance for the virtues of competition in design, the likely increased size of future nuclear stations and the correspondingly lower frequency of ordering made it desirable to establish a single new organisation. The urgent need to concentrate the export effort, since already the British Nuclear Export Executive set up in 1966 was not proving an adequate arrangement, also in the Authority's view pointed to the same conclusion. The new organisation the Authority saw as being formed from part of the Reactor Group, together with such industrial interests as wished to participate, including interests not represented in the consortia. This joint company would then take over from the AEA and the consortia essentially their complete capabilities in respect of commercial and near-commercial reactor systems. Responsibility for equipment manufacture and plant construction would remain with industry, and that for fuel with the resultingly slimmed-down AEA. The Authority suggested that they should be 'a substantial, not necessarily a majority' shareholder in the new organisation, but they did not see this as extending the boundaries of their remit, in that the new company would have its own independent management. In its relationship with the CEGB the new body would put forward detailed designs for the reactor island of a nuclear station, but the Board would have the responsibility for placing contracts, the objective being to bring the procedure for nuclear stations as quickly and as completely as possible into line with that for conventional stations. On the design side the Authority recognised that there was a sense in which the element of competition would be lost, but on the construction side, with the consortia no longer able to influence the placing of sub-contracts, competition would, the Authority thought, be enhanced. To extend it further Lord Penney would even have welcomed offers from overseas, even down to such components as turbo-alternators, provided only that it proved possible to ensure such offers were not subsidised.

In their views on the future structure of the nuclear industry the AEA and the CEGB were thus in 1967 in opposition. The CEGB felt that the AEA's proposals went too far in that they carried the AEA into areas where the latter enjoyed no longstanding pre-eminence, in that they effectively removed technical competition, and in that they left industry the role only of non-creative component-makers. The Board's counter-proposal looked to the Authority to act as consultants on the first station of each new type, specifying the nuclear island in detail for this station but increasingly generally in respect of subsequent stations, thereby permitting industry a growing freedom to innovate. 'Industry' in this context was to consist of at least two groups. The advantages the Board claimed for their scheme were that it offered the best way of guaranteeing sound and advanced basic design without duplication, while at the same time allowing competition in the development of this design and in the incorporation by industry of the results of practical experience as this was gained. The CEGB saw their scheme as bringing together 'by well-understood methods' what was best in the public and the private sections of the nuclear industry, and as being consistent with their objective of ending turnkey nuclear contracts. The export market was not of course the CEGB's concern, but even here they thought the Authority's proposal inferior to their own.

The CEGB's case was somewhat weakened by the fact that they had negotiated the second AGR station, Hinkley Point B, directly with TNPG rather than inviting open competition. This they had done they said because they had judged that APC had their hands full with Dungeness B, and NDC with Wylfa and the working up of a new AGR design. In the event, delay in receiving ministerial consent meant that there would have been time to allow competition at Hinkley B, but the CEGB said they had not anticipated this. As it happened, in the Magnox programme Hinkley Point A had also been a negotiated contract.

The proposals of the AEA, the CEGB and the consortia which have been outlined here for the most part emerged clearly from the evidence these bodies gave to the Science Committee during that Committee's inquiry of 1967, and in their report the Science Committee felt that they should put forward their own recommendation on the reorganisation question. In fact it was only on this question that the members of the Committee divided along party lines, six Labour members and the one Liberal voting for a single nuclear boiler company, with five Conservatives voting against. The majority based their recommendation on a combination of two types of factor, market prospects and practical considerations. It seemed to them that genuine competition between two or more companies was ruled out on both counts, that is, because of an insufficiency of orders and because of the fact that the AEA needs must participate closely in both. The Conservatives based their opposition to a single organisation on a number of points, in particular the many uncertainties still surrounding the nuclear industry and the known views of the CEGB. Among the uncertainties the Conservative minority cited were the scale and pace of the British nuclear programme, the size and type of reactors, the possibilities of cross-frontier links, and structural changes in the British electrical engineering industry. They were unhappy with the idea of a monopoly which could exclude interested parties, particularly when on the one hand it might have to be maintained by legislation preventing British companies from obtaining licences for foreign designs, and on the other would certainly require the acceptance of foreign competition in the domestic market without any safeguards that such competition would be fair. The Conservatives also regarded the single organisation as incompatible with two of the Committee's unanimous recommendations, namely that the AEA concentrate on research, and industry come into the development process earlier than had been the practice, and that nuclear station contracts begin to be treated like conventional ones. The experience of the consortia already demonstrated, these Conservative members felt, that more than one private organisation could work with the AEA, so that difficulties in that direction had been exaggerated. The Conservatives wanted in short what they called the 'market solution' in contrast to what the Committee chairman called the 'managed solution'. But members of the Committee stressed that their differences were not wide ones, one member specifically denying that they reflected the 'frozen political attitudes' to be found outside. The Committee also emphasised that their recommendation was not meant as 'an unalterable solution to be adhered to for all time', and Eric Lubbock, the Liberal member, had in fact changed his mind by the time that the report was debated, encouraged to pragmatism by the European links which two of the consortia had formed in the interim, links which he thought might not survive the creation of a single organisation.[2]

The Ministry of Technology had begun an examination of the nuclear industry in August 1966, the month after Anthony Wedgwood Benn became minister. In his appearance before the Science Committee in May 1967 Benn acknowledged that there were 'grave defects' in the structure of the nuclear industry, but asked not to be pressed for his view at that time: the problem was urgent, but not so urgent as to call for a rushed decision which might later prove ill-advised. The nuclear case, he said later,[3] illustrated a 'classic' British problem . . . brilliant research, generously funded and an inadequate structure for its exploitation'.

In his later appearance before the Committee in June 1969, Benn was more forthcoming. By this time the Committee's majority recommendation for a single organisation had been set aside and Benn was anxious to explain why this had had to be. It had, he now revealed, been his view too when he became minister that a single organisation would be the right arrangement, and when he had first met with the consortia in February 1967 it had been from this position that he had argued. There had indeed been press suggestions at that time to the effect that the minister was prepared to coerce the consortia into accepting his solution, either by refusing licences on later reactors to any recalcitrant company, or by ensuring that it did not receive further AGR contracts. However, Lord Penney had already described these as weapons only in theory and Benn now told the Science Committee that he could not have forced his view on the consortia because they might then have turned to foreign licences, and it would also have been a position of 'manifest absurdity' for a single design organisation to be seen to be withholding licences to British companies while pushing those same licences abroad.

What happened subsequently was broadly as follows.[4] In the autumn of 1967 the minister approached Sir Frank Kearton informally to discover whether, as chairman of the Industrial Reorganisation Corporation (IRC), he would be willing if asked to assist with the problems of reorganising the nuclear industry. Kearton had then for some thirteen years been a part-time member of the AEA, and was also on Mintech's Advisory Committee on Technology. Strictly, the IRC was at this time responsible to the Department of Economic Affairs, but this was a purely informal inquiry by the minister. The IRC chairman agreed in principle to help and in November, a few days after the Science Committee reported, the minister called him in and the IRC began preliminary work, a formal commission to them following in April 1968. The IRC were encouraged by the minister not to confine themselves to obtaining the views within the nuclear industry on the Science Committee's report, but to range more widely if this seemed necessary. In the early part of 1968 two IRC executives and two assistant executives worked almost full-time on the problem and in late April and early May they and the IRC chairman met with every company involved in the consortia, with some such as Rolls Royce and RTZ which were not, with officials of the AEA, the CEGB and the SSEB, and with outsiders, such as Duncan Burn, who offered to contribute an opinion. The IRC officials obtained reports on market prospects and alternative reactor systems and had confidential discussions with the consortia on their financial circumstances and European links. The view was formed that there was 'a strong case for reducing the consortia from three to two', but also that there was likely to be sufficient work for these two. A paper to this effect was presented to the IRC Board and was discussed by them at two Board meetings before a report was submitted to the Minister of Technology at the end of May. The negative views of the industry on the Science Committee's proposal for a single design organisation had been reported to the minister earlier.

In a Commons debate of 23 May 1968[5] on the Science Committee's report the minister, although setting out broad objectives to which he wanted any reorganisation of the nuclear industry to conform, declined to be drawn on the basic issue of whether there should be one or two nuclear organisations. His Parliamentary Secretary made it clear that 'some months of very difficult and protracted negotiations' still remained. In June and early July the IRC's report was discussed within the Government. The IRC's subsequent disclaimer that they were not the only source of advice was no doubt correct, but their assessment was in the nature of the circumstances virtually bound to be the decisive one. On 17 July the minister wrote formally to the IRC giving them a specific commission to assist in the establishment of two design and construction organisations to replace the three consortia and the AEA's design teams. He announced at the same time[6] that the Government proposed to put the AEA's fuel business on a wholly commercial footing by creating a public company to manage it, and he explained that it was the Government's intention that this company should have a minority shareholding in each of the two new design and construction organisations. He added that ultimately the Government meant to set up an Atomic Energy Board, with representatives from the AEA, the fuel company, the two private organisations and the generating boards, to consider r & d programmes, export questions and other matters of major policy.

The minister's directive to the IRC was not well received by many backbenchers of his own party, over a hundred of whom had tabled a Commons motion earlier in the year calling on him to implement the Science Committee's recommendation for a single organisation. Benn therefore met the Parliamentary Labour Party's Science and Technology Committee to further explain his reasons for adopting the IRC's quite different proposal. The main trouble was that the minister's proposal evoked the emotive concept of 'denationalisation'. Some observers felt that the minister had shown courage in setting aside the recommendation of the Labour majority on the Science Committee in favour of the Conservative minority, but his solution looked to others 'uncomfortably like a halfway house',[7] even less able to achieve export success than had the previous arrangement.

The IRC's immediate response to the minister's request was an attempt to promote a merger between International Combustion Holdings, Clarke Chapman and John Thompson, the first of these companies owning half of APC and the other two 22 per cent of TNPG. There were in the eyes of the IRC excellent grounds for such a merger, even leaving aside the need for nuclear rationalisation, in that there was excess capacity in the boiler-making industry. In fact, the IRC had independently been thinking in terms of a merger and the companies themselves had also for some time been considering one. A successful merger seemed certain and in presenting his annual report in October 1968 the new AEA chairman, Sir John Hill, described the principles as 'virtually all agreed'. But it was not to be. The precise reasons for the failure of the merger were to remain somewhat obscure, and this case is still one of the few in which the Science Committee has taken evidence in private session and permitted substantial sidelining. This was on the occasion of the appearance before the Committee of representatives from the IRC, itself the only instance of an appearance by this body before any parliamentary committee. The expressed reason for the failure of the three companies to merge derived from International Combustion's undetermined financial penalty arising out of the difficulties and delays at Dungeness B. Clarke Chapman's directors decided that they could not ask their shareholders to proceed with a merger when one of their proposed partners was caught in what they apparently called the 'bottomless pit of possible loss' at Dungeness B. In spite of this the IRC continued to make strenuous efforts to preserve the situation, but in attempting to find a formula which would have mitigated the effect of any loss on International Combustion's projected partners, although they offered 'finite amounts quite precisely', the IRC did not feel it right to undertake an open-ended guarantee. With 'great bitterness' they were then forced to accept that there was nothing they could do, their managing director afterwards referring to 'the disaster of Dungeness B' as 'a very, very serious setback'. But that the financial issue was not the only one involved was suggested by the remark of the responsible IRC executive, after the Dungeness B liability terms were known, that although the original scheme was now again feasible in theory, in practice it still was not. Clarke Chapman pulled out of the proposed merger in mid-November 1968, and the collapse of that between APC and TNPG automatically followed.

APC's position now became impossible. It had been announced in July 1968 that they were losing Colonel G.W. Raby, who as chairman and managing director had had so much to do with their earlier successful, but by 1968 disastrous, tender at Dungeness B. APC had also now

seen both their attempts to merge, with NDC and with TNPG, brought
to nothing. In the autumn of 1967, prompted by the CEGB, they had,
they later claimed, reached a substantial measure of agreement with
NDC. Their curious explanation to the Science Committee that, following that Committee's recommendation for a single organisation, there
had 'seemed no point in going ahead' with their negotiations with NDC,
must be seen as at least greatly overvaluing the significance of observations by a parliamentary committee. Thus it was in any case that when
the next round of IRC-sponsored negotiations also collapsed, APC
found themselves essentially excluded from the future of the nuclear
industry. They were unable to accept that the failure of the boiler-
makers' merger had been precipitated by the financial problems of
Dungeness B, and they rejected strongly all talk of a 'bottomless pit'
and of a 'Dungeness B disaster'. On the contrary, as they saw it, the
merger had fallen through because there had been a 'degree of disen-
chantment . . . after all, there was a battle over the control of the new
nuclear companies and it was not acceptable, quite obviously, to other
people who would find themselves no longer participating in the industry'. What they called the 'power game' had therefore been complicated.
Of particular interest was the fact that APC's new chairman, H.W.
Jackson, speaking in his other capacity as managing director of International Combustion, told the Science Committee that that company
had not been prepared to enter a merger without a 'clear understanding'
that the boiler-makers would take the majority interest in any reactor
island company. The Committee had however earlier learned from Sir
Edwin McAlpine, TNPG's chairman, that he did not think boiler-makers
were 'by heritage . . . people . . . designed to make colossal technical
progress in the nuclear field', their having, as he saw it, spent less on the
associated r & d than any other relevant industry.

Since APC had received no new order since Dungeness B and had
become less and less likely ever to receive another, it was hardly surprising that morale in the company fell quite drastically, almost a third
of their senior staff and a fifth of their total staff resigning between
July 1968 and May 1969. In the circumstances, it was inevitable that
they should seek assistance to complete their Dungeness B contract,
and this in due course took the form of an agreement under which
British Nuclear Design and Construction (BNDC), the new company
formed around NDC, undertook to manage the project on a fee basis,
one of their directors becoming APC's managing director. It was additionally agreed that APC's constituent companies would pay some
£10m compensation to the CEGB, that APC would remain formally in

being only to complete Dungeness B, and that they would therefore receive no further orders from the CEGB. APC had continued to hope for a complete merger with BNDC but it was easy to understand BNDC's lack of interest in sharing with them, especially since BNDC were bound anyway to pick up many of APC's remaining staff. APC, that is, the nuclear power interests of International Combustion and the Fairey Company, were slowly dying and the process while it lasted was painful to all concerned.

IRC's efforts to create the second new nuclear company were attended with more success, but here again there was a temporary hitch. This was Plessey's bid for English Electric, the latter owning 40 per cent of NDC. However, when the President of the Board of Trade decided not to refer the alternative of a merger between the General Electric Company (GEC) and English Electric to the Monopolies Commission, it was this merger which went through. With some adjustments, including a change of name from Babcock-English Electric Nuclear to British Nuclear Design and Construction Ltd, the original nuclear regrouping then went ahead in late 1968.

The other new company, TNPG II, was eventually registered in March 1969, with GEC, involved since their 1967 takeover of AEI and now also in BNDC, withdrawing. Both of the new organisations were squarely based on two of the three original consortia, neither Fairey nor International Combustion having, as it was put, 'found a place'[8] in either. The IRC and the AEA now had shareholdings in both groups. Those of the AEA, 20 per cent in each, were held on a permanent basis, though it was intended that they would eventually be transferred to the proposed new fuel company. The IRC's holdings by contrast were to be turned over as soon as possible: that the IRC holding in BNDC was 26 per cent and in TNPG II just 10 per cent reflected only the rather different circumstances obtaining in each of the groupings following the GEC-English Electric merger and the breakdown of the boiler-makers' merger.

On paper, then, the reorganisation of the nuclear industry had been carried through by early 1969. 'It will work and it will work well', Sir John Hill insisted.[9] But many practical problems remained. It was proving, as the *Financial Times* put it, to be a 'slow nuclear reshuffle'.[10] This particular editorial went on to add that 'the duopoly may gradually begin to behave so like a monopoly that the case against a monopoly disappears'. Getting this far had in the words of the minister been 'a very big job indeed', but he had not been 'pushed by events' into accepting the solution which had come about: rather, it had been reached by 'taking account of the realities'.[11] The Science Committee's opinion however was that apart from the elimination of APC, very little had changed: some forty AEA FBR staff had transferred to TNPG but otherwise the AEA showed 'little sign of a serious withdrawal'.

In January 1970 the Ministry of Technology published a Green Paper[12] dealing with the future organisation of r & d in government laboratories and in March 1970 a bill was introduced which provided for the transfer to separate companies of the AEA's fuel and radio-isotope businesses. The Green Paper proposed the creation of a British Research and Development Corporation (BRDC) to run the civil r & d laboratories of the AEA and Mintech, with the reactor development programme, on which the Government were to be advised by an Atomic Energy Board, forming the main element of the BRDC's programme: the distinction between the proposed Atomic Energy Board and the existing Reactor Policy Committee was not however made clear. In the event both proposal and bill were lost after the Conservative Party's return to power in July 1970. But as expected, with regard to the fuel and radio-isotope businesses, the new Conservative Government introduced substantially the same bills in December 1970. However, although as Opposition they had pressed an amendment allowing for majority participation in the new fuel organisation by private investors, the Conservatives in government, while still stressing their hopes for private participation, insisted on the retention of a majority public shareholding. British Nuclear Fuels Limited (BNFL) and the Radio-chemical Centre Limited came into being in April 1971.[13]

In late 1970 the Department of Trade and Industry (DTI) began a review of Britain's reactor development programme, with working parties on thermal and fast reactors.[14] The review body concerned with thermal reactors quickly became known as the Vinter Committee after its chairman, F.R.P. Vinter, a deputy secretary in the department; the other members were understood to be the AEA and CEGB chairmen. There was here a clear parallel with the Powell Committee of almost exactly a decade earlier. Also as with Powell, the Government declined to publish the Vinter Committee's report, on the grounds that it made use of commercially sensitive information, and Vinter himself cancelled a talk he was to have given to an industry lunch,[15] but the considerations which emerged from the report were in due course set out in a DTI memorandum to the Science Committee in March 1973.

Although the Vinter Committee's primary focus was the question of reactor choice, the Committee apparently found themselves forced to the conclusion that to discuss this in isolation from the structure of the industry would virtually amount to 'Hamlet without the Prince'. The Committee made their study during 1971, but although their report was in the hands of the minister by early 1972 no official statement was forthcoming until August. Inevitably, and again as had occurred with the Powell Committee, there were criticisms of the time the Committee had taken and of the fact that even people in the industry had had to rely on 'rumour and backdoor contacts' regarding the recommendations made.[16] There were criticisms too of the delay which resulted after the Committee had reported, and generally of the 'hiatus' to which they had contributed. And the official statement when it did come was really only an interim one as regards both reactor choice and industrial structure. With respect to structure the minister, John Davies, now announced that he intended to commence talks immediately, with a view to strengthening the industry by encouraging consolidation into a single unit.[17]

It took from August 1972 to October 1973 to carry through – and then only formally – this second consolidation, though the minister found it possible by March 1973 to reveal the basis of the new structure.[18] The solution which emerged was not the one for which the Science Committee were by now arguing.[19] They wanted a minimum 30 per cent public shareholding, with the remaining equity on open-tender and the Government 'under no circumstances' favouring any particular private commercial interest. They had been told by Sir Edwin McAlpine of TNPG that 'it would be a terrible disaster if any one company were to be seen to be in control of or influencing this new company unduly'. TNPG had nevertheless by now come round to believing that there must be only one British organisation, not least because there now looked like being only one fully European group, based on the German Kraftwerk Union, and not two as TNPG had earlier anticipated. In evidence to the Science Committee TNPG were not prepared to attribute blame for the continuing delay in carrying through the further re-organisation, but as they saw it the 'simple way' forward pointed to a straightforward amalgamation of the bodies with nuclear power interests, namely the two design and construction companies plus AEA/BNFL.[20]

Sir Arnold Weinstock of GEC in his evidence to the Science Committee in March 1973 also had some definite views about the future of the industry, though there were also points on which he said his views were flexible, and others with respect to which, because of continuing discussions with the minister, he refused to be pressed.[21] Weinstock saw the consortia system as neither successful nor logical. Under it, in his view,

firms interested in supplying equipment for reactors simply joined together and used the reactor business as a means of ensuring preferential treatment. A better arrangement would be a two-tier one, with
mixed public and private shareholding exercised through a management board, but not in such a way as to prejudice the effective management of the company through an executive board. Weinstock left the
Committee in no doubt that it was the latter which he envisaged as
taking the essential commercial decisions, on the grounds that policy
was not best decided by people divorced from detailed day-to-day
concerns.

Sir Hector McNeil, BNDC's chairman, took a similar line on reorganisation to that of Weinstock. Specifically, he looked for a 'much more
radical solution' than had McAlpine. This was understandable, since
GEC owned 25 per cent of the equity in BNDC and overall financial
management and supervision of BNDC was in GEC's hands. But McNeil
did think, given its national importance, that it would be very difficult
to allow any one organisation a majority holding in the proposed new
company, and he suggested a 51:49 ratio of private to public shareholding.[22]

The need for a further consolidation, and in effect contraction, of
the nuclear industry was expressed most directly to the Science
Committee by the new chairman of the CEGB, A.E. Hawkins, in
August 1972. The need sprang directly from the CEGB's downward
revision of projected growth in electricity demand. Until early 1972 the
Board had assumed a 5 per cent per annum growth rate, but the actual
growth over the preceding three to four years having been only some
3 per cent, they had lowered their target to 3½ per cent. For the
coming decade they therefore saw themselves as requiring only some
4GW, or three new station starts in addition to what was already
ordered, and of these they thought it likely that only one would be
nuclear, and that quite probably the fast reactor. They did not therefore see themselves having enough business for more than one nuclear
company — 'even if one'.[23]

Sir John Hill was clear that the nuclear industry's main problem was
still organisation.[24] There should have been 'less competition and more
replication'. Nuclear delays were 'little, if at all, more prolonged' than
ones with conventional stations, but they mattered more because of the
greater capital tied up in them. The industry needed continuity and this
led to the remorseless conclusion that there should be a steady ordering
programme.

The AEA regretted that what might seem the ideal solution, the creation of a British company along the lines of Westinghouse or GEC (US), was ruled out by the existing structure of the British industry, and by the inadequate order book. A simple merger between BNDC and TNPG was not enough, in that it would leave too many separate interests represented on the Board, and it was important that this Board run the company in the interests of the company and not, as with the consortia, in the interests of the separate parties. The AEA's deputy chairman did express the view that the new company should take over more responsibility for development.[25] The chairman of the Science Committee was to express surprise on just this point, that the first reorganisation into two design-construction organisations had in the event led to so little transfer of development effort from the Authority to industry.[26]

On his second appearance before the Science Committee in March 1973[27] the Minister for Industry, Tom Boardman, was able to be considerably more forthcoming than he had been on his first, nine months before. He now told the Committee that a variety of reorganisation proposals had been discussed with interested parties and that the 'overwhelming' opinion of industry had been that GEC should play a, or the, leading role in whatever new arrangement emerged. The Government had decided that there would be a two-tier structure along the lines which Weinstock had proposed three weeks earlier to the Science Committee. The main board of the new company would be agreed between the Government and GEC, GEC having 50 per cent of the shares, the rest of private industry 35 per cent and the Government 15 per cent. This board would then appoint the board of an operating company. There was to be no management contract but by agreement with the main board the operating company would draw on GEC for certain financial and supervisory services, and GEC would be paid a separate fee for these. The minister was confident that GEC would not on this account derive any unfair advantage — among the rights which the Government retained was the right to ensure there was no preferential treatment in the award of contracts. Boardman conceded that giving GEC a 50 per cent rather than a majority holding left open some possibility of deadlock. But to have given GEC 51 per cent he said would have turned the new company into a GEC subsidiary; yet on the other hand the Government had not felt it right, given that nuclear energy was now entering a commercial era, for the state to take 51 per cent — indeed the state holding had been cut to 15 per cent to accommodate the 'very large number' of private companies wishing to participate. This 15 per cent, the minister said, was sufficient to leave the Government the reserve powers they felt they must have, with respect especially to reactor choice, open purchasing policy, and international links.

When the shareholders of the new company, the National Nuclear Corporation (NNC), were eventually announced in October 1973 it was seen that all the private companies represented in BNDC and TNPG remained, with the exception of Reyrolle Parsons, and that no new private companies had entered. The seven private shareholders other than GEC were grouped in a holding company, British Nuclear Associates, and the NNC was of course itself a holding company, the operating company under GEC's management being known as the Nuclear Power Company (NPC). It was evident that the new arrangement was intended to be a much more closely disciplined one than had been the case with the consortia form of organisation, with direction firmly in the hands of GEC. The Government in particular had made it quite clear that they wanted so far as possible to get away from the consortia system: it was even suggested that they saw Weinstock as a latterday Hinton.[28]

The announcement of the creation of the NNC might have seemed the completion of the government-inspired reorganisation of the nuclear industry which had begun seven years earlier. But, just as the consortia had lived for some seven years before 1966 in a state of uncertainty, and from 1966 to 1973 in a condition of reorganisation, so the new arrangement of 1973 proved, with the reactor decision of 1974, to be considerably less than the final word on the structural question which had from the beginning been one of the main weaknesses of British nuclear power development.[29] For the 1974 decision in favour of the SGHWR led in due course to GEC reducing their holding in the NNC to 30 per cent. In addition, the NNC did not properly take over TNPG and BNDC until 1975, the Government then assisting with an *ex gratia* contribution of £1.4m. And even after that the NNC remained split between two centres, Risley, the home of TNPG, and Whetstone, headquarters of BNDC.[30] Finally, following the 1978 decision to return to the AGR, GEC indicated to the Energy Secretary their wish to withdraw from their supervisory role in the NNC. By then the three-tier arrangement, GEC-NNC-NPC, seemed to satisfy none of the parties.[31]

But setting these later developments aside for the moment, we can now sum up the place of the industrial reorganisation question in British civil nuclear power policy to 1973. By 1957 five consortia had been formed. Two pairs of mergers in 1960 reduced them to three, and GEC left one of these after Wylfa. There was however never really enough work, r & d and design or even construction, even for two, and the consortia were always the poor relations, uncomfortably sand-wiched between a public monopoly on the one hand and a virtual public monopsony on the other. Yet throughout the first half of the sixties the priority item on the nuclear agenda was reactor choice. Not until this was thought to have been settled after Dungeness B did the urgent need for a strong industrial structure become politically domi-nant. There was also by then a new general willingness on the part of government — as evidenced by the creation of the IRC — to involve itself in detailed questions of industrial reorganisation. But even so, after almost another decade the debilitating structural issue of the nuclear industry was still not fully resolved. In large measure this was because industrial reorganisation then proved not to be as conveniently separable from the question of reactor choice as it had previously been thought to be.

Notes

1. The opinions of the various parties are set out in detail in HC 381-XVII (1966-7). The reorganisation of the nuclear industry, like the fuel policy debate, was also very fully covered in the press: only the more important of the latter references are separately identified below.

2. Eric Lubbock, 'The Select Committee's First Report', *The Chartered Mechanical Engineer* (March 1968). HCD 765 c.1006.

3. HCD 765 c.951-1071.

4. See HC 401 (1968-9); HCD 765 c.973-4.

5. HCD 765 c.951-1071.

6. HCD 768 c.1428-38; also IRC Annual Report 1968/9, HC 286.

7. *Financial Times*, 18 July 1968; *The Times*, 22 May, 23 July 1968.

8. HCD 776 c.1317-20.

9. Sir John Hill, 'New Structure for the Industry', *NEI* (September 1969), pp. 717-18. Also *Atom* (November 1969), p. 278.

10. *Financial Times*, 10 October 1968.

11. HCD 774 c.485-7; HCD 776 c.1317-20.

12. *Industrial R & D in Government Laboratories* (Ministry of Technology, 1970).

13. HCD 808 c.1590-658; HCD 809 c.383-423; HLD 309 c.322-46, c.868-90; HLD 315 c.346-8.

14. See HC 444-i (1971-2).

15. *The Times*, 27 April 1972.

16. *The Times*, 10 May, 23 June 1972.

17. HCD 842 c.1491.

18. HCD 853 c.670.

19. HC 350 (1972-3).

20. HC 117-i (1972-3).

21. HC 117-v (1972-3).

22. HC 117-iv (1972-3).

23. HC 444-ii (1971-2).

24. Sir John Hill, *Atom* (November 1972), pp. 185-7; also 'The "Energy Crisis"

and Nuclear Power', *Atom* (May 1973), pp. 107-10, and 'The Increasing Role of Nuclear Power', *Atom* (September 1973), pp. 194-7.

25. HC 444-iii (1971-2); HC 117-vi (1972-3).
26. HC 117-iv (1972-3), Q 543-4.
27. HC 117-vi (1972-3) and HC 444-i (1971-2); HCD 857 c.287 (WA).
28. David Fishlock, *Financial Times*, 3 February, 1 May 1975.
29. Sir Richard Clarke, 'Mintech in Retrospect − II', *Omega*, 1, 2 (1973), pp. 137-63.
30. For example, Richard Masters, 'How the NPC is Being Organised', *NEI* (April-May 1976), pp. 58-9.
31. *Financial Times*, 6 March 1978. It was announced on 18 December 1979 that the NNC and NPC were being consolidated into a single structure and that GEC's management contract was being terminated.

9 NADIR OF THE AGR

'One more step in a gradual advance and not a sudden extrapolation from a small to a large reactor', was how one of the AGR's supporters saw the Dungeness B decision.[1] Another looked to the switch from Magnox to AGR as a 'smaller step than . . . in going from steel to concrete pressure vessels'.[2] These hopes were not to be borne out and the object of this chapter is to show why, the AGR having been selected for Britain's second nuclear programme in 1965, in 1974 the SGHWR was chosen for a third. This chiefly involves an examination of the opinions of the various parties to the decision in the period 1972-4. But it is convenient to preface this with a brief explanation of the SGHWR's role as seen by the AEA, and also with a short summary of the most important public critique the Authority's reactor strategy ever received, at the hands of the Public Accounts Committee, since this was directly relevant to the role of the SGHWR.

The AEA concluded in the late fifties that the expected nuclear demand in Britain in the early seventies justified the development of two separate thermal reactor systems.[3] Their attitude towards the SGHWR in 1962 was explained at that time by their chairman, Sir Roger Makins.[4] Following collaboration with the Canadians, and a closer study of water systems with the consortia, the Authority had concluded that the SGHWR concept represented their best prospect in water reactors, seeming to have better potential than BWRs and lower capital costs than CANDU. Makins found it necessary to stress that interest in water systems had not arisen because of doubts about gas-graphite reactors. On the contrary, confidence in Magnox and in the AGR had 'steadily accumulated'. It was the SGHWR's economics in smaller sizes which were attractive, and in deciding they wanted to build one the Authority were 'not thinking in terms of an insurance'. On the other hand, in the early sixties there were still doubts about graphite performance in the AGR, and also uncertainties about large steel pressure vessels, and the SGHWR did use heavy water instead of graphite as moderator, and did have as a distinguishing feature a pressure tube arrangement. Sir William Cook's opinion in 1963 was that the development potential of the AGR was such that it was 'going to set a difficult economic target for the SGHWR'.[5] The decision to build a SGHWR, a 'deliberate act of diversification', it was also said was 'not arrived at lightly': the reactor was 'born of intellect, not of expediency'.[6]

In sanctioning the prototype of the SGHWR the Government felt they were in part responding to concern over the narrow technical base on which British reactor development rested. The size of the prototype, 100MW, was chosen to enable the system to be developed 'as quickly as possible and avoid a further intermediate stage'.[7] There was not, of course, an intermediate stage between the Windscale AGR at some 30MW and the first commercial AGR at some 600MW but, as this quotation implies, it was always recognised that it would have been much more comforting if there had been.

In the autumn of 1967 an international conference was told that the SGHWR had gone 'well beyond the development stage' and was now capable of satisfying the exacting demands of electricity authorities.[8] The AEA were also confident that short construction times would be possible with it and, as the only body in a position to do so, they themselves in 1965/6 submitted SGHWR tenders to two Finnish electricity undertakings, the first time they had so acted. The prototype SGHWR began to operate on schedule late in 1967 and joint design studies by the AEA and CEGB that year confirmed the attractiveness of the reactor, particularly in intermediate sizes. Other studies, however, effectively ruled out a natural uranium version. In the late sixties there were AEA hopes of a sale to Greece, in a curious deal involving British purchase of Greek tobacco, and later, via The Nuclear Power Group (TNPG), to Australia. The Northern Ireland Joint Electricity Authority were also said to be interested in the reactor. In 1970 an SGHWR became a possibility for the North of Scotland Hydro-Electric Board's proposed station at Stake Ness.

The Authority's dilemma with the SGHWR was now that, hopeful of eventually achieving a low generating cost with the AGR, but believing also in the SGHWR for medium-sized reactors in the export market, they had to try to decide whether a large SGHWR could be justified in the UK.[9] Sir John Hill succinctly compared the merits of the two reactors in 1968.[10] The AGR was a high-temperature, high thermal efficiency reactor, ideally suited to base load operation, while the SGHWR had lower thermal efficiency but was very suitable for load following. The SGHWR also had a high specific production of plutonium and could be used for plutonium recycling. 'In my view,' Hill concluded, 'both reactors are the best in their respective fields and I regard them as complementary.'

The fourth Geneva conference in 1971 was told the SGHWR had now 'taken its place alongside the other LWRs' as a proven system, and the status of the reactor after five years of operation was detailed by four AEA authors in 1972.[11] They described the reactor then as being reliable, very safe, and flexible, and they stressed that, the prototype having been designed as a demonstration plant for commercial-size reactors, scaling-up called only for an increase in the number of already proven modules so far as the fuel elements and pressure tubes were concerned, and extrapolation 'well within the limits of normal engineering practice' for the ancillary equipment. It was a particular advantage that, unlike the gas-graphite reactors, most critical parts could be fabricated off site.

The critique of the AEA's reactor strategy by the PAC which was mentioned above came early in the seventies. The Authority had said in 1968[12] that a development programme was 'only authorised if, over a credible range of assumptions, benefits exceed costs by a factor judged against the probability of success'. And in their 1969 annual report[13] they had added that reactor development decisions were 'based primarily on comparisons between money still to be spent and reductions likely to accrue in generating costs', these reductions being appraised over a credible range of future assumptions, and the costs and benefits both being discounted to a common date. It was the reactor development policies which resulted from these criteria which were subjected to a searching review by the Comptroller and Auditor General in 1971.[14]

The Comptroller noted that while Treasury approval was required for the construction of prototypes, the Government had not otherwise exercised detailed control over the scale and content of the Authority's programme. Despite guidance offered by the Reactor Policy Committee, on which the generating boards and construction companies were represented, and the internal monitoring of projects by an AEA Reactor R&D Committee, the existing arrangements did not appear to the Comptroller to amount to an effective independent control over the Authority's use of public funds. It had seemed to him that if the Authority were required to relate their development expenditure to royalties, then they would have both an incentive to limit costs and a means of measuring their achievements, but the Authority had not agreed with this view. They saw royalty income as an incomplete measure of the benefits of reactor development and preferred instead to see resources allocated on the basis of economic analysis.[15] This involved forecasting electricity demand, the nuclear proportion of this, and the reactor mix 30-35 years ahead. The Comptroller's observations on this procedure were that it gave no indication of the rightness of past decisions on reactor development, and that the forecasts were the Authority's alone, since the generating boards had no need to look so far ahead and could therefore remain uncommitted. The Comptroller was told by the DTI that the department had no reason to doubt the effectiveness of the Authority's decision-making machinery for reactor development, and that the Authority's forecasting techniques were of a high standard. But the department did say they were looking for ways of increasing the responsibility of the generating boards and of industry in reactor development decisions, and they added that a new methodology of assessment was being introduced which would include the possibility of using foreign technology.

The Comptroller in his 1971 review summarised the 1954-71 costs of the Authority's reactor development effort, together with the economic benefits then expected from it. The costs were given as £20m for Magnox, £114m for the AGR, £25m for the HTR, £78m for the SGHWR, £205m for the FBR and £130m for other work, a total of £572m, fairly evenly incurred since 1954. The economic consequences of Magnox were still expected in 1971 to amount to a substantial loss, though with the out-turn possibly improved by the effects of inflation. The economic advantage of the AGR, HTR and SGHWR projects the AEA had estimated in 1969 at £1,000m, 1976 present worth. Sir John Hill told the Public Accounts Committee that these British expenditure figures were 'not large by international standards'.[16] The US was spending perhaps five times as much, West Germany three times, France twice, and Japan about the same. The Comptroller ended his 1971 report by observing that the gains from the reactor programme were dependent on the achievement of the AEA's development aims, and he added that for the HTR and the FBR, the systems expected to confer the largest benefits, this was 'still some way off'.

It should be said here that although there was much enthusiasm for the HTR in the late sixties, the AEA recognised that this reactor would have to possess 'outstanding features' if it were to win entry into the commercial market.[17] It was also largely with this consideration in mind that the emphasis in the Dragon HTR project was eventually switched from the thorium fuel cycle to more orthodox enriched-uranium ones.

In their report on the Comptroller's 1971 observations the PAC said they 'noted with concern that the Authority had recognised for some years that they had more reactor systems under development than were likely to be exploited commercially'.[18] The Committee said they had therefore wondered whether a choice between systems could not have been made earlier, but the Authority had maintained that a 'sound decision could not be reached until the development work had been taken far enough to remove some of the technical and scientific uncertainties in the different reactor systems'. In this connection, the Permanent Secretary at the DTI, Sir Anthony Part, in his evidence to the PAC had referred to the parallel development of the SGHWR and HTR as a 'belt and braces' policy, and he had admitted that there had been some impatience in 1971 that the two were being worn together for too long. The PAC also noted the large discrepancy between the AEA's estimate in 1969 of fast reactor benefits (£1,300-£1,500m, 1976 present worth) and an estimate in 1970 by a Study Group on which the generating boards and construction companies were represented (£220m). The Committee said they recognised the difficulty in assessing benefits so far ahead, but that they still thought 'rather too much of the control of the reactor development programme and the assessment of the potential economic benefits has hitherto been left in the hands of the Authority'.

The PAC were unable to pursue their inquiries as far as they would have liked in 1971-2 because of the two reactor reviews then being conducted by the DTI. They therefore returned to the subject the following year.[19] This was after a government announcement in August 1972 that there would be an 18-month delay in choosing a reactor. Of this delay the Committee said they were 'apprehensive' that the choice might be no easier at the end of it. There was, they thought, 'some danger that the complex relationships between the numerous interested parties . . . could . . . further slow up the process of reaching a decision'. The Committee discovered on this occasion that although the Vinter committee had found the thermal reactor situation 'extremely finely balanced' they had come out with a preference, but Sir Robert Marshall, Secretary (Industry) in the DTI, followed his minister's line in not revealing this preference. Marshall said that with hindsight it might have been possible to concentrate rather earlier on one or two reactor systems. Sir John Hill's view, again with hindsight, was that the five consortia arrangement had probably done more than anything else to hold up Britain's nuclear industry.

The CEGB's reactor policy in the late sixties was outlined by their chairman in June 1969.[20] The Board were not then actively considering LWRs since they could see no economic advantage in so doing, and also still had misgivings on safety grounds. The SGHWR they thought 'in all important respects developed to the degree which would be required by a power utility', so that a commercial SGHWR could probably be ordered for commissioning in 1974. The Board's interest in the HTR had been quickened by the possibility that it might be able to operate on a low-enrichment plutonium-uranium fuel cycle, and the availability of helium from North Sea gas they welcomed as making HTRs independent of American helium supplies. Fuel irradiation and certain design data had not been sufficient to allow them to encourage the HTR tender TNPG had offered them for Hartlepool in December 1967, but they saw the HTR 'evolving rapidly' into a Mark III gas reactor.

It therefore seemed to the CEGB in 1969 that both the SGHWR and the HTR could be adopted for commissioning in the mid-seventies, each offering a £5-10/KW saving over the AGR, with the SGHWR's immediate advantage in terms of its more complete development status being counterbalanced by the HTR's probable economic superiority in large sizes. In the words of their chairman, 'In such a finely balanced situation, the thought naturally occurs that both types of plant might be built until a definite preference could be established on the basis of experience.' But the HTR followed on more directly from Magnox and the AGR, and taking this and other matters into consideration, the CEGB decided to plan for its introduction, hopefully for service in 1975-6. They also decided to discuss with the AEA how they could both 'keep the SGHWR realistically available for rapid exploitation in the UK' and also help to ensure the necessary confidence in it for export purposes. (There was a striking parallel here between Sir Stanley Brown's wish to order an HTR as soon as possible and that of his predecessor a decade earlier in respect of an early AGR order.)

By 1970 the CEGB were further persuaded that SGHWR generating costs would not be as low as those of the HTR and they now looked to an HTR tender for an Oldbury B station to confirm the HTR figures. If the HTR's promise were confirmed then the SGHWR could be expected to have only a limited period of usefulness as a substitute for the AGR, and the Board doubted that the advantage would be great enough to outweigh diversification to 'yet another type of thermal reactor'. With the possibility of a first commercial FBR order in 1974, the CEGB were also becoming anxious that they should not then simultaneously be commiting a new type of thermal reactor.[21]

What meanwhile had been happening to the AGR?[22] Dungeness B having gone to Atomic Power Constructions (APC), TNPG received orders for 1,250MW stations at Hinkley Point B and Hunterston B (SSEB), essentially to the same design. The remaining consortium, British Nuclear Design and Construction (BNDC) as from 1969, meanwhile received orders for 1,250MW stations at Seaton Carew

(Hartlepool) and Heysham, again in principle to the same design. In February 1971 the CEGB postponed a proposed 2.5GW B nuclear station for the Sizewell site: this was to have been the first non-turnkey nuclear station. AGR sites at Portskewett, Stourport and Connah's Quay had also been sought. But no AGR exports materialised despite repeated high hopes and the formation of an AEA-consortia clearing house, the British Nuclear Export Executive, in 1966. Sir John Hill[23] was to tell the fourth Geneva conference that Britain had been short-sighted in introducing the term 'AGR' since the reactor was really an improved, or Mark II, version of Magnox. The avoidance of a new desig-nation might possibly have made better marketing sense, but it seems unlikely that this factor was at all decisive in preventing exports.

Technical optimism about the AGR continued until the late sixties. Gordon Brown,[24] APC's managing director, described the gas-cooled reactor in 1968 as 'the only system with true development potential'. From Calder to the latest AGRs reactor parameters had advanced greatly: pressure from 7 to 43 atmospheres, outlet coolant temperature from 340 to 675°C, thermal efficiency from 20 to 42 per cent, electri-cal output from 45 to 625MW, and fuel rating from 1 to 12MW/tonne. In addition had come on-load refuelling and the pre-stressed concrete pressure vessel, the latter making gross failure inconceivable. These developments in turn had led to a reduction in size, and hence cost, to the use of modern steam conditions, to decreased cooling water require-ments, and to straightforward maintenance. For the future there was the possibility of using silicon carbide instead of stainless steel cans, the possibility with coated particle fuel of the AGR merging into the HTR, and even the probability of a gas-cooled fast reactor system.

ICL, a constituent company of APC, later admitted[25] that because of the tight time schedule between APC's decision to tender for Dunge-ness B and the submission deadline of February 1965 'very little deve-lopment of the preliminary design was possible'. In addition ICL ack-nowledged that there had been valid criticisms about the scale of the extrapolation from the Windscale AGR — 'in particular the effects of increase in gas pressure and temperature and the full consequences of methane inhibition of graphite corrosion were not known at the time'.

By 1969 two major problems had been encountered, more or less in parallel, at Dungeness B. The first of these was specific to Dungeness B and resulted from distortion of the steel liner of the station's concrete pressure vessel. The distortion of this during fabrication was tolerable but further distortion during welding left inadequate clearance for the boilers. In the end the only solution proved to be the cutting out and rebuilding of the top halves of the liner walls, a costly remedy which inevitably entailed a delay of several months. The second problem also concerned the boilers. By 1968 the original design of these had been found for several reasons to be impracticable and the boiler casing, hangers and tube support system had all in the end to be redesigned, essentially around the existing components. The main trouble here was vibration produced by the high-pressure coolant gas, not in itself a new problem, but one which in this case had a highly significant effect both directly in delaying construction and indirectly in frustrating rationalisation of the nuclear industry. There had also in due course to be many other modifications to the Dungeness B design, and although they did not all contribute to delay, the more delayed the project became, the more modifications came to seem desirable.

Vibration induced by gas turbulence was in fact to prove a major problem with all the AGRs, and indeed with nuclear plant more generally.[26] Thus Hinkley B was largely finished in 1974, only two years late, when this kind of damaging vibration was discovered in the gas circuit, and with this solved yet another vibration problem arose with the gas valves. According to Arthur Jones, a director of projects with the CEGB, the 'enormity of the consequences' of this latter failure had gradually dawned when fortunately a solution was found, though admittedly one which involved 'watchmaking accuracy on great big stainless steel pieces'.[27] So serious initially had the problem in this case appeared to be that all relevant test facilities in the UK were mobilised.

Another AGR problem resulted from an unprecedented intervention in 1970 by the Nuclear Installations Inspectorate (NII). This led to modifications on safety grounds to both the Hartlepool and Heysham stations, the most important of these being the substitution of pre-stressed concrete for steel in the boiler closures, and the inclusion of secondary and tertiary shutdown systems.[28] By 1972 the CEGB also knew from experimental work that they had a new steel corrosion problem with their AGRs.[29] The Magnox corrosion problem had already led in 1971 to a decision that stainless steel should replace mild steel in certain core fittings at Dungeness B and Hinkley B. The new problem concerned the chrome steel of the boiler tubes and associated components. Unfortunately, the Dungeness, Hinkley and Hunterston stations, and the first of the Hartlepool reactors, were too far advanced at this stage to allow the substituting of more appropriate steels without unacceptable costs and delays. There was time to modify the design and materials at Heysham but otherwise the CEGB had to settle for what improvements were possible to the critical parts at Hinkley, while also accepting that the boilers at Hartlepool would have to be changed during the lifetime of the station if this became necessary. The Board's other initial response was to provide for a slight downrating of the reactors concerned so as at least to ensure their design life of 25 years. A contract for the investigation of helium as a substitute coolant was also let. Unhappily, controlling the corrosion of the chrome steel by lowering the operating temperature slightly necessarily meant a higher water level on the other side of the steam generator near the austenitic superheater section, where stress corrosion could be expected in the presence of excess water. It had also turned out that the addition of methane to the CO_2 coolant to control graphite corrosion led to carbon deposition on the fuel pins, and hence to a loss in performance, and there had as well been refuelling problems. On top of all this the CEGB also came to have serious reservations about AGR repairability, especially in respect of the highly complex area immediately above the core. Finally, the inherent complexity of the overall AGR design tended to exacerbate any weakness in project management. By 1973 *Nuclear Engineering* was describing the record as 'dismal . . . about as bad as it could be', and the morale of those working on the AGR as 'shattered'.[30]

R.A. Peddie, a member of the CEGB and a part-time member of the AEA, summed up the engineering problems with the AGR programme in 1976.[31] There had, he concluded, been insufficient industrial resources to design three prototypes concurrently and the greatest cause of delay had been the 'large amount of design innovation and the failure to ensure that all prototype features were properly proven before being committed to production'. Failure to produce and prove gas circulators had cost the Board £30m for their AGRs and the NII involvement at Hartlepool another £25m, the latter development having also lost that station its lead time over Heysham, so that problems eventually affected both simultaneously, with scarce resources also having had as a result to be spread more thinly.

By 1976, in constant prices, Dungeness B was 109 per cent, Hartlepool 72 per cent, Hinkley Point B 33 per cent and Heysham 23 per cent above their original estimates. What could be said in mitigation? Perhaps several things.[32] First, worsening the impact of their technical problems was the fact that the AGRs were constructed during 'a period of high inflation, rapidly escalating safety standards, and increasing site labour problems'.[33] Second, that the commissioning delays of the AGRs were much less consequential than they might have been because of the great excess of generating capacity in the UK in the seventies. Third, that although the Dungeness B appraisal remains a lasting embarrassment, the steep escalation of fossil generating costs, the thermal efficiency of the AGRs, and even possibly their on-load refuelling may all in the end confer important advantages: these reactors may also, despite their various corrosion problems, even exceed their design lives. Fourth, the purely nuclear parts of the AGRs have in any case behaved more or less according to expectation. And finally, fifth, when the Windscale AGR completed its first decade of operation in mid-1973 it had had the impressive overall load factor of 71 per cent, or 84 per cent allowing for deliberate outages.

Their experience with the AGR between 1965 and 1971 evidently taught the CEGB a great deal, as the conclusion to a paper at the fourth Geneva conference clearly showed.[34] The principal uncertainties in achieving estimated economics with nuclear plant, it was said in this paper, were engineering novelty, plant complexity, questionable replaceability, and use of materials where their behaviour was not fully understood over the plant lifetime. Furthermore, errors in assessing load factors and construction times could have larger effects than substantial departures from assessed capital costs. Where the cost difference between alternative projects was only some five per cent it was therefore worth expending considerable further effort on scrutinising the relative risks: 'In some cases it may be decided that what appeared to be the more expensive scheme will in fact be the better investment.'

R.A. Peddie, as was noted above, had joint AEA and CEGB membership from 1972, but the two-way arrangement, first established, as explained in the first chapter, in 1965, had temporarily lapsed when the two individuals initially concerned, J.C.C. Stewart and E.J. Booth, left the AEA in 1969 and the CEGB in 1971 respectively. Apart from Booth, the CEGB chairman and deputy chairman also left in 1972. The CEGB's other board member with AEA experience, L. Rotherham, had left in 1969.

By autumn 1972 the CEGB's opinion of the AGR was that it was 'inherently a difficult system . . . less economically attractive than was at first supposed'. In his evidence before the Science Committee at that time[35] the new CEGB chairman, A.E. Hawkins, identified the reactor's main technical problems as graphite-coolant reactions, steel corrosion, fuel deposition and endurance, fuel handling and circuit activity. (The graphite and steel problems were discussed above, and also fuel deposition, i.e., deposition of carbon on the fuel. Fuel endurance uncertainties arose from the build-up of fission product gas pressure in the fuel pins. 'Circuit activity' related not to the very safe operating level but to the collection of active oxide dust from the fuel in areas where access would be necessary for inspection and maintenance.) The AGR was proving, Hawkins told the Science Committee in 1972, to be a high-cost system which it was difficult to build. It had presented an unusually large number of difficult technical problems and the Board could not yet be confident that these had all been successfully overcome. More generally, the Board could not be sure of the AGR as a system until they actually had one working, but since they had £600-700m tied up in their four stations, 'these we must see producing power economically in the end for the consumer'. The Board definitely did not want to order another AGR until they had one of the first four working. With what he admitted was hindsight, Hawkins now suggested that the AGR had perhaps been 'adopted too quickly': the Windscale prototype AGR should possibly have been followed by a demonstration plant, a practice the Board might in future employ before going on to a full-sized commercial plant. The final decision to build the AGR had certainly been the Board's, but they had been 'very strongly' advised by the AEA, and 'If anybody was over-confident about the AGR it was the AEA.' By contrast with 1970, in 1972 the CEGB saw the HTR as essentially a new system with 'substantial' development potential, but also as a long-term rather than an immediate prospect. The SGHWR they now thought had less development potential than the HTR, and its other disadvantages included the problems associated with the switch from gas to water technology, the difficulties in ensuring heavy water supplies, and the other more general shortcomings shared by all water reactors. As the CEGB chairman succinctly put it, 'The SGHWR is . . . already out of date as a technology . . . a convenient stopgap if we needed one . . . we do not need one.'

In complete contrast, the Board now saw the advantages of LWRs as lying in 'their competitive generation costs and advanced state of development compared with other systems'. They acknowledged that 'some doubts' remained on safety grounds but 'every day, every month' more information was becoming available, and with 200 LWRs totalling 150GW being built in 18 countries, the Board were 'quite sure' that these doubts would, in due course, be resolved. The country should put everything it had into the fast reactor and not fritter away its technological capabilities following blind alleys. A satisfactory reactor system was one which could be 'built to time, achieve a satisfactory performance and life at a competitive price and still yield a profit to the manufacturer'. Ideally, overheads on it would be spread by collaborative development and export sales. As regards the specific issue of the next reactor to be adopted by Britain, the Board acknowledged that the

Government had to bear in mind additional factors to those which would influence them. Their position was that they had 'a very big task on board in terms of getting the AGRs working and fully developed', and that, since they saw no immediate need to order more reactors, there was 'no point in going into the argument' as to what type they should next order.

However, by December 1973 the CEGB's position had changed dramatically.[36] In view of what the Board's chairman now had to tell the Science Committee, it was hardly surprising that he received, in the words of the Committee's chairman, a 'very tough hearing'. For Hawkins maintained on this occasion that the time for a reactor decision, the time to order more nuclear power, had now come. Even more astonishingly, assuming a load growth of 4¾ per cent per annum up to 1980, and 5¼ per cent thereafter, the CEGB now said they wanted to order nine nuclear stations in the six years 1974-9 inclusive, each probably 2 x 12-1,300MW, and a further nine in the period 1980-3. Reconciliation of these figures with those the CEGB had given the Science Committee in August 1972 was not easy. In 1972 they had after all talked of only four nuclear stations for commissioning up to 1982, and this on the basis of a 5 per cent annual load growth. On the basis of a 3½ per cent rate, which in 1972 the CEGB chairman had seemed to see as just as likely, only one nuclear station would have been required, and this it had been thought might be a fast reactor station. Their changed outlook in 1973 the CEGB explained only in terms of a deterioration in projected coal and oil supplies, a small de-rating in the probable output of the AGR programme, and the need to withdraw more obsolete coal stations. Still more remarkable, Hawkins told the Science Committee that the Board had revised their plans *before* the Israeli-Arab war of October 1973, the latter having served only to add a special sense of urgency. No panic was implied by the Board's change of mind, he insisted, but he did accept that what was now proposed amounted to a 'crash programme'. He added that the change had been made reluctantly rather than with enthusiasm, in that he would have preferred on safety and security grounds to have continued with cheap fossil fuels had these only been available.

The CEGB also now had definite views as to the reactor they wanted for their expanded requirement. The AGR appeared to them even less favourable in 1973 than it had in 1972, and the four AGR stations they had built simply illustrated 'the inability of the manufacturers in varying degrees with this particular system to fulfil their obligations on construction time and cost'. The AGR was outside the international stream of reactor development, it would be 1975 at least before the Board had any operational experience with it, and several years more before its teething troubles were ironed out. Radical changes would be needed in any future AGR, and all in all the CEGB were positive that it would be a long time before they could again order the reactor with confidence. They had, they said, learned two hard lessons from their AGR experience. First, that it had been a 'major mistake' to extrapolate from a 30MW prototype to a 600MW commercial reactor; and second, that it had been a 'catastrophe' to allow what were in effect three different designs of AGR out of the CEGB's four stations. The CEGB chairman also made it clear that the Board did not like the engineering design of the AGR. It had already been necessary to de-rate projected output by 18 per cent in one case and by 10 per cent in the other three, and he strongly suspected that the Board would find it difficult to get an economic life out of the reactors.

On this occasion Hawkins was more blunt than any CEGB official had ever before been in public about the circumstances in which the CEGB had originally adopted the AGR. It had, he said, been 'under somewhat pretty heavy persuasion' that the CEGB had taken the AGR. Having now himself looked through the internal reports which had been written in 1965, he had formed the impression that there had even then been 'a very strong case for light water compared with the AGR'.

The CEGB's problems with the AGR in the early seventies need also to be seen in a wider context. Between 1961 and 1964 the Board had ordered 47 500MW turbo-alternators, though no unit larger than 200MW was commissioned before 1962. Five turbo-alternator manufacturers were involved, each working to a different design. The Plowden Committee[37] later described the Board as having in this case made a 'fundamental error', and one result was certainly the serious commissioning delays and voltage reductions of the late sixties. The CEGB's cumulative commissioning shortfall peaked at 13,635MW in 1969 and was down to 6,519MW by 1974 — but the rub was that the AGR units accounted for no less than 3,772MW of the latter figure.

The CEGB had not changed their view of HTR prospects during 1972-3, but in 1973 they were able to be more detailed in their assessment of this reactor. It offered 'possibly the greatest potential amongst thermal reactors' but considerable effort was still needed to develop it. The Board thought this justified and hoped it would be undertaken expeditiously, a full scale demonstration plant being built first, preferably on a basis of international collaboration. They were happy, with government financial support, to order one immediately, in fact regarding this as vital, and perhaps a second after an interval of three or four years to keep the design team together, but they could not rely on the HTR to meet their nuclear demand in the early eighties, and a substantial programme of HTRs should await successful operating experience.

The CEGB by 1973 did not think the SGHWR worth further development. It had been 'under the strongest pressure from the AEA' that they had decided in favour of the AGR and against the SGHWR in the late sixties, and there could be no going back on the fact that SGHWR had been set aside at that time. Although the Winfrith SGHWR had been operating successfully for several years it was of only 100MW and in that sense was obsolete. The SGHWR which had been proposed for Stake Ness in Scotland was a very different one, with substantial changes incorporated in it, changes sufficient to make it a demonstration plant rather than the first of a major programme.

As regards the fast reactor, the CEGB spoke in 1973 of 'disappointing progress', so that, by contrast with their hopes of 1972, they were not now expecting any fast reactor capacity at least up to 1982. The Board's general attitude to the FBR was now that it was unlikely to produce any significant reduction in electricity prices and that installation on just the national scale would only marginally improve world energy resources. The case for pressing on therefore rested on the overall merit of fuel breeding, and specifically, on judgements about the costs and benefits of capturing a part of the world FBR market.

It appeared that two other reactor types had by 1973 entered, or more correctly, re-entered, the CEGB's general picture, though only to be at once dismissed, namely Magnox and CANDU. Magnox they described as 'adequately proved' despite its corrosion problems, and they added that there was a comparable length of experience with it to that with LWRs, these two systems being, in their words, 'far more reliable' than any other available to them. But Magnox they regarded as almost 100 per cent more expensive than LWRs, and also as incapable of development much above 500MW, that is, to less than half the figure assumed possible with LWRs. CANDU they excluded on the grounds that it had not been a widely chosen system internationally.

All this left only the LWRs, and in particular the CEGB's new preference, the PWR. The Board now told the Science Committee that, given their need for a 'large tranche of reliable nuclear plant', they had 'reluctantly come to the conclusion that to meet this need economically and to the required time-scale they must seek from the National Nuclear Corporation a series of LWRs based upon American technology'. They had reached this conclusion because it seemed to them that there was no other reactor system which it had been demonstrated could be built on a commercial basis.[38] Some 40GW of LWRs had been ordered in the previous year and any British plant would be 'third generation'. Pressure and temperature parameters had long been standardised for LWRs, designs were proved, components were reliable, and these reactors were the cheapest available. In addition, more extensive access was possible for maintenance than was the case with AGRs. The import content would be less than ten per cent even for the first station, and would fall progressively. The CEGB wanted what their chairman called 'some bread and butter nuclear plant' and since LWRs were 'at least three years ahead of anything else' they were that much more likely to serve as such plant. They would be a stop-gap, the actual gap depending on HTR development. The CEGB were also impressed with the construction schedules they understood were now being achieved with LWRs. (*Nuclear Engineering* at this time found that a sample of 27 US plants and 18 non-US plants averaged 5- and 4¼-year construction periods respectively: the trouble as this journal saw it was that the CEGB's record on major construction projects was 'worse than the worst of the US utilities'.[39])

It is interesting to reflect here that if an LWR had been selected over the AGR in 1965 it would have been a BWR, and yet a decade later it was the PWR which the CEGB said that, as compared with the BWR, they 'marginally' preferred. France having opted for the Westinghouse PWR, following exploratory conversations the General Electric Company of the US were understood to feel there was no proposition on the BWR which they could reasonably offer to Britain to wean her away from the attractions of Anglo-French co-operation on the PWR.

Disagreement was inevitable between members of the Science Committee and their CEGB witnesses on the two most controversial questions surrounding LWRs, namely their economics in relation to their reliability, and their safety. Before outlining these issues it is convenient to explain the positions with respect to reactor choice which had been reached at the beginning of 1974 by the other main participants in the decision-making process.

In August 1972 the AEA indicated[40] that they still had hopes that the first AGRs would come on stream in 1973 and that they would then quickly establish themselves at the 'top of the league table' of economic performance. The HTR had considerable potential but was best regarded as a high risk technical problem, so that the Authority, always rather ambivalent about this reactor, did not feel justified in arguing for an immediate order. On LWR safety the AEA's representa-

tives told the Science Committee that they were careful not to criticise because they were sure that within a few years the Americans
would solve the outstanding problems.

Given that the introduction of the breeder would have to be slow
and very cautious, the AEA agreed there was room for an additional
thermal reactor, and their candidate had now to be the SGHWR. This
they represented in 1972 less as a new reactor than as a version of the
BWR with some important advantages. They also implied that, by comparison with the PWR, because of its design the SGHWR was inherently
safe. And they pointed out that unlike Magnox and the AGR, the
SGHWR was suitable for operation off base load. The SGHWR was a
'proven and established' technology which, allowing 9-12 months
working up, could be immediately ordered. Indeed, the North of
Scotland Hydro-Electric Board (NSHEB) having received an SGHWR
tender for their Stake Ness plant, the Authority implied that they
might have taken it had the SSEB approved, which in turn would have
required a commitment from the CEGB. The export future of the
SGHWR, in particular in Australia, depended on a domestic order. Only
in the sense that the SGHWR was ready for immediate construction at a
time when there was apparently no immediate requirement for a
nuclear plant could it be said to be obsolete. The Authority did not feel
it right to pressure the Government directly about the matter, but they
had, they said, strongly pressed the SGHWR's merits, through both the
Vinter Committee and the Department of Trade and Industry.

In eliciting the views in January 1974[41] of the AEA chairman, the
Science Committee experienced some difficulty. Sir John Hill made it
plain that he did not favour retreating to Magnox technology. If it were
a question of a 'single fill-in' station then he would rather an SGHWR.
The situation as he saw it at this time called first for an immediate decision as to which of the British thermal reactors, a newly designed AGR,
an SGHWR or an HTR should be commenced forthwith. Construction
of a large fast reactor could then start some two years later. Of the
thermal reactors it was evident that Hill's preference was for the HTR.
But whichever new reactor was ordered there would have to be, he
accepted, an interval of around two years before series ordering could
begin. A further decision was therefore necessary as to whether there
was need for a 'fill-in' reactor to meet electricity demand. But even then
there was no requirement for a decision binding beyond three years,
and Hill did not think the Government would or, by implication,
should, give advance approval for the reactors to be built over the next
ten. On LWRs he would not be drawn. He was certainly not prepared to

say that a move to these was necessary, but if the CEGB thought that it was, then it was for them to take it up with the Nuclear Inspectorate. Hill had asked the AEA's Member for Research to co-ordinate and make available to the Inspectorate all the Authority's information on the PWR. He did not believe that licensing authorities elsewhere were being irresponsible in allowing the construction of LWRs, but it was true that the problems posed were different in each country.

On the AGR and SGHWR Hill was more positive. The SGHWR was a very good reactor, its technology proven but not obsolete, and there were no questions about its safety. If it were adopted then there would be good grounds for close co-operation with the Canadians, whose not dissimilar CANDU had an excellent operational record. It would be a perfectly viable policy to build only the SGHWR until the fast reactor became available. But it would be much more difficult to launch the SGHWR in 1974 than it would have been even two years previously. And while important aspects of the Winfrith design could be retained, much detailed redesign would be necessary for a first commercial station.

Hill stressed that the particular difficulty of the AGR was that there had been no new design since the Hartlepool AGR order of 1968. He still insisted that the original commitment to the AGR by the CEGB had followed a truly objective appraisal, 'carried out on an absolutely meticulously fair and proper analysis'. It had been 'a joint decision completely'. Some of the AGR's problems had indeed been technical but the fragmented structure of the construction industry, involving the alternator and boiler-makers as well as the consortia, had also been a major contributing factor. The AEA had certainly not wanted to see three different AGR designs built, and had there been replication and progressive improvement, no question would have arisen of departing from the AGR. The AGRs had been a disappointment in terms of the time it was taking to get them working, but they would not be failures. The remaining problems which might arise with them would be operating ones, and there would be no difficulty in producing a tidied-up AGR which could 'fill in' as a reactor of established design. The most logical approach would be to continue with more of them before going on to the HTR, but since the HTR itself had almost reached the point where it could be introduced, the question arose of how far it was right to spread resources.

Turning to the views of private industry, TNPG in their final years were strongly in favour of the SGHWR.[42] It combined, they thought, the best of American BWR, Canadian and British technologies, and it offered safety at lower cost than did the LWR. It had been ready for exploitation in 1970-1 and such had been their confidence in it that they had tendered it both in Australia and for Stake Ness, though naturally no one else could be expected to buy it until the CEGB had done so. Following the Government's statement on reactors in August 1972, TNPG had established a joint working party on the SGHWR with BNDC. BNDC felt that the SGHWR design removed some of the safety fears attaching to the LWRs but were pessimistic about export prospects.[43] They really saw no reason in February 1973 to abandon the AGR, which could still, they thought, turn out to be a very good proposition. But it was the HTR for which at this time BNDC held out the best hopes, and they were therefore 'very concerned' that the momentum of HTR development in Britain should, as they saw it, have slackened following an unsuccessful HTR tender at Oldbury in 1971.

On his first appearance before the Science Committee in March 1973, Sir Arnold Weinstock was noncommital on the reactor question.[44] It seemed to him with hindsight that LWRs would have been a better choice for Britain in 1965, but this did not necessarily mean that the AGR should now be abandoned. It was true that £60m worth of reactor equipment had been supplied by the General Electric Company's Reactor Equipment Division in conjunction with a Westinghouse PWR being built in South Korea. This was also Britain's only commercial nuclear export for many years, and Britain needed a competitive reactor for the export market, but there remained safety questions with the LWRs, and the AGR might yet come up trumps. Weinstock hoped it would not be too long before a choice could be made, but it would not in his judgement have been responsible to make it then.

By the time of his second appearance before the Science Committee, in December 1973, Weinstock's position had very significantly changed.[45] Instrumental in this had been his talks with the CEGB in the late summer of 1973. (Lord Aldington, the chairman of NNC, also confirmed the impact of these talks.[46]) Such new evidence as had emerged since March, Weinstock thought, enhanced the position of the LWR *vis-à-vis* the AGR, but the critical consideration was that there had been a change in the demand situation. It was no longer a question of which was the best system, but of which system would produce most power in the least time. He had continued to hope that it would be possible to stay with the AGR but now thought it would be irresponsible to do so, since the AGR no longer had any prospect of competitive success and did not offer the necessary security of supply. Even if some of the AGRs had been in operation this would not necessarily have made a difference, though obviously the fact that none of them were was extremely important. In any case, the CEGB were not prepared to accept any of the existing AGR designs and a new one would simply add to the delay. The AGR was always available as an insurance system if the LWRs turned out at some stage to be unsuitable on environmental grounds. Weinstock would not acknowledge that the SGHWR was a commercially proven reactor – he did observe in a later interview[47] that it had taken Westinghouse twenty years to get from the existing stage of the SGHWR to where they were with the PWR in 1973 – but in any case for him the decisive thing was that the CEGB would not buy the SGHWR. The cost advantage of the LWRs was such that he could not accept TNPG's point that rendering the LWR sufficiently safe necessarily left the SGHWR with the advantage. Nor could the HTR serve as a stop-gap. A 1,300MW prototype of this was highly desirable, but there should be only one until enough was known about it, and there could not be a large programme until much later. Everything therefore pointed to the LWR. There was in fact no commercially feasible alternative in the short term. The LWRs were essentially a stop-gap, it was impossible to say how long this gap would be, and there were several reasons for thinking that in the long run LWRs would not keep their advantage. But as it was, with 300 LWR plants generating 250GW on order, ten countries using them, and future orders worldwide expected to run at 50GW per annum, an enormous stock of technology was at Britain's disposal. It was true Britain had nothing like the expertise on LWRs as had been built up on gas-cooled systems, and the National Nuclear Corporation (NNC) would initially be unable to guarantee LWR performance and completion dates unless these were backed by a licensor. Perhaps up to 20 per cent of the first reactor would have to be imported, including the pressure vessel at some £2m, but the nuclear steam-supply system was after all less than 15 per cent of the total station cost of some £150m. The four important decisional criteria as Weinstock now saw them were security of the electricity supply, development of the nuclear industry, collaboration fostering international trade, and balance of payments advantage.

At the end of 1973, asserting itself for really the first time, the SSEB differed from the CEGB on reactor policy in two very important respects.[48] First, Francis Tombs, the SSEB's chairman-designate, disputed the need for a crash programme of nuclear power. There was urgency certainly, but no compelling argument for moving immediately to a high ordering rate. It was unnecessary to run the risk of being stampeded into the wrong decision when fossil fuel supply provided a fair amount of freedom. Second, of the reactor systems available, Tombs's firm preference was for the SGHWR and not the LWR. The SSEB would have been reluctant to contemplate a further AGR at this time, but were 'less sanguine' than most about the LWRs. In buying an LWR one would be 'buying on the basis of expressed confidence, and the fact that there would be a large [international] financial commitment to the solution of problems'. And problems with the LWR there certainly were as the SSEB saw it, in respect of both availability and safety. The SSEB were impressed with CANDU, but, given Britain's access to enriched uranium, thought there was no occasion to spend more on heavy water than was strictly necessary. This was where the SGHWR came in. It was extreme and unrealistic to suggest this was not a proven system. The AGR programme had been a leap in the dark but this would not be true of a programme based on the SGHWR, where both fuel and pressure tubes were fully tested in commercial service, and where it would not be difficult to scale up to larger sizes. It was a pity the SGHWR had not been exploited in the late sixties, but it was still not too late. Even in regard to export potential Tombs thought that Britain was likely to do better with the SGHWR than with an LWR.

In his evidence to the Science Committee in July 1972 the Minister for Industry, Tom Boardman, would not be drawn on the question of reactor choice.[49] Boardman did however have Vinter with him and, in indicating the criteria his working party had kept in mind, Vinter suggested that the main arguments for and against the various reactors were well known, and that the real difficulty lay in the appropriate weight to give to each. It emerged that in assessing the LWRs the Vinter Committee had 'worked through the CEGB', using CEGB appraisals made in association with the AEA.

As was noted earlier, the Government, though unwilling to let the Science Committee see the Vinter Committee's report, did supply a memorandum outlining the considerations on which they were acting.[50] This identified the main technical points of comparison between the various reactor systems as being size considerations, steam conditions, fuel and general reactor performance, and safety and siting questions. The possibility of continuing to use the AGR in future construction was mentioned, but it was evident that this reactor's technical problems, with its construction delays, doubts about large versions, and its economic attractiveness relative to alternatives, were all points which had cast deep shadows. The memorandum noted that more was known about the SGHWR than had been known about the AGR when that had been commercially launched, and also that the LWRs raised new safety problems for Britain. It was emphasised that the customer cared more about reactors being built to contract and operating reliably than about development potential. And, of particular interest in the light of the position which the CEGB took up in mid-1973, the memorandum stated that 'A most important factor underlying the choice of thermal reactor is the prospective size of the country's nuclear construction programme.' The document concluded that the choice between reactors was 'finely balanced', and that developments in industrial structure as well as technology would affect the outcome. Thus it was that the Government finally decided in August 1972 to defer their reactor choice for another eighteen months, putting in hand, meanwhile, further SGHWR development, AGR improvement and LWR evaluation programmes to facilitate the eventual selection. They would, they said, have preferred to make a firm choice in 1972 but had come to the conclusion that this would have been premature. The parallel with 1964 was painfully obvious. The 1972 decision meant, *inter alia*, slippage in the FBR programme and a future for the HTR only in the medium term and as an international venture. It also led the NSHEB to abandon their plans for an SGHWR at Stake Ness.

In the reactor debate of 1972-4 the NNC was a force, though ultimately not a decisive one, as the consortia never managed to be in that of 1963-5. The Powell Committee of the early sixties as already noted had its parallel in the Vinter Committee of the early seventies, but the latter were superseded by a more formal institutional device, the Nuclear Power Advisory Board, on which all the major institutional actors were represented. The role of the NPAB is discussed below. There was also now the Science Committee, which produced two reports,[51] in June 1973 and January 1974, making recommendations on the structure of the industry, as well as on reactor choice. The Committee also, as usual, acted as a vehicle, forcing the more important bodies to some extent to react to each other publicly, and providing a channel for the more marginal actors. In addition, their hearings and reports informed and catalysed a wider debate.

It is worth noting some aspects of the Committee's approach. First, a single nuclear company having eventually come about more than five years after they had first recommended it, the Committee took pride in the soundness of their original view, though, as already explained, the industry was in fact ultimately reorganised along lines significantly different from those they had favoured. But a consequence of their having been, in the light of later events, 'right' when the Government had been wrong, or at least less positive, was that it served to increase

the Committee's self-confidence — like most such parliamentary committees they had from their inception in any case themselves tended to
value their recommendations more than their investigations. A second
feature of their approach in 1972-4 was their distinct predilection for
British technology. In their 1973 report, no nuclear order then being
contemplated, it was enough for them to say that 'it would . . . be unwise *at this stage* to do anything which might cause a rundown in the
UK reactor development effort: "buying American" might have this
result'. But in the face of the CEGB's huge projected LWR programme
of 1973 the Committee in their 1974 report found it necessary to be
firmer. No proposal to build LWRs in Britain should be approved by
the Government 'on the basis of the evidence at present publicly available'. To order LWRs on the scale proposed by the CEGB would,
except for the FBR, mean 'virtually abandoning the long-established
British nuclear r & d effort'. Even more in evidence in the questions put
to their witnesses than in the Committee's report, it is hard to resist the
conclusion that this preference for British technology sprang from
something more than the disquiet prompted by the safety aspect of
American LWR technology, and a more constructive scepticism would
in the circumstances have been more congruent with the role such a
committee must aspire to perform.

Comparing the Science Committee's reports of 1973 and 1974 it is
easy to see that they, like the Government and the construction industry, were the prisoners of the CEGB's nuclear projections. Thus in
1973, with the CEGB adamant that they had no plans for new nuclear
plant, the Science Committee recommended that the Board be required
to place a new order, the Government providing the necessary funds, so
that the newly-consolidated nuclear industry might receive a contract
at the earliest possible moment. But, faced with the great change in the
CEGB's projections between 1972 and 1973, the Committee concluded
that the Board had been mistaken in 1972, and that 'much greater
assurance' was needed before the 1973 plans were accepted. A closely
linked issue was the Committee's view on the SGHWR. In their 1973
report they described this as facing the 'overwhelming disadvantage'
that more than a hundred LWRs were operating or being constructed,
and they recommended that the Government 'undertake a serious reappraisal' of it. 'It might well be,' they said, 'that there is little point in
continuing it, sad as is such a conclusion after all the hopes of earlier
years.' But in their 1974 report, although they did not specifically
recommend which reactor should be adopted, they did suggest that 'the
way forward should be to use one of the British nuclear technologies

which is already proven', adding that 'in this connection we note the enthusiasm of the SSEB for the SGHWR'.

The Science Committee's treatment of the LWRs focused on three things: their economics in relation to their constructional and operational reliability; their safety, in particular the integrity of their pressure vessels and the efficiency of their emergency core-cooling systems; and the role of the Nuclear Inspectorate, an issue which it was clear any introduction of LWRs would throw into sharp relief.

It is outside the scope of this book, and also beyond the talents of the author, properly to assess the technical questions surrounding LWR economics and safety as these stood in 1973-4. It is actually not unreasonable to suggest that, within Britain at least, there was at this time no fully authoritative source on these questions. This followed from the fact that, apart from the PWRs in Britain's nuclear submarines, there was no direct national experience with LWRs. As the chairman of the NNC said in evidence to the Science Committee, everyone was in the position of relying on reports and newspaper stories. This is not to suggest, of course, that where there is direct national experience then there is necessarily an authoritative source in an absolute sense. Thus in 1964 the AEA were an authority on the AGR in the sense that no body was in a position to challenge their opinion of it, except generally, but as events were to show, they had thereafter much themselves to learn about this reactor. However, even in the limited sense, there was no British authority on LWRs in 1973-4. For the purposes of this book it is sufficient to outline the techno-economic status of the LWRs only as this was represented by their supporters and opponents in Britain in 1973-4. But before doing that it is convenient properly to introduce the Nuclear Installations Inspectorate.

The NII were created under legislation of 1959, their chief function being to advise the relevant minister on the licensing of nuclear installations (other than those of the AEA), their regulatory activity covering everything connected with such installations. In 1973 the Inspectorate had a technical staff of 67 and were headed by the Chief Inspector, E.C. Williams, who was also Chief Scientist (Energy). There had been many occasions before 1973 when the Inspectorate had exercised an influence on safety questions arising in the British nuclear power programmes, the downrating of the Magnox reactors and the design of the boiler closures of the Hartlepool AGR design for example, but not until the prospect arose of introducing LWRs into Britain did the potentially key *policy* role of the Inspectorate fully emerge.

The Chief Inspector appeared twice before the Science Committee in 1973, in February and in December.[52] The issue which the Committee were anxious to clarify when Williams first appeared before them was how far discussions between himself and the CEGB had proceeded on the subject of LWRs. The Committee had learned from the Board that there had been some discussions and the Chief Inspector confirmed this. He implied that as a precaution he had begun to initiate a review by his staff of American work on LWR safety, but from the figures he gave it was apparent that very little work on LWRs had up to this time been done by his organisation. There was, to be fair, no compelling reason why it should have been done, in that he had no occasion to take a view of any kind until he had received a formal application for an LWR licence. In advance of this, in his view he was the one man who could have no opinion lest he later be held to have prejudged the issue. Yet he did not feel there was any particular difficulty about the minister taking a decision on reactor choice before the Inspectorate had pronounced. As he saw it, the electricity authorities could put their case to the minister on a range of station outputs and, while starting ambitiously and downrating a reactor was costly, starting with conservative assumptions about reactor output need not be. He added that 'When the chips were really down, my Secretary of State would have to make a judgement as to whether his Chief Inspector was being unduly cautious or whether the Generating Board was being unduly optimistic, and it is for anybody to judge which view he would take.'

The Chief Inspector thought it was 'nigh impossible to get a real judgement as to relative safety between different types of reactor', and he urged the Science Committee 'not to get into a slanging comparison of the relative safety of different reactor types', a 'glass house situation' in his words. He did however think that it would be 'very unwise' of a generating board to announce an order for any kind of reactor until they were 'pretty sure' that they would get a licence for it, and he accepted that it might take two years to amass the necessary information on LWRs. Striving to remain unbiased, he observed that LWRs in large numbers had operated satisfactorily from the safety point of view, albeit there were restrictions on the operating parameters of most of them. For any new reactor introduced in Britain a cautious siting policy would be pursued, and it would therefore take 'many years' to get back to the confidence levels which had come to be attached to the pre-stressed concrete pressure vessels of the AGRs and later Magnox stations.

The day before the Chief Inspector's second appearance before them the Science Committee heard from the CEGB that the Board were seeking an approval in principle for an LWR, having put in a licence application for all types of water reactor on the Sizewell site.[53] The Board's position was that if they received government approval they would then be able to obtain the necessary data for a full submission to the Inspectorate. They had hopes of a licence in December 1975 and full operation by September 1981. The Committee had already heard from Sir Arnold Weinstock that he had no doubts, 'given all the requirements he will lay upon the supplier', that the Nuclear Inspector would in due course authorise an LWR on a named site.[54] The margin of advantage enjoyed by the LWR Weinstock thought so great that he could not imagine any safety requirements which would wholly remove it: the more important issue was the delay likely before the Inspector gave his approval.

Questioned about this, the Chief Inspector stuck by the period of two years which he had tacitly agreed to at his earlier meeting with the Science Committee. He might, he said, shorten it a little, but he did not see how he could shorten it by much. A blanket application of the sort the CEGB had made for the Sizewell site was a new procedure intended to shorten the planning process in the event that the Board elected to depart from their original reactor choice. The procedural change had been agreed between the CEGB and the Electricity Division of the DTI.

It emerged that, the CEGB's preference for the LWR having been declared after their blanket submission, there had still been no detailed discussions between the Board and the NII, nor had LWRs been considered by the Nuclear Safety Advisory Committee. Before he could 'talk turkey' with the CEGB, Williams made it plain he would have to see the actual LWR design the CEGB were proposing. It was apparent to him that he might have to redeploy his staff 'very rapidly' onto LWRs in that there would be 'a devil of a lot of work' to be done if the CEGB's choice settled upon them, and he was already recruiting more staff in connection with this possibility. Unique among nuclear regulatory authorities, the Inspectorate would be starting from scratch on LWRs. As it was, the only advice on LWRs that he had given the Secretary of State was that it would take him quite a long time to formulate any advice at all. Until then the CEGB could have no assurance that he would approve LWRs. It was not his business to know on what the CEGB and NNC's existing confidence in LWRs was based. His Inspectorate would not issue an initial licence unless they believed the project likely to be acceptable from a safety viewpoint right through to the end. Nor, 'unless specifically instructed otherwise', would they wish to depart from their normal approach involving discussions 'in considerable detail' with the generating board, designers and manufacturers. The Chief Inspector told the Science Committee that for much of nuclear technology there was no way of gaining experimental evidence except on a real reactor. As well as using all overseas information he would insist on re-examining all data, recalculating all theoretical calculations, and if necessary would even resort to having the AEA or some other authority carry out experiments for him. Still struggling to preserve his impartiality, he also this time ventured some more specific remarks on LWRs. Not the least significant of these was that he would expect to insist on the CEGB's importing, at least at the outset, most of the pressure parts of any LWRs they might build. He accepted that a programme of standardisation was beginning in the United States, but there was 'no such thing' as a 'bread and butter reactor', the expression the CEGB chairman had used before the Science Committee the previous day.

One of the two main uncertainties surrounding LWRs as seen from Britain in 1973-4 concerned their economics in the context of their operational status. In mid-1972 the Science Committee were informed by the CEGB and the DTI that there were some 200 LWRs totalling 150GW being built in some eighteen countries, 11GW of LWR capacity already being in operation and 1971 orders for LWRs amounting to 41GW.[55] In December 1973 the CEGB updated these figures, quoting 26 BWRs and 49 PWRs totalling 82GW as having been ordered since August 1972.[56] At the same time the Board gave comparative figures for the various reactor systems in a twin 1,320MW power station (4 x 500-600MW in the case of Magnox). Construction costs, electricity costs in p/KWh, and total present worth were projected to be as follows:

Magnox £500m, 0.72, £366/KW; AGR £400m, 0.57, £293/KW; SGHWR £-, 0.51, £262/KW; PWR £300m, 0.46, £233/KW.

The CEGB further claimed that their PWR figures were conservative, in particular in that they assumed a fuel rating 25 per cent below that of plants actually running at full capacity, and in that they allowed for 'the modifications thought to be necessary to meet British safety standards'. Sir Arnold Weinstock thought 'quite a lot of work' would have to be done to make an LWR design suitable for Britain, and Tombs of the SSEB felt it was easy to underestimate the difficulty in translating foreign designs to British practice, but the CEGB chairman stressed that there was no intention of redesigning. The Board's plan was simply to take Westinghouse's latest design, much of the technology necessary to make it suitable for British conditions being already in existence. The chairman of the NNC acknowledged that if the Inspectorate required 'very significant changes' to the LWR, an hypothesis he evidently thought unlikely, then the case for building LWRs was 'not proven'.

As regards load factors and reactor sizes, a discrepancy emerged between the CEGB and SSEB figures. The CEGB referred to LWRs and Magnox as having achieved load factors of just above and just below 60 per cent respectively, but the SSEB talked of 60 and 80 per cent. The SSEB thought in-service experience with LWRs 'very limited' and compared the 200 reactor years of experience registered by Magnox with only about 20 reactor years for large PWRs. Their figures were supported on this point by the Chief Nuclear Inspector, who quoted the total reactor years of experience with PWRs above 500MW as only seven and a half. But the CEGB chose to stress operating experience in all sizes, on which basis their figures showed that there was a total experience of 90GW years with 47 LWR reactors compared with 50GW years with 27 Magnox ones. However, the CEGB figures did also show that there had been only 26 reactor years of experience with LWR reactors above 600MW operating at an annual load factor of 50 per cent or above.

That substantial delays had occurred in commissioning LWRs the CEGB chairman accepted, but he implicitly agreed with Sir Arnold Weinstock that 'any date postulated for a light water reactor is intrinsically more reliable than that postulated for any other type of reactor'. The NNC chairman said he understood there had been virtually no delays in the United States comparable to those which had been experienced with the AGRs.

Safety was the second main LWR uncertainty in 1973-4. The Chief Nuclear Inspector told the Science Committee in December 1973 that the sum total of the technical information he had received from the CEGB on their proposed LWR was contained in the wording of their blanket application for Sizewell B. This simply referred to provisions for the reactors and their associated primary cooling circuit to be 'suitable contained', a phrase which he agreed begged an enormous number of questions. Williams identified for the Committee the three most important safety questions attaching to LWRs. These were the integrity of the reactor pressure vessel, the emergency core-cooling system (ECCS), and what he described as a relatively new issue, the functioning of the automatic emergency shutdown arrangements under certain special conditions. Belief in the validity of existing designs of ECCS was 'entirely theoretical', laboratory testing having provided little real information, but the US Atomic Energy Commission (AEC) were building a test reactor to confirm the system. Of the emergency shutdown arrangements the Inspector said he had heard a new set of requirements were to be imposed by the AEC which it was his understanding would be 'very much more difficult' to meet on the PWR than on the BWR. As to pressure vessel integrity, it was the 'cardinal assumption' of LWR designs that the pressure vessel would not fail catastrophically, and so no provision was made against its doing so. But there was 'some foundation for concern' here in that 'a number of eminent metallurgists' rejected the fundamental assumption. It might be possible to put the reactor into a pre-stressed concrete pressure vessel, though he believed this to be 'very, very difficult', or to satisfy the Inspectorate over pressure vessel containment in some other way. There was even apparently a 'magic gadget' called a core-catcher which might serve, but he still had to learn about this.

The Chief Inspector tacitly encouraged the Science Committee to take up pressure vessel integrity with the Government's Chief Scientist, Sir Alan Cottrell, an internationally distinguished metallurgist, and in due course Cottrell submitted a memorandum.[57] The essence of his professional opinion was that rapid and catastrophic failure of steel pressure vessels was possible, that Magnox reactors with such vessels enjoyed the safety feature that they would leak before breaking, but that LWR pressure vessels, because they had to be made of much harder steel, lacked this failsafe advantage. Cottrell's conclusion was that it was 'a matter of judgement, for those with responsibilities for reactor safety, of the conditions under which it is justifiable to waive the need for the leak-before-break feature'. In these circumstances security of an LWR pressure vessel depended on stringent manufacturing standards, proof-testing at 125 per cent of design pressure before bringing the vessel into service, and thorough and regular examination of the vessel by a special crack-detection technique. There appeared to be good prospects of such a technique being available, but because of the 'unique requirement to eliminate all possibility of major failure' this technique would need careful checking. A further complication was that the size of a critical crack was estimated from theory, yet this theory could not be applied accurately to LWR conditions and therefore 'an element of uncertainty and judgement' remained. Altogether Cottrell's memorandum, if not exactly ominous, was distinctly sobering.

Nor did Cottrell leave matters there. In June 1974 he wrote to the *Financial Times* arguing that it would be 'wise to choose a system less critically dependent on human perfection than the steel pressure-vessel water reactor'.[58] The AEC were naturally quick to deny the validity of his views, but his intervention was an important one. (It is also of interest that in 1964 he had been a member of the Emeléus Committee.)

Apart from the observations of the Chief Nuclear Inspector and of the Government's Chief Scientist, the Science Committee also received written submissions touching on LWR safety from Friends of the Earth and two important private sources. The FoE memo is dealt with in Chapter 11. The private submissions were from L. Rotherham, formerly Research Director of the AEA's Industrial Group before following Sir Christopher Hinton to the CEGB in 1958 as a board member, and from Lord Hinton himself.[59] Both recognised the limitations of their positions, Rotherham that he could be accused of prejudice and Hinton that it was fifteen years since he had been intimately concerned in the design of nuclear power plants. But both came down in favour of the SGHWR, Rotherham with confidence and detailed arguments, Hinton more reluctantly, describing his choice as a 'gamble' acceptable only because of the urgent need for nuclear power. Yet more important than their opinions of the SGHWR were certain remarks each made with general reference to the LWR. Rotherham felt that comparisons between reactors had gone on for twenty years 'bedevilled by pseudo-economic arguments, differing ground rules, emotional and political judgements'. It was 'virtually impossible to advance quantitative reasons for any conclusion to be generally acceptable since any set of calculations can invariably be matched by a comparable set leading to a different conclusion'. More specifically, LWRs could not be regarded as proven systems. Furthermore, on the assumption that some LWRs would have components made by inexperienced manufacturers and be managed by inexperienced operators, the number coming into use meant that it was 'statistically, not unlikely that one day there will be a serious accident. This would be the time when we would be happy to say we had no such reactors'.

Hinton made essentially the same point: 'If I were responsible for an electrical utility, I might feel that I should like to be in a position to tell the public that they need not worry about my reactors because none of them were of the type involved in the accident.' Because he accepted that LWRs were probably the cheapest reactors available, and in order to explain why in spite of his doubts these reactors had sold so well throughout the world, Hinton gave a considered explanation of their commercial success: 'American salesmanship has been extremely clever, they used "loss-leaders" to establish a market and then steeply escalated prices . . . the engineers of many of the utilities which have bought [LWRs] have no first-hand knowledge of nuclear power, they can only rely on what is published and on what is told to them by consultants and by salesmen . . . most of the leading consultants who advise on nuclear power plants are American and are likely to have a bias in favour of American designs . . . if a reactor proves to be unsatisfactory, the Board of the utility which has installed it can always argue that, in buying an LWR they have done as most other utilities have done, whereas, if they buy any other type, they may be criticised for being out of step with the majority of buyers.'

On the other side of the safety argument to Rotherham and Hinton were the CEGB, the NNC and Sir Arnold Weinstock. It should in all fairness be reiterated that each of these fully recognised that LWRs gave rise to safety fears. Where they differed from Rotherham, Hinton, and ultimately the Science Committee, was in the weight they gave to this issue. Thus Weinstock described the safety question as 'the only inhibiting factor' in the choice of LWRs, adding that it did not seem to him that there was 'anything in the possibility of the United States environmentalists being right in the face of the most informed authoritative opinion'. Not all of the LWR's opponents were cranks, but some of the arguments being put forward were rather exaggerated. Pretty well all the LWR safety issues seemed to Weinstock either already overcome or in the course of being dealt with 'to the satisfaction of more or less everybody', the one possible exception being fast fracture of the pressure vessel, which Weinstock also thought a soluble problem. An incident at San Onofre in the United States, put to Weinstock by a member of the Science Committee as illustrating the danger of LWRs, struck him as being instead a 'convincing demonstration of the safety of the system', in that the reactor had, he understood, shut itself down. He did not accept that there were intrinsically greater doubts about LWR safety than about that of other systems. There was no completely safe reactor but those in public life had a special responsibility 'to be careful what words they use' lest they aroused unjustifiable fears. The Science Committee were doing their duty in trying to grapple with a very difficult problem but they should not be 'unduly swayed by reports of things which may heighten suspicion and do not rest on fact'.

The CEGB chairman felt that satisfying the public on safety was largely an emotive matter: the very fact that LWRs were being built all over the world naturally attracted critical attention to them. Further, since they were essentially the only reactors in the United States, controversy had inevitably settled on them because the whole argument about reactor safety had originated there. Hawkins acknowledged that pressure vessel integrity was 'perhaps the most important question', but it was a 'well-known technology' and the CEGB felt they could handle the problem. The Board were especially impressed by the fact that the reactor they were proposing to order was the first type they had examined in which it would be possible to carry out regular in-service inspection of vital parts. Their Health and Safety department were working on reports for the NII covering both pressure vessel integrity and emergency core-cooling.

In November 1973 the Secretary of State, Peter Walker, promised a reactor decision by February 1974. Pressures mounted.[60] US Atomic Energy Commission scientists defended LWR safety at a colloquium organised by the Conservative Party. Lorne Gray, president of Atomic Energy of Canada Ltd, pressed the advantages of CANDU and co-operation with Canada before the Nuclear Power Advisory Board and the British Nuclear Energy Society. One ex-Minister of Power, Roy Mason, described the possible purchase of LWRs as a 'disastrous idea'. At a press conference on the Science Committee's report Arthur Palmer, chairman of the subcommittee which produced it, suggested it would be a rash minister who ignored Sir Alan Cottrell's views. Palmer and Airey Neave, chairman of the Science Committee during the Conservative Government, saw the Trade and Industry Secretary, and several of the Committee's members wrote to him. The Lords had a debate and the BBC's 'Panorama' a full report but the reactor crisis was soon overtaken by other crises of more immediate political magnitude, the miners' strike, three-day week, General Election and Conservative defeat.

The Government having announced the establishment of a Nuclear Power Advisory Board (NPAB) in August 1972, in September 1973 asked their advice on thermal reactor policy. The Board were chaired by the responsible minister and the ten members included the chairmen of the AEA, NNC, electricity boards and Electricity Council. Since the Chief Nuclear Inspector also attended NPAB discussions as an adviser, NPAB deliberations effectively brought together all the main official nuclear interests. The Board's report,[61] published as a White Paper in September 1974, can therefore be taken as a virtually complete summary of the contending positions as they stood in mid-1974 when the decision for the SGHWR was made. The Board were able at that time to agree that the options for the next nuclear programme should be narrowed to the PWR and SGHWR, but were unable to reach a unanimous recommendation as between these two. This was because in effectively all of the issues relating to these reactors, and indeed in many of those relating to the other reactors under consideration, the CEGB and NNC were on one side of the argument, the SSEB, often with support from other members of the Board, on the other. The Conservative Government had feared deadlock of exactly this sort even when they set up the NPAB.

The PWR proponents maintained that a decision in its favour would bring Britain into the mainstream of world nuclear activity, while allowing development to concentrate on the HTR and FBR. They were confident the PWR would prove acceptable to the Nuclear Inspectorate, and that a rapid nuclear build-up would be possible with it. By contrast, choosing the SGHWR would have grave implications. It was outside the mainstream, there were major problems in scaling up the prototype, its heavy water would have to be imported, it would detract from effort on the HTR, and finally, it would allow only a slow nuclear build-up, thereby adversely affecting the balance of payments when fossil fuels had to be used in its stead. Those who wanted the SGHWR on the other hand pointed to the success of the prototype and to the prospect of co-operation with Canada. They doubted that the PWR could be quickly established for use in Britain. They accepted that choosing the SGHWR would not allow a substantial effort on the HTR, but questioned whether choosing the PWR would either. They did concede that 'as a matter of prudence' the Inspectorate should carry through to completion a generic study of PWR safety. And some members of the NPAB even thought that, provided full commitment to the SGHWR were not undermined, the PWR option might usefully be retained until the relative merits of the two reactors could be reexamined in the light of later information.

Some of the considerations which led the NPAB to their inconclusive conclusions were of great interest. They described their 'key criteria' as including safety and public acceptability, and in particular the requirement for a nuclear system which inspired confidence both in its construction and in its operation, so that a strong nuclear industry could be established on a sustained programme. Britain had in the past 'tried to develop too many systems and taken insufficient account of industrial and commercial needs'. At least 2.5GW a year of nuclear capacity needed to be ordered on a long-term basis, and design repetition too was of great importance. The NPAB also saw that the demand forecasts they had been given called for a much higher rate of nuclear ordering than Britain had previously had. Fossil fuel prices would mean that nuclear would have to meet the bulk of a minimum of 42GW needing to be ordered in the following decade.

The Board reviewed all the available reactors. There was general agreement that a return to Magnox would be 'retrograde and wasteful', and that to order more AGRs without operating experience would be 'an unwarrantable risk'. Some NPAB members were less pessimistic than others about the AGR, and the Board's overall conclusion was that it might be a fallback or supplement to the main system. The HTR was generally agreed to have the greatest potential but it was accepted that only a demonstration plant was immediately feasible, and not series ordering. It was recognised that it might in any case not make sense to switch back to the HTR if water reactors became established in Britain.

It was perhaps surprising that all members of the NPAB felt that as between the two possible heavy water reactors, the SGHWR and CANDU, the SGHWR was to be preferred. The Canadians, after all, had by this time had three years operating experience with a 514MW reactor and had another 8,300MW under construction, whereas there was only the 100MW prototype SGHWR. The reason for the Board's unanimous decision was that CANDU was more expensive in capital cost and also, perhaps begging an important question, that CANDU 'would conflict with the UK's established position as an enriched uranium producer'.

The CEGB's case for regarding the PWR as the most tried system emerged even more clearly from the NPAB's report than it had from the Board's evidence to the Science Committee. More resources had been devoted to the LWRs worldwide than to any other system. The CEGB and NNC both preferred the Westinghouse PWR but PWRs were also offered in the US by the Babcock & Wilcox Co. and by Combustion Engineering Inc., and there was a separate West German design. The PWR proposal was effectively for a third generation system, yet the basic technology had not changed. Not including the Soviet bloc, 30GW of LWRs were operating and 250GW were on order in a total of 26 countries. 40GW had been ordered in 1973. Westinghouse had 13GW of PWR in operation and 115GW on order – 'more than for any other system'. Of the 25 operating Westinghouse plants, one had 16 years experience, and 15 were in excess of 500MW. 33 of the 1,150MW PWRs the CEGB wanted had been ordered, the first being planned for commissioning in 1976 and 10 by 1980, all before the first CEGB PWR would commission. Westinghouse had shown in France and Japan that their method of manufacture and quality control could be transferred, and the present might be a 'uniquely favourable' time for co-operation with European interests on the PWR. The PWR had had more technical effort applied to it over 20 years than had any other system.

This last point the SSEB in fact saw as a source for concern, in that, despite all this effort, important problems remained with the PWR. But the NPAB report pointedly brought out that the two main uncertainties, pressure circuit integrity and loss of coolant accidents, arose also with the SGHWR. The Chief Nuclear Inspector's position on the LWR was now that he expected to be able in due course to license it, but that he had only in 1974 begun receiving information on this reactor, from the AEC, Westinghouse and the CEGB, and that it could take him up to 20 months from the time he received a detailed submission before he was able to say what changes in it he would want. The CEGB had suggested that if they were allowed to take the risk of issuing a letter of intent to the NNC, subject to the Inspector's eventual clearance, this would speed things up and allow 16GW of PWR to be constructed by 1985/6, as compared with only 13GW if they had to await a safety clearance.

The NPAB report argued that, for several reasons, in scaling up the SGHWR, experience with the Winfrith prototype was of more relevance than experience with the Windscale AGR had been in moving to the commercial AGR programme, though it was seen as more sensible to start with a 660MW SGHWR than with the 1,150-1,300MW units the CEGB wished to build in the PWR case. The SSEB thought possible a 5GW SGHWR programme over the first four years, with series ordering then following. The CEGB and NNC however, thought this 'much too risky' given the 'immaturity of the system'. Even if all went well, series ordering could not begin until six years later than would be possible with the PWR. The AEA were said by the NPAB to regard the SSEB proposal as 'practicable', but also to have recognised the LWR case. The SSEB thought the SGHWR would cost 8-10 per cent more than a PWR, the CEGB 12 per cent, but the NPAB stressed that construction cost estimates could easily be outweighed by differences in construction and operation — as an awful warning, the CEGB had now estimated that the fuel costs of replacing electricity production lost through AGR delays would exceed the original capital cost estimate for these stations. With regard to the balance of payments, the NNC believed that while the first PWR would cost £15-25m, a net balance could be achieved after the third PWR, except for the 1-2 per cent licence fee. By contrast, the SGHWR would continue to cost £15m a station, mainly for heavy water. It was recognised that exporting complete reactors would be very difficult whichever were chosen, but the NNC saw a strong opportunity for fuel and component sales if Britain adopted the PWR.

Since the NPAB could thus not agree as between the PWR and SGHWR which to recommend, the decision was thrown back to the minister. It is of some interest in this connection that several in the academic nuclear engineering community were rather annoyed in 1974 at not having been consulted. Some of this group wanted the SGHWR, some the LWR, and some even Magnox.

On 2 May 1974, fulfilling a promise given both by the new Labour Government and by the previous Conservative administration, that no decision on reactor choice would be made until the Commons had had a chance to discuss the issue, the Energy Secretary, Eric Varley, opened a debate on the question, conscious, he said, of the immense responsibility he carried.[62]

The minister discussed electricity demand, the various strategies open and the main advantages and disadvantages of the relevant reactors. His department did not accept the CEGB estimates of future electricity demand, reckoning on 56.7GW by 1980-1 and 84.1GW by 1990-1 as compared with the CEGB figures of 61.9 and 103GW respectively by those dates, and indeed it now appeared that the CEGB themselves agreed that their figures should be revised downwards. Nevertheless, the figures amounted to a minimum of 3GW of nuclear plant being ordered each year for the CEGB, or 4GW a year when the programme got into its stride and taking into account Scotland. Varley underlined the fact that though no decision could affect actual nuclear capacity before 1980, there were marked differences between the various authorities concerning the rate at which nuclear capacity should be built up. In the minister's own very candid words: 'on electricity demand, as on almost everything else to do with this highly charged and controversial subject, the evidence is sometimes confused and sometimes disputed, and sometimes both'. Of the choices open the minister thought that not one emerged as clearly best, but there were in principle three main technological routes, gas reactors, HWRs or LWRs, and these were not mutually exclusive. Thus it was possible to have LWRs alone – the CEGB strategy – or CANDU alone, or AGR alone – 'a high risk option' – or SGHWR alone – the SSEB strategy which would also require additional fossil fuel capacity. Or on the other hand one could have LWR with SGHWR as an insurance against licensing difficulties; or LWR with AGR and a decision between them in 1976, a policy which would provide somewhat greater security than LWR alone; or

CANDU with SGHWR, the former bridging the gap until the latter could with confidence be ordered in numbers.

The advantages and disadvantages of the contending reactors were set out in some detail by the minister. Varley reminded the Commons that all cost figures were 'hotly disputed', though he thought it reasonable to say that the LWRs looked cheapest. He also reaffirmed the fundamental importance of safety. Of the LWRs he said that the results of major work on safety being done by the US Atomic Energy Commission would not be available until 1975 but that he had meanwhile had an interim report from a team which Walter Marshall, director of the AEA's research establishment at Harwell, had headed, and which had visited the US to investigate the integrity of LWR pressure vessels. Varley also announced that, though uncertainty remained about rating and reliability in service, as well as with respect to commissioning dates, the Hinkley Point AGR station was now expected to commission in 1974, and the rest between 1975 and 1977. As to the SGHWR, following John Davies's statement as minister in August 1972, a £5m proposal had been submitted by TNPG and NDC to make the reactor acceptable to the Nuclear Inspectorate by late 1974. On the HTR a reference design had been formulated.

Since this debate was taking place only two months after they had left office, Opposition speakers were almost as well briefed as the Government spokesmen. Patrick Jenkin, who led for the Opposition, had been minister in the Energy Department in the previous Government and stressed that that Government had been fully conscious that the choice of reactor was a decision of immense complexity and importance and one of the most difficult technological and industrial questions which had ever faced any Government. Reminding his listeners that he had been the only Commons speaker to propose in 1965 that LWRs might have been a better choice, Jenkin now suggested that while the AGRs had failed to live up to their high promise and the British nuclear industry was demoralised, these reactors could still turn out well. But he would not have wanted to be the minister who told the CEGB chairman that he must order a further large AGR programme: he suspected that the answer would be that it could be 'either Hawkins or AGRs but not both!' The nub of the problem was the choice between LWRs and HWRs, and by far the most important factors in the choice were proven capacity and safety. Britain was confronted 'not only with the technical, economic and safety merits, but with pressures of economic and technical nationalism'. As between LWRs and HWRs there was a colossal difference in experience. The SGHWR was probably more suitable for Britain than CANDU, but was it right to base a whole new programme on SGHWR when the consequences of a similar decision on the AGR were still unresolved? On the other hand there were big questions about the safety of LWRs. Might it not be possible, without any compromise on safety, for the Nuclear Inspectorate to shorten the time they needed to pronounce on the LWR, since it appeared from the interim report, which the minister had arranged for Jenkin to have, that much of the information on pressure vessel integrity was available in the AEA?

The bipartisan approach of the Science Committee was well illustrated in the speeches in this debate of their then and previous chairmen, Arthur Palmer and Airey Neave, though these speakers did not advocate quite the same solution. Palmer (an electrical engineer) pointed out that among the things which the Committee had demonstrated was that it was a mistake to suppose that somewhere there were impartial experts to whom the decision could be left. He sympathised with the minister's difficulty if he should decide to refuse the CEGB the LWRs they wanted, and although he did not accept at face value the CEGB's case, he recognised that the latter were acting from their proper but narrow terms of reference. Neave (who had declared interests in one of the consortia) was much more censorious of the CEGB. He objected to the fact that they were already advertising for scientists to work on LWRs; he suggested that in assessing the CEGB's judgement it should be borne in mind that the Board's representatives had appeared before the Science Committee without even knowing that the reactors they proposed to order were not in service; and he quoted with approval an Institution of Professional Civil Servants memorandum to the effect that the CEGB had attacked British products outrageously.

This was undoubtedly the best-informed debate the House of Commons had ever had on nuclear power policy; nearly all speakers paid tribute to the Science Committee for their work; and nearly all admitted that they did not envy the minister his decision. Perhaps the most valid general conclusion was drawn by David Howell, Minister of State at the Energy Department in the previous Government, summing up for the Opposition. Howell thought that the Commons had over the years played a creditable role in an otherwise sad saga, and with deliberate humility drew the lesson that 'if we have learned anything from the stories of the last 20 years in nuclear reactor systems, it is that in government our decision-making procedures have been weak'.

The Government announced their decision in July 1974. A White Paper[63] acknowledged that the discussions on reactor policy had been 'prolonged' and that 'strong views and positions' had been taken. But the period of uncertainty was now said to be over: the Government had decided in favour of the SGHWR. The initial programme would be 'relatively modest', not more than 4GW over the ensuing four years, but subsequent to this orders were to be built up as rapidly as progress allowed. The SGHWR offered 'substantial advantages'. It would provide power reliably, could be ordered quickly, posed no fundamental difficulties as far as the Nuclear Inspectorate were concerned, and offered particular scope for British technology. The White Paper stressed the importance of maintaining public confidence and acceptability, and argued that the SGHWR decision met these tests.

The Government had accepted the NPAB's advice that there were not sufficient resources for a substantial HTR effort while the SGHWR was being launched. Britain was by this time paying some 48 per cent of the Dragon HTR costs and now offered to extend the period of her commitment to allow her European partners to consider whether they were prepared to assume greater financial responsibility. This they declined to do and the project therefore ended in November 1975. Thus the HTR, the one reactor favoured by virtually everybody in the early seventies, was the one decisive casualty of the 1974 decision.[64]

The White Paper was careful to note that although the Government had decided against an LWR commitment, this did not imply any judgement about the validity of the technical doubts which had been expressed regarding LWR safety. In line with the NPAB's advice, the White Paper also revealed that the Nuclear Inspectorate had been asked to carry through to a conclusion their generic study of LWR safety.

Varley's decision had undoubtedly been, as Hugh Stephenson said in *The Times*, a 'miserably difficult' one. Questioned in the House on his statement of 10 July the minister explained that a decision in favour of the SGHWR had been reached on the basis of reactor reliability and public acceptability, with the added consideration of 'giving a boost to British technology'.[65] It had not been possible to get a unanimous decision out of the NPAB and he accepted that Sir Arnold Weinstock would now wish to reduce the General Electric Company's shareholding in the NNC. Later in the year, the Under-Secretary for Energy, Alex Eadie, defending the SGHWR decision on the grounds that it 'was not only right but the only one possible in the circumstances', described the new reactor as being 'at a significantly more advanced point of development than was the AGR when it was chosen in 1965'.[66]

Notes

1. G.H. Greenhalgh, 'Big Future for the AGR', *NE* (October 1965), pp. 381-2.

2. S.A. Ghalib, *BNESJ* (1963), 2, p. 336.

3. For example, P.T. Fletcher, 'Nuclear Power – The Future', *Atom* (February 1969), pp. 4-10.

4. Sir Roger Makins, 'Nuclear Energy: A Year of Promise', *BNESJ*, 1 (1962), pp. 161-7; see also symposium on 'Water Reactors for Power Generation' (Risley, 4 July 1962, *BNESJ*, 1 (1962), pp. 323-73; 'The SGHWR – An Assurance not an Insurance', *NE* (June 1963), p. 186.

5. *Atom* (December 1963), p. 369; also Sir William Cook, 'Reactor Development in the UK: The Present and Future Pattern', *Elec. Rev.* (17 November 1961), pp. 771-4; 'The Development of the Nuclear Power Programme in the UK', *Atom* (January 1962), pp. 7-12.

6. Tom Marsham, quoted in *Financial Times*, 21 September 1967.

7. A. Firth and J.E.R. Holmes, 'SGHW Prototype Reactor', *Atom* (February 1965), pp. 34-40; See also R.H. Campbell, 'Fuel for the SGHWR', *Atom* (April 1966), pp. 88-94; HCD 673 c.23-4 (WA); *New Scientist*, 8 September 1966; H. Cartwright, 'The SGHWR', *Atom* (December 1966), pp. 274-81.

8. H. Cartwright, 'The Design of the SGHWR', *Atom* (February 1968), pp. 26-37 (March), pp. 49-55; also E. Gabriel and D. Smith, 'The SGHWR: Technical Status and Operating Experience', *Atom* (December 1970), pp. 254-72.

9. Sir William Penney, 'Nuclear Power', *Atom* (1967), pp. 136-44. Also *NE* (May 1968).

10. Sir John Hill, *Atom* (1968), pp. 286-8.

11. J. Moore *et al.*, 'Status of the SGHWR', *Atom* (January 1973), pp. 7-19; G. Brown *et al.*, 'SGHWR', IV Geneva, 5, pp. 255-67; also R. McKeague, 'The Suitability of the SGHWR for the Power Requirements of Developing Countries', *Atom* (September 1974), pp. 200-14; J.C. Phillips, 'Eight Years' Operation of the SGHWR Prototype', *BNESJ* (January 1976), 15, pp. 21-33.

12. Annual Report; HC 359 (1967-8), para. 191; see also M. Phillips, 'A Broader Approach to Benefits from Nuclear Power and Associated Social and Other Costs', *Atom* (November 1968), pp. 297-306; *Atom* (November 1968), p. 295.

13. HC 328 (1968-9).

14. HC 552 (1970-1), C & AG's Report, paras. 24-44.

15. See also P.J. Searby, 'Present Worth Evaluations as an Aid to Nuclear Power Decisions', *BNESJ*, 10 (1971), pp. 177-89.

16. HC 273 (1971-2), Q 142.

17. Sir William Penney, 'High Temperature Reactors and DRAGON', *Atom* (July 1966), pp. 162-4; also *High Temperature Reactors and the DRAGON Project* (Symposium Institution of Mechanical Engineers, 23-24 May 1966), *BNESJ*, 5 (1966), pp. 235-450, 491-550; *Advanced and High Temperature Gas-cooled Reactors* (IAEA Symposium 21-25 October 1968), *BNESJ*, 8, pp. 18-30; G.E. Lockett, 'Using the HTR for Power Generation Below 500 MW', *Atom* (March 1971), pp. 67-76; L.R. Shepherd, 'Development of HTR Technology in the Dragon Project', IV Geneva, 5, pp. 317-30.

18. HC 273 (1971-2), paras. 42-51.

19. HC 385 (1972-3), paras. 105-9.

20. Sir Stanley Brown, 'Future Nuclear Reactors for CEGB', *BNF Bulletin* (October 1969), pp. 1-5 and 'The Next 25 Years in the Electricity Supply Industry', *BNF Bulletin* (December 1970), p. 5; 'Nuclear Power on the Grid', *NEI* (September 1969), pp. 714-17; also Eric Booth, 'Whither Nuclear Power? The Dilemma', *BNF Bulletin* (May 1971), pp. 1-5; also CEGB Newsletters, nos. 75 and 81.

21. J.O. Grieves, 'The Place of Fast Reactors in the UK Power Programme', *NEI* (August 1971), pp. 630-1.

22. Of general use: *The Construction Commissioning and Operation of Advanced Gas-cooled Reactors* (Institution of Mechanical Engineers, London, 1977), Symposium 26-27 May 1977.

23. Sir John Hill, 'Nuclear Power in the UK', IV Geneva, 1, pp. 331-42; see also for example, J.H. McLoughlin, 'An AGR for Export at £36/KW', *NE* (April 1967), pp. 286-92.

24. Gordon Brown, 'Advances in the Gas-cooled Reactor System', *BNESJ*, 8 (1969), pp. 46-59; also R.V. Moore, 'Review of Experience with Gas-cooled Reactor Power Stations', *BNESJ*, 8 (1969), pp. 123-32; R.D. Vaughn, 'Future Technology of the Gas-cooled Reactor', *BNESJ*, 8 (1969), pp. 134-48; G.R. Bainbridge, 'Gas-cooled Reactors,'Performing and Prospective', TRG Report 1924 (R) (May 1970).

25. HC 401 (1968-9), p. 219.

26. Special Keswick Conferences, *BNESJ*, 12 (1973), pp. 469-70 and *Atom* (August 1978), pp. 210-14, were held on this subject. Also W. Rizk and D.F. Seymour, 'Investigations into the Failure of Gas Circulators and Circuit Components at Hinkley Point Nuclear Power Station', *Proc. Instn. Mech. Eng.*, 179 (1964-5), no. 21, p. 61.

27. *Guardian*, 4 March 1976.

28. J.D. McKean *et al.*, 'Heysham Nuclear Power Station', *NEI* (November 1971), p. 916.

29. J.E. Newell, 'Corrosion of 9% Chromium in AGR Boilers', *NEI* (August 1972); also *NEI* (April 1971), p. 307 (March 1972), p. 137.

30. *NEI* (November 1973), p. 841; see also Bill Gunston, 'What Went Wrong with Dungeness B?', *Science Journal* (November 1970).

31. R.A. Peddie, 'Management of Large High-technology Projects', *Electronics and Power* (July 1976), pp. 419-21; See also, W.J. Prior *et al.*, 'Gas-cooled Reactor Operating Experience', *BNESJ*, 14 (October 1975), pp. 287-92; *NEI* (July 1978), pp. 31-3.

32. For example, Simon Rippon, 'The AGRs Make a Start', *NEI* (April-May 1976), pp. 54-7.

33. J.R.M. Southwood, 'The Engineering Development of Thermal Reactors in the UK', *Proc. Instn. Mech. Eng.*, 192 (1978), no. 34.

34. K.P. Gibbs, 'Economic Assessment of Nuclear Power Plant', IV Geneva, 2, pp. 465-73. But see Sir Stanley Brown, 'The Nuclear Power Programme' in Lord Sherfield (ed.), *Economic and Social Consequences of Nuclear Energy* (OUP, London, 1972), Ch. 3, p. 41.

35. HC 444-ii (1971-2).

36. HC 73-iii (1973-4).

37. Cmnd. 6388; see also Committee of Inquiry into delays in commissioning CEGB power stations (chairman Sir A. Wilson), Cmnd. 3960; and also HC 223 (1969-70).

38. In this context see C.E. Larson, 'Technology and economics of LWRs', *BNESJ*, 12, 1973, pp. 277-95.

39. *NEI*, January 1974, p. 5.

40. HC 444-iii (1971-2).

41. HC 73-vi (1973-4).

42. HC 117-i (1972-3).

43. HC 117-iv (1972-3).

44. HC 117-v (1972-3).

45. HC 73-i (1973-4).

46. HC 73-v (1973-4).

47. *Financial Times*, 21 March 1974.
48. HC 73-ii (1973-4).
49. HC 444-i (1971-2).
50. HC 117-vi (1972-3).
51. HC 350 (1972-3); HC 145 (1973-4).
52. HC 117-iii (1972-3); HC 73-iv (1973-4).
53. HC 73-iii (1973-4).
54. HC 73-i (1973-4); HC 73-iv (1973-4).
55. HC 444-i and -iii (1971-2).
56. HC 73-iii and -vii, Appendix 6 (1973-4).
57. HC 73-vi (1973-4).
58. *Financial Times*, 7 and 25 June 1974.
59. HC 73-vii, Appendices 2 and 3.
60. For example, *Sunday Times*, 2 October 1973 and 31 March 1974; Norman Dombey and John Surrey, 'Nuclear Reactors — Britain's Choice', *New Statesman*, 26 April 1974.
61. Cmnd. 5731.
62. HCD 872 c.1344-450.
63. Cmnd. 5695.
64. HC 534 (1976-7) Q 342; also 'The Dragon Project 1959-76', *Atom* (June 1976), p. 166.
65. HCD 876 c.1357-70.
66. HCD 883 c.2014-35.

Part IV: 1974-8

10 RETURN OF THE AGR

When the SGHWR was adopted in 1974, Donald Clark, a member of the CEGB Board, resigned, giving as his reasons that an opportunity of great importance had been lost, and that the SGHWR was not in a state of industrial readiness comparable to that of the LWR.[1] There were many others at the time who believed the whole reactor question would shortly have to be reopened yet again, and so it proved.

In February 1965 a 4 x 660MW SGHWR station was approved for the CEGB at Sizewell and a 2 x 660MW station for the SSEB at Torness, but with electricity demand much reduced by the summer of 1975, there came the first suggestions that the SGHWR programme should be halted. Delays in producing a reference design were explained to Tony Benn when he became Energy Secretary following an exchange of jobs with Eric Varley. Amidst increasing speculation, in January 1976 Westinghouse were reported willing to build a 1,300MW PWR in Britain for £200m, a figure they contrasted with their estimate of £370m for a 2 x 650MW SGHWR.[2] Then in May 1976 came much-quoted remarks by another CEGB board member, R.A. Peddie, to the effect that the SGHWR was proving 'more difficult than Concorde': the Board had 'not got the measure of it at all'. It could be built, but Peddie implied that he did not know when, or at what cost. By mid-summer 1976 the Energy Secretary was saying in answer to Parliamentary Questions that while he was satisfied there had been no obstruction of the SGHWR programme, its launching was indeed giving more trouble than had been anticipated in 1974.[3] Benn later added that apart from this 'technical slippage' a reduced electricity demand made practicable a longer time-scale than had originally been envisaged, and in a not unexpected move, the Chancellor included in his public expenditure cuts of July 1976 a £40m deferment in respect of the SGHWR programme. There had in effect been a one-year delay in the project. Such was the general background against which the General Purposes Sub-Committee of the Commons Science Committee began a review of the SGHWR programme, the Committee's fifth venture[4] into the nuclear power field.

The Committee had before them a short AEA report, the product of discussions in which the SSEB, though not represented on the AEA board, had also participated.[5] The report began from the position that 'it was hardly possible for [the Government] to have come to any

241

other decision' in 1974 than to proceed with the SGHWR. It had not been possible to advocate a continuing commitment to the AGR, and it would have been 'extremely difficult' for the Government to have switched to LWRs in advance of an approval in principle of them by the NII, and in the light of Sir Alan Cottrell's objections. In full knowledge that it was a difficult recommendation to make, and could lead to new uncertainty and a slump in morale, it was now suggested that the SGHWR programme be halted. The much lower electricity demand projections of 1976 would mean a slow installation programme, and the launch expenditure of the SGHWR was money better spent elsewhere on nuclear energy. There was confidence that technically the SGHWR would work, but there had been more difficulties in producing a 660MW design than had been anticipated; it would be significantly more expensive than alternatives, with no clear advantages; and there were no prospects of export orders. The SSEB, the report noted, dissented from these opinions.

The AGR was now said to look more promising than it had in 1974, but experience with it was acknowledged to be still very limited. A detailed review of its prospects was needed but pending that it could, the report suggested, be 'considered seriously' as an alternative to the PWR. The PWR itself was seen as dominating immediate export prospects. An AEA study group had now satisfied itself that Cottrell's questions about the reactor could be answered, and he himself was understood to have accepted this. It ought thus to be possible for the NII to be satisfied about PWR safety. 'Some of us,' the report continued, 'are therefore driven to the judgement that any thermal reactors we do build should be PWRs.' It was recognised that this would be a hard decision for the Government to take, and that there would also be repercussions for the AEA.

Fundamental to this critical conclusion were said to be the severe difficulties of the power engineering industry. In view of the low ordering projections for the UK there appeared to be 'no alternative to a vigorous export policy in the short and medium term', though this would not be easy, and it was 'not obvious' how the UK could, 'at this late date', become a substantial exporter of LWR components. The realities of the export opportunities needed to be established, but in any case the views of the nuclear design and power construction industries ought to be given 'high weight' in settling thermal reactor policy. It would be tragic if the nuclear industry were to disappear, especially given the large nuclear programme anticipated for the nineties.

It will be remembered that despite making a decision in favour of the SGHWR in 1974, the Government had requested the NII to complete their examination of the general safety issues relating to the LWR. At the AEA Sir John Hill separately asked Walter Marshall to undertake a study of PWR pressure vessel safety, and this was the study referred to in the AEA's 1976 report. Marshall produced his report[6] in mid-1976, and although Cottrell had by this time left the public service, Marshall sent him a copy, Cottrell's views on PWR pressure vessels having been so influential in the 1974 decision. Cottrell replied that the report was 'first class . . . impressively thorough and objective'. He was in general agreement with its technical content but made the point that the necessary standards with PWRs could be attained 'only in engineering and operational organisations of outstanding technical excellence'. However, in a letter to Benn, Cottrell continued to maintain that the technical position did not guarantee that PWR pressure vessels would operate safely for the full design life of the reactors. The difference between the SGHWR and CANDU on the one hand and the LWRs on the other was that the pressure tubes of the former were replaceable, whereas the pressure vessels of the latter were not. Marshall later summed up the situation as he saw it in a further letter to Cottrell in which he stated that he had initially been unable to reconcile Cottrell's letters to him and to Benn, but following a clarification by Cottrell now felt that strictly both he and Cottrell were saying the same thing, but with a different emphasis. Marshall also said at this time that he expected the NII to approve the PWR by spring 1977, subject to conditions similar to those applied by the US regulatory agency. Cottrell for his part wrote to the *Financial Times*,[7] referring to the need with LWRs for 'almost superhuman' engineering and operational qualities: there was 'little to gain and a lot to lose' with the PWR.

Questioned by the Science Committee in August 1976, Benn explained that the need to economise in public expenditure and technical slippage in developing a commercial SGHWR design had between them pointed to the deferment in the SGHWR programme which had been announced. He was emphatic that the Government had taken no new decision on the SGHWR, and repeated that there had been no attempt elsewhere to frustrate the earlier government decision in favour of this reactor. The suggestion that the decision be looked at again had, however, come from Sir John Hill, and not from the minister himself. Benn said that he had responded to this initiative by asking for the considered opinion of the AEA board, leading to the report which had been published. He had pointed out that exactly the same problems could occur if the PWR were now adopted as had arisen with the

SGHWR, and also that if the SGHWR were cancelled it 'might not even be a nuclear station at all that was adopted'. He would be only 'very reluctantly driven off a decision taken after so much care and attention'. He had also been candid in pointing out to all concerned that once the question were raised as to whether the SGHWR should be cancelled, it was bound to undermine 'the credibility of British technology and the quality of the advice that comes in'. Still more specifically, he had drawn Hill's attention to the fact that for the AEA now to recommend cancellation of their own SGHWR could well threaten their case on the FBR, in that the Government would in turn be encouraged to scrutinise that proposal more sceptically.

Hill, in effect, replied to this latter point in presenting the Authority's annual report the following month.[8] Without referring to Benn by name, he chose to 'totally reject' criticisms that the AEA's behaviour over the SGHWR had damaged their credibility on the FBR: was it really being suggested that the AEA should have ignored the changed circumstances in respect of the SGHWR?

The CEGB chairman, Sir Arthur Hawkins, stressed in his new evidence to the Science Committee that the SGHWR would be much more expensive than alternatives, though the Committee found that he was 'singularly unforthcoming' in giving details. The CEGB had been unable, Hawkins said, to get the Energy Department to 'come clean' and accept that the taxpayer should bear some of the SGHWR development costs. (Between 1965 and 1975 the Board had spent some £630m on their four AGR stations for, at that time, no return.[9]) The Board had satisfied the minister that they were trying diligently to apply the SGHWR decision of 1974, but they had no need of any reactor in the near future and had been happy to join the AEA in recommending that the SGHWR programme be abandoned. Hawkins said he did not expect Francis Tombs of the SSEB to agree, in that it had no doubt been his opinion in part which had influenced the Government in their original decision for the SGHWR, but time would show, if it had not already, that the CEGB were backed by better resources and experience than were the SSEB. The CEGB's own changes of plan, from 1972 to 1973 and then to 1976, were 'not anywhere near as bad' as they appeared. The Board had changed 'reasonably' and not 'wildly' and their policy, Hawkins thought, had been 'consistently right'. The existing excess capacity had arisen from efforts in the late sixties to smooth plant orders to help the manufacturers. The latter were again making the 'same bleats', but these should perhaps be ignored and the manufacturers be made to face up to the reality of life. Certainly the CEGB had an interest in ensuring that the manufacturers stayed in business, but it was not in the Board's interest to prop them up at the expense of electricity prices. On the subject of reactor choice, while it was a matter for the Government to decide as between nuclear power and alternatives, confusion resulted when the Government became mixed up in reactor technology. Here they could be taking on rather more than they understood. This issue needed flexibility and not the rigidity of a White Paper. In a specific response to this the Science Committee were later to describe it as an 'obvious political impossibility' for the Government to treat reactor choice as they would the selection of coal or oil systems.

The CEGB chairman's observations on this occasion were a useful guide to the uneasy relationship he had with the Government, and perhaps with Benn in particular. The CEGB's reports for 1975-6 and 1976-7 made the point even more bluntly. The Board welcomed the Energy Secretary's initiatives to enhance consultation but felt that executive decisions could be taken successfully only by those experienced in the industry 'and within the discipline that comes from being accountable'. The Board looked for a 'more thorough application of the original Morrisonian or "arms-length" approach' — they 'must be allowed to carry out . . . statutory duties without day-to-day interference'. In the light of these various opinions it is understandable why it was not thought surprising when the CEGB chairman was allowed to retire in 1977.

Hawkins also told the Science Committee in 1976 that it was 'complete nonsense' to suggest that some reactors were more safe than others: all of them could, at different costs, be built to the same safety standard.[10] In this context he also said that he had never understood what had seemed to him 'almost an emotional bias by Sir Alan Cottrell against the American reactor'.

Sir John Hill and Walter Marshall in giving their evidence to the Science Committee had a rather hard passage. Hill accepted that there had been some overselling by the AEA in 1964, but again blamed Britain's nuclear problems squarely on the earlier 'totally unsatisfactory' fragmentation of the British industry and on the small scale of the country's nuclear programme.

Hill had previously taken the offensive in regard to the AEA's performance before the 1974/5 Public Accounts Committee.[11] The Magnox stations, he had then claimed, were a success, in that with costs about half those of fossil plant, the CEGB were making £60m per annum profit on them. The 'overriding lesson' of Dungeness B had been that there had been inadequate design and component development effort before work had started on site, and there had also been the fact of APC's inadequate resources. But the AGR was technologically sound and these lessons would not be repeated. Delay in the prototype fast reactor (PFR) project was due to many things — the AEA for having been too ambitious, rationalisation in the heavy electrical and boiler-making industries, the enormous reduction of power plant orders in the late sixties forcing industrial contractions, and perhaps six months due to the transfer of the PFR project management to TNPG in 1968-9. But the UK was fortunate to have chosen liquid metal cooling for the FBR in 1953, the PFR was the world's cheapest, and it had been built within 15 per cent of the 1966 cost estimate. With the elimination of the HTR following the 1974 SGHWR decision the AEA would hence-forth be concentrating on a narrow front approach: resources, he told the Science Committee on another occasion, had indeed been spread 'a bit widely in the past'.[12]

Before the Science Committee Hill also defended as completely con-sistent the advice which the AEA had given the Government during his chairmanship: it had changed only as circumstances had changed. The Nuclear Power Advisory Board had not met since 1974 — the Commit-tee were later told that it had really been designed specifically to meet the particular thermal reactor situation of 1973-4 — and Hill explained that it had been on his own initiative that he had approached the Government with a proposal for a new review of reactor policy. It had been the only proper thing to do, but the Authority's subsequent advice to the Government had not been palatable for them to give. Ideally Hill said he would have liked simply a quiet look at the new information and circumstances since 1974, but it was not possible to have such a review without its becoming public knowledge.

Marshall defended his own review of PWR pressure vessel safety. It had seemed to him at the outset of his work that Sir Alan Cottrell had made some very powerful points, though pressure vessel integrity had not been a serious question in the US, where the issue of emergency core-cooling had dominated. But Marshall's long study had satisfied him about the pressure vessel, subject to the conditions and qualifica-tions in his report. He had also come to accept the strong business argument for adopting the PWR. Both Hill and Marshall made the point that cost calculations were too uncertain to be relied on alone in reactor choice: the judgement, they maintained, had rather to be a broad one.

Lord Aldington and N.L. Franklin gave evidence to the Science

Committee on behalf of the NNC/NPC. (At Eric Varley's request[13] Franklin had resigned as chief executive of BNFL to manage NPC.) The NPC had a development contract from the AEA for the SGHWR. There was, according to Franklin, a cost difference of the order of 30-40 per cent between the SGHWR and a PWR, but there were hopes that the SGHWR capital cost might be cut by around 15-20 per cent. CEGB safety criteria had added to SGHWR costs, and these had also been affected by more general safety considerations. The NPC lacked good direct knowledge of the PWR, but it was the purpose of a comparative exercise which the NNC had proposed to bring the NPC's knowledge of this reactor into line with their knowledge of the SGHWR and the AGR. Hitherto, only one or two staff had worked on the PWR. That would now be increased to around thirty, and to ensure that the comparative exercise was unprejudiced, it would be conducted with the same people looking at each reactor. Franklin was not, he said, precommitted to the PWR, but he did think that most people would find satisfactory the results of recent American full-scale tests on PWR safety.

As they had done before the 1974 decision, in their evidence to the Science Committee, the SSEB took a very independent line. One of their representatives, the chairman Francis Tombs, had just been appointed chairman of the Electricity Council. By the SSEB's account, the CEGB having concentrated on the PWR before the decision of July 1974, it had taken until January 1975 for them to form a view on a basic SGHWR design. A General Electric Company management review had then reopened a number of questions and the appointment of the new chief executive at the NPC in May 1975 had led to a new fuel element being adopted. This and another change requested by the CEGB had led to further delay. The CEGB had also applied to the SGHWR more severe safety criteria than those relevant to other reactors, and their unhappy experience with the AGR had led them to insist on excessive design margins. The SSEB did not therefore regard the resulting SGHWR design as optimised, though it retained 'unique features of good operational flexibility and repairability'.

Essentially the SSEB were saying that the SGHWR was not being compared on an equal basis with its rivals. The Institution of Professional Civil Servants (IPCS) in a memorandum to the Science Committee made the related point that SGHWR standards had been set higher than the NII were likely to require: the correct relationship between the NII, NPC and generating boards had not, the IPCS affirmed, been established. The Committee were to agree that imperfect relationships had indeed contributed to the delay and cost escalation of the SGHWR.

The SSEB did not think that the doubts which had attached to the AGR in 1974 had as yet been removed. The issues now seen to be crucial — corrosion of tubing, insulation of the pressure vessel, graphite integrity and increasing contamination levels — were all long term. Any further AGR programme would require substantial redesign and more stringent safety standards, and even given wholehearted national commitment, it would be two years before manufacture could start. As to the PWR, the SSEB felt that the Marshall report on pressure vessels provided 'no ground for believing that these vessels are safer than was believed to be the case a few years ago'. Sir Alan Cottrell they felt shared their view. On the other hand, they recognised that they were in a minority. They thought this might be because the issue was marginal, in that they were not saying that the PWR was unsafe or would not work, only questioning whether it was better than alternatives.

As the SSEB saw it, a safe pressure vessel required almost perfect manufacture from almost perfect materials, as well as almost perfect inspection, and even the Marshall report had drawn attention to the need for operational restrictions and for more investigation. The Ludwigshaven PWR design in West Germany, it was true, allowed for failure and had superior safety features to the Westinghouse PWR. The SSEB also continued to see the performance of the emergency core-cooling system in the PWR as a major uncertainty: the evidence on this was still mostly derived from computer analysis rather than actual experiment. As to the relative construction costs, acknowledging the unreliability of the estimating process, and that in effect it involved guesses, the SSEB put them at £400/KW for the existing SGHWR design, £325-350/KW for an optimised SGHWR and much the same for a redesigned AGR, with the PWR coming out around £350/KW, or slightly above. So unreliable was the estimating exercise, the SSEB thought, that the apparent ten per cent difference between the three reactors was within the limit of uncertainty, and not significant as far as a choice between them was concerned. There might be no export prospects for the AGR, but the SSEB found it difficult to believe there were big ones for the PWR either. There might, however, be hopes here for the SGHWR, in that the LWR had hitherto commanded the world market in the absence of a competitor. The SSEB did not regard themselves as entirely dependent on the CEGB — they had the most reliable Magnox station and had commissioned their Hunterston AGR only eleven hours after the CEGB's Hinkley AGR, though starting construction seven months later. But they could not proceed with the SGHWR unless the type were nationally agreed. They had not advocated a large nuclear programme in the early seventies, just 5GW. But neither were they pessimistic now. They accepted that their actions affected the welfare of the manufacturing industry and were persuaded that a new nuclear plant by 1985 was justified. Inflation made nuclear power even more attractive.

The SSEB having given the Science Committee reactor cost estimates in their oral evidence, the CEGB and NNC both made the point in memoranda that the absolute figures were, for many reasons, of uncertain precision but that the relative levels, while still uncertain, were more dependable. The NNC thought that the differences between their own estimates and those of the SSEB and CEGB were of no great significance. Their own best figures for the three reactors were: SGHWR £336/KW, AGR £312/KW, PWR £270/KW, with capitalised fuel costs of £173-185, £167 and £141/KW present worth respectively. Their PWR figure was for a 1,100MW reactor, the comparable figure for a 2 x 660MW station like those assumed for the SGHWR and AGR being £352/KW. Their conclusion in respect of this was that 'the economies of scale for the PWR . . . are substantial and account for most of the cost advantage of the PWR, though perhaps not all when account is taken of fuel cycle costs'. They could not say whether the SGHWR and AGR might eventually yield equal economies of scale, but it was in any case clear that they could not do so for at least some years. The NNC also emphasised that cost estimates, even if reliable, should not alone be decisive. Degree of provenness, export potential, suitability for a small UK programme, longevity and accessibility for maintenance, all had to be taken into account.

Reactor size was thus critical and it was significant that in this connection the SSEB had major reservations about a 1,100MW PWR reactor and turbine on their system. Their system was expected then to have a maximum demand of 9.6GW, so that a single, large PWR would amount to 18 per cent of capacity. This they feared could adversely affect security of supply even if the unit were fully proven, which it would not be, and it would also lead to system inflexibility. The SSEB did not feel they could quantify all the resulting effects but judged that the apparent cost savings of a 1,100MW unit would prove illusory, and that there might even be an actual cost penalty. It is also of relevance in this connection that when in 1977 the CEGB increased their plant margin from 20 to 28 per cent, apart from the desperate need of the manufacturers for orders, the long construction timescale and inherent unreliability of large plant also played their part in forcing the move.[14]

The Science Committee were to complain that the NNC/CEGB estimates contained a 'surprising omission', and were misleading, in that although they claimed to be based on a 'common safety standard', the PWR had not as yet been redesigned to this standard. The Committee also noted that the NPC chairman had said that LWRs were 'not likely to meet the release criteria as specified by the CEGB for the SGHWR', while on the other hand the AEA had referred to 'unnecessarily stringent radioactivity release criteria' in the SGHWR design.

The NNC described the SGHWR as the least favourable reactor as regards exports. It was at a disadvantage both as compared with other enriched uranium reactors, which did not require heavy water, and as compared with the CANDU heavy water reactor, which did not need enriched uranium or, possibly, reprocessing. The AGR might have certain export advantages, but not until proven reliability had repaired the damage done by adverse UK publicity. It must be at least some years before the UK would be accepted as a PWR prime contractor, and it could be a mistake to suppose that the potential market here was substantial, except in relation to the fuel cycle and component supply. But if a relationship closer than that implied by a licence could be created, then the UK might be allowed the lead by the licensor in those countries where history, finance or language gave the UK an advantage. The AEA's opinion in respect of PWR equipment exports was that as regards 'wet steam' turbine plant British prospects should expand as the PWR market expanded, whether or not PWRs were chosen in Britain. As regards reactor plant however, a UK PWR programme would give added credibility when in the long term the existing world over-capacity vanished.

The evidence given to the Science Committee by the Electrical Power Engineers Association was significant in that this organisation represented 95 per cent of the engineers, scientists and managers in the electrical supply industry. Their assessment was that the weight of professional opinion in the industry was not in favour of the SGHWR. They accepted that 'continued controversy, based on a resumption of old battles', was harmful, but said they had come around to believing that serious questions about the viability of the 1974 programme were being raised, and that this was not simply 'an attempt by a defeated lobby to reverse a decision with which it disagreed'. It was essential that there be a 'genuine commitment' to any new decision, based on a general consensus between government, the industry and Parliament, otherwise there would remain a major risk that the decision might later be reopened yet again. Drawing attention to the lower radiation exposure levels to operators with gas as against water reactors,[15] the Association still saw the main argument as lying between the SGHWR and the PWR, though they could see it might be right to include the AGR in any new comparison. There was not much in the British/non-British technology argument where the AGR and SGHWR as against the PWR was concerned, since about the same percentage of technology would have to be imported in each case, and the overall import cost with the SGHWR would be higher because of this reactor's heavy water inventory.

The Health and Safety Executive having absorbed the Nuclear Inspectorate in 1975, explained to the Science Committee in 1976 that they had only recently received an SGHWR reference design, and that they had specifically been asked even then not to deal with it because it was to be further amended. The CEGB and NNC were collaborating in the Inspectorate's generic study of the PWR, and Westinghouse had assigned two staff to answer questions as they arose. Kraftwerk Union, West German manufacturers of the PWR, also had offered to supply information, and the Inspectorate were making use of their own independent consultants. Their study was based on a specific PWR but it could be expected to have a general applicability. On the other hand, if the PWR were adopted for use in Britain, there would still have to be a further review of the actual design selected.

The reactor argument in late 1976, lying mainly between the SGHWR and the PWR, could be summed up as follows. The SGHWR's opponents maintained that this reactor was more expensive, both because of its design and because of its heavy water requirement; they considered that this disadvantage would be increased by the small programme which was projected; and they were persuaded that there were no SGHWR export prospects. The reactor's proponents on the other hand were arguing that there was scope for cost reduction; that the PWR advantages were not proven; that the domestic programme might in the event be larger than was foreseen in 1976; and that the SGHWR might even prove to have export prospects, those of British PWRs having in any case been exaggerated. The safety argument as between the two reactors was confused. They were both water reactors, but, the doubters asked, were the SGHWR's pressure tubes an easier proposition than the PWR's pressure vessel, and were the reactors being compared on the same safety basis? Whatever the relative merits of the SGHWR and PWR in 1976, it was difficult to dismiss the point made in another memorandum which the Science Committee received at this time, to the effect that the Government had been 'seriously misled' in 1974 by those who had advised that the SGHWR was then 'ready to build'.

The Science Committee themselves saw the overall debate as centring on three main issues, the costs of the different reactor systems, their safety, and the impact of any choice on manufacturing industry. Their overall conclusion was severe: 'It is a sad reflection on our decision-making machinery, and on the quality of the expert advice given to successive governments, that, seven years after the last nuclear station was ordered, and after extensive private and public debate, sufficient information is apparently still not available on any of these points for the country to proceed with confidence . . .' And more specifically, two and a half years after the adoption of the SGHWR: 'the reactor has neither been designed to agreed parameters nor accurately costed, and, in consequence, neither the opponents nor the supporters can argue their case with the ability to carry conviction in the minds of others'.

The Science Committee felt that it was essential to maintain a viable nuclear design and construction industry, as well as a turbogenerator industry, and that taxpayers' money should be used to these ends. Here they found themselves broadly in agreement with the recommendations of the Heavy Electrical Machinery Working Party of NEDC and those of the Central Policy Review Staff,[16] to the effect that power station ordering should be advanced. The Committee also thought it 'perfectly respectable' for the CEGB to want government financial assistance for the SGHWR programme, though it was unfortunate that this had not been made clear from the start, since the 'circuitous method' by which it had subsequently been proposed had increased uncertainty and damaged confidence. The Committee said they wanted the SGHWR cancelled only if it could be shown to be more expensive at a given safety standard, if there were clearly better export prospects with an alternative, and if a construction start could be made with such an alternative no later than would have been possible with the SGHWR. If the SGHWR had to be cancelled then, given another year of satisfactory experience with the AGRs, the latter should be the preferred alternative. A 1,100MW PWR instead of the SGHWR, the Committee concluded, was likely to cause unacceptable delays and involve additional costs which might cancel out any notional cost advantage it appeared to have.

The Science Committee were not the only parliamentary committee concerned about the AEA's reactor policy in the mid-seventies. As they had some years previously, the Public Accounts Committee also took the matter up. The 1975/6 Committee[17] heard that a much more cautious approach was now being applied in nuclear power development than had been the case a decade previously, the Committee's particular concern at this time being the financial responsibilities of the various parties in the SGHWR programme. The 1977/8 Committee[18] were told by the Energy Department that the £145m spent on the SGHWR, viewed in context, 'represented a substantial insurance premium'. The expenditure should not be seen as having been wasted in that the prototype produced electricity and in that the project as a whole had contributed to the AEA's understanding of water reactors. Noting that the Authority's Reactor Group, in a review of the SGHWR project had referred to 'frequent changes in concept', and suspecting that because they were not paying for it, the generating boards had been tempted to elaborate the SGHWR design excessively, the Committee found it 'clearly unsatisfactory' that the Energy Department had borne costs it normally would not have done, and this without the AEA being final arbiter on their necessity even when the Authority thought some of them unreasonable. Sir Jack Rampton, permanent secretary of Energy, agreed one could argue about a few millions either way, but thought SGHWR expenditure overall about as small as could have been expected. The Energy Department doubted that the fact that they were not paying had made much difference to the generating boards' requirements. Discussion at official and ministerial levels to get the boards to contribute had, it was true, been 'inevitably difficult' until overtaken by the reduced prospective demand for electricity, but Rampton did not want to suggest that this meant the boards had not supported the programme. However, following this experience it had now been arranged that two CEGB members would in future sit on the AEA board, and one AEA member on the CEGB board.

But this is to get slightly ahead of events. The Hinkley Point B and Hunterston B AGR stations having at last begun to produce electricity in February 1976, by the spring of the following year, despite the continuing uncertainties associated with corrosion, carbon deposition and maintenance, it was being suggested that the AGR was again a possibility for the third British nuclear programme.[19] In this context some commentators chose to see a special significance in the appointment of Sir Hermann Bondi as Chief Scientist in the Department of Energy, Walter Marshall giving up the part-time post he had held there since July 1974 and returning full time to the AEA as deputy chairman. Presenting their 1976-7 report the AEA emphasised that the new AGR stations were producing electricity substantially more cheaply than contemporary fossil ones. On the basis of historic costs CEGB figures were now 0.69p/KWh nuclear, 1.07 coal, 1.27 oil: the AEA conceded that on current and estimated future costs the difference was 'not so great'. The total estimated cost of the five-station AGR programme, excluding fuel, was now £1,150m, prices as paid or anticipated.[20]

The Secretary of State had in October 1976 accepted the NNC's proposal that it should assess the merits of the three thermal reactor systems in dispute, on the clear understanding that this would 'in no way jeopardise' an SGHWR start in 1979.[21] The resulting survey by the NPC ran to ten volumes and its main features were published in July 1977.[22] Its clearest conclusion was that there was no longer a case for the SGHWR. It would be a decade before there could be operational experience with this reactor, there were no foreseeable export prospects, it was the costliest system — its further development would cost more than development of the AGR and the PWR together — and its heavy water inventory would be a major charge on the balance of payments. The SGHWR thus eliminated, the report advocated the programmatic adoption of the PWR, with another AGR station being ordered in the interim. To choose the AGR instead of the PWR would indeed be building on experience, and would lead to an earlier construction start, but this would be at the expense of exports: the AGR appeared to have no particular advantages to justify this course. Nor could the UK leave it until some future time to introduce the PWR if the object were to establish an industrial capability. Outright adoption of the PWR could be expected to lead to the cheapest electricity, and would be an important contribution to Britain's industrial strategy, but there was a tactical argument against it. This was that since the PWR was a new technology in Britain, a construction start on a station could not come before 1980, leaving the industry very short of work in the interim. Continuing with both the AGR and the PWR would offer the export advantages of the PWR, would keep the options open, and would allow an early start on a new AGR station. But it would divide the total effort available and it was not likely to be a sensible policy beyond the early eighties. The NPC report judged that all three systems could meet UK safety requirements, though with clearance for the PWR taking longer. For a four-station programme the import bills were estimated at £7m for the AGR and £104m for the PWR. The PWR was expected to be 15 per cent lower in capital cost than the AGR, and also to have a generating cost advantage of 10-15 per cent.

There were, however, still real differences within the nuclear industry and the original NPC study apparently reflected some preference for the AGR, the General Electric Company as a shareholder in the NNC then insisting on the more pro-PWR line eventually adopted.

A short version of the NII's report on 'The Generic Safety Issues of PWRs', like the NNC's report, was published by the Energy Department on 29 July 1977.[23] It defined 'generic' to mean inherent in the concept or likely to be common to any PWR, and its main conclusions were clear: 'there is no fundamental reason for regarding safety as an obstacle to the selection of a PWR . . . in Britain'. Existing information on certain safety aspects was inadequate, but such issues were 'not such as to prejudice an immediate decision in principle about the suitability of the PWR . . .'

One criticism of the NNC review was, as *The Times* put it, that 'by some quirk' it had not included an assessment of the CANDU reactor.[24] In an interesting intervention, two members of the Science Policy Research Unit at Sussex University argued that while LWRs might have made economic sense in 1965, this no longer held.[25] Pressure vessels for these reactors would have to be imported for the foreseeable future, and since Britain could not establish LWR reliability in operation before 1990, export orders were unlikely, the Americans having already had fifteen years experience with these reactors and the West Germans ten. These critics also pointed out that CANDU made much better use of uranium than did LWRs, and that, with relatively few changes, it would allow the future use of thorium if uranium became too expensive. Other observers pointed out that while CANDU reactors did indeed need an initial stock of heavy water, they used natural uranium, thereby obviating the need for enrichment, and were designed without a requirement for fuel reprocessing, thereby conforming with President Carter's newly declared objectives in this respect.

Another criticism of the NNC's terms of reference was entered by C.A. Rennie, former head of the Dragon HTR project.[26] Rennie was concerned that the latter reactor had not been reconsidered. The arguments in its favour were as valid in 1978 as they had been in 1974. It had good safety characteristics, made good use of uranium resources, had promise for process heat and direct cycle applications, and as a gas reactor was a logical UK choice. A demonstration plant in conjunction with one or two new AGR stations held out much better export prospects than were likely with PWRs.

The chief arguments for the PWR continued to be much rehearsed. It might be 15 per cent, or £75m, cheaper than the AGR for each 1,300MW station; unlike the AGR it was a system proven by the number of stations functioning; it was less complex and allowed better access for maintenance; more of it was manufactured in factories, there-

by lessening on-site problems of both the technical and industrial relations kinds; it would allow Britain to join the larger international
community of PWR operators, so ending technical isolation and
opening the way to exports. For those who believed that the argument
should turn on export prospects, the NNC's studies accepted the inevitability of international over-capacity in LWR technology but still saw
hopes for Britain, especially in Australia, Ireland, New Zealand and
Iran. Against the PWR the main arguments continued to be those of
safety and the view that much of its cost advantage over the AGR was
due to its size, 1,300 as against 660MW.

The debate had the usual confusing developments. Under the headline '£130m Nuclear Station may be Written Off' *The Times*[27] for example reported the accidental entry of salt water into the reactor
system at Hunterston, suggesting a repair bill of up to £14m after
allowing for the use of alternative generating capacity. The SSEB chairman immediately protested 'in the strongest of terms'; the 'damaging
implication' of a write-off was 'completely without foundation'.[28]
Only one of the two reactors was affected in any case, the fault was the
result of an error which could have occurred with any type of reactor,
and the salt deposit could and would be removed.

Had this accident really been a direct consequence of the AGR
design, then it might very well have tipped the balance in favour of the
PWR, since the only other AGR station working at this time, Hinkley
Point B, also had technical troubles. Later, in an editorial advocating
endorsement of the PWR, *The Times* suggested that the AGR development cost was over £3,000m, with a cost overrun in excess of £1,000m
— 'higher than that for Concorde'.[29] This time it was the AEA secretary
who wrote to complain of a 'totally incorrect' figure: the Authority
had borne nearly all of the AGR development costs, and they totalled
only some £150m.[30]

It became known in October 1977 that the CEGB had advised a start
on a redesigned AGR station in 1980 and on a PWR station in 1982.
The CEGB were understood to want an insurance against continuing
difficulties with the AGR — load factors with the two operating stations were still only around 30 per cent — and to believe that a reliable
cost comparison between the AGR and the PWR could come only from
actual orders. It seemed that they now felt that 1982 was the earliest
a start could be made on a PWR station, allowing for design changes to
win Nuclear Inspectorate approval, and a possibly difficult planning
inquiry.

Also in October 1977 came an announcement by the Energy Secretary of a new Energy Commission. Seven of this Commission's 22 members were drawn from the energy industries, seven were members of the TUC Fuel and Power Industries Committee, and eight represented other relevant interests. It did not go unremarked that while the SSEB and the Electricity Council were represented on the Commission, the CEGB were not. The Commission held their first meeting in November and immediately showed themselves to be strongly in favour of the AGR.

The Electricity Council chairman was now Sir Francis Tombs. It was, Tombs argued, 'crucial' that all sides of the nuclear industry agree on what was to be built: 'the area of political choice grows with technical uncertainty . . . governments are often, quite unfairly, put in a position of having to take decisions against a background of conflicting advice'.[31] This was exactly what Sir William Penney had said in 1964.

The new reactor crisis reached its height with Cabinet deliberations in December 1977 and January 1978. There were by now those unequivocally pro-PWR, those firmly pro-AGR, and between, those prepared to countenance both reactors, this group in turn dividing between some wanting only further design study of the PWR as a back-up to a new AGR commitment, some wanting a clear commitment to both types, and some wanting AGRs only as a stop-gap until PWRs could be built in quantity. It was generally understood that Sir Arnold Weinstock remained the main force behind the PWR, closely supported now it was thought by Sir Kenneth Berrill, head of the Central Policy Review Staff and Sir Kenneth Keith of Rolls Royce, a firm already very experienced in PWRs and now interested in possibly joining NPC. Towards the other pole of the argument were known to be the Energy Secretary, Sir Francis Tombs the new chairman of the Electricity Council, and the TUC Fuel and Power Committee. Benn made it clear that, since both the CEGB and SSEB wished to order AGRs, for him the discussion was really about what would follow this.[32] There were the leaks and inspired reports which by 1977 had become the typical accompaniment of major government decisions.[33] This group of Cabinet ministers was in favour of the Weinstock position; this group was behind Benn; the Prime Minister wanted a quick decision and was going to lend his decisive weight to the PWR; Benn, supported by his political advisors but opposed by his senior officials had failed to have his permanent secretary, Sir Jack Rampton, moved; the minister had found a formula which deferred a final decision on the PWR and which had won him the CEGB's support. Some thought that a half-switch to the PWR would be disastrous, both because the available resources were inadequate to cover the two reactor systems, and because Britain would not be taken seriously by Westinghouse or Kraftwerk Union, the potential suppliers of PWR technology. Others felt that yet again only an interim decision could be expected and that the final choice would have to come in the early eighties. There was a further round of talks.

The Government's decision was finally announced on 25 January 1978,[34] but it still contained an important ambiguity. Some £50m having been spent on the SGHWR since 1974 the discontinuation of work on it was formally approved and authorisation was given to the CEGB and SSEB to order one AGR station each, they and the Government being persuaded, it was said, that two early nuclear orders were needed and that these should be AGRs. Then came the critical and controversial paragraph of the Energy Secretary's statement: 'The electricity supply industry has indicated that, to establish the PWR as a valid option, it wishes to declare an intention that, provided design work is satisfactorily completed and all necessary Government and other consents and safety clearances have been obtained, it will order a PWR station. It does not consider that a start on site could be made before 1982. This intention, which does not call for an immediate order or a letter of intent at the present time, is endorsed by the Government.' Benn added that all future orders beyond those he had indicated would be a 'matter for decision at the appropriate time'. His statement had been 'written with great precision' and it was not a case of the Government being devious but only of their reflecting faithfully what it was open to any Government to reflect given the time scale and the uncertainty of clearance by the Nuclear Inspectorate. Neither the CEGB or SSEB on the one hand, nor Kraftwerk Union or Westinghouse on the other, had sought more.

Later,[35] answering parliamentary criticism that his announcement had left the industry in a state of uncertainty, the Energy Secretary turned upon his critics. Before PWR construction could begin the generating boards would need various clearances, in particular consent to the construction of a power station, deemed planning permission and capital investment approval, all from him, and a nuclear site licence from the Nuclear Inspectorate. The implication that the decision which had been taken was 'simply a way of slithering into a permanent decision on PWRs' was 'entirely without foundation'. The Government's wish was rather to leave a genuine option open. It was the PWR's supporters who claimed there was uncertainty, and this simply because they had failed to persuade the Government, 'or even the customer', to switch immediately and fully to this reactor.

The world's most serious nuclear accident, at Three Mile Island,

Harrisburg, Pennsylvania, in March 1979, was to leave Benn fully convinced that the AGR decision of 1978 was among the most significant British decisions ever taken in the energy field. Several times after this accident he reiterated that the decision had been taken in the face of intense pressure, from within the industry, from Fleet Street, and even from the (by then deposed) Shah of Iran.

Benn also said more than once in 1978-9 that the thermal reactor argument as a whole had 'involved a greater use of pressure' on him than he had seen in almost any other issue and had as well included a 'systematic attack upon British technology'. He was 'fed up' with reading that British gas reactor technology had no export value.[36] It would be 'highly irresponsible' to write that experience off in favour of a system which had not been developed to British safety standards. Britain was henceforth going to be double-banking on her reactor systems and other countries might want to do the same. It was also important to be realistic about export possibilities with the PWR — worldwide projections for it had been cut by about half in the previous four years, while industrial capacity to produce it had perhaps doubled. Benn also accepted the point that the CEGB wanted compensation for the Drax B coal station on the grounds that no more capacity was needed, yet had been pressing for a nuclear decision. Of the FBR he now argued that with £60-70m a year being spent on its development, the Government should be acquitted of delay. A decision on this reactor's future had not been possible before one had been arrived at on the thermal reactor situation, but the Government had said they were committed to a full public inquiry in respect of the FBR, and this was now 'next on the agenda'.[37]

Notes

1. *NEI* (September 1974), p. 701.

2. *Sunday Times*, 2 May 1976: Westinghouse offer mentioned *Sunday Times*, 18 January 1976.

3. HCD 913 c.8-9; HCD 914 c.23-4 (WA); HCD 914 c.181-2 (WA); see HLD 906 c.362 (WA).

4. HC 89 (1976-7); HC 623 (1975-6). All references below are to this inquiry except as separately footnoted.

5. See *Atom* (September 1976), pp. 231-5; also *The Times*, 16 September 1976.

6. AEA, *An Assessment of the Integrity of PWR Pressure Vessels*, report by a study group under the chairmanship of Dr W. Marshall, October 1976; see also J.G. Collier and W. Marshall, 'How UK Experts Assessed the Integrity of PWR Pressure Vessels', *NEI* (July 1977), pp. 41-5; Cottrell/Benn/Marshall correspondance was published in HC 89 (1976-7), memo 1.

7. *Financial Times*, 22 February 1977.

8. *Atom* (November 1976), p. 275.

9. HCD 896 c.278 (WA).

10. Here see also John A. Richardson, 'Reported Experiences of US Plant Designs for Light Water Nuclear Power Reactors in Relation to Current USNRC Regulations', *BNESJ*, 14 (July 1975), pp. 201-11; the American Physical Society's review of LWR designs was published in *Review of Modern Physics*, 47, supplement 1 (1975). See also Simon Rippon, 'Reactor Safety at a Cost', *New Scientist*, 23 September 1976.

11. HC 374 (1974-5), Q 35-46.

12. HC 534 (1976-7), Q 1021.

13. *Atom* (October 1975), p. 189.

14. *Energy Policy* (June 1977), p. 86.

15. But see also Alan Martin, 'Occupational Radiation Exposure in LWRs Increasing', *NEI* (January 1977), pp. 32-4; Robert O. Pohl, 'Radiation Exposure in LWRs Higher than Predicted', *NEI* (February 1979), pp. 36-8; P. Woollan, 'The Main Radiation Problem — Protecting the Workers', *NEI* (February 1979), pp. 38-40.

16. Central Policy Review Staff, *The Future of the UK Plant Manufacturing Industry* (HMSO, London, 1976).

17. HC 555 (1975-6), paras. 34-48.

18. HC 621 (1977-8), paras. 12-21.

19. For example, of many suggestions, Richard Masters, 'First Hunterston AGR should have High Availabilities', *NEI* (June 1977), pp. 25-7; *The Times*, 4 April 1977.

20. HCD 933 c.219 (WA).

21. HCD 917 c.562-3 (WA).

22. Short summary, *Atom* (September 1977), pp. 207-13.

23. Printed in *Atom* (September 1977), pp. 218-26.

24. *The Times*, 15 February 1977.

25. *The Times*, 5 November 1977.

26. *The Times*, 20 January 1978.

27. *The Times*, 3 December 1977.

28. *The Times*, 6 December 1977.

29. *The Times*, 3 January 1978.

30. *The Times*, 6 January 1978.

31. *NEI* (April 1977), p. 16.

32. HCD 941 c.1242-6.

33. For example, *Observer*, 18 December 1977; 15 January 1978; *Sunday Times*, 8 January 1978; *The Times*, 23 January 1978.

34. HCD 942 c.1391-408.

35. HCD 944 c.10-12, c.66-7 (WA).

36. These particular quotes HCD 942 c.1391-408.

37. It was not to be. In May 1979 the Conservatives replaced Labour and the new PM, Margaret Thatcher, quickly made clear her support of nuclear power in general and of the fast reactor in particular. The outgoing Government's two new AGR orders were confirmed and on 18 December, following a Cabinet leak, the Energy Secretary, David Howell, announced that the Government had made clear to the generating boards that, subject to the necessary consents and safety clearances, and a public inquiry, the PWR should be the next nuclear order. The Government were also endorsing a 15GW nuclear programme over the ten years from 1982, the reactor for the bulk of this being left open for the time being. A report from the AEA on the FBR, including the prospects of international collaboration, was expected 'fairly soon'.

11 THE WINDSCALE DECISION

The Opposition

We have now followed the political decisions relevant to British thermal reactor policy over rather more than a quarter of a century. We have been concerned almost exclusively with official institutions and with individuals acting in an official capacity, and in that sense have justified the epithet 'private' which was used in the first chapter as a shorthand description of the politics of Britain's civil nuclear development. It is time now to turn, briefly, to the 'public' politics of British nuclear power in the period 1974 to early 1978, the politics in short of what came to be called the 'nuclear debate'. Five positive government decisions fall to be considered in this period, the thermal reactor decision of July 1974; the decision in March 1976 to allow BNFL to accept foreign reprocessing contracts for oxide fuels; the decision in December 1976 to hold the Windscale Inquiry; the thermal reactor decision of January 1978; the decision in March 1978 to accept the Inspector's affirmative report on the Windscale Inquiry. The first and fourth of these decisions were discussed from a different perspective in Chapters 9 and 10 and the other three all relate to BNFL's Windscale project. We should also note a significant 'non-decision' between 1974 and 1978; no positive decision on a commercial fast breeder reactor was taken during this period, despite the apparent possibility of one, at least until the report by the Royal Commission on Environmental Pollution (the Flowers Report) in September 1976. The question of a first commercial fast reactor (CFR1) must nevertheless be understood throughout this chapter to lie waiting in the wings.[1]

One should also not overlook two other developments during this period. First, between 1974 and 1978 strong local opposition emerged to AEA geological research aimed at proving suitable rock formations for the final disposal of nuclear waste. By late 1978 permission to drill exploratory boreholes had been granted to the AEA in Caithness, but applications had been refused in Northumberland and south-west Scotland. These cases had, however, still not by this time seriously impacted on national politics. Nor had the second development, local opposition to actual nuclear stations. The first significant demonstration here occurred in May 1978 at the proposed Torness site for one of the new AGRs announced the previous January. An SGHWR had been approved for this site in 1974 after a public inquiry and in 1978 the Scottish Secretary refused a new inquiry in approving an AGR instead. The matter was later raised in an adjournment debate by Robin Cook, who argued that there was already excess generating capacity in Scotland and that nuclear energy continued to be more expensive than conventional power, but the Government's spokesman would not bend: critics, he felt, would not be satisfied with ten public inquiries.[2]

This chapter is in four parts. It looks first at the sort of things the 'nuclear opposition', and particularly Friends of the Earth, were saying between 1974 and 1976, and second, at the AEA's response. The third section then introduces the official reports which provided bench marks for the debate. Finally, the fourth part summarises the course of the Windscale affair proper. The fourth part would in fact stand on its own, but it has seemed right here to put it into full context.

The British nuclear opposition first effectively mobilised in respect of the 1974 thermal reactor decision – occasional earlier developments had wholly failed to stimulate public interest. Friends of the Earth (FoE) were from the outset in the van of this opposition. FoE were founded in 1969, the UK branch in 1970, and by 1976 there were said to be groups in twelve countries, and in Britain some 8,000 members in 160 local branches. An FoE group was formed in West Cumbria in 1973 but failed to get representation on the Windscale local liaison committee. FoE's principal initiative in 1974 was a memorandum of over 30 pages and with some 80 footnotes which two of their members, Amory Lovins and Walter Patterson, submitted to the Science Committee.[3] Lovins was to become one of nuclear power's chief international opponents, while Patterson was effectively to lead the British campaign for FoE.

Lovins and Patterson were scathing about the CEGB's case for a large tranche of LWRs, seeing it as a tribute only to Westinghouse's salesmanship. No reasonable man who understood the US safety controversy could possibly order LWRs. Of the CEGB chairman's opinion that matters of this sort were best left to experts Lovins and Patterson argued that 'Democracy is dead when the people are told that they cannot understand or participate in the gravest public decisions.'

By December 1977 FoE's nuclear aims in Britain had for more than two years been firmly centred on Windscale. Nevertheless, with the UK's thermal reactor policy again then in the melting pot, the organisation sent an open letter to the Prime Minister pointing to what they claimed were some 200 unresolved safety issues with the PWR. Lovins also wrote a covering article for *Nature*[4] in which he explained the

PWR's worldwide dominance as being due to 'mutual intoxication'. British advocates of the PWR might still not have consulted the principal original sources, preferring to rely 'as in 1973-4' on American summaries. PWRs were now 'proving all but unsaleable throughout the industrial world', and this was 'the most dramatic collapse of a major industrial enterprise in history'.

These interventions apart, the British nuclear opposition between 1974 and 1978 was firmly focused on the future of the fast breeder reactor and the expansion of the Windscale reprocessing plant. In the nature of the case, the British nuclear debate in its essentials had to be more open to scrutiny than is true for so much of the thermal reactor story. An offsetting complication was that the debate from the first became embedded in the international nuclear controversy to an extent which was only ever marginally true of the thermal reactor question. But if the thermal reactor case demonstrated the British capacity to be insular in more than geography, then the nuclear debate found the British authorities again determined that Britain's response should spring only from her own traditions.

Opposition to nuclear power had increased throughout the seventies in all the liberal democracies,[5] drawing strength from a substantial measure of international co-ordination, but the movement in Britain remained distinctly muted until the Windscale issue in 1976-7. What were the main reasons for the lower political sensitivity of the nuclear question in Britain? Or put another way, what were the main influences which shaped public attitudes to nuclear energy here?

At the level of technology there were two dominating features: the health and safety record of the nuclear industry, and communication to a wider public of professional beliefs about the technologies and procedures adopted in the UK nuclear programmes. The health and safety record, both occupational and environmental, of the British civil nuclear undertaking is widely recognised to have been without parallel in any other major industry, and also to have been internationally unsurpassed. Serious incidents have been rare, so much so that the Windscale reactor fire of October 1957 and the irradiation of 35 workers in the small oxide fuel reprocessing plant at the same centre in 1973, neither of which involved loss of life, stand out. As to the actual technology, British designers, whatever their other problems, have never doubted their ability to produce safe reactors; the governmental functions of control and sponsorship became institutionally separate as long ago as 1959; and even the sponsoring agency virtually from the outset realised that, unique among technologies, nuclear engineering could not expect to advance through its mistakes. Beyond all this the British nuclear community, for technical as well as chauvinistic reasons, for long at least tacitly regarded the reactor types on which the country's first two programmes were based, and that projected in 1974 for the third, as in a basic sense safer than the two established varieties of American reactor. (The Harrisburg accident of 1979 served to underline this, as well as drawing attention to the looser operating regimes of certain US utilities as compared with those of the CEGB and SSEB.) The special dangers of the fast reactor were from the beginning fully acknowledged, but the official position even here was that such a reactor could not be built commercially unless it were at least as safe as any other, and the AEA's Safety Directorate even considered this as 'potentially the safest reactor system'.[6]

The essential point, then, is that good historical reason convinced the British nuclear engineering fraternity that risk and the consequences of accident could be held well below a nominal, publicly acceptable level. This attitude also came to be confidently shared throughout the relevant British decision-making circles, the media, and beyond. As regards fuel reprocessing for example, the MP Tam Dalyell was far from alone in his belief that, if reprocessing there must be, 'then let it be done by us British, here in Britain, because it is likely that we do it better, and more safely, than anyone else on the face of the globe'.[7] Or in the words of the Energy Secretary, 'Britain with its record of political stability and social responsibility and expertise in nuclear power is quite clearly from a world point of view a much better place to do a lot of nuclear activity than some countries.'[8]

Looking beyond technology, a key factor in explaining the limited politicisation of nuclear energy in Britain is the prevailing socio-political culture, which, broadly, has encouraged trust in public authorities, and also consensus, except in those cases which lend themselves to party political argument. Nuclear energy has always been regarded as almost the ideal type of technical, non-party political issue, and party differences in regard to it have been fairly minor. A related circumstance is that, the allocation function of the Research Councils and a very few individuals apart, scientists and engineers are uncommon participants in British policy-making processes. In *Science and Technology in British Politics*, Vig[9] described British scientists as an interest group 'only in the broadest and loosest sense', with no developed positions on public questions. Written in the sixties, that conclusion still held in the seventies, the British Society for Social Responsibility in Science and the Council for Science and Society notwithstanding. This of course is in marked contrast to the general policy awareness of the American technical community.

To be fair, for the scientist, as for others, access to the political decision-making system is less routine in Britain than it tends to be in the United States. In regard to technical subjects the creation in 1966 of the Science Committee certainly helped, though few enough seem to have seen it as a vehicle for drawing in outsiders. That the Committee could in part provide a forum for controversial technical views was evidenced by the written submissions they received when they examined nuclear power policy for the fourth time in 1973-4.

It remains true that it is proximity to the executive and not to the legislature which really counts in Britain, and what could a scientist or technical group offer, or what deny, which the administration might want? For scientists outside government are mobilised, so far as they are felt to be needed, through the Research Council system and via *ad hoc* committees and commissions. As an independent force, only the Royal Society could perhaps have been expected to play a major advisory role, as being essentially congruent with the style of British government, but it has never seriously exerted itself.

When participatory access is constrained one naturally thinks of more formal arrangements, and specifically of the legal possibilities. This is certainly not unimportant in Britain and there have been test cases, for example, over the deaths of former workers at the Windscale plant. In addition, the law provides for many of the grievances which might be expected to arise from the development of nuclear power, and the various planning controls allow for an airing of proposals like that to expand Windscale. Nevertheless, the British legal system appears to be distinctly less amenable to citizen initiatives than is the American one, though it is probably also true that less imaginative demands have been made of it.

Despite the test cases mentioned above, the development of nuclear energy in Britain has overall been greatly facilitated by the union support which it has received, from the General and Municipal Workers Union (GMWU), from the Electrical Trades Union (ETU), from the Institution of Professional Civil Servants (IPCS), and from the TUC itself. Now it can be argued that unions the world over pay too much attention to the economic and employment aspects of a situation and too little to the health and safety dimensions. It can also be said, though, as explained below, the initial handling of the Windscale radiation leak in late 1976 must constitute a lapse here, that the union and public relations policies of the British nuclear authorities have been very competently conducted. It would still be grossly unfair to imply that the British unions have ever been other than extremely watchful of the risk element in nuclear energy as they understood it. It follows that their steady, if cautious, approval has left little room for manoeuvre by those who have wished to halt or redirect Britain's nuclear development.[10]

Perhaps the most basic obstacle of all facing the anti-nuclear lobby, at least in Britain, has been that, to stop what they see as the nuclear juggernaut, the onus has lain with them to establish that there exist other options, for it is in that currency alone that ministers can deal. The urgent need for nuclear energy may well have been repeatedly oversold, and the post-war concentration of energy r & d in the nuclear sector have been excessive, but the low-energy, high-conservation, non-nuclear alternative society advocated by environmentalists in the seventies has seemed too vague a concept for ministers to act much in accord with its requirements, at least immediately.

Having touched on FoE's intervention in the 1974 and 1978 thermal reactor decisions and indicated some at least of the reasons why the nuclear opposition found the going hard in Britain, we can now review the opposition's broad approach during the early phases of the debate.

Following their memorandum to the Science Committee both Lovins and Patterson went on to write books opposing nuclear power. Lovins preceded his with another heavily footnoted public memorandum and an influential article in *Foreign Affairs*.[11] Lovins's own memorandum and that with Patterson, if more than polemic masquerading as fact, were also distinctively different from orthodox science, and naturally attracted criticism on this count. Lovins's book *Soft Energy Paths: Towards a Durable Peace*[12] was directed primarily at US policy-makers but was also published as a Penguin and became a basic text for the British nuclear opposition. Lovins in this book saw the world as having to choose between a 'hard' energy path, based effectively on nuclear power, and a 'soft' one consisting instead of conservation and renewable energy sources, coal being capable, he thought, of providing a bridge from the 'hard' present to the 'soft' future. Lovins's core conclusion was that 'the technical, economic, and social problems of fission technology are so intractable, and technical efforts to palliate those problems are politically so dangerous, that we should abandon the technology with due deliberate speed'. Most informed observers also considered civil nuclear energy to be 'the main driving force behind the proliferation of nuclear weapons'. Fortunately, the nuclear industry worldwide was already 'collapsing under its own weight'. By phasing out nuclear power and giving a firm international lead the US could therefore 'get the world speedily and permanently out of the nuclear business'.

Patterson was a platform speaker for FoE in a public debate[13] of January 1976 on BNFL's Windscale proposal, and he and an FoE colleague made the organisation's first appearance before the Science Committee in May 1976.[14] On the first of these occasions Patterson described plutonium as an 'unthinkably dangerous' industrial material. Before the Science Committee the Energy Department's current projection of an additional 50 large reactors by 1990 was described by the FoE representatives as 'so far out of touch with economic and technical reality as to cast serious doubt on the Department's competence'. That Britain had already spent up to £400m on FBR development was 'so far out of proportion as almost to defy comprehension'. FoE did not believe in an energy gap in the foreseeable future, and coal in particular had an important part to play in the transition to 'small-scale decentralised systems in a conservation context'. Patterson admitted to the Science Committee that some of his FoE colleagues would have liked even the Magnox stations closed. He himself thought this puerile, recognising it would take a long time to get out of nuclear power. In July 1976 he wrote an article for the *Observer*[15] to open that newspaper's nuclear debate. Completely eschewing measured argument in this instance he looked, he said, to creative imagination to provide many options 'cheaper, easier and safer than the atom bomb economy'.

Patterson's book *The Fissile Society*[16] was published in mid-1977 and amounted to a savage indictment of Britain's electronuclear development. Dismissed as polemic, it received little attention. The essence of Patterson's argument was that Britain's civil nuclear decisions had been taken in a framework which ignored economic criteria and discouraged public discussion. The habit of secrecy associated with nuclear weapons had been carried over into civil nuclear engineering, producing an 'inner sanctum effect' as nuclear policy-makers became used to taking major decisions with little public interest and no public dialogue. The AEA, though having no explicit forecasting responsibilities, had 'always exerted a powerful influence on the official view of nuclear electricity in forward planning'. They had 'pressed on regardless' with no less than five different reactor types when no comparable public finding was available for other energy technologies, and without having to answer for the consequences. The Government's support of nuclear energy since 1955 had itself been 'obsessive' and 'misguided' and the further growth of the technology could lead to 'the insidious establishment of an electronuclear technical oligarchy', with a 'broad community of interest between nuclear and electric interests'. Yet nuclear electricity remained 'inordinately complex, difficult, expensive, vulnerable and risky'. To suggest it was the only option was, in Patterson's view, an 'indefensible doctrine of fatalism'.

The best-received publication by the nuclear opposition was *Nuclear Prospects: A Comment on the Individual, the State and Nuclear Power*[17] which appeared in autumn 1976, issued jointly by FoE, the Council for the Protection of Rural England (CPRE) and the National Council for Civil Liberties. (The involvement of the CPRE neatly underlined the change in public attitudes which had occurred in respect of nuclear power: a decade earlier the CPRE's Berkshire branch had pressed for a relaxation of nuclear siting restrictions so that a proposed power station at Didcot might be nuclear rather than coal.[18])

Nuclear Prospects examined nuclear sabotage, plutonium diversion and tension between the public and electricity authorities seeking sites for nuclear development. Drawing attention to developments which might accompany nuclear expansion and which must, if they materialised, threaten civil liberties and hence liberal democracy, it specifically argued that nuclear security demanded an unacceptable degree of public and parliamentary ignorance. An effective coalition between those opposed in principle to nuclear power and those with local amenity objections had not so far occurred only because no new nuclear site had recently been sought in Britain. Civil liberties were the concern of all and not only of experts, yet the public record suggested that the Government apparently had not tackled these matters 'in any but the most superficial way'.

Justice (the British section of the International Commission of Jurists), found *Nuclear Prospects* 'profoundly disturbing', and following a meeting with the Energy Secretary its spokesman described the document's scenario as 'far from fanciful'. Paul Sieghart, joint chairman of *Justice* went on to warn that 'the easiest path towards a police state would be . . . to opt for a plutonium economy'. The AEA naturally rejected this, arguing *inter alia* that nuclear power would require no more stringent precautions than those judged necessary for other industrial activities, and that the fast reactor would even protect civil liberties by preventing competition for scarce energy resources. Sieghart remained unsatisfied. He found especially worrying the Government's statement that surveillance would be confined to those whose activities were believed 'subversive, violent or otherwise unlawful', for who was to be judge of this?[19]

Another 'civil rights' issue which attracted critical comment in the course of the nuclear debate was the Atomic Energy (Special Constables) Act of 1976. This Act provided a direct statutory authority for arming the AEA's 400-500 special constables, the Energy Secretary undertaking specifically to answer in Parliament for any incident, other than training, in which a weapon came to be fired by AEA police.

There were several pronouncements during the debate by distinguished scientists speaking outside their professional fields and the AEA chairman replied to at least three of them.[20] Lord Rothschild, former head of the Central Policy Review Staff, wrote an article for *The Times* headed 'I think the future will (not) look after the future', making the point that these, without the negative, were Sir John Hill's own words. The burden of Rothschild's article was that 'No British Government since 1939 has had a greater responsibility put on its shoulders than the present one — by the Flowers report.' (John Biffen, Opposition energy spokesman, had already suggested it was perhaps the most portentious report since Beveridge.) The involvement of Z. Medvedev, a dissident Soviet scientist, resulted from an article in which he made an apparently incidental reference to a major nuclear catastrophe which he said had occurred in the Soviet Union in 1958 following the burial of nuclear waste. This incident was unknown in the West, at least publicly, and Medvedev's disclosure was received with much scepticism. Hill in particular denied that waste burial could have led to an accident even remotely resembling the one Medvedev had described, making clear his object in refuting Medvedev's claim was to dispel fears it might stimulate about the burial of waste in Britain. Stung by dismissals of his story, Medvedev thereupon wrote two further articles offering proof that an accident had occurred, and insisting that the facts best fitted nuclear waste as the probable cause. It was Hill's original response to Medvedev which disturbed Sir Martin Ryle, the Astronomer Royal. Ryle felt that if the policy of public discussion were to have any meaning, then it was important that the AEA chairman should not attempt to keep the public unaware of a nuclear accident. Ryle himself wondered whether the FBR was necessary and whether Britain could afford it: Britain had a damaging obsession with nuclear power and North Sea oil.

As against Rothschild and Ryle, Fred Hoyle's book *Energy or Extinction*[21] argued a powerful case *for* nuclear energy, though for the slow rather than the fast breeder, but Hoyle's analysis was spoiled by his political approach. Terms such as 'friend of the earth' were word-labels used by political manipulators. The real motive of political environmentalists was connected with a world energy struggle: they were operating 'right to the last letter of . . . Kremlin inspired instructions'. Hoyle's supporting argument was however too sketchy to convince, and was also undermined by a stuck-in disclaimer which accepted that FoE at least were motivated by genuine concerns and were not a Soviet tool.

The Defence

The British Nuclear Forum strengthened its role as a pro-nuclear spokesman in mid-1976 and a pro-nuclear information centre, 'A Power for Good' was established in late 1977, but otherwise the AEA and BNFL had naturally to bear the brunt of the response to the nuclear opposition, and in lectures, articles and press conferences between 1974 and 1978 their chairman in particular led for the defence. A brief review of his statements[22] is therefore particularly helpful in understanding the Authority's evolving attitude to the nuclear debate.

October 1974 found Sir John Hill convinced that the world would eventually have a 'vast nuclear programme'. The need to conserve uranium dictated a switch to fast reactors and a commercial prototype should now be constructed. Nuclear power was safer and had less environmental impact than any alternative. Storage of fission products caused great public concern but the nasty problems were really ones of management and design: 'They do not really impinge upon the public because the public is neither exposed nor involved.' It was right to exercise great caution in nuclear development, and to provide for independent regulation, but there must be a proper degree of objectivity.

By mid-1975 Hill was describing the attacks on nuclear power as 'very worrying', and in November 1975 he suggested that the nuclear industry had not yet reached maturity in terms of public understanding. This was the fault of the media and of the jargon used by nuclear engineers rather than of the public. Occupational safety in the industry was extremely high, nuclear power had the lowest human damage rate per energy unit, and the existing weighting in the country's health services towards the hazards of atomic energy indicated that public concern about nuclear power was not being sensibly directed. There was an enormous amount of expertise available to impartial bodies such as the Health and Safety Executive, the National Radiological Protection Board and the International Atomic Energy Agency: 'Let there be public debate if the public wants it, but let us pay due weight to these independent reports . . . and perhaps a little less to those who have

studied oratory.' Reprocessing had turned out to be much more difficult than had earlier been assumed, and at current uranium prices there
was no economic pressure to reprocess immediately. But prices would
rise and time was short if the fast reactor were to be made ready.
Despite commissioning difficulties with the PFR, the really important
thing was that the twenty years of fast reactor development had 'done
nothing but confirm the essential correctness of the choice made by Mr
Hinton, now Lord Hinton, in 1953 when we started on the project'.

Hill's basic axiom at this time was that world energy demand would
rise for at least 30 years, and that neither conservation nor renewable
sources could do much to help. In 20-30 years, with the production of
oil and natural gas in decline, there would have to be a rapid transfer
to coal and nuclear power. Part of nuclear energy's problem was that
the mystique of its scientific and defence background had led to lay
suspicion. Its promise had meanwhile begun to be fulfilled, with the
first nuclear stations generating at approximately the same cost as their
fossil competitors. But the fast reactor was the ultimate in fuel utilisation in that it could in principle make possible a 50-fold increase in
uranium utilisation. Even more important, it could burn all the waste
uranium, mostly U238, left over from the first reactors. Britain's stock
of this, burnt in fast reactors, was equivalent to 20,000mtce, more than
the country's total coal reserves. Since the radiation dose to the general
public from the nuclear programme was about a thousandth that from
natural background radiation, and only a third that caused by TV and
luminous dials, all Hill asked was 'that environmentalists, who for some
reason seem to have picked on nuclear power, should be rational in
relation to the claims they make'.

More than once during the nuclear debate Hill argued for the ordering of new power stations in relation to the replacement and expansion
of installed capacity rather than to meet anticipated demand. Thus he
urged before the Energy Resources subcommittee of the Science
Committee in the spring of 1976 that the FBR should not be delayed
because the CEGB happened temporarily to have excess generating
capacity. Nor did he feel that it greatly mattered whether the AEA, the
CEGB or the Government paid for CFR1 since it was all in the end
government money. (The AEA's estimate at this time was that CFR1
might cost £700-770m, though possibly much more.)

Hill told a *Financial Times* conference in July 1976 that while man's
history had been influenced by the search for greater power, he was
conservative, suspicious, and very resistant to any change in the period
of his own lifespan. Nuclear power was admittedly a fairly big step but

nuclear weapon proliferation was easily its most worrying aspect, and since the solution to this was political and international, banning nuclear power stations would not help. There was less to fear from terrorists, but it had to be accepted that somewhere, sometime, nuclear terrorism would be attempted. Critics of nuclear power had certainly abused the technology as regards plutonium hazards, occupational health and environmental pollution. Irresponsible attacks were more than an abuse, they were a national disservice.

In mid-1976 Hill wrote newspaper articles making a still more spirited defence of nuclear power. The Authority advocated no 'crash programme' of fast reactors, just the next step in a careful step by step approach. This reactor was the 'ideal nuclear incinerator . . . science putting immense resource at man's command'. The development of nuclear power would leave an asset rather than a liability to future generations, and those whose professional lives had been devoted to the study of the 'real problems' of nuclear power should also be accepted as 'friends of the earth'.

Hill's suggestion to a professional audience in July 1976 was that in their attitude to the final disposal of waste, nuclear engineers had fallen into a trap of their own making. Vitrification might be the best disposal route, but this was still uncertain and it was important meanwhile to avoid where possible both unnecessary exposures and irreversible processes. There was a danger of being driven by short-term pressures into adopting inadequate disposal measures, but also of having nuclear programmes paralysed until a final solution was found. Those involved knew there was plenty of time to reach the best solution, but this very satisfactory situation was being used against nuclear power by its critics, and one disposal method had therefore to be established to answer them, whether or not it eventually proved the best and most economic.

Hill said in September 1976 that expenditure on safety in the nuclear industry was already 'far higher in regard to incremental effectiveness than in any other industry'. He also admitted on this occasion that he was 'concerned about the form of the public debate on nuclear power . . . the audience can hardly avoid being confused if the debate is always 50:50. A second problem is that it is much easier and, more important, quicker to make an allegation than it is to answer it fully and accurately. This is particularly true of television . . .'

Hill made one of his most explicit public statements about the nuclear opposition in November 1976. The principal problems were now ones of 'political will and public acceptability' rather than of

engineering. The debate in Britain was largely about 'non-problems
. . . the public debate of science fiction . . . Much of it is uninformed
but it is there and it is holding up perfectly sound projects . . . We must
therefore answer the questions that are being posed, recognising that as
soon as one question is answered another will be asked.' It was not
incumbent upon objectors actually to meet the energy shortage a
decade ahead: 'At the time of plenty it is easy to argue that nothing
need be done.' The British public in particular was erroneously being
led by environmentalists to believe that the country had so much fossil
fuel that it could pull up the drawbridge. The nuclear industry should
also have foreseen the attack on plutonium. It was 'typical extrapolation of future requirements being met with today's practices'. If terrorism proved a problem, irradiating the plutonium fuel for fast reactors
would make it no more dangerous to transport than spent fuel from
existing reactors. Talk of loss of civil liberties was therefore 'quite
irrelevant because the problem can be avoided'. Referring specifically
to FoE, Hill said he believed that they were 'through misguided good
intentions doing a great disservice to the next two generations'.

Hill felt in February 1977 that even detractors could no longer
seriously challenge the economic advantage of nuclear power. The
debate had now shifted from nuclear stations to plutonium, but a Medical Research Council report had laid the 'hot particle' theory to rest,
and what the several tons of plutonium distributed by weapons tests
had failed to do would not be accomplished by the proverbial piece the
size of an orange. The world had in fact already learned to deal with
most of the problems of a plutonium economy. It had also been an
'unsatisfactory characteristic of the nuclear debate' that some had
assumed the programme would grow rapidly while the technology
remained static. Questions posed too far into the future could not be
answered. Hill's overall prognosis for Britain was now optimistic: 'The
British are fundamentally a sensible people. Facts eventually speak for
themselves . . . In due course the emotion surrounding this subject will
subside . . . My only regret is that we are allowing so much time to go
by when so much needs to be done.'

In the spring of 1977 Hill found another way of illustrating the
importance of the fast reactor. Reasonably assured uranium reserves
would, if consumed in thermal reactors, produce rather less energy than
the world's oil supplies. Thermal reactors alone could not therefore
transform the world's energy position, only the fast reactor could do
that. An immediate decision to build CFR1 would however still mean
that there would have been a 14-year gap since the PFR was started,

and this was already too long.

Hill said in May 1977 that the world energy picture would become increasingly grim from about 1985. He wanted therefore to urge pressing ahead not only with nuclear power, but also with new mines such as were proposed for Selby and Belvoir, and with renewable energy sources as well. Of President Carter's decision to halt reprocessing and fast reactor development, he noted that the US was especially well endowed with coal and uranium and that no other country took such an optimistic view of uranium's availability. The fast reactor could provide Britain with energy more economically than fossil fuels, and with a higher standard of safety and less environmental impact than any alternative. He continued to wish that the issues might be discussed with more quantitative argument and less emotion.

In a paper to the Royal Institution's Nuclear Energy conference in October 1977, a meeting jointly sponsored by the AEA, FoE and other pro- and anti-nuclear bodies, Hill argued that reprocessing was justified because otherwise more storage facilities for spent fuel would be needed, there might have to be limited processing even to allow such storage, and anyway, over time it would become easier to extract plutonium from stored spent fuel, so that there could then be a greater security danger than if spent fuel were simply reprocessed directly and the plutonium used in fast reactors. The latter in turn were called for because only four countries had uranium reserves large enough to do without FBRs if their energy needs were to be met. Furthermore, there was insufficient time to develop alternative approaches to that represented by the fast reactor — the only possible competitor was the thorium breeder and that would re-introduce the proliferation problem in a different way. It could even be argued that a halt to reprocessing and fast reactor development might increase the risk of proliferation, as disadvantaged countries sought energy independence. The PFR, Hill said on another occasion, was the most stable and docile reactor the AEA had ever built, with the most robust and tolerant of fuels.

Having followed Sir John Hill's observations over some three years it is natural to end with his views of the Windscale Inquiry and of the overall position following it. Speaking in January 1978, Hill said the nuclear industry could have no complaint about either the fact or the conduct of this Inquiry, but only about the circumstance that the Government had set it up a year after they had originally approved the project. Its great merit had been that claims there had had to be substantiated. The public debate had by contrast been more emotional and less successful in getting at the facts. The fast reactor, he said later, was the 'one and only nuclear incinerator'. Nuclear energy had arrived 'just in time to save the world's industrial society from a devastating collapse'.

Sir John Hill apart, the nuclear debate produced no AEA or BNFL tendency to compromise. Thus T.N. Marsham,[23] Managing Director of the AEA's northern division, described the introduction of the FBR as of more economic significance than North Sea oil. Since it had been decided to make all the major engineering changes in the transition from the DFR to the PFR, the final step to the CFR would technically be small. It would be possible for FBRs to be operated as net plutonium producers only so far as this was thought appropriate for the expansion of the electricity programme. Plutonium recycling in any case kept most of the plutonium where it was safest — inside reactor cores, and technical fixes and physical security measures rather than police methods could be relied upon to safeguard it from terrorists when it was outside.

Walter Marshall,[24] then Chief Scientist at the Energy Department as well as Director of the AEA's Research Group, in 1975 saw nuclear power as the only energy source apart from fossil fuels which could be planned upon for 1990, and the fast reactor as economically essential. In 1977, in response to the Flowers Report, he argued that while to drop out of FBR development and rely on foreign licences later would meet the sense of the Commission's recommendations, such a course would have 'very serious industrial implications and in practice might well close the option of fast reactors altogether'. In 1978 he addressed himself directly to the proliferation issue. There were many routes to nuclear weapons, only some involving plutonium, and a determined government could manufacture weapons whether or not plutonium were available. There was therefore merit in the argument that civil nuclear power 'should not be saddled with problems which are political and not actually related to nuclear power at all'. On the other hand, it was prudent to consider how nuclear power might evolve given pessimistic assumptions about future world stability. Marshall's key point was that the fast reactor fuel cycle could, if necessary, be developed such that when these reactors were fully established, recycling would take place so quickly that plutonium would effectively be continuously inaccessible for weapons purposes. The best non-proliferation policy was thus to build FBRs, and 'with all commendable speed'.

When it became apparent that a debate with regard to Windscale was going to precede one on CFR1, BNFL found themselves even more in the front line than the AEA. Their Managing Director, C. Allday,[25] insisted in March 1977 that reprocessing was essential to energy conservation and was environmentally, and probably economically, more acceptable than the 'throw away' alternative. The world must remain committed to an expanding nuclear programme, but unless the FBR were developed it could be argued that the entire nuclear programme would have been a misuse of resources: 'it would be ridiculous to stop now'. Reprocessing capacity must be available to meet the demands of the FBR as and when these arose.

Many other AEA and BNFL personnel also contributed to the nuclear debate and it is instructive to consider a few of the points they made. L.G. Brookes,[26] for example, of the Authority's Economics Branch, offered a 'Plain Man's Case for Nuclear Energy'. Brookes could sympathise with the 'prevalent near-puritanical reaction to the rapid growth of the post-war world', but this was not to see this reaction as rational. The associated political movement had now attracted 'a great deal of organised thought' and was 'backed up by intellectual analysis that is often of very high quality', but it still relied on attitudes which were mostly irrational and emotional. It was unkind to say so, but the movement was also 'predominantly elitist and middle class in origin' and a product of affluent societies. The coming energy shortage meant however that vigorous programmes of fission power were the only viable option, and even on optimistic assumptions FBR development needed to be pursued 'with all possible speed' so that it could be introduced 'at the maximum feasible rate'. Nuclear electricity was already 'quite a bit' cheaper than that from fossil stations – and here the AGRs were no exception. Misdiagnosis of the energy problem as one of gaps rather than of high prices could be harmful if it led to the pursuit of sources such as wave and solar power as alternatives to 'real solutions like the uninterrupted development of nuclear energy'. The real benefits of nuclear energy were very hard to quantify but were 'vastly greater than the figures arrived at by somewhat oversimple comparisons between generating costs'.

The risk associated with nuclear power having been a main theme of the opposition case, discussion of it had naturally to be part of the AEA's response. The Rasmussen Report[27] on nuclear safety had proved a highly controversial document in the US but the probabilistic approach to safety developed by the AEA's Safety and Reliability Directorate, set up under F.R. Farmer after the Windscale incident in 1957, never became the centre of a comparable storm in Britain. In part this was probably because the AGR and SGHWR seemed safer to nuclear opponents than did the LWRs, in part probably because in

Britain there was no single specific document to attack.[28] On International Commission on Radiological Protection standards the AEA's position was that UK environmental and occupational exposures were both extremely low and based on the conservative assumption that there was no threshold dose. Nuclear power the Authority saw as susceptible to criticism precisely because, as compared with other hazards, there was so much quantified information about the effects of radiation, and it was also wrong to consider the impact of nuclear energy in isolation from the much worse effects of other power sources. This last point was repeatedly made throughout the nuclear debate by the advocates of nuclear energy, some also suggesting that the material discharged from the stacks of coal stations exceeded in its natural radioactivity the (man-made) emissions of nuclear installations.[29]

The AEA's attitude to the nuclear opposition by late 1977 was summed up by one of their senior staff, P.M.S. Jones.[30] Opponents had conceded the extreme safety consciousness of the British nuclear industry and referenda and polls in the US, UK, Sweden and West Germany had shown positive levels of support for nuclear energy. Why then be worried about the opposition? Not because of their arguments but rather because in the course of the debate they had switched from outright opposition to deceptively credible delaying tactics. Yet it was precisely time which was critical, and procrastination in the present could well compel sub-optimal decisions in the future.

Official Aspects

Having briefly sketched the general positions of the two sides in the British nuclear debate we can now turn, equally briefly, to the official reports which helped shape it. Here, in addition to the Royal Commission report already mentioned, there were in particular the report by the Advisory Council on R&D (ACORD), *Energy r & d in the UK*; the Royal Society's response to this; the Energy Department's *Energy Policy Review*; and the official position of the CEGB as set out in their annual reports. President Carter's nuclear policy of 1977 must also be introduced in this context.

For the CEGB[31] three considerations in the nuclear debate stood out. First, Britain had an unsurpassed nuclear regulatory system; second, British operators had demonstrated they could develop nuclear power responsibly, reliably and economically; and third, the people most involved, the workforce, trade unions and local populations, all had 'accepted nuclear power in their stride'. Nuclear power should certainly be debated, but neither the industry's track record nor the 'dismal consequences' of nuclear abstention should be overlooked. The energy r & d study by ACORD[32] was published as a contribution to the National Energy conference of 22 June 1976. Chaired by Walter Marshall, the ACORD report concluded that 'in most perceived views of the future nuclear power will be essential'. The polar nuclear scenarios outlined in the study were shown as having on the one hand only 20-25GW nuclear by 2000 and nil by 2025 as all nuclear plant was phased out, and on the other, figures of 210-240 and 820-890GW by these target dates.

The future role of nuclear power as seen by the Energy Department in late 1976 was spelled out in the department's *Energy Policy Review*.[33] In the short term there was excess capacity. Coal stocks stood at 34m tons and, no new power stations having been ordered for nearly three years, none was needed on demand grounds before 1980. Since for some years after 1980 Britain would possibly be a net energy exporter this was an uneasy context against which to take long-term decisions. The Energy Department's report made estimates of primary fuel demand and of electricity demand in the year 2000, and concluded that if electricity demand were near the maximum then nuclear power was the only established source which could cope. But on the figures in the report the *maximum* nuclear programme on construction grounds, itself justifiable on demand grounds only if electricity demand were high, was roughly equivalent to the estimated *minimum* residual primary fuel requirement in the year 2000. It followed that, if the residual primary fuel demand were above the minimum, not even nuclear power could cope. The public debate on nuclear power should, the document argued, be based on a full understanding not only of the dangers of nuclear power, but also of 'the consequences which deciding against the nuclear option would have for the country's economy and its ability to achieve social and other objectives'.

Nuclear Power and the Environment,[34] the sixth report of Britain's standing Royal Commission on Environmental Pollution, was published in September 1976 and was the first official study of its kind to be produced anywhere. The Commission's chairman at the time was Sir Brian (later Lord) Flowers, previously an AEA staff member and also then a part-time member of the AEA. Apparently under the impression that an early decision on CFR1 was contemplated, Flowers had written to the Prime Minister during the course of the Royal Commission's study, pointing out the serious and fundamental difficulties associated with the fast breeder. He had also given the nuclear establishment, as they saw it, a 'stab in the back' with trailer remarks on the Commission's report at the National Energy conference in June 1976.[35]

The Royal Commission's work did considerably more than catalyse an existing debate. It put the main arguments for and against nuclear power on a basis which thereafter made reasoned criticism of fission energy almost orthodox. It is doubtful whether even by extensive quotation one could adequately communicate the complete sense of the Royal Commission's report, such was its complexity and balance. It does however seem possible to provide a sufficient summary to allow the report's major contribution to the nuclear debate to be appreciated.

The Commission's most important general conclusion perhaps concerned their assessment of the opposition to nuclear power: 'It seems that nuclear power has in some ways become the whipping-boy for technological development as a whole . . . Nuclear power provides a dramatic focus for opposition in some countries to technological development and we have no doubt that some who attack it are primarily motivated by antipathy to the basic nature of industrial society, and see in nuclear power an opportunity to attack that society where it seems likely to be most vulnerable, in energy supply.' Contacts with the British proponents and opponents of nuclear power suggested to the Commission that the arguments of both deserved to be heard with greater mutual understanding.

On reactor safety, although anxious that the Government should have independent expert advice on hazardous technological developments generally, the Commission did not consider the hazards of nuclear power either so unique or so great that it should be 'abandoned for this reason alone'. On the other hand, they did not find inconceivable terrorist action against nuclear facilities which might then lead to desperate political measures and chronic economic disruption. Judging that plutonium had a 'unique and terrifying potential for threat and blackmail against society' the Commission were moved to one of their most provocative statements: 'We are sufficiently persuaded by the dangers of a plutonium economy that we regard this as a central issue . . . We should not rely for something as basic as energy on a process that produces such hazardous substances as plutonium unless we are convinced that there is no reasonably certain economic alternative . . . We should also be aware of the advantages that nuclear power offers . . . though we do not think that these outweigh the risks . . . they are real and should not be minimized.' However, elsewhere in their report, revealing that they had considered whether Britain should try to abandon fission power altogether, they concluded that 'even if it could be confidently supposed that this could be done without risk of unacceptable restrictions on energy supply in the future, we should not think that such a strategy was wise or justified'.

It was 'entirely credible' that terrorists might fabricate plutonium into a 'crude but very effective weapon', but the Commission were 'by no means convinced' that the British Government had realised the full implications of this. Feeling they had to look fifty years or more ahead they also feared 'an insidious growth in surveillance', and the unquantifiable effects on civil liberties of such requirements 'should be a major consideration' in any nuclear expansion. It was all the more remarkable therefore that, in all the official documents they had encountered, nowhere had they found 'any suggestion of apprehension about the possible long-term dangers to the fabric and freedom of our society'.

The Commission made another of their more controversial statements in connection with highly radioactive wastes: 'it would be irresponsible and morally wrong to commit future generations to the consequences of fission power on a massive scale unless it had been demonstrated beyond reasonable doubt that at least one method exists for the safe isolation of these wastes for the indefinite future'. The Commission were confident an acceptable solution would be found to the waste problem, but they were surprised so little attention had hitherto been given to it. In addition, they looked for a more systematic approach in the future to the problems of gaseous emissions, discharged liquid wastes and low-level solid wastes.

The Commission also had serious practical doubts about the official strategy of a 'high-nuclear, high-electric' future. AEA projections[36] given to them for the year 2000 ranged from a desirable high of 210-285GW nuclear down to a practicable 104GW, including 33GW of FBRs. This the Commission thought would be 'exceedingly wasteful' in energy terms and there were as well 'very considerable environmental objections' to it. The need for a major nuclear expansion with FBRs they judged 'by no means so clear cut' as they had been told. And although they themselves were not advocating a non-nuclear future, it was 'highly desirable' that there be the fullest discussion even of this. Their 'basic concern' was that 'a major commitment to fission power and the plutonium economy should be postponed as long as possible, in the hope that it might be avoided altogether'. Here they feared that the Energy Department's passivity would lead gradually to an 'overriding dependence on nuclear power through tacit acceptance of its inevitability'. It was not for them either to propose or oppose CFR1, but they viewed 'with misgivings' the 'highly significant first step which it would be'. If CFR1 did proceed, and they accepted it was not too soon if FBRs were to be in operation by 2000, then they hoped it would be regarded 'as being in the nature of an insurance policy, albeit an expensive one', with it clearly understood no inevitable commitment was being undertaken.

Such a commitment should instead be preceded by one of a different kind which they wished the Government to make. Nuclear power raised 'long-term issues of unusual range and difficulty', these were 'political and ethical, as well as technical' and there had so far been 'very little official consideration' of them. More was needed than 'bland unsubstantiated official assurance' and a special procedure, perhaps along the lines of US environmental impact statements, was called for: 'The ultimate aim is clear; it is to enable decisions on major questions of nuclear development to take place by explicit political process'.

It should be clear from this brief digest that the Royal Commission's report amounted to an authoritative questioning of nuclear power. But the Commission's scepticism was applied equally to the arguments of the nuclear opposition. Two of the latter's objections to nuclear power were that the carcinogenic potency of plutonium particles in the lung had been grossly underestimated (the 'hot particle' theory[37]), and that there would be a net energy deficit during a rapid nuclear expansion.[38] The Commission took steps to satisfy themselves that both these hypotheses were invalid.

In their response to the Royal Commission[39] report the AEA noted that the study gave a generally clean bill of health to the existing nuclear industry, and said they disagreed with the Commission's assessment of the future. The fears which the Commission had expressed on this were 'greatly exaggerated'. Building CFR1 would not prejudge the FBR issue, other energy sources could not make a major contribution in the time available, and the Royal Commission's alternative energy strategy was unsound. The Authority could not accept the conclusions drawn on the dangers of plutonium and also saw no grounds for expecting that the impact of nuclear energy on society would ever be significantly greater than it already was. They did however accept that they had a responsibility to explain 'fully and in public' the implications as well as the advantages of nuclear power.

Inevitably, for months afterwards the Royal Commission's report was widely quoted, and abroad as well as in Britain. Only an outline of this response can be given here.[40] *The Times* judged the report 'a distinguished contribution' to the nuclear debate and broadly accepted its arguments, though Britain could not by lone abstention escape the 'plutonium economy'. To the *Guardian* the report was 'enthralling'. If such commissions had a valid part in forming public policy, 'it must now be inconceivable that Britain should commit itself in the next few months or years to the use of plutonium for the production of energy'. *Nature* saw the document as containing both 'excellent reasoning' and 'sloppy thinking'. It made outstandingly clear the need for more discussion, and that the Energy Department had delayed a decision on CFR1 was already more than a token response. The British Nuclear Energy Society's *Journal*, by contrast, saw the report as a 'masterpiece of confusion' and the Commission as 'facing in all directions'.

The Lords debated the Royal Commission report in December 1976[41] and, as usual with this House's debates on nuclear energy, there were several very well-informed speeches. Lord Sherfield thought one could find in the report quotations supporting 'almost any point of view'. As a former AEA chairman, he found the report lucid and valuable, and it was useful to have various misconceptions removed. But the Commission's chapter on energy was not convincing, and it was difficult to believe nuclear power could threaten civil liberties. The report gave the Government every encouragement to delay, and Governments needed little encouragement in that direction.

Baroness White, who had been a member of the Royal Commission, attributed much of the report's merit to Sir Brian Flowers. As he had admitted, it had set him at odds with some of his colleagues. The 'most disappointing aspect' of the Commission's investigations had been 'that we felt that the attitude of those concerned with the administration of our nuclear endeavours in this country was simply not geared to the quite understandable apprehensions of the general public . . . some of us, at least, were often depressed by what we felt was the blinkered outlook which could preclude adequate consideration of matters not directly in the line of vision. We were depressed by a certain rigidity of mind, and in some cases by what I have called the impenetrable complacency of those in high places.' The Commission had clothed their observations in restrained language, despite 'a bromide from the Cabinet Office', but 'bland assertions' were very unconvincing. On security, waste management and energy strategy the Commission's witnesses had failed to convince. It would have been irresponsible for the Commission to have rejected the nuclear option, but lay members had not been able to swallow the assumption shared by the Energy Department and the AEA that the FBR was the only real option. Too many of the official witnesses had appeared to have virtually closed minds on alternatives to this.

Lord Hinton thought the report was surprisingly wrong in suggesting that it was the fast reactor which led to the plutonium economy: thermal reactors had already introduced that. Nor were fast reactors inherently more dangerous than thermal ones. It had been right to draw attention to the risks, but some of the Commission's paragraphs had been 'so over-cautious as to be timid and almost contradictory'. The fast reactor must proceed so that uranium resources were not squandered as fossil fuels had been. Lord Aldington, chairman of the National Nuclear Corporation, found the report 'balanced and clear'. Flowers had said the nuclear industry should be retained at the lowest viable level, and there should be an 'unequivocal commitment' at least to this, but the AEA's reference programme was neither 'possible or probable, either in the requirement or in the achievement'.

Lord Zuckerman, formerly Chief Scientific Adviser to the Government, was highly critical of the Royal Commission's report. It was indeed all things to all men, but the overwhelming impression it gave was that nuclear power was too dangerous to be acceptable. The Commission had exceeded their terms of reference, which was good practice only if done with competence. The report was inconsistent and peripheral parts of it were sometimes naive to the point of being science fiction. It was also wrong to complain of official complacency. It was all too easy to criticise technical advisers, and easier to ask for independent and authoritative supervisory bodies than to find them. Zuckerman had been 'shattered' to read the Commission's implied criticism of the Medical Research Council. He had also had a letter from a member of the Commission, Sir Frederick Warner, to the effect that the latter had signed the report only on the assumption that there would be no delay to Windscale. A close reading of the paragraphs relating to Windscale did not necessarily give reason for delay but Sir Frederick apparently felt that they had been so used. Zuckerman also referred to the study being conducted in the US by the Ford Foundation. This was 'highly professional' and 'a much more extensive' one than had ever been attempted before.

The Commons also debated nuclear power in December 1976,[42] but at 4.39 in the morning. Here again there was substantial quotation from the Flowers Report, as well as complaints that the Government had failed to arrange a proper time for a full discussion. This debate was initiated by Nigel Forman, the Conservative MP throughout most involved in the nuclear question.[43] The further development of nuclear power was, Forman thought, both 'necessary and inevitable', in that a virtual consensus had emerged that the country would eventually face an energy gap. But common sense, public criticism and the passage of time had forced the AEA to become more realistic in revising downwards the nuclear projections they had given the Royal Commission. There had been 'growing doubts' about the AEA's previous advice to the Government but the body remained a 'well-established and powerful institution' backed by a 'mystique of professional expertise' not readily available to the lay politician. Nuclear power could easily become a 'fearful institutional tapeworm' and Britain could not and should not allow CFR1. If there really were no alternative to the FBR it would be better simply to stretch the existing PFR design. Politicians were 'uniquely placed to deliberate and to decide' the environmental and social objections to nuclear power, and a generation which failed to give exhaustive thought to the consequences of irreversible nuclear decisions would stand convicted of a 'peculiarly wicked selfishness and shortsightedness'.

Other speakers in this debate suggested that it was the 'height of obscenity' to bury waste in areas like the Western Isles and Galloway (Donald Stewart); that a 'new ethical dilemma' was introduced when industrial communities contemplated transporting their waste to communities with a different lifestyle (Robin Cook, one of Labour's most active nuclear critics); and that there was bound to be public unease about the profound polarisation of views exhibited by Sir Brian Flowers, Lord Rothschild and Sir John Hill (Geoffrey Johnson Smith). A further short debate[44] on the environmental aspects of nuclear power took place at 7.49 the same morning, the Scottish nationalists insisting that there was a 'welling tide of public disapproval' at the prospect of depositing waste in Scotland, but the Commons did not address themselves fully to the Royal Commission's report until December 1977,[45] and even then the occasion was a Friday debate initiated by a backbencher, Leo Abse.

In a lecture of December 1976 Sir Brian Flowers expanded somewhat on the Royal Commission's report.[46] The Commission, he said, had not hoped to resolve the 'Faustian bargain', only to expose it. Their report had not been written with a view to detailed textual criticism and he was disappointed the public debate had not subsequently reached a higher level. There was a decade before Britain need become 'irretrievably committed' to nuclear power, and waste disposal called for agreement on 'at least one specific site', if only as a fallback. Flowers agreed that the Commission's report was not as explicit as it might have been on the connection between the FBR and the plutonium economy. Thermal reactors did indeed introduce the latter, but the really important point was that the FBR, through reprocessing, might increase dependence on nuclear power a hundred fold. It was clearly vital that advice to ministers should be seen to be independent of the major factions in the argument about energy, and it should be a matter of public concern that currently this did not obtain. The Government should also cease to 'skulk behind the Official Secrets Act'. If the Commission's proposals were accepted then a 'cautious development of nuclear power could be seen in a more acceptable light'. There was still 'no need for undue speed', in that the existing PFR would yield information for 5-10 years, and CFR1 could not in any case be started for 3-4 years. The conditions under which CFR1 should be built would hardly make it 'commercial', but it would be environmentally acceptable. However, thermal reactor development had proved 'only just' within Britain's resources and fast reactor development was likely to be beyond those resources unless pursued collaboratively. There was, in Flowers's opinion, time in the meanwhile to effect 'a reconciliation between views that at present are merely polemical — according to the standards and values of a society that is both technological and humane'.

Flowers also drew attention in this lecture to a study in some respects paralleling that of the Royal Commission. This was a report by a three-man Commission chaired by Mr Justice Fox which had been set up by the Australian Government in 1975 to examine proposals to exploit uranium deposits in the Ranger area of the Northern Territories.[47] Published in October 1976, this report like that of the Royal Commission, offered a broad view of nuclear power. Its most provocative conclusion was that the nuclear power industry was unintentionally contributing to an increased risk of nuclear war, and that this was the most serious hazard associated with nuclear power. Like the Royal Commission, the Fox Report also saw fit to criticise a lack of objectivity in the proponents as well as the opponents of nuclear energy. This report too was therefore grist to the mill of the British nuclear opposition.

The Royal Society had been invited by the Energy Department to comment on the ACORD study of energy r & d, and in response a group chaired by Sir Harrie Massey reported early in 1977.[48] This group accepted that the nuclear option needed to be kept open. A credible nuclear policy for Britain had to be based on the fast reactor, and a higher priority should be given to this than to further thermal reactor development. Britain had only to maintain a strong position on the FBR to have an excellent chance of participating in a future EEC venture. Reprocessing, at least within the UK, need not increase the hazards of nuclear power. The group's report also urged a stronger nuclear waste disposal programme and asked that fossil and nuclear r & d should not be at the expense of other energy sources. The fact that Sir Brian Flowers was a member of this Royal Society group naturally attracted attention — some saw it as a return to orthodoxy.

The Government's reply to the Royal Commission was published in May 1977.[49] The Government said they were accepting most of the Commission's recommendations and itemised several institutional changes. The Commission's proposition that any large-scale commitment to nuclear power should be conditional upon the demonstration of a safe waste containment method was 'bound to be the dominant factor' in the relevant decisions, but the Government said they noted the Commission's own confidence that such a method would be found. Of the terrorist threat the White Paper argued that 'by giving careful attention to security considerations at the design stage . . . we could ensure that [plutonium's] availability in an accessible form remained severely restricted'. This would both discourage terrorism and reduce the threat to civil liberties. Overall, surveillance to counter terrorism depended 'more on the prevalance of terrorism than on the availability of plutonium' — which made irrelevant any unilateral British decision not to use the material. In response to the Commission's request for an 'explicit political process' of consultation the Government said they wished to think further, but they did accept that such a process should be 'settled and announced' before any decision on CFR1.

Subsequent to the Royal Commission report the Energy Secretary published a list of 19 questions he had addressed to the Nuclear Installations Inspectorate (NII). These concerned the comparative safety of thermal and fast reactors, the kinds of accidents possible with the latter and their consequences, the problems arising from the use of plutonium, nuclear waste, and the balance of advantage in respect of CFR1. The only MP to take up Tony Benn's invitation to contribute questions was Nigel Forman, who asked 23 mostly covering aspects of the same ground. FoE also submitted a list of questions, some 45 in all, again centring on the FBR but also taking in other reactors and more general issues. In due course a document was produced offering answers to these questions, the NII taking primary responsibility for most of it.[50]

Many of the questions were said to call for unconditional assurances of safety and the Inspectorate observed that absolutes of this sort were unobtainable. British nuclear development had since 1960 been taking place under their eye, and so the general tone of their document was naturally one of confidence. Of the FBR they suggested that the conservationist argument was perhaps even more important than the relevant economics. They could see no reason why a commercial fast reactor could not be made safe enough for licensing, and this without becoming uneconomic.

These three sets of questions to the NII were shortly followed by two other sets.[51] One of these resulted from a meeting in February 1977 between the Energy Secretary and the three organisations responsible for the monograph *Nuclear Prospects*. Benn agreed to accept from these organisations a set of questions dealing with security, siting and terrorism, and drawing on the various departments concerned, subsequently published answers to the 23 they submitted. The essence of these answers was that a large nuclear programme would create no security problems materially different from those already existing. The second set of follow-up questions, posed by Dounreay personnel, were intended to balance things up by drawing attention to the health hazards of conventional energy sources. Replies to these too were published.[52]

We have now noted the principal official reports which bore on the British nuclear debate and need to look finally at relevant events abroad. All participants in the British debate were, of course, aware of the continuing general opposition to nuclear power, and especially to the FBR, in Western Europe and North America. Britain was also among 15 countries to introduce uniform controls over nuclear exports. But it was only President Carter's nuclear policy which impinged directly and significantly on British policy-makers.

In March 1977 the Ford Foundation released their study *Nuclear Power Issues and Choices*.[53] The main conclusions of this were that LWRs were economically and environmentally acceptable; that uranium supplies were sufficient to fuel these reactors to the end of the century without plutonium; that weapons proliferation was enough of a risk to justify the indefinite postponement of reprocessing and recycling; that the economics of reprocessing were in any case marginal; and that the commercial exploitation of the FBR should be delayed.

Two of the Ford study group soon afterwards joined President Carter's administration, one, Joseph Nye, as deputy Under-Secretary of State, and the President and his energy adviser, afterwards Secretary, met with the Ford panel on the day the report was published. It therefore came as no surprise when the Ford study's main recommendations were adopted in a policy statement on 7 April. The President specific-

ally stated on this occasion that the country's leading reprocessing
plant, a private venture, would receive 'neither federal encouragement
nor funding' for its completion. The FBR programme would be restruc-
tured away from plutonium fuelling and would receive a lower priority.
Steps were also to be taken to increase supplies of enriched uranium
and to make these available internationally. Carter said that in addition
he wanted to establish an international nuclear fuel cycle evaluation
(INFCE) programme, in the hope of proving new fuel cycles with less
serious implications for proliferation.

Two major criticisms of the Ford Report were that it took a much
more optimistic position on uranium supply than did official projections; and that reprocessing of spent fuel in any case was the least
attractive, because most costly and slow, of many existing technological routes to weapons, with yet others likely to appear in the eighties.[54]
These criticisms were repeated following the President's statement and
many others were added. Among the 'more squalid if more understandable'[55] motives attributed to the US was the consideration that if the
US proposals were adopted internationally, then given its lead in
thermal reactors and enrichment and its lag in the FBR and reprocessing, the US stood to gain a significant commercial advantage. Yet
another critical political view was that at the very least President Carter
had gratuitously strengthened the anti-nuclear lobby.

Nye subsequently explained the Carter stance to an International
Atomic Energy Agency conference in Salzburg. He confirmed there
that permission for spent fuel of US origin to be reprocessed elsewhere
was being considered on a 'case-by-case' basis. When he added that he
did not think a case-by-case approach and 10-year contracts were consistent, he was seen to be striking specifically at the basic premiss of
British and French reprocessing policies, since these depended on long-
term contracts from customers like Japan using US-supplied fuel. Nye
admitted there was no guarantee that alternative fuel cycles would
prove viable, but argued that it was essential they be explored while
there was still time.

INFCE was in due course set up, Britain and Japan were appointed
co-leaders of its working group on reprocessing and plutonium recycling,
and a final plenary conference was scheduled for 1979/80. Later, in the
context of the Windscale Inquiry, Nye wrote to the Foreign Office suggesting that official testimony at the Inquiry had drawn unwarranted
conclusions about US policy. When news of this letter eventually
became public the initiative was seen as tantamount to asking Britain
not to proceed with Windscale, and this was naturally seized upon by

objectors. That US policy on reprocessing had been badly misrepresented by official participants in the Windscale debate was also the theme of a letter sent to President Carter by five US legislators. This too was highlighted in the British press as a 'boost to the anti-nuclear lobby', though there were by now some rather contradictory noises coming out of Washington.

Windscale

The first three sections of this chapter constitute, in a sense, background to the three key decisions on the Windscale expansion identified earlier. We can now examine those decisions in a little more detail.

The British nuclear debate first developed some momentum in 1975. At the start of the year the *Guardian* and Independent Television drew attention to the deaths from cancer of two Windscale workers, and Britain's first formal anti-nuclear group, *Half Life*, was set up in mid-year in Lancaster, among its first initiatives being the organisation of a 'nuclear awareness' week and a demand for the abandonment of the Heysham AGR station. At about the same time FoE began a newsletter offering advice on involvement in the gathering debate. The debate began in earnest on 21 October 1975 with a *Daily Mirror* 'shock report on lethal imports', its education correspondent referring to the UK in this front page report as the 'world's nuclear dustbin'. This was a 'scoop' in a communication rather than an information sense, in that BNFL's wish to construct a major new thermal oxide fuel reprocessing plant (THORP) at Windscale, and to accept for reprocessing there increased quantities of spent fuel of foreign origin had since late 1974 been public knowledge.[56] A 1,500 tonne/year plant at Windscale had long been handling spent uranium metal fuel from the domestic Magnox stations and those the consortia had sold in Italy and Japan — the latter with provision for return of plutonium but not for return of waste. And a small 'head-end' oxide fuel reprocessing facility had also been built at Windscale when the improved performance of Magnox fuel left spare reprocessing capacity: this facility had operated until the accident of 1973 mentioned earlier. In 1975 there was also no secret even about the imminence of a large Japanese contract for oxide fuel. In November 1975 the *Mirror* followed up with another half-front page headline, 'Sign Here for Japan's Atom Junk.' Reaction was quick. From an average of one Parliamentary Question on the subject every month or so, the number jumped to eleven in October. There were stories in other newspapers, on radio and on TV. The nuclear industry responded bitterly to what it saw as sensationalism, though oddly enough the term 'world's nuclear dustbin' had been applied unpejoratively to Windscale by members of the industry themselves. FoE and *Half Life* organised a protest demonstration at Barrow in December and BNFL a public meeting. On 8 December a short, late, and ill-attended adjournment debate[57] was moved by the MP for the Windscale area, John Cunningham, afterwards a junior minister. Cunningham drew attention to local and union support for BNFL's plans, regretted that fellow Labour members had put down Early Day motions without consulting him, and suggested that what he called the 'Daily Dustbin' should take a lesson in objective reporting from the *Whitehaven News*.

The Energy Secretary had a pivotal role in the subsequent debate and there is therefore particular interest in his public position as this emerged.[58] Tony Benn had become firmly identified with the concept of 'open government' while in Opposition in the early seventies, and when he and Eric Varley exchanged posts in 1975 the nuclear field at once provided him with an ideal opportunity for his ideas. He later said that initially he was concerned that the nuclear debate seemed slow to mature in Britain, and that his aim was always to ensure that nuclear questions were handled more rationally and reasonably in the UK than was the case elsewhere.

BNFL's proposals reached Benn in September 1975 and he hoped at first that the Science Committee would take up the whole reprocessing issue. He made clear that he was concerned Britain should not become a permanent repository for foreign waste, and there were accusations both that he had become ambivalent in his overall attitude to nuclear power, and that he had himself inspired press interest in the reprocessing question. In any event, he personally instigated the public debate which BNFL organised in London in January 1976.[59] Opening this he stressed that, given the full availability of information on which he was determined, the public airing of the reprocessing question marked a departure from past practice in the handling of major technological decisions. It would have been preferable had there been a public debate before the first nuclear programme had been authorised, but since there were still real decisions to be taken as between nuclear and non-nuclear energy systems, and as between different nuclear systems, debate was even now not fruitless.

The first Windscale decision followed in due course. On 12 March 1976, after a visit to Tokyo, Benn announced — in a written reply[60] — that the Government had decided to allow BNFL to enter into new overseas reprocessing contracts, provided suitable understandings could be reached to give the company the option of returning residual radioactive waste. He added later that he had come to think it right that Britain should get a proper share of the rapidly expanding reprocessing business,[61] but he also maintained that the January debate had helped in getting appropriate arrangements for handling the waste problem. Dissatisfied, FoE ran a protest 'nuclear excursion' to Windscale.

Several times during 1976 and 1977 Benn gave clues to his broad attitude towards nuclear power. Comparing his experiences as Energy Secretary in the seventies and as Minister of Technology in the sixties his role as 'statutory elector' had, he felt, grown. The ministerial responsibility for nuclear decisions was a lonely one. These decisions required an understanding, 'as far as that is possible for laymen', of very complicated issues. The only way the Government could respond to public anxiety was by 'adopting policies of the greatest possible openness', and then listening attentively to the ensuing discussion. There must be wide knowledge and understanding of the facts about nuclear power in order that a broader public than previously might participate in the formation of energy policy. By publishing all relevant information ministers had the opportunity of knowing public feeling in advance of making decisions, and the public were in a position to appreciate the basis for those decisions. (The Energy Department in fact received some 600 letters and 12 petitions on nuclear power in 1976.[62]) Uncertainties about safety, together with lower demand forecasts and a healthy supply situation, justified Britain, Benn felt, in taking time. Certainly this was true in respect of the FBR. Quite different considerations did however apply in the choice of thermal reactor, where industry needed urgently to know where it stood.

In June 1977 Benn told the Commons that he had been assured by Sir John Hill that the rate of spending on the FBR had thus far been such that its development could not be said to have been delayed. He did not, he said, intend to preempt a decision either way, but he did believe that in nuclear policy 'there must be absolute ministerial control'. The questions at the core of the nuclear debate, he said on another occasion, could not be dismissed as the work of cranks or subversives. He personally made no claim to understand 'more than something of the jargon of this science', but the 'decision must be a political one, otherwise we are abdicating our responsibilities to experts'. Ignorance had been bred by the tradition of security surrounding the nuclear industry.

On 13 December 1976 Benn gave the Commons details of a radioactive leak which had occurred at Windscale.[63] The leak had been discovered on 10 October but he himself had not been informed until early December, the Environment Secretary having been told shortly before. Given that this had happened while BNFL were waiting for approval for their Windscale project, the media naturally suspected a cover-up. Benn now said he had given instructions that in future he was to be immediately informed of any similar incident, however apparently trivial. It must be for ministers and not those managerially responsible to decide whether a report should be made to the House. Again re-affirming his commitment to openness, he made plain his embarrassment at what had occurred.

Following the decision of December 1976 to hold the Windscale Inquiry, Benn stressed that, while reprocessing was needed even with the existing nuclear programme, he strongly supported the setting up of the Inquiry. Prior statutory authority to assist BNFL was essential to prevent later delay — THORP was projected to cost £500-600m — but these powers would not be activated unless planning permission were forthcoming as a result of the Inquiry.

On renewable energy sources and conservation Benn's view was that it would take time and effort to bring them to where they might merit expenditure comparable to that already going into established technologies. Full-scale nuclear development he described at another time as 'neither self-evidently inevitable nor self-evidently wrong'. His Sunningdale conference[64] in July 1977 found him wondering what effect £2b would have spent on conservation as compared with the FBR. It was easy to talk of keeping options open but what he needed was guidance on priorities. His objectives were energy self-sufficiency for Britain for as long as possible, industrial strength and export success, but also security and peace of mind. He would be very nervous, he told a Royal Institution conference in October 1977, were he in the nuclear industry with its high rate of spend, and yet not subject to a corresponding degree of scrutiny. (The AEA's nuclear r & d had cost £310m in the five years to 1976, the 1976-7 figure was £102m, and between 1973 and 1977 the Energy Department had spent £47m on the centrifuge.)

Probably Benn's most pointed parliamentary observations came in a parliamentary debate late in 1977. In his whole political life he had, he said, 'never known such a well-organised scientific, industrial and technical lobby as the nuclear power lobby. It is not so much the Friends of the Earth as what Eisenhower might have called the nuclear industrial complex of which I am aware . . .' In publishing every document he had acted partly in self-defence. He had also been delighted at President Carter's initiative, which he saw as an attempt to exert political control over 'a body of expertise which, I suspect worldwide, has had its business too much unchecked'.

Still more remarkable were two in particular of Benn's revelations in a lecture of January 1979.[65] He then said he believed the AEA had known at the time of the Soviet nuclear accident of the late fifties, made public by Medvedev only in 1976. And of the Magnox corrosion difficulty in the late sixties he disclosed that there had been 'very strong pressure not to reveal the full extent of this problem for fear of creating alarm'. Benn also in this lecture made quite clear his position on the FBR: 'If I am very doubtful about the FBR, as I am, and believe that any proposal to build one should be delayed, as I do, it is because I am not yet satisfied that our democratic machinery is strong enough to control this new development and not because I doubt the technical competence of those in the industry to construct and operate one.' The environmentalists, the minister said, had 'a very strong case' when they argued that the public 'were never kept informed that the technology to process, by vitrification, high toxic nuclear waste has not yet, even now, been fully perfected'.

These remarks were later followed up in a *Nature*[66] interview. It had been, Benn then said, a 'great mistake' in the creation of the AEA to hive-off policy formation as well as execution. Sir John Hill had recently recently asked him how the situation could be improved and he intended to write to the AEA chairman outlining 'a new list of areas of legitimate ministerial interest'. There were 'some very serious defects', though they did not arise from wickedness. There was also a second problem in that the control of nuclear power had not been institutionalised in such a way that all the real arguments came to the top. In a democratic society there was 'no escape from the ultimate provision of consent' and to evade debate was to be 'destructive of the whole democratic process'. His 'main interest in politics', said the Energy Secretary, was to 'get democratic control established effectively' over those areas where high complexity and security made the normal operations of democracy 'very very difficult'. (During the 1979 General Election, a new leak of radioactive material at Windscale led him to call for a full inquiry.)

On 1 June 1976 BNFL applied to Copeland Borough Council for outline planning permission for their proposed Windscale expansion. This application was passed to Cumbria CC as a county matter and on 13 August Stephen Murray of the Town and Country Planning Committee of Cumbria CC wrote to *The Times* giving his personal view that the matter should be called in by the Secretary of State for the Environment. There had, he revealed, been a view in the early stages that the application should be approved by the County Council without the assistance of an expert adviser, and even in principle before BNFL had formally applied, but wiser counsels had prevailed and the Council now had professional advice. Opposition had in the interim arisen to such an extent that he had arranged a public meeting for 29 September in Whitehaven. He himself proposed to keep an open mind until all the arguments had been examined to an extent which justified a conclusion, and he believed his committee would take the same line.

The meeting arranged by Murray was attended by over 600 people, BNFL citing Flowers as in favour, the environmentalist groups refusing to accept the occasion as an adequate mechanism for the full discussion they wanted. Following this meeting the Cumbria CC planning committee postponed their decision on the BNFL application for two weeks. On 3 November[67] the Environment Secretary, Peter Shore, told the Commons that he understood Cumbria CC had decided the previous day that while they were minded to approve BNFL's proposals, the matter should be referred to him as a departure from the development plan. It was, he added, only fair to say that at the public meeting which had been held in Cumbria the 'overwhelming opinion' had been in favour of going ahead. In a written reply on 25 November,[68] the last of the 21 days legally allowed him for action, Shore indicated that he had decided he must take more time over the application.

The unions, in particular the GMWU, the ETU and, with qualifications, the IPCS, were in favour of the scheme, and with an inquiry in prospect BNFL were arguing that such a check to settled government policy would be 'tragic' in that it could lead to the loss of £500m worth of overseas business: there had been enough public debate about reprocessing.

One particularly interesting exchange occurred at this time in the columns of *The Times*[69] between Anthony D. Woolf, chairman of the Lawyers' Ecology Group and A.I. Scott, BNFL company secretary. To Woolf the handling of the Windscale application had been an 'indecent charade'. The application itself was 'the sketchiest ever offered for any major development', and it had also not been advanced until all the other options were closed. This flew in the face of the recent recommendations of the Advisory Committee on Major Hazards, and of the DoE's own inquiry, since between them these reports called for both rigorous safety studies and full public participation in advance of major decisions. Scott's reply to these strictures was to the effect that the Major Hazards Committee had in fact been recommending for general applicability something approaching nuclear industry practices. BNFL's planning application was 'a development of existing Windscale activities, not a new departure'. And, of particular interest as underlining the often unforeseen political implications of technological development: 'The need to handle oxide fuel has been known since the early 60's when the second nuclear power programme was approved.'

The Environment Secretary was now under growing public and parliamentary pressure for an inquiry. FoE, *Half Life*, the Socialist Environment and Resources Association, the National Association for Freedom were all among the groups demanding one. The minister received two petitions, one of some 18,000 signatures for the Windscale project, and another of some 27,000 asking for an inquiry. A rally against the project was held in Trafalgar Square.

The press were also by now fully involved.[70] *Nature* was persuaded that it was at least right to 'pause and think' about reprocessing. Nuclear decisions should be taken only after 'the fullest possible informed debate before the widest possible public'. The *Sunday Times* also thought that Britain had time to think before processing. The AEA was a 'hard-liner' in the energy field, but energy forecasts in the past had 'proved as often wrong as right'. The Windscale leak, disclosed 'with a tardiness at which Mr. Benn is rightly incensed', was only the least of the hazards entailed in nuclear development. The decisions involved were special and 'A generation which took them without exhaustive thought about the consequences might stand convicted of a peculiarly wicked selfishness.' Much could be done, and in public, to ensure the right decisions were taken, and Peter Shore could make a start by calling in the Windscale application. *The Economist* by contrast feared an inquiry would scupper the Japanese contract. It was unlikely that expansion at Windscale would affect proliferation and a decision in principle should therefore be taken. This would still leave the Nuclear Inspectorate with absolute powers if necessary to prevent the plant operating, and the public, having a right to full information, should be brought into this latter decision. *The Times* considered that Shore should resolve his dilemma, as in the event he did, by holding an inquiry on the third part of BNFL's proposal, allowing the first two parts to proceed. The planning laws provided — 'fortuitously' — a means of airing the issue, and the risk that Japan would take her business elsewhere had perforce to be accepted. Following Shore's decision the *Financial Times* argued that the UK's chance to play a leading role in the reactor business had been 'thrown away by a series of ill-judged decisions', and there would now be 'serious doubts' as to whether Britain would be able even on the fuel side to maintain her strong position. There was 'legitimate public anxiety' and it was right that BNFL should provide 'all reasonable assurances', but ministers must realise that nuclear decisions could not be delayed indefinitely. (A general fear at this time was that France, associated since 1971 with Britain and West Germany in United Reprocessors, would take full advantage of any British hesitation.)

The various departments were widely understood to be divided over the merits of a Windscale inquiry, and it is easy to understand why this should have been so. The commercial, export and energy aspects must on the one hand have strongly inclined those with this as their chief concern to press for straight approval, while on the other hand many of those to whom environmental responsibilities were paramount must have appreciated that not to call in the Windscale application would be to set an impossible precedent. Given the form in which Cumbria CC had passed the application to the Environment Secretary — as a departure from a fundamental provision of the county development plan — there was also the possibility, if he failed to call it in, of legal intervention by the objectors, and this at the least would have meant further delay. The planning committee fully recognised this, and that they were leaving the minister responsible for the long-term safety aspects of the project. On top of all this, the Windscale leak and its handling by BNFL undoubtedly further strengthened the hand of those voices within the Government arguing for an inquiry.

In any event, and whether or not he initially lost out in Cabinet Committee, Shore eventually carried the Cabinet and announced his decision to hold an inquiry on 22 December 1976.[71] Had BNFL's proposals related only to Magnox fuel and waste vitrification Shore said he would have been unlikely to have called them in, but the reprocessing of oxide fuels raised major issues. Since he had no power to call in just one part of an application, to avoid delay he was inviting BNFL to resubmit in separate parts. The part providing for an oxide plant would then be called in for a public inquiry under Section 282 of the Town and Country Planning Act 1971. There were special features which made it hard to decide procedure, but the minister said he looked for a thorough and speedy conclusion. He had been influenced in his decision by study of Cumbria CC's planning report, and not by the 'less authoritative voices that have been casting doubt on the development of nuclear energy'. It was explained in the Lords that the Government had decided against setting up a Planning Inquiry Commission under Section 48 of the 1971 Act on the grounds that this was an untried procedure and might take too long.[72]

BNFL withdrew that part of their application relating to a thermal oxide reprocessing plant (THORP) on 21 January 1977 and outline planning permission for the rest was granted on 1 March. That same day BNFL submitted a new four-part THORP application. As a result of this new submission, full planning permission was immediately granted for plant developments which would allow receipt of oxide fuel under existing overseas contracts; conditional permission was granted for an outlined first phase of new and expanded receipt and storage facilities; action was deferred on an outline application for the whole of the latter; and the outline application for the operational THORP plant was on 25 March called in under Section 35 of the 1971 Act.

Mr Justice Parker was appointed Inspector on 31 March, according to Bugler[73] the third lawyer to be asked, with Sir Edward Pochin and Sir Frederick Warner nominated as his technical assessors. Parker had very successfully chaired the Flixborough disaster inquiry of 1974, Pochin was a former chairman of the International Commission on Radiological Protection, and Warner, a distinguished chemical engineer, had been a member of the Royal Commission during its study of nuclear power. The Environment Secretary issued a statement on 5 April indicating the points he expected would be relevant to his consideration of the application: after protests the deadline for objections was extended. BNFL published an outline of their case on 11 May, the Inspector held a preliminary meeting at Whitehaven on 17 May, the inquiry proper opened there on 14 June and closed on 4 November, its hundredth day. 146 witnesses gave oral evidence, there were 161 written objections, over 1,500 documents were submitted, and at the behest of the objectors the Inspector also saw five films. BNFL were legally represented at the inquiry by Lord Silsoe QC and were backed by the AEA, the CEGB, the SSEB and, broadly by Copeland Borough Council and Cumbria CC, all legally represented. The opposition consisted of FoE, represented by Raymond Kidwell QC; the Windscale Appeal, an umbrella organisation for various environmental groups centred around the Conservation Society, and represented by David Widdicombe QC; the Isle of Man Local Government Board and the Town and Country Planning Association, both legally represented; the Lancashire and Western Sea Fisheries Joint Committee; and individuals and various other environmental and public interest groups mostly not legally represented, such as Network for Nuclear Concern and the Oxford Political Ecology Research Group. The three government departments most involved, Energy, Environment, and Agriculture, Fisheries and Food were represented, and certain other organisations, for example, the Council for the Protection of Rural England and the

Friends of the Lake District maintained a watching or more neutral brief. With finance threatening to be a serious problem for them, the opposition groups launched a public appeal in April, the financier Sir James Goldsmith in response creating a fund on their behalf and undertaking to raise whatever was necessary to ensure that the full facts emerged.

At the outset of the inquiry the Inspector posed three questions which seemed to him to cover all the issues. These concerned whether oxide fuel should be reprocessed at all in Britain; if yes, whether this should be at Windscale; and again if yes, whether the plant should be double the size needed for Britain's own needs. He also made two formal departures from normal procedure. All the parties and not only the proposers were allowed to make opening speeches, to assist him and to allow them to get their case before the public as soon as possible; and all evidence was taken under oath. In a less formal sense the conduct of the inquiry as a whole was unusually innovative, sometimes to its great advantage, sometimes not.

BNFL's case was, in brief, that reprocessing was inherently desirable on energy conservation grounds and that the uranium and plutonium recovered annually in the proposed plant if re-used in thermal reactors would be the equivalent of about a third of UK coal production or a quarter of North Sea oil production in 1980. UK needs by the late eighties made essential a 500 tonne per annum plant but a 1200 tonne plant would cost only 20 per cent more. Building the latter and accepting foreign fuel would lower the unit cost of British reprocessing, substantially reduce the UK capital required because of advance payments by overseas customers, and contribute £600m to Britain's balance of payments. The plant would so operate that the worst affected members of the public would receive less than 10 per cent of the internationally recommended radiation dose limit, and the total population dose would be only a fraction of the genetic dose limit. THORP would not preempt a decision on the FBR, but it was essential if the FBR option were to be retained. To deny reprocessing services to foreign customers might actively encourage proliferation. Terrorists were already not short of targets and the additional risk from THORP would be negligible. There were no problems of visual amenity and the plant would provide upwards of 750 jobs. BNFL also argued that they had the requisite experience to build and operate the plant safely, and that the Nuclear Inspectorate accepted this to be the case.

The objectors rejected many of these points. THORP would increase rather than decrease the likelihood of proliferation, and it would also force a choice between an enhanced risk of terrorism and unacceptable interference with civil liberties. Normal emissions from the plant would constitute an intolerable radiation burden on the workforce, local population and future generations, and risks from plant or transport accidents would be excessive. Whatever was said to the contrary, THORP would effectively preempt the FBR decision. The jobs it would create would be of the wrong kind to assist local unemployment, would put new strains on local services, and would strengthen BNFL's overall grip on the area.

The objectors also had other grounds for their position. THORP was not actually needed, might never be needed, and would anyway be unsound financially. It was too ambitious technologically and it also had still to be established that vitrification of waste would work and that reprocessing was preferable to simple disposal of spent fuel. The institutional arrangements for setting standards and monitoring performance were insufficiently independent. Windscale was a bad location. Given the public hostility, to proceed might lead to civil unrest and violence, and the inquiry form and its general circumstances had anyway loaded the scales against the opposition.

Before the publication of his report Mr Justice Parker earned high praise from most quarters for his conduct of the inquiry. In addition, despite the particular difficulties of the inquiry – the haste with which it was organised, the dynamic complexity of the issues, the sharp divisions of opinion, the remoteness of Windscale – the immediate impression it appears to have left on participants was one of reasonable tolerance, openness and fairness. The inquiry was throughout given extensive media coverage, and the efforts of the *Guardian* and *New Scientist* reporters in particular also led to early paperbacks on the event.[74]

This is the point as well to make two general observations about the media coverage of Britain's nuclear debate. The first is that while the Windscale Inquiry provided easily the most important instance of direct contact between the two sides, between 1975 and 1978 there were also innumerable radio and TV confrontations between them and, in addition, as the table of events shows, several major public seminars and hearings, a number of which were officially stimulated. The second point is that while media interest naturally peaked at key events like the publication of the Flowers and Parker Reports, much lesser events, even down to the discovery of a radioactively contaminated cat at Trawsfynydd, also attracted substantial news and editorial coverage, and the media were sometimes moved as well to make their own more original contributions. A few examples must serve to illustrate what was an impressive level of sustained media interest.[75] Thus *Nature* editorialised at length on both the National Energy conference and the circumstances of Walter Marshall's departure from the Energy Department. There was, it thought, an enormous difference between the well-ordered procedure of fifty-six speeches, which the National Energy conference had been, and open government. Analysing possible reasons for Marshall's departure it again found that as a result of this development Benn's advocacy of open government looked that much thinner. *The Times* carried several major articles during the debate, including one by six senior engineers who sought to establish in non-technical terms that the advantages of nuclear power outweighed the risks, and this like most such contributions generated a substantial correspondence. *The Economist's* fear by March 1977 was that the nuclear opposition were fighting a war of attrition, each defeat carrying the seeds of future victory. Among the more original contributions were the reports in the *Daily Express* in May 1976 about that newspaper's experiments in commissioning an outline A-bomb design, the *Observer's* attempt in July 1976 to initiate its own nuclear debate, and the BBC's dramatisation of the Windscale Inquiry in March 1978.

New Society's contribution[76] to the debate was the commissioning of a public survey in March 1977. This found that a representative quota sample of 1,081 adults gave 'guarded approval' to nuclear energy, though the 'don't knows' tended to hold the balance. About two-thirds thought nuclear power stations reasonably safe, and a similar percentage would have been prepared to accept one within ten miles of their home. Half were unhappy about the burial of nuclear waste at sea or underground. Respondents were much more alarmed at the prospect of a new police force to prevent nuclear terrorism than about nuclear terrorism itself. 69 per cent had confidence in the judgement of scientists, as against only 26 per cent in the Government, the media and the manufacturers. There was a 'startling degree of indifference' about what future generations would think. In general, women, those over 65, and the DE group were most opposed to nuclear power. There was no significant difference in the view of Conservative and Labour supporters, but almost half the Liberals questioned were against, as compared with only a third overall. The AEA reported the results of this survey in their house journal *Atom*, but among the opposition groups the Conservation Society in particular were unhappy about it.[77] The survey, like many other events in the nuclear debate, should perhaps have suggested that the social psychology of nuclear power deserved more systematic attention, a more subtle and complicated problem, one commentator suggested, than any in nuclear physics or technology.

To repeat, the items mentioned here are no more than examples of the media's attention. The impact of the great media coverage is also uncharted. In the absence of such a study one is forced back to highly subjective generalisations. In those terms it may be said that while some of the coverage was either simply inaccurate or biased, much of it was, given the complexity of the issues and the heat they raised, really very reasonable. But that is not a judgement with which either side in the debate is likely to agree, for this was not an argument which was kind to neutrals.[78]

FoE's post-inquiry reflections were rehearsed in *What Choice Windscale?*, a booklet by Czech Conroy issued jointly with the Conservation Society.[79] Conroy described the Windscale expansion as having nearly been 'steamrollered through without any proper public consultation', only very strong public pressure having prevented a controversial £600m decision being left in effect to fifteen part-time councillors and a public meeting. FoE continued to regard BNFL's aims as being far ahead of their technical capabilities, the FBR as discredited, and the proliferation question as bedevilled with inconsistencies. FoE had succeeded at the inquiry in having their QC see the Japanese contract, and Conroy admitted they had been surprised to see how watertight and financially favourable it had turned out to be. His main economic complaints therefore turned on the fact that BNFL had had, as he saw it, to be pressured into producing what even then had turned out to be a 'totally inadequate economic appraisal' of their proposed expansion.

Mr Justice Parker's report on Windscale was forwarded to the Environment Secretary on 26 January 1978 and published on 6 March[80] The report's main conclusions were that a new plant to reprocess oxide fuel was desirable and should be started forthwith, that Windscale was its obvious location, and that it should be double the size required for the UK's own needs to allow reprocessing of foreign fuel. Basic to the reasons given for these conclusions was the assumption that the nuclear industry must survive and be capable of expansion. Stocks of spent oxide fuel would therefore continue to grow and, if not reprocessed, would require storage. The latter procedure was unattractive on grounds of cost, the waste of energy it entailed, and the greater risks of plutonium or waste escaping than would be incurred with the alternative of reprocessing and solidification of highly active waste. Since oxide reprocessing was going to be necessary eventually, the sooner a start was made the better, to allow time for suitable techniques to be evolved without the risks which would attend a later crash programme. The dangers from terrorism were not significant: spent fuel would in any case be carried to Windscale and the plutonium arising from reprocessing would either be stored there or else be transported in the form of fuel, an unattractive target. If radiation hazards had been seriously underestimated, this was likely to have been recognised before the plant began to function and it would then have to operate to new limits or not at all. The extra risks to local inhabitants were so small as not to outweigh the overall advantages.

The main justification for building a plant capable of reprocessing foreign wastes was financial. If the plant were to be limited so that it could meet only Britain's needs this would mean redesign and delay, and when further capacity became necessary it would have to be financed without foreign assistance. There were also the considerations that reprocessing foreign waste would lessen the pressure on non-nuclear weapon states to develop their own facilities, and would show Britain was prepared to honour at least the spirit — 'and as I think the letter' — of the Non-Proliferation Treaty (NPT) obligations.

The disadvantages of reprocessing foreign fuel were 'clearly outweighed' by the advantages. The risks from the additional routine emissions were small, those from the movement of plutonium could be overcome by technical fixes, and the total highly active waste from British and foreign fuel combined would contain only a fraction of the plutonium which British waste alone would have without reprocessing. The 'one substantial objection' was that non-nuclear-weapon states would be put nearer the bomb. Since this could be partially alleviated by technical fixes, would not in any case happen for ten years, and since a refusal could undermine the NPT and put pressure on the non-nuclear-weapon states, leading them to produce their own plutonium, it could not be regarded as an overriding objection. In addition to these broad conclusions, Mr Justice Parker's report also made a number of detailed recommendations: all were intended to tighten up the conditions under which Windscale would in future function.

The Parker Report, quite different in approach and conclusion from the Flowers Report, like the latter, naturally received substantial editorial coverage.[81] The *Daily Telegraph* had suggested at the end of the inquiry that its hundred days might prove as disastrous as those following Napoleon's escape from Elba. Many facts had been established which had been well known before the inquiry had begun. Export contracts worth £600m had been imperilled and 'an intolerable degree of self-importance' given to 'pseudotheorists', some of whom would prefer 'millions of hideous and unproven windmills'. Sympathising in February 1978 with Peter Shore's new dilemma of how to handle the report, *The Times* concluded that the inquiry had been unique and that a ministerial decision before public debate would arouse deep suspicion. A decision only after debate was to be preferred, even at the risk that one of the disputants then tried to have the decision set aside by the courts. *The Economist* was also clear that the report should be published in advance of a decision — new evidence was in any case constantly coming forward on nuclear power, so that the courts could technically intervene were they so minded irrespective of whether or not the report were published. When the report was in due course published, *Nature* felt that having decided in favour of BNFL, Parker had then gone out of his way to find for them on almost every count. The two major grounds on which the report could be criticised were its assumptions regarding the need for nuclear energy and its treatment of proliferation. *The Economist* saw the report as clearing away many myths but it too found the report least convincing in its treatment of proliferation.

The Times reckoned that parliamentary debate of the report was especially desirable given the 'uncompromising way' Parker had dismissed most of the objectors' arguments, and it again felt that the section of the report dealing with proliferation commanded 'rather less confidence' than did the rest. (Proliferation was also the point which most worried Sir Brian Flowers, by now chairman of a newly-created Commission on Energy and the Environment.) The FBR must in time, *The Times* argued, be the subject of an inquiry 'at least as searching'. The *Guardian* saw the Parker Report as condensing a 'great deal of arcane argument into manageable form' and as making 'no attempt at the uneasy compromises' which might have arisen had Parker sought to please all sides. The report contained a 'clear analysis' of the NPT, and if Parliament and public now approved they could do so 'with a deeper knowledge of what they are embarking on than countries which have decided to skip the democratic process . . . to that extent, Mr. Justice Parker's report, which fully sets out the issues before giving an opinion on them, could stand translation into several European languages'. The *Financial Times* now thought it right that a public inquiry had been held, and right that its report should be debated in Parliament. But the Government must accept the implication of the report — that there was a need for nuclear power. Mr Justice Parker was to be congratulated. No known aspect of the problem had failed to be discussed at the

inquiry and the report itself was a 'model of clarity'. *New Society* felt
that the report had unreservedly endorsed the integrity and intentions
of the nuclear establishment. It had also suggested that there might be a
socially responsible case for nuclear energy. Previously even FoE, at
the 'infinitely saner hub' of the opposition movement, had sought to
radiate a moral superiority. On the evidence, Parker had reached the
only conclusion open to him. What was surprising was how little com-
fort he had given to objectors: opponents of nuclear power would in
future have to make altogether a stronger case.

Discussing the ensuing Commons debate *Nature* thought it frightening that matters of such consequence could be dealt with so perempt-
orily. Parliament ought to have been the place to resolve the essentially
political aspects of reprocessing, 'blatantly prejudged in the Parker
report', but the bulk of its members were too ill-informed. Nor could
the Science Committee serve, not least because their chairman was
partisan. (The Committee had reported in favour of CFR1 in July
1977, Nigel Forman and Frank Hooley dissenting.[82])

Shortly before the Parker Report was published the Prime Minister
told the Parliamentary and Scientific Committee that he found it 'most
cogent and clear, with well-argued conclusions',[83] and in his own statement to the Commons accompanying publication, the Environment
Secretary described the report as analysing 'in a masterly way' all the
issues which had been raised by objectors. Shore said he found the
Inspector's conclusions 'persuasive and broadly acceptable', and
ordinarily would have proceeded to a final decision. However, conscious of the House's desire to discuss the report — there had been an
Early Day motion signed by some 200 MPs — to allow this and enable
ministers to take part while yet preempting any resulting demand for a
reopening of the inquiry on the technical grounds that he might then be
held to have been influenced by events subsequent to the inquiry, he
had agreed with the Opposition on an unusual course. Under this he
was refusing planning permission on the existing application. A debate
would then be arranged and following that a special development order
would be laid under Section 24 of the Town and Country Planning Act
1971, in effect authorising the project.

The consequent debate took place on 22 March 1978.[84] Opening for
the Government, Shore's argument was that the reprocessing case could
be judged on its own merits and without reference to an FBR programme, both because reprocessed plutonium could be recycled in
thermal reactors and because the Magnox reprocessing plant alone
would produce sufficient plutonium for eight FBRs. The minister now

said that he had established the inquiry both because he had not been satisfied that all the relevant information had previously been available, either to Cumbria CC or to himself, and also because he believed strongly that major new nuclear power developments should be publicly scrutinised. He doubted whether any other country had had such an open and thorough review of a major nuclear proposal and he thought most people would approve the cautious approach the Government were adopting, reposing confidence 'but not blind faith' in the nuclear professionals, and conscious of 'but not paralysed by' the risks and benefits of nuclear power. Winding up, the Foreign Secretary, David Owen, said there should be no misunderstanding about the American view: the Americans had conveyed their wish that there should be no British decision until after the INFCE report. For himself he thought the Americans were wrong and he hoped to convert the Carter Administration to his view, either through INFCE or otherwise.

The special development order promised by Shore was laid on 3 April and debated in the Commons on 15 May, the Government's detailed response to the Parker Report having been published – as a written answer – on 8 May.[85] Shore again said he found the Inspector's conclusions persuasive in respect of the three major issues at the heart of BNFL's proposal, the environmental risk, the security problems, and the proliferation consequences. Twelve of the Inspector's fifteen detailed recommendations had been accepted outright by the Government, and they also accepted the underlying purpose of the other three. The Government had taken objections to Windscale 'with the utmost seriousness'. It would have been amazing given the nature of the issue had the Inspector's finding not come under attack, but it could not be said that the public were being put upon by technical expertise when the parliamentary and public procedure had been preceded by the longest and most thorough investigation which had ever taken place anywhere into such a subject. The Windscale Inquiry had been no charade.

Winding up this debate, the Energy Secretary also vigorously denied that the inquiry had been a charade. Benn said he understood the disappointment of the environmentalists, but it must be remembered that it was ultimately neither BNFL, nor Mr Justice Parker, nor even the Government which would decide, but the Commons themselves in an exercise of political judgement. If alternatives to nuclear energy were available many might take a different view, but it was internationally accepted that the nuclear component could not be abstracted without running the kind of risk no Energy Minister could recommend. The

issues raised by the environmentalists would always be on the agenda
and it also had to be said that there could be no certainty about the
rightness of the present decision.

The Government had majorities of 186 to 56 in the debate of 22
March and of 224 to 80 in that of 15 May. In the debate of 8 February
1977 to increase to a possible £500m the support available to BNFL
they had had a majority of 196 to 22.[86] The Windscale votes were not
party ones, except for the Liberals, who were opposed. (A strong anti-
nuclear amendment had carried at the Liberal Party assembly in October 1977 despite platform objections.)

Britain's nuclear opposition groups were happy neither with Mr
Justice Parker's conclusions nor with the manner in which, as they saw
it, he had misused their contributions to the inquiry.[87] The Town and
Country Planning Association for instance complained that by day 75
the inquiry had become an administrative shambles. The only decision
Parker had seriously considered was one of approval for BNFL, and
despite disclaimers, the report made policy. The Political Ecology
Research Group saw the report as a clear exposition of the author's
views but felt it was of little value to anyone wishing to decide the
matter for themselves. This was because there was only a modicum of
cross-referencing and because the report was highly selective in regard
to the evidence which it quoted. FoE too were dismayed by the Parker
Report. It contained many omissions, misrepresentations and inconsistencies, and it also did much to strengthen the hand of those who
preferred action to argument. One of the witnesses for the Network
for Nuclear Concern, who since the inquiry had become chairman of
the US National Academy of Science's Committee on the Biological
Effects of Ionizing Radiation, wrote to *The Times*, challenging Sir
Edward Pochin to public debate. And another of the Network's witnesses questioned the appropriateness of Pochin's having acted as assessor
for the inquiry while also a senior member of the International Commission on Radiological Protection. Witnesses for all these organisations, and others who had appeared for the Isle of Man Government,
the National Peace Council, the National Resources Defence Council
and the Windscale Appeal, in due course wrote a joint letter to *The
Times*. Their position was that since their evidence had been either
misunderstood, misinterpreted, distorted or ignored, the Parker Report
was not even remotely adequate.

The new nuclear opposition cannot be pursued here and the post-
script to this chapter is more fittingly another official document, the
Green Paper on Energy Policy, published in February 1978.[88] Like the

National Energy conference[89] of 1976 and the creation of the Energy Commission in 1977, this it was said was meant to facilitate 'an improvement in the quality of future decisions and, if possible, a substantial degree of consensus on what those decisions should be'. The Green Paper stressed that series ordering even of thermal reactors was still years away, but affirmed that an ability to expand in nuclear power must be an important element of any flexible energy strategy. Three objectives were now laid out: the establishment of a thermal reactor and the re-establishment of an industry which could build it; the guaranteeing of fast reactor technology, whether by proceeding with CFR1, foreign purchase or otherwise; and the finding of answers to the problems of waste disposal and proliferation. The Paper's estimated nuclear target for 2000 was only 40GW, 'low in comparison with those which are sometimes made . . . but even so . . . a substantial industrial effort'. After the much higher figures of earlier years, here clearly was a more cautious modesty.[90]

Notes

1. See for example, J.S. Forrest, *The Breeder Reactor* (Scottish Academic Press, Edinburgh, 1978); J. Rotblat (ed.), *Nuclear Reactors: To Breed or Not to Breed* (Taylor and Francis Ltd, London, 1977); John Francis and Paul Abrecht (eds.), *Facing up to Nuclear Power* (St Andrew Press, Edinburgh, 1976).

2. HCD 955 c.1185-96.

3. HC 73-iii (1973-4); see also Lovins's article and reply, *Sunday Times*, 25 November, 2 December 1973.

4. *Nature* (5 January 1978), p. 2.

5. See for example, J. Surrey and C. Huggett, 'Opposition to Nuclear Power: A Review of International Experience', *Energy Policy* (December 1976), pp. 286-307; C. Ickerman, 'Perspectives on the World-wide Debate and Public Opinion on Nuclear Power', *Science and Public Policy*, 4 (October 1977), pp. 465-82; J. Davoll, 'Controversy over Nuclear Power', *BNESJ*, 15 (July 1976), pp. 200-2; L.D. Smith, 'Evolution of Opposition to the Peaceful Uses of Nuclear Energy', *NE* (June 1972), pp. 461-8.

6. See T.N. Marsham, 'A UK View on Fast Reactors', *Atom* (July 1973), pp. 150-63.

7. *New Scientist*, 13 January 1973.

8. Hugh Montefiore and David Gosling, *Nuclear Crisis* (The Gresham Press, Old Woking, 1977), p. 7.

9. Norman J. Vig, *Science and Technology in British Politics* (Pergamon Press, Oxford, 1968).

10. But see Dave Elliot *et al.*, *The Politics of Nuclear Power* (Pluto Press, London, 1978).

11. *Nuclear Power: Technical Bases for Ethical Concern* (FoE, London, 1974); 'Energy Strategy: The Road not Taken', *Foreign Affairs* (October 1976), pp. 65-96.

12. Amory B. Lovins, *Soft Energy Paths* (Penguin Books, Harmondsworth, 1977).

13. For an AEA view of this debate see *Atom* (March 1976), pp. 58-69.

14. HC 24-XV (1975-6).
15. *Observer*, 25 July 1976.
16. Walter C. Patterson, *The Fissile Society* (Earth Resources Research, London 1977); his *Nuclear Power* (Penguin, Harmondsworth, 1976) was a much less polemical, and indeed very useful, introduction to nuclear energy.
17. M. Flood and R. Grove-White, *Nuclear Prospects* (FoE etc., London, 1976).
18. *The Times*, 28 February 1966.
19. *The Times*, 31 March, 11 April, 2, 12 and 23 August 1977; see also *Plutonium and Liberty*, a report by *Justice* (London, 1978).
20. Lord Rothschild in *The Times*, 27 and 30 September, 9 October 1976; but see Rothschild's 'Risk' (Dimbleby Lecture, 1979), *Atom* (February 1979), pp. 30-5. Medvedev in *New Scientist* (4 November 1976), pp. 264-7 (30 June 1977), pp. 761-4, 10 November 1977, pp. 352-3, and in *The Times*, 23 December 1976, 8 February 1977; Ryle in *The Times*, 14 and 20 December 1976, 5 October 1977. See also, L. Grainger, 'The Nuclear Issue as seen by a Competitor', *Energy Policy*, 4 (December 1976), pp. 322-9.
21. Fred Hoyle, *Energy or Extinction* (Heinemann, London, 1977); see also Edward Teller, 'Pollution by Poverty', *Atom* (February 1977), pp. 14-17, and H. Hunt, 'Thorium as a Substitute for Uranium', *Atom* (March 1977), p. 48.
22. Hill's speeches mentioned in the text are as follows, all references to *Atom* unless otherwise indicated: (January 1975), pp. 2-7; *New Scientist* (17 July 1975), p. 159; *BNESJ* (April 1976), pp. 105-9; (February 1976), pp. 34-5; HC 534 (1976/7), Qs 992, 1042: (September 1976), pp. 236-41; *Observer*, 1 August 1976; *The Times*, 29 July 1976; (January 1976), pp. 2-10; (October 1976), pp. 250-3; (November 1976), pp. 292-6; (January 1977), pp. 2-4; (April 1977), pp. 59-62; (June 1977), pp. 106-9; (July 1977), pp. 126-31; (October 1977), p. 248; (November 1977), pp. 290-6; (March 1978), pp. 46-55; (May 1978), p. 122; (June 1978), p. 159; also (May 1973), pp. 107-10; (September 1973), pp. 194-7; (January 1974), pp. 2-35.
23. T.N. Marsham, 'The Fast Reactor and the Plutonium Fuel Cycle', *Atom* (November 1977), pp. 297-311.
24. W. Marshall, 'Self-sufficiency in Energy', *Atom* (May 1975), pp. 62-6; 'Nuclear Power and the Proliferation Issue', *Atom* (April 1978), pp. 78-102; 'Proliferation and the Recycling of Plutonium', *Atom* (September 1978), pp. 234-41; 'Energy Research', *BNESJ* (1977), 16, pp. 13-20.
25. C. Allday, 'The Importance of Nuclear Fuel Reprocessing', *Atom* (July 1977), pp. 136-9 and *BNESJ*, 16 (April 1977), p. 108; P.W. Mummery, 'Health and Safety and the Nuclear Industry', *Atom* (March 1974), pp. 40-1.
26. L.G. Brookes, 'Energy Accounting and Nuclear Power', *Atom* (September 1975), pp. 164-8; 'The Plain Man's Case for Nuclear Energy', *Atom* (April 1976), pp. 95-105; 'Energy Prices and the Role of Nuclear Power', *Atom* (August 1977), pp. 171-8.
27. *Reactor Safety Study — An Assessment of Accident Risks in US Commercial Nuclear Power Plants*. USAEC, Report, Wash-1400. See also R.F. Griffiths, 'Reactor Accidents and the Environment', *Atom* (December 1978), pp. 314-25, and *NEI* (December 1978), pp. 41-2 (European Nuclear Society/American Nuclear Society meeting on Nuclear Power Reactor Safety).
28. For example, F.R. Farmer, 'Advances in the Reliability of Reactor Systems', *Atom* (December 1975), pp. 218-26; See also, B.A.J. Lister, 'Nuclear Power — The Perspective of Risk', *Atom* (May 1975), pp. 68-75.
29. For example, *Nuclear Energy* (January 1978), p. 10.
30. P.M.S. Jones, 'Nuclear Energy Prospects', *Atom* (February 1978), pp. 26-30.
31. CEGB Annual Report. See also Sir Francis Tombs (Electricity Council),

'Nuclear Power and the Public Good', *Atom* (January 1978), pp. 2-7 and R.R. Matthews (CEGB), 'The Safety of the Fast Reactor', *Atom* (May 1977), pp. 86-9.
32. *Energy R & D in the UK*, Dept. of Energy, Energy Paper No. 11, 1976.
33. *Energy Policy Review*, Dept. of Energy, Energy Paper No. 22, 1977.
34. Cmnd. 6618.
35. HC 534-ii (1976-7), Q 1010; *NEI* (July 1976), pp. 6-7.
36. See also, L.G. Brookes, 'Towards the All-electric Economy', *Atom* (August 1973), pp. 174-83; R.L.R. Nicholson, 'Meeting Future World Demand for Energy: The Role of Nuclear Power', *Atom* (July 1974), pp. 158-63; C.E. Illife, 'Economic and Resource Aspects of Fast Reactors', *Atom* (August 1973), pp. 163-70.
37. See for example, Amory B. Lovins and Walter C. Patterson, 'Plutonium Particles: Some Like Them Hot', *Nature* (27 March 1975), pp. 278-80; MRC, *The Toxicity of Plutonium* (HMSO, London, 1975); B.A.J. Lister, 'Safe Working with Plutonium', *Atom* (February 1979), pp. 36-9.
38. For example, Peter Chapman, 'The Ins and Outs of Nuclear Power', *New Scientist* (19 December 1974), pp. 866-9; John Wright and John Syrett, 'Energy Analysis of Nuclear Power', *New Scientist* (9 January 1975), pp. 66-7; Malcolm Slesser, 'Accounting for Energy', *Nature* (20 March 1975), pp. 170-2; L.G. Brookes, 'Energy Accounting and Nuclear Power', *Atom* (September 1975), pp. 764-8; John Price, *Dynamic Energy Analysis and Nuclear Power* (FoE, London, 1974).
39. *Atom* (November 1976), p. 287; also Annual Report and *Guardian*, 23 September 1976.
40. *The Times*, 23 September 1976; *Guardian*, 23 September 1976; *Financial Times*, 23 September 1976 (David Fishlock); *Nature* (30 September and 9 December 1976), pp. 494-6 (R.H. Mole , 'The Flowers Report: Opportunities Missed'); *BNESJ*, 16 (January 1977), p. 4.
41. HLD 378 c.1308-440.
42. HCD 923 c.293-339.
43. See his *Towards a More Conservative Energy Policy* (Conservative Political Centre, London 1977), CPC No. 615.
44. HCD 923 c.354-69.
45. HCD 940 c.884-981.
46. Sir Brian Flowers, 'Nuclear Power and Public Policy', *BNESJ*, 16 (April 1977), pp. 113-21.
47. Ranger Uranium Environmental Inquiry (First Report) (Australian Government Publishing Service, Canberra, 1976).
48. *Energy R & D in the UK* (Royal Society, London, 1977).
49. Cmnd. 6820.
50. HCD 917 c.1208-10 (WA); Health and Safety Executive, *Some Aspects of the Safety of Nuclear Installations in Great Britain* (1977).
51. For example, *BNESJ*, 16 (October 1977), pp. 295-8.
52. Report by the Health and Safety Commission on the Hazards of Conventional Sources of Energy (HMSO, London, 1978).
53. *Nuclear Power Issues and Choices* (Ballinger, Cambridge, Mass., 1977). See also Abram Chayes and W. Bennett Lewis, *International Arrangements for Nuclear Fuel Reprocessing* (Ballinger, Cambridge, Mass., 1977); also Edward F. Wonder, *Nuclear Fuel and American Foreign Policy* (Westview Press, 1977); *Nucleonics Week* (24 March 1977).
54. For example, Chauncey Starr, 'Nuclear Power and Weapons Proliferation', *Nuclear News* (June 1977), pp. 54-7.
55. Tam Dalyell, quoted in *Nucleonics Week* (21 April 1977).
56. For example, *New Scientist* (8 May 1975), pp. 310-12 (26 June 1975), pp. 710; also T.G. Hughes and E.F. Kemp, 'Reprocessing of Oxide Fuel at Windscale', *Atom* (October 1970), pp. 206-11; T.G. Hughes *et al.*, 'Development,

Design and Operation of the Oxide Fuel Reprocessing Plant at the Windscale Works of BNFL', IV Geneva, 8, pp. 367-73.

57. HCD 902 c.192-204.

58. Sources for Benn's views include *Sunday Times*, 20 March 1977; HCD 906 c.81-89; HCD 909 c.378 (WA); HCD 913 c.6-8; HCD 915 c.1255-7; HCD 917 c.208-10 (WA); HCD 918 c.2-4; HCD 925 c.1253-67; HCD 940 c.970-8; HCD 940 c.1563-74; HCD 934 c.291-2.

59. For an AEA summary see 'Reprocessing: The Public Debate', *Atom* (March 1976), pp. 58-69.

60. HCD 907 c.341 (WA).

61. HCD 908 c.9-10.

62. HCD 921 c.461.

63. HCD 922 c.310-11 (WA), c.967-72.

64. Summary in *Atom* (September 1977), pp. 199-206.

65. Tony Benn, 'Technology's Threat to Parliament', *Guardian*, 20 February 1979.

66. *Nature*, 278 (15 March 1979), p. 201; *Guardian*, 5 April 1979.

67. HCD 918 c.1386-8.

68. HCD 921 c.2-3 (WA).

69. *The Times*, 5 and 10 November 1976.

70. *Nature* (23-30 December 1976); *Sunday Times*, 12 December 1976; *The Economist*, 18 December 1976 (but see 13 November 1976) and 6 August 1977; *The Times*, 19 January 1976, 7 June 1976 and 26 November 1976; *Financial Times*, 22 December 1976.

71. HCD 923 c.672-82.

72. HLD 378 c.1389-92.

73. Jeremy Bugler, 'Windscale: A Case Study in Public Scrutiny', *New Society* (27 July 1978), p. 183.

74. *Guardian, Windscale* (London, 1978); Ian Breach, *The Windscale Inquiry* (*New Society*, London, 1978); Ian Breach, *Windscale Fallout* (Penguin Special, Harmondsworth, 1978); *The Times*, 2 August, 28 September 1977.

75. *Nature* (1 and 15 July 1976, 7 July, 29 September, 1 December 1977; *The Times*, 6 February 1978; *The Economist*, 19 March 1977.

76. *New Society* (31 March 1977).

77. *New Society* (12 May 1977); see also Richard Baker and Leonard Taitz, *Nuclear Power and Society* (Conservation Society, February 1977, mimeo).

78. Peter Chapman, *Fuel's Paradise* (Penguin Special, Harmondsworth, 1975) makes this point.

79. Czech Conroy, *What Choice Windscale* (London, 1978); see also G.R. Bainbridge and Czech Conroy, 'Reprocessing Nuclear Fuel: For . . . and Against', *Nature* (2 March 1978), pp. 2-3.

80. *The Windscale Inquiry* (HMSO, London, 1978).

81. For example, *Daily Telegraph*, 7 November 1977, 24 January, 7 March 1978; *The Times*, 4 February, 7 March 1978; *The Economist*, 4 February, 11 March 1978; *Nature* (9, 23 and 30 March 1978); *Guardian*, 7 March 1978; *New Society* (9 March 1978).

82. HC 534 (1976-7).

83. *Daily Telegraph*, 23 February 1978 and HCD 945 c.981-91.

84. HCD 946 c.1537-676.

85. HCD 950 c.111-82.

86. HCD 925 c.1253-360.

87. For example, *The Times*, 8, 10, 21 and 22 March; 7, 27 and 29 April; 10 May 1978; *Observer*, 30 April 1978; see also Simon Rippon, 'The Windscale Report – A Review', *Atom* (May 1978), pp. 131-3.

88. Cmnd. 7101.

89. See Department of Energy, Energy Paper No. 13, 1976 (2 vols.).

90. See also Gerald Leach *et al.*, *A Low Energy Strategy for the UK* (International Institute for the Environment and Development, Science Reviews, London, 1979). Also *Coal and Nuclear Power Station Costs*, Energy Commission Paper No. 6, January 1978.

12 CONCLUSIONS

The structural argument of this book can now be summarised. By 1978 there had been three British thermal reactor crises, 'resolved' respectively in 1965, 1974 and 1978. The first of these had economic, technological and political dimensions, and was further complicated by the intrusion of the two American light water reactors. The economic uncertainties were represented as having been removed by the results of the 1965 appraisal; the technological doubts also largely by this, but in part also by the device of the Emeléus Committee; and the overall political problem was solved by going through the motions of a nominally commercial appraisal, and perhaps also indirectly by the changes at the top in the AEA and CEGB. The international aspect, involving as it did a comparison between British and American technologies, was not satisfactorily resolved by the elaborate ballet of the appraisal and the combination of a crisis plus appraisal process also diverted attention from two more fundamental questions – how much nuclear power to aim for in the context of a wider fuel policy, and how best to structure the nuclear industry. The events of 1964-5 also presented the matter of reactor strategy itself in a highly contrived fashion.

The issues of fuel policy and the nuclear industry's structure quickly became urgent as a direct result of the 1965 decision for the AGR, but the shortcomings of the reactor strategy did not fully surface until the early seventies, when it at last became painfully clear that the AGR had been far from ready for commercial construction in 1965. The new reactor crisis which then followed again temporarily diverted attention from overall fuel policy, but in this instance the questions of reactor choice and industrial structure were unmistakably more interdependent than they had been in the earlier crisis.

Now this book has, for the most part, throughout treated the AEA as if the Authority were monolithic. But of course this was not the case. They cannot be fully documented but over the years there were inevitably rivalries and schisms of greater or lesser moment within the Authority, between scientists and engineers, between the different Groups, especially the Research and Reactor Groups, between the geographically very separated sites, and between different technical philosophies. In particular, the water reactor fraternity within the AEA always found itself overshadowed by the advocates of gas-graphite and the SGHWR was not an option in 1965. Nor was Hinton[1] alone later in believing that the AEA were playing this reactor down in order not to create a competitor for the AGR. For the SGHWR to be adopted commercially the AGR had to be thought unsuitable at a time when the CEGB wished to have a substantial new tranche of nuclear power, when even the AEA's gas-graphite proponents might be expected to prefer it to the alternative of an LWR, since the adoption of an LWR at any time would be viewed publicly and politically as undermining the fundamental rationale of the AEA. These circumstances eventually occurred in 1973-4 and in due course the SGHWR was adopted. This decision however, unlike that of 1965, was not allowed to be tested by practice. It proved rather to be a holding operation, the AGR being readopted in 1978, though there were those who thought the 1978 decision would itself prove in the end to have been less than final. Most of the book having thus dealt with the various thermal reactor crises, the Windscale decisions were then treated separately as having been part of an altogether more public process. Let us next try to sum up that political part of Britain's nuclear record.

From the perspective of government the public nuclear debate of the mid-seventies could be viewed as having facilitated the discharge of two distinctively different functions. First, a controlled debate bringing in Parliament and with a good availability of information and adequate opportunities for involvement − itself quite different from participation − was a politically attractive way of accommodating conflict. The ensuing delay in making decisions had then to be tolerated as a necessary cost of securing at least a grudging, and of particular importance, non-violent acceptance. Second, public debate was also a genuine means, in circumstances involving at least some uncertainty, of getting all relevant questions identified if not answered, and of testing BNFL's case. The first of these functions no doubt amounted to a form of manipulation, but government is in part about that. Furthermore, the two functions were not mutually exclusive. On the contrary, Tony Benn and Peter Shore quite evidently had both in mind in 1975-8. In line with this interpretation, it was noticeable that the public debate was not allowed by Benn to embrace the new re-examination of thermal reactor policy when this took place in 1976-7. This was understandable given the nuclear construction industry's desperate need for work, but hardly in keeping with the minister's declared objectives in regard to public involvement, the more so given the country's excess generating capacity.

Participation having been mentioned here a separate word needs to be said about it. This was very much a vogue concept of the seventies, but an unsatisfactory one. To participate in any activity one needs greater or lesser amounts of expertise and of time, and these are very unequally distributed. There must also be a readiness to use one's time for this purpose rather than for that or some other.the interests of those who cannot, or at any rate do not, participate also need to be considered — and these may now include other states and even other generations. Quite apart then from the existence of adequate opportunities to participate, the general public evidently needs protection from the special publics which in any given case elect to participate — who exactly for instance were FoE and similar groups actually 'representing'? In a liberal democracy the usual course is to settle for the rough and ready method of primary participation through the electoral system, supplementing this with various devices, such as public inquiries, which allow scope for the secondary circuit of representation, the pressure group system, to operate. This is a necessarily imperfect arrangement, not least because it frequently leaves the detailed definition of the public interest to appointed bodies, and it is certainly worth trying to improve it. Nevertheless, it is difficult to be optimistic about what may be possible, and it is for that reason that this chapter will conclude with a plea for more accountable systems of decision-making, rather than more participatory ones.

From the perspective of the nuclear opposition there was a spectrum of objectives to be attained in the nuclear debate. For some within the opposition the debate was simply the best instrument available for a general attack on technological society. At the other extreme were those concerned about only some and not all nuclear activities. Between these poles objectives ranged from securing the total abolition of nuclear energy, through the winning of a strategic moratorium, to the gaining of a tactical delay.

The socio-psychological origins of the nuclear opposition movement are, in fact, of great interest,[2] and especially intriguing was the movement's failure or unwillingness properly to confront the question of comparative risk: nuclear energy is by no means the only hazardous technology. But if nothing else, the nuclear opposition of the seventies should have shown the science and engineering community, and government, that public attitudes towards science and technology can probably not any longer be taken for granted. Government, in its handling of information, needs to show that there are no grounds for residual suspicion, the media have a responsibility to report accurately and with balance, and the academic has a duty to analyse and investigate all issues of moment.

Considering specifically the Windscale affair, one could even prospectively have claimed for it a high degree of inevitability. BNFL had in 1974 to prepare themselves for handling an increasing quantity of spent oxide fuel of British origin and, whatever Britain's other nuclear problems, they at least could point to a record of some considerable success. As part of the nuclear establishment they also fully shared in the high expectation of the fast reactor. What more natural then than that they should wish to proceed with THORP, and as an internationally oriented commercial proposition? On the other hand, FoE were five years old, in their way they too had enjoyed a reasonable amount of success, and yet, despite developments abroad, the nuclear issue had not caught the public imagination in Britain. How could FoE possibly pass up an opportunity like THORP? Then in 1975 there arrived a minister who had preached open government and who evidently had in mind at least the two motives identified above, conflict accommodation and a 'long-stop' check, and in 1976 a Royal Commission report probably unique in its unorthodoxy.

The Windscale debate did not really have time to build up much momentum between autumn 1975 and spring 1976 and therefore, since he had then, as he saw it, obtained satisfaction on the most important immediate issue involved in accepting the Japanese contract, Benn had no reason in March 1976 not to make a positive decision. By the end of the year, however, things were very different. The media had by then had plenty of material questioning nuclear power on which to feed, the Royal Commission report especially, and Cumbria CC were quite properly unwilling themselves to assume full responsibility for what was by now a highly controversial as well as a national undertaking. In turn therefore it is hard to see that in his decision of December 1976 Shore had any real choice.

The responsibility then passed to Mr Justice Parker. The case he had to consider had political, economic, social, scientific and technological components, and BNFL were the responsible public body who must be presumed to be acting in the public interest. The opposition naturally believed before, during and after the inquiry that there were glaring weaknesses in BNFL's case, and the Inspector indeed found a few shortcomings but, on what had to be a matter of judgement, he did not consider them of sufficient seriousness to indicate rejection. It would have been remarkable had he thought otherwise. He had technical advisers, but his decision was not a technical one; he was a leading specialist barrister, but except in a peripheral sense his decision was not a legal one; nor certainly was it an economic one. Indeed it is difficult to see what other word to apply to it than political — the word trans-scientific has been coined for such cases, and this can be a convenient euphemism, but the essential point about trans-scientific questions is that they have in the end to be resolved by political decisions. So, if this argument is correct, Mr Justice Parker made a political decision, a decision informed certainly by his legal erudition and experience, and with the assistance of technical advisers, but a political decision nevertheless. In addition, it is not clear that either the scope or the depth of the Windscale Inquiry was as internationally unprecedented as ministers tended to claim.

This is also the point to comment on two of the main criticisms levelled by the nuclear opposition against the inquiry procedure, namely the speed with which it was arranged and the professional standing of the Inspector's two assessors. It is possible, but not really very likely, that the opposition case would have been substantially better had there been more time, but in any case the Inspector did not find the evidence marginally in BNFL's favour, he found it overwhelmingly so. On the second point, because one does not know the exact relationship which obtained between the Inspector and his technical assessors, one cannot know with certainty whether the Inspector would have come to a different conclusion had one or both of the assessors been professionally competent technical critics of nuclear power. But that is anyway an irrelevant consideration, for why would the Environment Secretary have appointed such a person, supposing one existed in Britain? Surely he would have done so only if he looked in advance for a negative decision, and this he clearly did not do. On the contrary, he looked for a positive one.

The Inspector was virtually bound therefore to find for BNFL. He would have had to be deeply troubled to have found against them. He made in short the decision he was expected to make, the decision any orthodox man would have made. The only surprising thing about Mr Justice Parker's report was perhaps that it was as unequivocal as it was. Yet this itself can be regarded as excellent evidence that the Inspector in no way saw the exercise as a charade, but rather was personally fully convinced of the merit of BNFL's proposals.

It was then left only for the Government and Parliament to approve, and Shore for the former evidently had no reason not to do so forthwith. Some subsequently expected more of the Commons, but it is hard to see on what grounds. Few MPs could be expected to think themselves sufficiently expert to oppose BNFL, the Inspector and the

Government on technical grounds, and the nuclear opposition had made far too little parliamentary impression for the Commons as a whole to have done so purely on political grounds.

So all turned out as expected. Was the Windscale affair then, despite denials, merely a charade? There are good grounds for arguing that it was not. Take first the disappointment of the objectors, for whom it was all too easy to see the process as a farce. It remains the case that the demand for participation is usually at root a demand for a different decision. If, as suggested above, the outcome really were all along virtually inevitable, the opposition were certain to be disappointed, and the fact of the inquiry and of their great efforts there only made their disappointment the deeper. Their opinion of the inquiry and its outcome cannot therefore be regarded as other than understandably partisan.

The real significance of the Windscale Inquiry is to be found rather in what it bequeathed to the future. Thanks largely to the determination of the nuclear opposition, BNFL were forced to provide a quite detailed public justification of their proposals. There is consequently a comprehensive plan against which subsequent performance, technical, economic and above all safety, can be continuously monitored. The Windscale episode will not have been a charade if that is done. Ministers and officials will of course move on and if things go wrong with THORP it will not necessarily be those who advocated and supported it in 1975-8 who are then held responsible. But the Windscale Inquiry began an important learning process and *provided the out-turn is kept equally open*, then it should, in principle, be possible for corrective action to be taken if this is ever necessary. If it never is necessary then of course BNFL will have been triumphantly vindicated. This was not participatory government, whatever that might be, but it was in the end something approaching accountable government.[3]

There are at least two qualifications which must be made to this opinion. They concern the FBR and proliferation. It should be remembered, for it was said often enough in the debate, that THORP in no way need preempt an FBR decision. Despite the feasibility of plutonium recycle in thermal reactors, it is true that the FBR cannot be represented as technically a wholly separate matter from THORP, but it can certainly be handled as a wholly separate one for purposes of political decision.[4] In this context Shore in fact acknowledged in 1978 the twin objectives of accommodation and check in indicating how he would propose to handle a CFR1 proposal.[5] He appeared then to have in mind a consolidation of the decisional route in effect 'discovered' in the course of the Windscale affair, comprising a general background study by, say, a commission (the Flowers Report in the Windscale case), followed first by a site-specific inquiry (the Parker Report at Windscale), and then by a special development order. Such a procedure would make any CFR1 commitment a politically separate undertaking. It could still prove difficult to resist the technical logic of proceeding with CFR1 given the fact of THORP, provided, that is, the safety argument were sound and that a sufficient case could be made on grounds either of economic need or of developmental necessity overriding the short-term absence of such a need. Here Britain's overall energy situation, and particularly the excess electricity generating capacity, would be important, as would the feasibility, and even more the relative desirability, of obtaining an FBR licence at some later stage from, probably, France if France proceeded with FBR development and the UK did not.[6]

There remains the question of nuclear weapon proliferation. Even if this occurs more rapidly in future it seems very doubtful that it will ever be possible to lay any part of it directly at THORP's door, and in that sense the opposition are unlikely ever to be able to say, and have it accepted, that they were right in their fears on this score. While therefore it should in principle be possible to monitor THORP regarded as an isolated project, it may well not be possible to determine its contribution to proliferation, one way or the other. His conclusions in this regard were thus the most political, because least legal, technical or economic, of the Inspector's report, and the matter remains one on which each man is entitled to his own view. It is clearly essential to ensure that the plutonium produced by THORP is used only for civil purposes, but it must be faced that the nuclear genie is out of the bottle and it is extremely doubtful that there is any prospect of conjuring him back in, short of a second experience of nuclear war, some major nuclear accident not involving terrorists, or the discovery that radiation standards are wrong by orders of magnitude – and even then it could fairly be argued that only the first of these would prevent nuclear weapon proliferation. In short, from the point of view of world peace, if not regional security, the most dangerous proliferation has already taken place.

The accountability in regard to Windscale which the nuclear debate brought about was by any criterion, and particularly when compared with past example, a major achievement. But it should be remembered that the debate also forced the nuclear industry to re-examine its procedures, standards and assumptions, and in some cases, as with waste disposal, compelled it to proceed differently from the way it would have preferred. The debate also led to changes in institutional responsibilities and practices. It is impossible so close to events to judge the ultimate effect of these various developments, but they were scarcely negligible. There is at least one other point a political analyst would want to make about the public debate. FoE in particular demonstrated during it that it was possible for a group to have a significant impact on public policy despite lacking privileged access to the inner circle of British decision-making. Much of this success was due to their approach and strategy. They took care to be well informed, generally to do their technical homework, and where possible, though this was much more difficult, to be constructive. They tried hard to appear reasonable, responsible and even pleasant in their opposition. They sought not to miss a tactical opportunity, and they made every effort to develop good relations with the media, with politicians and officials, and with the public at large. Walter Patterson in fact even won the right to be, in a strictly limited sense, on the 'inside' − he was for instance the only completely non-official person at Tony Benn's Sunningdale conference, though this itself could be construed as part of the process of accommodation referred to above.

Speaking quite generally, after an initial decision has opened up some new policy area, all later decisions form with it a chain, each decision making unique one of a set of options and each limiting the subsequent range of choices. In that sense *all* of the British civil nuclear decisions, including Windscale, can be traced right back to the immediate post-war years. There remains a temptation to see the period from 1955 to 1957 as especially important, since it was then that the Government, having decided upon a nuclear programme, quickly trebled it, and then also that the AEA, having earlier been forced by circumstances into gas-graphite reactors, freely confirmed their preference for this technology in its enriched uranium, oxide fuel, form. Writing in 1971, J.C.C. Stewart[7] found it 'quite remarkable' how the forecasts of the Trend Committee of 1955 had been borne out, yet to a large extent, as we have seen, these forecasts were self-fulfilling.

It can certainly be argued that, in particular, any of the main 'crisis-resolving' decisions, 1965 (AGR), 1974 (SGHWR), 1978 (AGR and Windscale), might have gone the other way. Or it can be argued that in between these decisions a minister or a Government might have somehow put right the fundamental nuclear problems from which it became increasingly more apparent Britain suffered. But in the real world, politics, or decision-making, is the art of the convenient, not to mention survival, even more than it is of the possible, and faced with the great technological momentum of the nuclear programmes, successive ministers understandably settled for the incremental best they could get. Some critics have severely condemned ministers for this, Burn especially in regard to the thermal reactor decisions. Yet it is all too easy to see oneself as one of these ministers. No doubt some were better than others, but the striking thing remains their difficulty as a whole in freeing themselves of the constraints in the situations they inherited. This was an unusually rigid policy subsystem and virtually throughout the period from 1955-78 the balance of capabilities, responsibilities and rights as between the various elements, AEA, generating boards, consortia and Government was inadequate and confused to an extent which made sound policy almost by definition unattainable. The clockwork mechanism once wound up in 1955-7 thereafter remorselessly unwound.

It is therefore really only a partial diagnosis to argue that Britain

- should have relied on companies not consortia;
- should have ensured that the centre of gravity of the nuclear programme became industrial as soon as possible, also designing for a world rather than a domestic market and possibly collaborating with France;
- should never have proceeded by programme, or alternatively should have aimed at replication instead of nine Magnox stations each slightly different built by five consortia and three AGR designs built by three consortia;
- should at least have managed not to repeat the chief errors of the first programme in the second a decade later;
- should have avoided creating an AEA altogether, or made it an r & d subdepartment of the CEGB, or made it an energy rather than a nuclear energy agency, or at least left nuclear ordering decisions to the generating boards;
- should not have given such a monopoly position to the CEGB either;
- should have switched to light water reactors in 1957/65/74/78 — France, after all, eventually did so, and there were many parallels between the French situation in the late sixties and the UK one in the early seventies;
- should not have persuaded herself that extrapolation from a 30MW experimental AGR to a full-scale 600MW one was a short step, and then repeated the error with the 100MW prototype SGHWR.

The consortia were indeed a bad idea, the nuclear programmes were an expensive and unnecessary constraint, an energy r & d agency, or an AEA fully subservient to the CEGB would undoubtedly have led to a more balanced role for nuclear power, and light water reactors have enjoyed vastly more international success than have gas-graphite ones. It is also easy to agree that the British nuclear experience — 'dearly bought'[8], in the AEA's own words — also provides a 'perfect example of the difficulty of pursuing an independent path in face of American influence and technological skill'.[9] But the decisions which led to gas-graphite, the AEA, programmes and consortia all appeared to have some, and often a great deal, of logic on their side at the time they were made. What really was wrong was that the decisions were not for the most part framed with a view to enhancing policy flexibility later, they were insular and primarily designed to maximise gains rather than minimise losses, they demonstrated a general naivety about the political ramifications and momentum of technology fully characteristic of the period in which they were made, and above all, they were formulated in a system which lacked sufficient public accountability to pick up and fully address weaknesses as these revealed themselves. Despite many requests for example, there was not even a publicly available, independent, report of all that happened at Dungeness B.

It is also of some marginal relevance in this connection that Britain's civil nuclear development has received comparatively little academic analysis. Here nuclear energy is unhappily all too typical of British industrial and technological policies generally. The absence of independent scholarly analysis was especially marked in the critical years to 1965. Thereafter a few academics did begin to take an interest — Webb, Pryke, Franks, Wonder, Sweet, Rush, Henderson and in particular Burn, though at least two of these were non-British. (Patterson's views, since they were more those of an actor than of an analyst, were outlined in Chapter 11.) Let us briefly consider some of the points these analysts made.[10]

Webb[11] drew attention to the absence of representatives from the electricity authorities on the committee which drew up the first nuclear programme; argued that nuclear generating costs should have been recognised in 1957 as being 50 per cent up on the 1955 figures, and suggested that much of this rise was foreseeable in 1955, and that the fall in conventional generating costs was also predictable. Franks[12] noted that while the UK was criticised at the first Geneva conference for excessive optimism in regard to nuclear power costs, this did not lead to a debate within Britain because, he thought, no one wanted it. Of the 1957 expansion Franks suggested that with the Flett committee deliberating 'well below the level of public visibility' it 'would not have been seemly' for those who had doubts to say so in public, and that the political parties in particular 'did not have access to the sort of inside information' which would have encouraged criticism. The AEA had had a 'practical monopoly over effective communications on nuclear energy' and this could only have accentuated the 'pre-existing faith in the magic of nuclear power'. Franks also argued that in regard to nuclear power Treasury civil servants had revealed themselves to be quite simply 'bad economists', and that this was reinforced by the fact that ministers were 'bemused by the octopus-like appeal of nuclear power'.

Pryke[13] saw the 1957 decision as an 'extraordinary' one, the Government having in his view acted 'in a panic of its own making'. Hinton's public arguments in 1960 for not cutting the nuclear programme still more decisively Pryke considered 'persuasive rather than conclusive', in that the construction industry could have been run down further and then been built up again later as need arose. Discussing the eventual reorganisation of this industry in the late sixties/early seventies Wonder[14] concluded that 'so long as reactor policy remained sacrosanct the possible impact of reorganisation was intrinsically limited'. And reactor policy, Wonder judged, was fully tied up with what he saw as the high expectations, vested interests and political dogmas of nuclear nationalism.

In a major paper discussing both Concorde and the AGR programme, Henderson[15] put the loss on the latter, as compared with a notional LWR programme, at £2,100m (1975 prices, discounted to 1975/6 at the test discount rate). Henderson felt British institutions might be especially liable to 'errors' of the Concorde and AGR kinds. This was because the administrative culture emphasised secrecy, anonymity and bureaucratic tidiness rather than accuracy in individual judgement. The information flow as a result was restricted, individual initiative discouraged, and no built-in checks operated to prevent bias — the only authorised and acknowledged sources of expert advice tended to be parties to a decision or else predisposed to particular policies. Henderson's solution to these problems would have included a body outside government specifically created to analyse and review British public expenditure programmes. Rush[16] too looked to a more open decision-making process to prevent a repetition of the AGR decisional process, while Sweet wanted a better information flow in order to improve significantly the quality of research on the costing of nuclear energy. Sweet[17] could not accept the official cost-benefit analyses of nuclear power for the decade 1967-77, or CEGB figures given to Parliament and quoted by the AEA to demonstrate the economic superiority of nuclear power. Published information was inadequate to allow an independent check, but Sweet was unhappy about several cost elements, in particular nuclear load factors, capital and fuel cycle costs, and the failure to include r & d expenditure.

Burn[18] published severe and book-length challenges to British civil nuclear policy in 1967 and again in 1978. Burn's central thesis was that Britain had experienced a relentless nuclear disaster and that this was the failure of government enterprise rather than of the consortia or of British industry in general. It ought never to have been thought that ministers — experts in 'justification by words' — were qualified to take the kind of technical and commercial decisions they had taken. The positions now known to have been mistaken could easily have been recognised for what they were from 1955 onwards. Later, AGR development, having consisted of one mistake after another, had been crowned by the bizarre award of the Dungeness tender to the weakest consortium for a sketch design. There had been no ruthless public probing of what had gone wrong and those responsible for the 'colossal misjudgements' which had led to 'extraordinary irresponsible behaviour' by the AEA and CEGB in 1965 had gone unnamed. Eric Varley's 1974 decision had then come as the most categorical assertion of ministerial power in the nuclear field to date, deciding between two groups of engineers of which the larger had been on the side of the LWR. It would, however, have been impossible to conceal what was happening had competition been encouraged and entrenched groups, and particularly the AEA, not been allowed to dominate policy.

The thesis of Burn's 1967 book was somewhat contemptuously dismissed at the time both governmentally and by the AEA — it was said to contain 'pretty glaring inaccuracies' and to be 'vitiated by the failure to ensure strict comparability', and there was bipartisan support for these views in Parliament, though some, like Sir Keith Joseph, had doubts.[19] But at least the book *was* dismissed. That of 1978, and Patterson's of 1977, except for a small amount of media attention, were effectively ignored. Neither, for example, even managed a mention in the AEA's house journal *Atom*, though Pocock's authorised and essentially non-political version of events was reviewed there, as was the easy target *The Nuclear Disaster*.[20] Admittedly both Burn and Patterson wrote as polemicists, but even polemicists deserve a reply.

Now both Burn and Patterson castigated what might be called Britain's nuclear-electric monopoly, Burn above all because it had prevented competition, Patterson in particular because of the role it had preempted for nuclear energy. Both believed a better political and industrial structure would have led to better decisions — though naturally their expectations of those decisions were quite different. Clearly, one cannot agree fully with both Burn *and* Patterson. Equally clearly, from quite different perspectives and with quite different objectives, they came to some of the same conclusions. The official and general indifference which greeted both books should therefore be seen as a more disturbing indictment of Britain's nuclear-electric institutions, and of political awareness about such matters in the country at large, even than the contents of the books themselves. In a truly healthy political environment books like Burn's and Patterson's would be vigorously discussed.

Which is not of course to say that one agrees either with Burn or with Patterson. In particular, and among other reservations, it seems to me that public acceptability is far more important than Burn appears to think, and energy security much more complex than Patterson wants to admit. More to the point, it is to be hoped that readers of this book will now have views of their own on Britain's nuclear development, and anyone who writes about nuclear energy must also remember that there are many chapters still to come.

For me the central issue remains that of public accountability. I stress this because, unlike Burn, Patterson and others, I am distrustful of simple solutions which, one is told, would have produced better results, and persuaded only that better accountability of the whole policy system, and especially of the AEA, would have contributed significantly at the time to finding such solutions. In the atomic energy field in Britain one feels that secrecy having begun as a necessity continued as a convenience and eventually became an obsession. In my view, only since 1975 and in respect of Windscale has British civil nuclear power approached real accountability. Judged by the criterion of openness — itself the first requirement in public accountability — each of the main political reactor decisions — 1955, 1957, 1960, 1965, 1974 and 1978 — was an improvement on the one before, with the last two markedly more open than the other four, though even then far from fully open. But always one must remember that the reactor choice questions — 1955 (Magnox), 1965 (AGR), 1974 (SGHWR) and 1978 (AGR) — were squarely based on much earlier, and exclusively internal, AEA decisions. And always too one must remember the obscurity with which the CEGB conduct their affairs.

To ask for enhanced public accountability is to be directed first, and often last, to Parliament. What in this respect can Parliament claim to have achieved?

Incredible though it may seem, the first full parliamentary investigation involving the AEA was conducted by the Estimates Committee in 1958-9, when the Industrial Group of the Authority was examined.[21] The Estimates Committee proved an 'affable watchdog'[22] and the ensuing report mostly commended the AEA, but it has been suggested[23] that the great pains taken by the Authority to assist the Committee and the complexity of the subject matter together ensured the Authority a favourable report. The AEA, by this time committed to the AGR, were also then considering the reactor concept which later became the SGHWR, but the Committee felt incompetent to judge whether resources could in fact be spared to develop this extra system, though they did think the AEA should encourage more and earlier consortia participation in r & d.

The AEA has fallen outside the province of the Nationalised Industries Committee and this Committee in 1962[24] dealt with the Authority only peripherally in looking at nuclear energy. In spite of this, it has been said that the Committee 'exhibited considerable ability'[25] in tackling the technical issues at stake, and as was shown in Chapter 4, they certainly revealed real areas of difference between the AEA and the CEGB, concluding that 'the evidence which has been recited suggests defects in the existing structure and organisation which may mean that money is not being spent to the best advantage'.

The Public Accounts Committee, using the reports prepared for them by the Comptroller and Auditor General, as noted in this book have frequently investigated the AEA's accounts. Confining themselves to the financial side of nuclear energy, and so ordinarily avoiding the technical arguments for particular policies, the Committee have in this field, as in others, usually offered valuable and searching criticism. Their analyses have, of course, been retrospective, and also there have been some important time gaps in their work. It is of particular interest that until the early sixties they found the AEA's accounts to be at best mostly unintelligible, and strongly, and ultimately successfully, urged their reform.[26]

The new Science Committee, having in 1967 chosen nuclear energy for their first study, also in that inquiry found themselves confronting the matter of public accountability. They were told[27] then by the Minister of Technology that 'there has been every reason for relying on the advice of the Authority as the chosen instrument, in all questions of atomic r & d . . . the AEA contains within itself the machinery for giving advice to the Government'. It was not thought 'necessary, right or proper, or possible' for Mintech to duplicate the advisory machinery of the AEA, though individual projects were evaluated in Mintech 'to the best of our ability'. The AEA were much closer to Mintech than were other public corporations to their ministries and although Mintech was developing a techno-economic analysis unit, the technical side of nuclear proposals currently could not be assessed other than by the AEA: 'when the Authority decides what particular reactors it wishes to build for research purposes, than I would be glad to leave it to them because at this stage one would not even have the facts upon which an economic assessment could be made. Their decision . . . would be one based entirely upon a scientific assessment . . . and here I do not think it would be open to me to have a sensible alternative view unless the expenditure . . . was so great as really to be beyond the capacity of the country to pay for it.'

Sir Friston How, Secretary of the Atomic Energy Office, had told the Estimates Committee[28] essentially the same thing in 1959: it was inevitable that the Authority should have a fair margin of freedom because 'in this curious sphere' only the people available to them had sufficient knowledge to know what was worthwhile; there had naturally, therefore, been no attempt to create a parallel bureaucracy in Whitehall. Or as a minister put it in 1960,[29] he was 'advised by the best experts available' and was bound to take their advice since it was rather higher than his own knowledge of the subject.

The Science Committee's opinion of all this in 1967[30] was that 'neither the Minister of Power nor the Minister of Technology appeared to have any very effective technical check on the activities of the AEA and the consequent allocation of public funds for the Authority's purposes'. The Committee were 'not satisfied that, between them, the two Ministers are adequately equipped to assess the value and significance of what the Authority are doing'. Thus it could even be argued that the entire gas-cooled reactor technology line might not have been the best one to follow. The Committee therefore recommended 'a technical assessment unit capable of advising the Government on the merits and prospects of particular projects proposed to be undertaken by the Authority'. The minister's reply[31] was that he 'foresaw very real difficulties in establishing such a unit', and that the Authority were 'the repository of nearly all the national expertise in the nuclear field'. He did, however, intend to set up an Atomic Energy Board to advise him and he hoped this would meet the Committee's objective. The Committee persisted on that occasion that such a board was not the sort of independent agency they had in mind, but in their subsequent studies they took their own opinions of policy more seriously and never properly returned to the accountability theme. The Committee's investigations, as this book's indebtedness to them shows, were of considerable value, but as should also be clear, they were far from adequate in getting full accountability. Judged against that objective there were too many subjects which the Committee did not address, their inquiries were for the most part insufficiently thorough , and they mostly failed to see themselves as primarily an instrument of inquiry. It might have helped had they been able to draw on some permanent techno-economic expertise located, say, in the Comptroller and Auditor General's office, if such an arrangement could have been made.

The work of these various committees apart, one can pass quickly over Parliament's other devices for securing public accountability. In the nuclear field debates, especially in the Lords, though infrequent, were often interesting and even informative; statements and answers to Parliamentary Questions were as usual under close ministerial control.

Now the quest for more accountability is never a popular one to make. Lord Rothschild found that in the early seventies with his report on civil science, and he also encountered on that occasion a reluctance or refusal even to acknowledge what accountability might mean. Certainly an annual report, answerability to ministers who are themselves never culpable to the point of resignation, and occasional appearances before parliamentary committees do not add up to the real thing. Yet common sense alone suggests that there is likely to be a strong, though obviously not infallible, correlation between the extent to which proposals are analysed and criticised in advance of a commitment and their soundness in practice afterwards. Even then nuclear decisions, in common with others in technology, emphasise the contrast between the horizon of decision-makers, measured at best in years, and the timescale of the technology, measured in decades.

Unhappily, it is basic to human nature to shy away from full and public accountability, and in Britain there are the Official Secrets Acts, the 30-year rule, a multiplicity of lesser devices and the whole political culture to reinforce this trait. It is all grotesquely inadequate when millions, even billions, of public money are at stake, but it is going to be very hard indeed to change. By comparison, Britain's other nuclear problems, technological, organisational, and industrial have really all been derivative. Many would have arisen no matter what the policy system, but their form, severity and chronic character all were greatly affected by the particular closed system in which they arose.

It may be necessary to say here that one is not suggesting that government should not 'govern', that it should abdicate from responsibility. One is saying rather that in respect of Britain's nuclear development, government mostly amounted to ratification, indifference or bewilderment. One might have thought that, faced with matters which they could not really be expected to understand, decision-makers would have sought safety in opening out policy arguments so that outsiders might identify weaknesses insiders were either not qualified to assess or which they were prevented from even acknowledging because of institutional affiliations. Instead, on grounds of commercial security or constitutional propriety, the arguments were repeatedly closed up and decisions made on an inadequate basis of true knowledge.

In any mature polity the wise use of power must involve the sharing of information and the uncertainties and costs of technology have only underlined this. But in Britain, at least until the mid-seventies, healthy debate was not to be. Instead the AEA inherited on their creation a tradition of high priority and deep secrecy. The organisation was from the first a powerhouse of ideas and enjoyed wide outside support, amongst the public and media and within Westminster and Whitehall. The civil service backgrounds of the AEA's first two chairmen perfectly bridged the internal demands and the external supports. The net result was that the level of nuclear spending was set independently rather than by evaluation against alternatives, and this having been the way things began, this was how they continued. The Authority's later position that 'massive government financial support is essential to the satisfactory launching of a development programme for nuclear power'[32] was obviously correct but, remembering that in the post-war period Britain has found it increasingly difficult to hold a position in the second rank of states, less costly routes to nuclear power than a large development programme would certainly have had attractions.

The civil nuclear enterprise appealed on many different grounds, as exciting science, as challenging engineering distinct from weapons work, as a more or less urgent social need, and last, but by no means least, as a symbol of national vigour. Commitment once entered into on these kinds of consideration, technological momentum took care of the rest and the Authority grew from 17,000 in 1954 to a peak of 41,000 in 1961. In the end, a good case can be made out that not only was British energy r & d strategy thrown out of balance, but British technology much more generally as well.[33]

On the other hand, there never was created, and understandably there never spontaneously developed, in Britain a capacity to criticise the development of nuclear power, cogently, constructively and with full techno-economic rigour. Policy was much the worse for this lack and it was this gap which in part the nuclear opposition of 1974-8 and also the Royal Commission attempted, albeit very imperfectly, to fill. But where might a critical capacity have established itself? Possibly it might have arisen within government itself had not the AEA and CEGB been regarded from that perspective as both in a sense themselves part of government and simultaneously a mutually monitoring binary system. Possibly it might have developed within Parliament had not all the committees which investigated nuclear power, with the partial exception of the Public Accounts Committee, both lacked professional assistance and valued their own opinions above their ability to ferret out information. Possibly the party system might have served had politicians known how to relate the various issues, technical, economic, industrial and ethical, to party ideologies, or at least to party lines. Possibly the university world could have helped had it been officially thought worthwhile encouraging there on a continuing and disciplined basis a faculty for public policy analysis.

What is particularly remarkable in this connection is how differently nuclear safety and nuclear economics were handled in Britain. Sponsorship had been separated from regulation by 1960 and although the AEA gave substantial assistance until at least 1962, a deliberate effort was thereafter made by the Nuclear Installations Inspectorate (NII) to establish an independent regulatory capacity. No doubt there were weaknesses in the NII's approach, and the Inspectorate did not become fully separate from the nuclear sponsoring department until the creation of the Health and Safety Executive in 1975. Nevertheless, it was thought possible to create an organisation with an informed view of safety, and distinct from the AEA. The creation of the National Radiological Protection Board in 1970 was another step in the same direction, and even within the AEA the Safety and Reliability Directorate enjoyed a far-reaching independence. Yet similar moves as regards nuclear economics were repeatedly refused and a policy monopoly tolerated, and even defended, as being inevitable. The point is sharply brought out by considering, as one of many similar examples, some words by N.L. Franklin,[34] chairman of the Nuclear Power Company but formerly of the AEA and BNFL, made in 1977 in respect of the public acceptability of nuclear power. Franklin was of course concerned with the safety aspect and here he felt that the public could be educated in the generality of the subject, to the point where they could realise there was a problem. But beyond that, evaluation of risk, especially at low levels, he saw as depending centrally on skills and specialisations which could not be acquired by the public at large through educa-

tion. Such evaluation was a matter rather for experts, and this arrangement could be publicly acceptable 'provided the public can be reassured
in clearly visible ways that the organisational and institutional arrangements are such as to promote checking of one group of experts by
others who are as well qualified and suitably independent'. It is, as
should now be very clear, exactly such an independent check which has
been totally missing in regard to nuclear power economics. Yet protests
such as those of Lord Robens apart, nuclear power clearly has been
publicly acceptable in Britain in the economic sense. It is perfectly
understandable why the safety rather than the economic aspects of
nuclear power should eventually have come to be a major matter of
public concern, but one can still regret the possible overemphasis on
this as compared with the virtual indifference on the part of the public
to the economic questions. At the same time, nuclear power as well as
government having lost most of its mystique in the seventies, one can
suggest that the long-term failure to deal fairly with the public as
regards nuclear economics substantially worsened suspicions when these
eventually arose about nuclear safety.

Certainly, so long as it is considered enough to rely on the amateurs
which ministers and MPs — and in this type of case officials too — must
be, on journalistic investigation which however good is necessarily inter-
mittent, and on academics and private individuals, then so long will
policy continue to be essentially unaccountable, and because unaccountable, inadequate more often than it need be. This book might well have
dwelt at greater length on the technological success and safety of
British nuclear power. It is certainly easy to overlook the enormous
technical achievements of the last quarter century. But it remains the
author's conviction that Britain can have a much more successful industrial future than she has had an immediate past, especially where
nuclear power is concerned. It is also vital that public decisions should
aim at social effectiveness as well as commercial efficiency. The structure in which decisions are taken and implemented is thus for two quite
separate reasons absolutely fundamental. With due respect to such
bodies as the Waverley, Powell and Vinter Committees, and the Nuclear
Power Advisory Board, if a small fraction of the detailed effort which
went into designing British nuclear reactors had gone into designing
an adequate policy system and getting the responsibilities right, the
benefits must surely have been enormous. But then, the design of
reactors is obviously a highly specialised matter, whereas it has been
traditional to regard the design of a policy system as a matter of reflex
common sense and experience. Unfortunately, tradition and technology

seem to make poor bedfellows, which has been so much the worse for Britain where tradition has enjoyed such a special place.

Notes

1. Lord Hinton, 'What Next for Nuclear Power?', *New Scientist* (June 1968, pp. 525-7.
2. But see for example, H.J. Otway, 'Risk Assessment and the Social Response to Nuclear Power', *BNESJ*, 16 (October 1977), pp. 327-33.
3. For other views see Brian Wynne, 'Nuclear Debate at the Crossroads', *New Scientist* (4 August 1978), pp. 349-52; Philip Gummett, 'Some Lessons of the Windscale Inquiry', *R & D Management*, 9 (October 1978), pp. 23-7; David Pearce *et al.*, 'Energy: How to Decide', *Nature* (9 March 1978), pp. 115-16.
4. I have found A.J. Surrey, 'The Policy Background' (Science Policy Research Unit, 1978, mimeo), very useful.
5. 'Major Planning Inquiries', *Atom* (November 1978), pp. 307-9; see also C. Allday (BNFL Managing Director), 'Nuclear Power, Politics and Public Opinion', *Atom* (February 1979), pp. 44-5.
6. See remarks of M. Garner in Hugh Montefiore and David Gosling (eds.), *Nuclear Crisis* (Prism Press, Dorchester, 1977), pp. 96-9.
7. J.C.C. Stewart, 'The Development of Power Reactors in the UK', *Engineering for Nuclear Power* (Bulleid Memorial Lectures, University of Nottingham, 1971,) pp. 1-5.
8. C.C. Hood, 'Experience in the Introduction of Nuclear Power', *Atom* (August 1974), pp. 176-90 (190).
9. Nigel Hawkes, *Science* (17 February, 1978), pp. 755-6.
10. In addition to sources cited, see also Roger Williams, 'The Select Committee on Science and Technology: The First Round', *Public Administration* (Autumn 1978), pp. 299-313, and Roger Williams, 'Accountability in Britain's Nuclear Energy Programmes', in D.C. Hague and B.L.R. Smith, *The Dilemma of Accountability in Modern Government* (Macmillan, London, 1971); W.G. Jensen, *Nuclear Power* (Foulis & Co., Henley, 1969); K.D. George, 'The Economics of Nuclear and Conventional Coal-fired Stations in the UK', *Oxford Economic Papers*, 12 (1960).
11. M.E. Webb, 'Some Aspects of Nuclear Power Economics in the UK', *Scottish Journal of Political Economy*, xvi (February 1968), pp. 22-42.
12. C.E.S. Franks, *Parliament and Atomic Energy*, D.Phil. thesis, Oxford, September 1973.
13. Richard Pryke, *Public Enterprise in Practice* (MacGibbon & Kee, London, 1971).
14. E.F. Wonder, 'Decision-making and the Reorganisation of the British Nuclear Power Industry', *Research Policy*, 5 (1976), pp. 240-68.
15. P.D. Henderson, 'Two British Errors: Their Probable Size and Some Possible Lessons', *Oxford Economic Papers* (July 1977), pp. 159-205.
16. Howard J. Rush *et al.*, 'The Advanced Gas-cooled Reactor', *Energy Policy*, 5, 2 (June 1977), pp. 95-105.
17. Colin Sweet, 'Nuclear Power Costs in the UK', *Energy Policy*, 6, 2 (June 1978), pp. 107-18, with reply and rejoinder 6, 4 pp. 40-1; and see also H. Hunt, and G. Betteridge, 'The Economics of Nuclear Power', *Atom* (December 1978), pp. 326-30.
18. Duncan Burn, *The Political Economy of Nuclear Energy* (Institute of Economic Affairs, London, 1967) and *Nuclear Power and the Energy Crisis*

(Macmillan, London, 1978).

19. HLD 282 c.1071-3; HCD 746 c.1263-4 and 749 c.1541-5; HC 381-xvii (1966-7), Appendices 16 and 22.

20. R.F. Pocock, *Nuclear Power* (The Gresham Press, Old Woking, Surrey, 1977); *The Nuclear Disaster* (Counter Information Services, London, 1978).

21. HC 316-I (1958-9).

22. *NP* (September 1959), p. 81.

23. Nevil Johnson, *Parliament and Administration: The Estimates Committee 1945-65* (Allen and Unwin, London, 1966), p. 60.

24. HC 236 I-III (1962-3).

25. David Coombes, *The Member of Parliament and the Administration: The Case of the Select Committee on the Nationalised Industries* (Allen and Unwin, London, 1966), p. 111.

26. HC 252 (1960-1), report, paras. 105-9.

27. HC 381-XVII (1966-7), p. 188, para. 3 and Q 970-84.

28. HC 316-I (1958-9), Q 1-9.

29. HCD 625 c.952.

30. HC 381-XVII (1966-7), report, para. 154.

31. HC 40 (1968-9).

32. E.P. McTighe, 'The Development of the UK Nuclear Power Industry', *Atom* (December 1970), pp. 242-53 (53).

33. See for example, Mary Goldring, 'The Atomic Incubus', *New Society* (28 October 1965).

34. N.L. Franklin, 'Nuclear Power in Western Society', *BNESJ*. 16 (October 1977), pp. 303-14.

Summary of Main Actors, Reactors and Programmes

Institutional Actors

AEA (1954)	Atomic Energy Authority: the r & d organisation
BNFL (1971)	British Nuclear Fuels Ltd: the fuel company
CEGB (1957)	Central Electricity Generating Board)
	) the utilities
SSEB (1955)	South of Scotland Electricity Board)
The consortia	originally five company groups, evolving first to TNPG, NDC and APC, then to TNPG and BNDC, and finally to the NNC-NPC arrangement
NNC (1973)	National Nuclear Corporation: holding company
NPC (1973)	Nuclear Power Company
NII (1959)	Nuclear Installations Inspectorate
NCB (1946)	National Coal Board
SCST (1967)	Select Committee on Science and Technology
RCEP (1970)	Royal Commission on Environmental Pollution
FoE (1970)	Friends of the Earth
BNF (1963)	British Nuclear Forum
BNEX (1966-9)	British Nuclear Export Executive

Reactors

Magnox	Based on Calder Hall and used for the nine stations of the first programme: two exported
AGR	(Advanced gas-cooled): used for the five stations in the second programme: the Windscale AGR (WAGR) was the basic experimental/prototype version
SGHWR	(Steam-generating heavy water reactor): chosen in 1974 for the third programme but later abandoned: prototype at Winfrith
FBR	(Fast breeder reactor): planned for the longer term: the Dounreay experimental fast reactor (DFR) was succeeded by the prototype fast reactor (PFR) also at Dounreay, and a first Commercial Fast Reactor (CFR1) has long been discussed
LWRs	(Light water reactors): American types considered in the 1960s and 1970s

BWR   (Boiling water reactor)   )
) the two versions of LWR
PWR   (Pressurised water reactor))
HTR   (High-temperature (gas-cooled) reactor): Dragon at
                       Winfrith was developed with European co-operation
                       but shut down in 1975
CANDU   (Canadian Deuterium Uranium): Canadian type con-
                       sidered in 1960s and 1970s

Programmes

I	1955	1,500-2,000MW over 10 years
Ia	1957	5,000-6,000MW by end 1965
Ib	1957	5,000-6,000MW by end 1966
Ic	1960	5,000MW by end 1968
II	1964	5,000MW by end 1975
IIa	1965	8,000MW by end 1975
III	1974	4,000MW of starts by end 1978
IIIa	1978	2 AGR station starts immediately, plus possible PWR station(s) in 1980s
Iv	1979	15,000MW 1982-91

For comparison: the total net capability of the CEGB's power stations in March 1978 was 56.3GW, the (record) maximum system demand in 1977-8 was 42.8GW, and there were 13.7GW of plant under construction at the end of this period.

APPENDIX 2

Principal Events in British Nuclear Power Development, 1953-79

March 1953	Approval for construction of Calder Hall
July 1954	Establishment of the AEA
February 1955	First programme announced
August 1955	First Geneva conference
October 1956	Opening of Calder Hall
November 1956	Suez
March 1957	Nuclear programme trebled
October 1957	Windscale accident
July 1959	Estimates Committee report on AEA
June 1960	Nuclear programme cut back
December 1961	Hinton's *Three Banks* article
May 1963	Nationalised Industries Committee report
July 1963	'Wylfa debate' in the Lords
December 1963	Oyster Creek 'breakthrough' (US)
April 1964	Decision to have an appraisal
September 1964	Third Geneva conference
October 1964	Labour Government elected
May 1965	AGR wins Dungeness B appraisal
October 1965	First Fuel Policy White Paper
October 1967	Science Committee's first nuclear report
November 1967	Second Fuel Policy White Paper
July 1969	Science Committee's second nuclear report
June 1970	Conservative Government elected
April 1971	Creation of BNFL
June 1973	Science Committee's third nuclear report
October 1973	Yom Kippur war
January 1974	Science Committee's fourth nuclear report
March 1974	Labour Government elected
July 1974	Decision for the SGHWR
October 1975	*Daily Mirror* — UK as 'World's nuclear dustbin'
March 1976	Government approves oxide reprocessing contracts
September 1976	Royal Commission report on nuclear power
December 1976	Decision to hold the Windscale Inquiry
January 1977	Science Committee's fifth nuclear report
June-Nov. 1977	Windscale Inquiry

January 1978	Decision to return to the AGR
March 1978	Parker Report published
May 1978	Commons approve THORP
March 1979	Harrisburg nuclear accident (US)
May 1979	Conservative Government elected
December 1979	PWR commitment, 15GW programme

APPENDIX 3

Principal Events in the British Nuclear Debate, October 1975-May 1978

1975

Oct. 21	*Daily Mirror* headlines 'Plan to Make Britain World's Nuclear Dustbin'
Dec. 8	Commons debate the Windscale project
Dec. 12	BNFL arrange a public meeting in Barrow

1976

Jan. 15	Church House debate on the Windscale project
Jan. 29	Lords debate nuclear safety
Feb. 23	Commons debate nuclear safety
Mar. 12	Benn approves Windscale project
Apr. 24	FoE organise a 'nuclear excursion' to Windscale
May 18	Second reading of AEA special constables bill
June 1	BNFL seek Windscale planning permission
June 8	GMWU defeat anti-Windscale motion
June 22	National Energy conference
July 7	*Financial Times* conference 'Nuclear Power and the Public Interest — The Implication for Business'
Sep. 8	DHSS recognise malignancy claim for ex-Windscale worker
Sep. 22	Publication of Royal Commission report
Sep. 28	Pugwash debate on FBRs (Royal Society)
Sep. 29	Public meeting at Whitehaven
Oct. 26	Publication of FoE/CPRE/NCC study *Nuclear Prospects*
Oct. 28	President Ford questions reprocessing
Nov. 2	Cumbria CC tacitly approve BNFL Windscale application
Nov. 5	Lawyers Ecology Group query legality of Cumbria CC action
Nov. 20	Trafalgar Square rally against Windscale
Nov. 25	Shore postpones immediate decision
Dec. 9	Benn announces Windscale radiation leak of October 10
Dec. 13-14	British Council of Churches Hearings on CFR1
Dec. 20	Commons debate nuclear power development

Dec. 22	Lords debate nuclear power and the environment
Dec. 22	Shore decides to have an inquiry

1977

Jan. 21	BNFL withdraw controversial part of application
Feb. 8	Second reading of Nuclear Industry (Finance) Bill (to fund BNFL)
Mar. 1	Cumbria CC approve non-controversial aspects of Windscale project
Mar. 1	BNFL submit new THORP application
Mar. 11	Benn intervenes to end Windscale strike
Mar. 25	Fourth part of THORP application called in
Mar. 31	*New Society* nuclear survey
Apr. 7	Commons debate radiation waste in the Dee estuary
Apr. 8	President Carter announces his energy policy
May 10	BNFL publish details of their THORP case
May 13-14	Sunningdale seminar on nuclear policy
May 28	DOE publish response to Royal Commission Report
May 27	Dr Marshall ceases as Chief Scientist at Energy Department
June 14	Windscale Inquiry opens
June 28	Commons debate energy
Oct. 11-12	Royal Institution forum 'Nuclear Power and the Energy Future'
Nov. 3	Windscale Inquiry closes
Nov. 15	High Court award for radiation death, BNFL admitting liability
Dec. 2	Commons debate nuclear energy
Dec. 8	Commons debate nuclear energy
Dec. 12	Benn announces a 10-year energy conservation package

1978

Jan. 25	Decision announced to halt SGHWR, build two AGRs
Jan. 26	Mr Justice Parker reports to Shore
Mar. 6	Parker Report published
Mar. 22	Commons debate the Parker Report
Apr. 3	Windscale special development order laid
Apr. 29	Trafalgar Square demonstration against nuclear power
May 7	Torness demonstration against a nuclear station
May 15	Commons debate Windscale special development order

APPENDIX 4

The Nuclear Reactor: A Highly Simplified Outline

In a nuclear power station a nuclear reactor replaces the coal or oil furnace of a conventional power station. In a conventional station the energy release (in the form of heat) results from chemical combustion whereas in a nuclear station it results from nuclear fission. Nuclear fission occurs when the nuclei of certain atoms are split by sub-atomic particles called neutrons. Atomic nuclei are in fact made up of these particles together with others called protons. During fission a minute part of the atom's mass is converted into a comparatively very large amount of energy according to the famous equation due to Einstein: Energy = Mass x c^2, where c is the velocity of light. During fission neutrons are also released and these, by splitting further atoms, can under appropriate conditions (sufficient material and a sufficiently low neutron loss) initiate a chain reaction. This is the fundamental process involved in the atomic bomb as well as in a nuclear reactor. A nuclear reactor is said to have gone critical when the chain reaction becomes established. Materials which readily undergo fission are described as fissile. Other substances capable of being converted by neutrons into fissile materials are said to be fertile.

The development of nuclear power has so far depended for fuel almost completely on the naturally occurring element uranium, though, as explained below, alternative types of reactor using the element thorium are feasible. Natural uranium consists of atoms of two distinct types known as isotopes, written U235 and U238. These occur in the ratio 1:139 — isotopes are chemically the same but physically slightly different. U235 is fissile whereas U238 is fertile.

In contemporary nuclear power reactors the fuel is contained in fuel elements, there being an appropriate canning material to protect the fuel from corrosion and to retain the products of fission (the nuclear waste). Also present is a material known as a moderator whose function it is to slow down the neutrons emitted in fission — more of this in a moment. If, as in a power reactor, the heat generated in a nuclear reactor is to be used, then a coolant is also necessary. This coolant is circulated through the core of the reactor in order to remove the heat, which is used subsequently to generate steam in boilers. (The steam is then passed through turbogenerators in essentially the same way as with a coal station.) It is important that the moderator and coolant should be poor neutron absorbers — otherwise the nuclear reaction would be more difficult to sustain — but it is also necessary to have control rods present composed of material which is a very effective neutron absorber. These can then be pushed in (absorbing more neutrons) or pulled out (absorbing less), as necessary to operate the reactor. The reactor vessel containing fuel, moderator, coolant and control rods is then surrounded by concrete shielding because of the high radiation flux. A nuclear station naturally also comprises many safety, monitoring and other devices. It may be built by the organisation which expects to operate it placing contracts with many separate specialist firms, or else by the organisation placing a turnkey contract with one firm which itself then subcontracts.

Operation of a reactor, even for substantial periods of time, still leaves much fissile material unused. Further fissile material can also be produced by neutron absorption in any suitable fertile material present. After removal from the reactor and temporary storage to allow their radiation to decay somewhat, spent fuel elements can be reprocessed to separate out the unused and new fissile materials from the nuclear waste. The former is then available for recycling but as yet no permanent means of dealing with waste has been proved.

Some types of reactor use natural uranium fuel (in metal form) while others use enriched uranium fuel (in particular as oxide). In enriched uranium fuel the percentage of fissile U235 has been increased above the natural level of 1 part in 140 by one or other of the highly complicated enrichment processes. The two best known of these involve separation of U235 from U238 by diffusion through a very large number of special screens or by centrifuging. The most important new fissile material created in a reactor is plutonium, in particular the Pu239 isotope.

It was stated above that a moderator is used to slow down the neutrons in a reactor. The neutrons emitted in fission are said to be 'fast'. Collisions, especially with a good moderator, gradually slow them to ordinary or 'thermal' speeds, and reactors using such a moderator are thus sometimes called thermal reactors. Thermal neutrons are much more easily absorbed by U235 than are fast neutrons and indeed in a natural uranium reactor there are too few U235 atoms to allow a chain reaction without the use of a very good moderator.

Since in a thermal reactor fertile material is being converted into fissile material even as existing fissile material is being used to produce energy, such reactors are also known as converters: they produce less fissile material than they consume, typically around 50-60 per cent. But reactors can also be designed to produce more fissile material than they consume. Of particular interest here is a reactor without a moderator, so that it operates with fast neutrons, i.e. a fast reactor. ('Fast' has nothing to do with the speed of operation.) Given such a reactor is meant eventually to produce more fuel than it consumes, it is also known as a breeder (or fast breeder) reactor. Intermediate between thermal reactors and breeders are the advanced converters or near-breeders.

It was mentioned above that reactors using thorium are feasible. Natural thorium is all Th232 and in a suitable reactor this material, which like U238 is fertile, is converted into U233. U233, like Pu239, is fissile. Provided with a charge of enriched uranium or plutonium as fissile material, thermal reactors can convert Th232 to U233 more efficiently than they can U238 to Pu239, and indeed in principle the possibility of a thermal (i.e. slow neutron) breeder is opened up.

Reactor coolants may be gases (carbon dioxide, helium etc.) or liquids (light or heavy water, or organic liquids) or liquid metals (e.g. liquid sodium). Graphite and light and heavy water turn out to be the most important moderators. Boron and cadmium have been the materials most used for control rods. Heavy water is so called because its molecules are composed of two deuterium atoms and one oxygen atom (D_2O), whereas the molecules of ordinary or light water are composed of two hydrogen atoms with the one oxygen atom (H_2O). Deuterium is an isotope of hydrogen in which the nucleus consists of a neutron as well as the single proton which comprises the nucleus of ordinary hydrogen, i.e. the deuterium nucleus is twice as heavy. D_2O makes up only about one part in 6,000 of ordinary water, but deuterium can be separated from hydrogen more easily than U235 from U238.

APPENDIX 5

United Kingdom Nuclear Power Stations

Name	Reactors (type and number)	Net Output (MW)	Year of regular power operation	Owner	Consortium
Calder Hall	Magnox 4	200	1956	BNFL	
Chapelcross	Magnox 4	200	1959	BNFL	
Berkeley	Magnox 2	280	1962	CEGB	NEC
Bradwell	Magnox 2	250	1962	CEGB	NPPC
Windscale AGR	AGR 1	30	1963	AEA	
Dounreay DFR	FBR 1 (shut 77)	13	1963	AEA	
Hunterston A	Magnox 2	340	1964	SSEB	GEC-SC
Winfrith Dragon	HTR 1 (shut 75)	20MW(th)	1964	Europe/AEA	
Trawsfynydd	Magnox 2	390	1965	CEGB	APC
Dungeness A	Magnox 2	410	1966	CEGB	NPPC
Sizewell A	Magnox 2	420	1966	CEGB	EE-BW-TW
Hinkley Point A	Magnox 2	460	1965	CEGB	EE-BW-TW
Oldbury	Magnox 2	420	1967-8	CEGB	TNPG
Winfrith SGHWR	SGHWR 1	93	1968	AEA	
Wylfa	Magnox 2	840	1971	CEGB	EE-BW-TW
Hinkley Point B	AGR 2	1,240	1976-7	CEGB	TNPG
Dounreay PFR	FBR 1	250	1976	AEA	TNPG
Hunterston B	AGR 2	1,240	1976	SSEB	TNPG
Dungeness B	AGR 2	1,170	1980?	CEGB	APC(BNDC)
Hartlepool	AGR 2	1,250	1981?	CEGB	BNDC
Heysham	AGR 2	1,240	1981?	CEGB	BNDC
Sizewell B1-4	AGR 4	2 x 1,330	?	CEGB	NPC
Torness	AGR 2	1,330	?	SSEB	NPC
Tokai-Mura	Magnox 1	160	1966	Japan	GEC-SC
Latina	Magnox 1	200	1964	Italy	NPPC

APPENDIX 6

Selected Reactor Characteristics (Indicative Only)

Characteristic	Magnox	AGR	HTR	Reactor FBR (PFR)	SGHWR (Winfrith)	PWR	BWR	CANDU
Fuel	U	UO_2	UO_2	$PuO_2 + UO_2$	UO_2	UO_2	UO_2	UO_2
Coolant	CO_2	CO_2	He	Na	H_2O	H_2O	H_2O	D_2O
Moderator	C	C	C	None	D_2O	H_2O	H_2O	D_2O
Fuel Cladding	mgnx	ss	C	ss	Zr	Zr	Zr	Zr
Enrichment (% fissile nuclei)	nat (0.7)	2-2.6	10	20	2-2.3	2-3.4	1.8-2.8	nat (0.7)
Burn-up (MWd/te)	3-4,000	18,000		61,000	21,000	33,000	17-28,000	7-8,000
Coolant pressure (Atmospheres)	8-28	34-42	20	7	67	150	70	60-90
Coolant outlet $^{\circ}C$	350-410	635-675	720	620	280	310-320	285-290	300
Efficiency	25-31	40	39	42	30	33	33	29
Average power rating (MW/m^3)	1	2	5	500	10	100	40-50	10
Core size	15	10	10	2	3	3	4	7
(m) (d x h)	8	7	6	1	4	4	4	6

Key:

U	—	uranium	UO_2	—	uranium dioxide
Pu	—	plutonium	C	—	graphite (carbon)
Na	—	sodium	ss	—	stainless steel
Zr	—	zircaloy	mgnx	—	magnox
H_2O	—	water	D_2O	—	heavy water
nat	—	natural	Mwd/te	—	megawatt days per tonne
MW/m^3	—	Megawatts per cubic metre			

The table is meant only to illustrate a few selected characteristics of the main reactor types, but note that it shows:

(a) the much more compact cores of the LWRs, as compared with the gas-cooled reactors — a principal reason for their lower capital cost;

(b) the much higher coolant outlet temperatures with gas cooling as compared with water cooling, hence their higher efficiencies;

(c) the much higher fuel burn-up possible with UO_2 as compared with U fuel;

(d) the lower power rating of Magnox and the AGRs, the much higher ratings of the LWRs, and the very high rating of the FBR;

(e) the sense in which Magnox, the AGR and the HTR are Marks I-III of gas-graphite reactors.

Note also,

(f) Magnox, AGRs and CANDU refuel on load. LWRs are typically shut down every 12-15 months for a refuelling period of approximately 20-40 days;

(g) early Magnox stations have stainless steel pressure vessels 5-7.5cm thick, the later stations and the AGRs prestressed concrete pressure vessels up to 6.5m thick; the stainless steel pressure vessel of a BWR is some 11-17cm thick, that of the PWR around 21cms; the Dragon HTR had one of 5.1cm; the PFR has a 1.6cm stainless steel containment vessel which is virtually unpressurised; the SGHWR is a pressure tube reactor.

APPENDIX 7

The Consortia, etc.

1954

(1) Nuclear Energy Company Ltd (NEC)
AEI – John Thompson Ltd (67-33%)
(associated: Balfour Beatty & Co. Ltd, John Laing & Son Ltd, Morgan Crucible Co. Ltd)

(2) Nuclear Power Plant Company Ltd (NPPC)
C.A. Parsons & Co. Ltd (31.5%)
A Reyrolle & Co. (21.0%)
Head Wrightson & Co. (15.8%)
Clarke Chapman (5.3%)
Sir Robert McAlpine & Sons (15.8%)
Whessoe Ltd (5.3%)
Strachan & Henshaw (5.3%)
(Alexander Findlay & Co.)

(3) Atomic Power Group (association only, not a limited company) (APG)
English Electric Co. Ltd (33 1/3%)
Babcock and Wilcox Ltd (33 1/3%)
Taylor Woodrow Ltd (33 1/3%)

(4) Atomic Energy Group (association only, not a limited company) (AEG)
GEC Ltd (dominated)
Simon-Carves Ltd
(associated: Motherwell Bridge and Engineering Co. Ltd and John Mowlem Ltd)

(5) Atomic Power Constructions Ltd (APC)
International Combustion (Holdings)
Richardsons Westgarth and Co. (withdrew)
Fairey Engineering
Crompton Parkinson (withdrew 1961)
(associated at outset: Elliot Bros., Trollope and Colls Ltd, and Holland & Hannen and Cubitts; agreement with Babcock & Wilcox for steel pressure vessels)

1959-60

(1) The Nuclear Power Group (TNPG)
     NEC
     NPPC
(2) United Power Co. Ltd (UPC)
     AEG (50%)
     APC (50%)
(3) APG continued (later Nuclear Design and Construction Co. Ltd)
     (NDC)

1964-5

GEC — Simon-Carves withdrew from UPC, leaving APC

1968-9

(1) TNPG (AEI, taken over by GEC left; AEA 20%; IRC 10%)
(2) Babcock-English Electric Nuclear, became British Nuclear Design
     and Construction (BEEN/BNDC)
     (GEC entered through take-over of English Electric; AEA 20%;
     IRC 26%)
(3) APC excluded

1973

National Nuclear Corporation (holding company) (GEC 50%; BNA 35%;
     AEA 15%) (NNC)
     Nuclear Power Company (operating company) (NPC)
     British Nuclear Associates (BNA)
     Babcock & Wilcox
     Clarke Chapman
     Sir Robert McAlpine & Sons
     Taylor Woodrow
     Head Wrightson
     Strachan & Henshaw
     Whessoe
After 1974 GEC holding in NNC reduced to 30%, AEA holding increased to 35%.

SELECT BIBLIOGRAPHY

Official Sources (all London, HMSO, except as indicated)

Command Papers

Report of the Committee on National Policy for the Use of Fuel and Power Resources (Ridley Committee)	Cmd. 8647 July 1952
The Future Organisation of the UK Atomic Energy Project	Cmd. 8986 Nov. 1953
A Programme of Nuclear Power	Cmd. 9389 Feb. 1955
Report of the Committee of Inquiry on the Electricity Supply Industry (Herbert Committee)	Cmd. 9672 Dec. 1955
Capital Investment in the Coal, Gas and Electricity Industries	Cmd. 132 Apr. 1957
Accident at Windscale No. 2 pile on 10 October 1957	Cmnd. 302　1957
Report of the Committee appointed by the Prime Minister to examine the Organisation of certain parts of the United Kingdom Atomic Energy Authority (Fleck Committee)	Cmnd. 338 Dec. 1957
Final Report (of the Committee on the Windscale Accident)	Cmnd. 471　1958
The Control of Radioactive Wastes	Cmnd. 884　1959
The Nuclear Power Programme	Cmnd. 1083 Jun. 1960
The Financial and Economic Obligations of the Nationalised Industries	Cmnd. 1337　1961
The Second Nuclear Power Programme	Cmnd. 2335 Apr. 1964
Fuel Policy	Cmnd. 2798 Oct. 1965
Nationalised Industries: A Review of Economic and Financial Objectives	Cmnd. 3437　1967
Fuel Policy	Cmnd. 3438 Nov. 1967
Report of the Committee of Inquiry into Delays in Commissioning CEGB Power Stations (Wilson Committee)	Cmnd. 3960 Mar. 1969
Ministerial Control of the Nationalised Industries	Cmnd. 4027　1969
Nuclear Power Policy (Government observations	

on HC 350 (1972-3)	Cmnd. 5499 Nov. 1973
Nuclear Reactor Systems for Electricity	
Generation	Cmnd. 5695 Jul. 1974
Report by the Chief Inspector of Nuclear	
Installations on the incident in Building B204	
at the Windscale Works of BNFL on 26	
September 1973	Cmnd. 5703 Jul. 1974
Choice of Thermal Reactor Systems (NPAB)	Cmnd. 5731 Sep. 1974
The Structure of the Electricity Supply	
Industry in England and Wales: Report of the	
Committee of Inquiry (Plowden Committee)	Cmnd. 6388 1976
Royal Commission on Environmental Pollu-	
tion, 6th Report, Nuclear Power and the	
Environment	Cmnd. 6618 Sep. 1976
Nuclear Power and the Environment	Cmnd. 6820 May 1977
Energy Policy: A Consultative Document	Cmnd. 7101 Feb. 1978
The Reorganisation of the Electricity Supply	
Industry in England and Wales	Cmnd. 7134 Apr. 1978

Commons Committees

1. Select Committee on Science and Technology
   (i) *United Kingdom Nuclear Reactor Programme*, Report, Evidence and Appendices, HC 381-XVII (1966-7).
   (ii) *Comments on letters from the Minister of Power and the Minister of Technology*, 3rd Special Report, HC 40 (1968-9).
   (iii) *United Kingdom Nuclear Power Industry*, 4th Report, Evidence and Appendices, HC 401 (1968-9).
   (iv) Fifth Special Report, HC 222 (1969-70) (The Minister of Technology on BRDC).
   (v) *Generating Plant Breakdowns: Winter 1969-70*, 1st Report, with Evidence and Appendices, HC 223 (1969-70).
   (vi) *Nuclear Power Policy*, Second Report, HC 350 (1972-3), Evidence and Appendices, HC 444 (1971-2) and HC 117 (1972-3).
   (vii) *The Choice of a Reactor System*, First Report, HC 145 (1973-4), Evidence HC 73.
   (viii) *Energy Conservation*, First report, HC 487 (1974-5), Evidence, HC 127 (1974) and HC 155, 156 (1974-5).
   (ix) *The Development of Alternative Sources of Energy for the UK*, Third Report, HC 534-I (1976-7).
   (x) *The SGHWR Programme* together with memoranda submitted to the General Purposes Subcommittee, HC 89 (1976-7), Evidence

HC 623 (1975-6).

(xi) *Fast Breeder Reactor*, Special Report 4, HC 625 (1975-6).

2. Select Committee on Nationalised Industries

(i) *The Electricity Supply Industry*, HC 236 I-III (1962-3).

(ii) *Ministerial Control of the Nationalised Industries*, First Report, HC 371 I-III (1967-8).

3. Select Committee on Estimates

United Kingdom Atomic Energy Authority (Production Group and Development and Engineering Group), Fifth Report, HC 316-I (1958-9).

4. Committee of Public Accounts

6th Report, HC 348, 1955-6, paras. 91-102.

2nd Report, HC 256, 1959-60, paras. 128-40.

3rd Report, HC 252, 1960-1, paras. 105-9.

3rd Report, HC 251, 1961-2, paras. 152-66.

3rd Report, HC 275, 1962-3, paras. 149-51.

Report, HC 113, 1965-6, paras. 29-39.

Report, HC 71, 1966-7, paras. 29-39.

3rd Report, HC 314, 1967-8, paras. 162-80.

3rd Report, HC 362, 1968-9, paras. 141-59.

2nd Report, HC 297, 1969-70, paras. 199-205.

2nd Report, HC 537, 1970-1, paras. 171-86.

2nd Report, HC 273, 1971-2, paras. 36-51.

8th Report, HC 385, 1972-3, paras. 105-9.

3rd Report, HC 374, 1974-5, paras. 154-66.

5th Report, HC 556, 1975-6, paras. 34-48.

8th Report, HC 621, 1977-8, paras. 12-21.

Some other Official Documents

Report by the Hon. Mr Justice Parker, *The Windscale Inquiry*, 1978.

Health and Safety Executive, *Some Aspects of the Safety of Nuclear Installations in Great Britain*, 1977.

Dungeness B AGR Nuclear Power Station (CEGB, London, 1965).

An Appraisal of the Technical and Economic Aspects of Dungeness B Nuclear Power Station (CEGB, London, 1965).

Energy Policy Review (Department of Energy, Energy Paper No. 22, 1977).

Energy Research and Development in the UK (Department of Energy, Energy Paper No. 11, 1976).

National Energy Conference (22 June 1976), 2 vols. (Department of Energy, Energy Paper No. 13, 1976).

Health and Safety Commission, *Advisory Committee on Major Hazards*, First Report, 1976.

Conferences and Symposia (Selected)

Proceedings of the International Conference on the Peaceful Uses of Atomic Energy, Geneva, 8-20 August 1955 (16 vols.).

Proceedings of the Second United Nations International Conference on the Peaceful Uses of Atomic Energy, Geneva, 1-13 September 1958 (33 vols.).

Proceedings of the Third International Conference on the Peaceful Uses of Atomic Energy, Geneva, 31 August-9 September 1964 (16 vols.).

Proceedings of the Fourth International Conference on the Peaceful Uses of Atomic Energy, Geneva, 6-16 September 1971 (15 vols.).

Calder Works Nuclear Power Plant, November 22-23 1956, *J. Brit. Nucl. Energy Conf.* (April 1957).

Symposium on the AGR, London, March 14-15 1963, *J. Brit. Nucl. Energy Soc.*, 2 (1963), pp. 98-294, 335-54.

The Construction, Commissioning and Operation of AGRs, The Institution of Mechanical Engineers, London, May 26-27 1977.

Industrial Challenge of Nuclear Energy, OEEC, April 1957.

Semi-specialist and Specialist Journals

The Economist, New Scientist and *Nature*
Nuclear Power, Journal of the Institution of Nuclear Engineers
Nuclear Engineering (incorporated *Nuclear Power* in 1963, later became *Nuclear Engineering International*)
Journal of the British Nuclear Energy Conference (later *Journal of the British Nuclear Energy Society*, and later still *Nuclear Energy*)
Nucleonics (ceased publication)
Nucleonics Week
Nuclear News
Atom

Annual Reports, Accounts etc

AEA, BNFL, BEA, CEA, CEGB and NCB

Parliamentary Debates and Statements (Selected)

Lords

23/10/46	Atomic Energy Bill 143 c.569-90
5/7/51	Atomic Energy 172 c.670-708
14/12/53	Atomic Energy Project 185 c.14-64
11/5/54	Atomic Energy Authority Bill 187 c.469-519
15/2/55	Peaceful Uses of Atomic Energy 191 c.4-7
5/3/57	Nuclear Power Programme 202 c.184-94
2/4/57	The Fuel and Power Industries 202 c.965-1017
10/7/63	The Nuclear Energy Industry and the CEGB 251 c.1380-457
10/6/64	The Second Nuclear Power Programme 258 c.894-959
8/12/64	Electricity, Gas and Atomic Energy Industries 262 c.14-85
25/5/65	Dungeness Nuclear Power Station 266 c.793-7
9/12/65	Reactivation of Capenhurst Atomic Energy Plant 271 c.418-21
9/2/66	Atomic Energy (PFR) 272 c.760-2
13/4/67	Fuel and Energy Policy 281 c.1417-514
14/2/68	Fuel Policy 289 c.106-94
8/5/68	The Nuclear Reactor Programme 291 c.1477-549
17/7/68	The Nuclear Power Industry 295 c.333-42
14/4/70	Atomic Energy Authority Bill 309 c.321-46
23/4/70	Atomic Energy Authority Bill 309 c.863-90
26/1/71	Atomic Energy Authority Bill 314 c.822-62
4/2/71	Atomic Energy Authority Bill 314 c.1449-65
28/2/73	Energy Policy and World Supplies 339 c.626-726
22/3/73	Nuclear Industry Reorganisation 340 c.811-86
10/7/74	Nuclear Reactor Policy 353 c.563-71
2/12/75	EEC (Energy) 366 c.482-562
29/1/76	The Technological Problems of Nuclear Safety 367 c.1174-216
22/12/76	Nuclear Power and the Environment 378 c.1308-440

Commons

28/4/53	Atomic Energy Project (Reorganisation Committee) 514 c.1958-64
10/12/53	Atomic Energy (Ministerial Responsibility) 521 c.2286-323
1/3/54	Atomic Energy Authority Bill 524 c.844-967
29/4/54	Atomic Energy Authority Bill 526 c.1795-886
15/2/55	Atomic Energy (Peaceful Use) 537 c.187-91
25/2/55	Atomic Energy (Peaceful Purposes) 537 c.1625-77

13/6/55   Debate on the Address 542 c.342-9
5/3/57   Nuclear Power (Revised Programme) 566 c.184-90
30/4/57   Nuclear Power and Oil Supplies 569 c.33-159
8/11/57   Atomic Energy Establishment, Windscale (Accident) 577 c.465-8
19/12/57   Atomic Power Stations (Siting) 580 c.667-83
20/3/58   Atomic Energy (Peaceful Uses) 584 c.1565-76
11/7/58   Nuclear Power Stations (Plutonium) 591 c.779-94
21/1/59   Nuclear Power Stations (Safety) 598 c.369-78
9/2/59   Nuclear Installations Bill 599 c.861-938
1/7/59   Nuclear Installations Bill 608 c.516-68
1/7/59   Nuclear Power Programme 608 c.569-82
30/7/59   Nuclear Power Stations 610 c.765-77
18/11/59   Atomic Energy Authority Bill 613 c.1217-39
3/2/61   Nuclear Power Programme 633 c.1327-93
22/2/62   Atomic Energy and Radioactive Substances 654 c.783-99
8/6/62   Hunterston Nuclear Power Station 661 c.880-97
12/7/62   Science and Industry 662 c.1555-8
19/11/62   Atomic Energy Establishment, Capenhurst 667 c.965-76
24/7/63   Nuclear Power Station, Wylfa 681 c.1667-80
25/5/65   Nuclear Power (Dungeness B Station) 713 c.236-41
20/3/67   Nuclear Power Stations 743 c.1339-53
18/7/67   Coal Industry (Borrowing Powers) 750 c.1859-2036
6/2/68   Nuclear Power Stations (Siting) 758 c.235-8
26/3/68   Fuel and Power Policy 761 c.1398-427
23/5/68   Science and Technology 765 c.951-1071
17/7/68   Nuclear Power Industry 768 c.1428-38
14/5/69   Uranium (Gas Centrifuge Process) 783 c.1600-12
17/12/70   Atomic Energy Authority Bill 808 c.1590-1658
15/1/71   Atomic Energy Authority Bill 809 c.383-423
20/6/72   Nuclear Reactor Industry (Vinter Report) 839 c.430-40
8/8/72   Nuclear Reactor Policy 842 c.1491-1500
22/3/73   Nuclear Design and Construction Industry 853 c.670-8
2/5/74   Nuclear Reactors 872 c.1344-450
10/7/74   Nuclear Reactor Policy 876 c.1357-70
20/12/74   Nuclear Energy 883 c.2014-35
8/12/75   Nuclear Fuel Reprocessing 902 c.192-204
18/12/75   Nuclear Reactor Project 902 c.1716-40
23/2/76   Nuclear Safety 906 c.81-151
26/2/76   AEA (Special Constables) Bill 906 c.701-56
13/12/76   Windscale (Radioactive Contamination) 922 c.967-72

20/12/76	Nuclear Power 923 c.293-339
20/12/76	Environmental Pollution (Nuclear Power) 923 c.354-69
22/12/76	Windscale 923 c.672-82
8/2/77	Nuclear Industry (Finance) Bill 925 c.1253-360
27/5/77	Nuclear Power and the Environment 932 c.1766-76
28/6/77	Energy 934 c.280-388
2/12/77	Nuclear Energy 940 c.884-981
8/12/77	Energy Policy and Nuclear Energy 940 c.1563-606
25/1/78	Thermal Reactor Policy 942 c.1391-408
21/3/78	Windscale Inquiry Report 946 c.1537-676
15/5/78	Windscale (Special Development Order) 950 c.111-82
5/12/78	Torness (Nuclear Power Station) 955 c.1185-96

NAME INDEX

SUBJECT INDEX

Printed in the United States
by Baker & Taylor Publisher Services